THE ANABAPTIST STORY

The Anabaptist Story

An Introduction to
Sixteenth-Century Anabaptism

Third Edition, Revised and Enlarged

WILLIAM R. ESTEP

WILLIAM B. EERDMANS PUBLISHING COMPANY
GRAND RAPIDS, MICHIGAN / CAMBRIDGE, U.K.

© 1975, 1996 Wm. B. Eerdmans Publishing Co.
2140 Oak Industrial Drive N.E., Grand Rapids, Michigan 49505

First edition published 1963 by Broadman Press, Nashville, Tennessee
Revised edition published 1975 by Wm. B. Eerdmans
Third edition 1996
Printed in the United States of America

22 21 20 19 18 17 16   19 18 17 16 15 14 13

Library of Congress Cataloging-in-Publication Data

Estep, William Roscoe, 1920-
The Anabaptist story: an introduction to sixteenth-century Anabaptism /
William R. Estep. — 3rd ed., rev. and enl.
p.   cm.
Includes bibliographical references and index.
ISBN 0-8028-0886-7 (pbk.: alk. paper)
1. Anabaptists — History. I. Title.
BX4931.2.E83 1995
284'.3 — dc20   95-42241
                                      CIP

To two who have walked
in the steps of the
Anabaptists, both physically and
spiritually, I dedicate this third
edition of The Anabaptist Story

John Allen and Pauline Willingham Moore,

Dienern des Wortes
in
Europe, 1938-1978

Contents

Preface to the Third Edition

*T*he *Anabaptist Story* FIRST MADE ITS APPEARANCE IN 1963. TWELVE years later, more than thirty years ago, the first revised edition was published. Since that time increased interest in the sixteenth-century Anabaptists has led to renewed research that in turn has produced a flurry of recent books with fresh insights from a variety of perspectives. Even though *The Anabaptist Story* was still in print and in use in a number of churches and schools, it was dated. In the light of more recent research, I was faced with three options. First, I could ignore the recent works and let *The Anabaptist Story* run its course; second, I could produce a new volume that would largely be given to a critical historiography of the last twenty-five years; or third, I could bring out a new revision. I decided on the third option.

A number of reasons persuaded me to attempt a revision rather than a new work. First, *The Anabaptist Story* has been so well received, particularly since the second edition, that it seemed unwise to replace it with some other title. It has become a standard textbook (or reference work) in many colleges and seminaries in the United States, and in other countries as well. Spanish, Italian, Serbo-Croat, Czech, and Korean editions are now available. Such a work remains new for each succeeding generation of students. Also, since the reasons that prompted its publication in the first place are still relevant, it appeared a matter of wisdom to bring out another revised edition rather than some other option.

Translations of Anabaptist Sources

In the last half century many Anabaptist sources have come to light, but they remained closed documents to those who could not read German, Dutch, or Latin. Fortunately for those whose knowledge of these languages is greatly limited or nonexistent, many of these sources are now available in English. This development is due to a number of dedicated scholars in both Europe and North America who organized the *Tauferaktenkommission* for the purpose of publishing critical editions of source documents in the history of Anabaptism *(Quellen zur Geschichte der Täufer)*. A number of scholars, largely Mennonite, have been enlisted to translate several of these documents into English. Among these are: Leland Harder, ed., *The Sources of Swiss Anabaptism;* H. Wayne Pipkin and John H. Yoder, eds. and trans., *Balthasar Hübmaier: Theologian of Anabaptism;* and William Klassen and Walter Klaassen, eds. and trans., *The Writings of Pilgram Marpeck.* The Hutterian Brethren have translated and published in English two significant works: Peter Rideman, *Account of Our Religion, Doctrine and Faith;* and *The Chronicle of the Hutterian Brethren,* volume one.

Other collections of sources now available in English translations include Clarence Bauman, *The Spiritual Legacy of Hans Denck: Interpretation and Translation of Key Texts;* W. R. Estep, ed., *Anabaptist Beginnings, 1523-1533: A Source Book;* W. R. Estep, ed., *Luther and the Anabaptists;* J. C. Wenger, ed. and trans., *Conrad Grebel's Programmatic Letters of 1524;* and George Huntston Williams, *The Polish Brethren: Documentation of the History & Thought of Unitarianism in the Polish-Lithuanian Commonwealth and in the Diaspora, 1601-1685.*

Recent Monographs

A number of significant monographs on various facets of the Anabaptist and related movements have appeared in recent years. Although it is not possible to mention all of them here, some are too significant for the serious student to overlook. They are: Willem Balke, *Calvin and the Anabaptist Radicals;* Torsten Bergsten (Irwin J. Barnes and William R. Estep, ed. and trans.), *Balthasar Hübmaier, Anabaptist Theolo-*

gian and Martyr; Neal Blough, *Christologie Anabaptiste;* Claus-Peter Clasen, *Anabaptism: A Social History, 1525-1618;* Kenneth Ronald Davis, *Anabaptism and Asceticism: A Study in Intellectual Origins;* Mark U. Edwards, Jr., *Luther and the False Brethren;* Abraham Friesen, *Reformation and Utopia: The Marxist Interpretation of the Reformation and its Antecedents;* Abraham Friesen, *Thomas Muentzer, A Destroyer of the Godless: The Making of a Sixteenth-Century Religious Revolutionary;* Eric W. Gritsch, *Thomas Muentzer: A Tragedy of Errors;* Leonard Gross, *The Golden Years of the Hutterites;* Irvin Buckwalter Horst, ed., *The Dutch Dissenters: A Critical Companion to Their History and Ideas;* Irvin Buchwalter Horst, *The Radical Brethren: Anabaptism and the English Reformation to 1558;* Werner O. Packull, *Mysticism and the Early South German-Austrian Anabaptist Movement, 1525-1531;* James R. Coggins, *John Smyth's Congregation: English Separatism, Mennonite Influence, and the Elect Nation;* Arnold C. Snyder, *The Life and Thought of Michael Sattler;* James M. Stayer, *Anabaptists and the Sword;* James M. Stayer, *The German Peasants' War and Anabaptist Community of Goods;* Christof Windhorst, *Tauferisches Taufverstandnis: Balthasar Hübmaier Lehre zwischen traditioneller und reformatorischer Theologie.*

Reference Works

In a category all its own is the encyclopedic third revised edition of *The Radical Reformation* by George Huntston Williams. The first edition, published in 1962, consisted of 940 pages, 57 of which were indexes of topics, persons, places, and biblical references. The second edition, revised and greatly enlarged with an extensive bibliography, was translated into Spanish by Antonio Alatorre and published in 1983. The third edition, enlarged again to a total of 1,559 pages, is the most complete single volume devoted to the Radical Reformation yet to appear in English. Its usefulness is enhanced by 128 pages of indexes and a bibliography of over 1,600 sources.

The *Mennonite Encyclopedia,* volume five, edited by Cornelius J. Dyck and Dennis D. Martin, is a welcome addition to the highly acclaimed four-volume encyclopedia published from 1955 to 1959. Volume five (1990) contains nine hundred new entries and four hundred other articles, updating those previously published. Edited under the auspices of the Institute of Mennonite Studies, this volume is as indispensable to Anabaptist research as were previous volumes of *The Mennonite Encyclopedia.*

Trends in Anabaptist Studies

The last thirty years have seen some interesting developments in Anabaptist studies, as reflected in substantial volumes, articles in historical journals, and scholarly conferences. Prior to the 1960s, theologically oriented historians largely dominated the field of Anabaptist research. Although most of these historians were Mennonites, A. H. Newman, H. C. Vedder, Roland Bainton, Frank H. Littell, and George Huntston Williams were not. But it was Harold Bender of Goshen College and Fritz Blanke of the University of Zürich who led in the rediscovery of the Anabaptist movement as a separate identifiable current within the Protestant Reformation. In their writings the Anabaptists were sharply distinguished from the *Spiritualisten* and the rationalists. The origins of the movement were found within the Swiss Reformation under the leadership of Zwingli. According to their reconstruction of the historical scenario, the Swiss Brethren first, under the leadership of Conrad Grebel and Felix Manz, and later Michael Sattler, constituted normative Anabaptism, by which all forms of the movement were to be judged. The criteria by which "normative Anabaptism" was determined were not only historical but also ethical and theological. As Blanke stated it, "Only at the source of a movement do the waters run pure." Many contemporary, even Mennonite, historians have reacted against this position.

Social historians have gradually replaced church historians and are in the process of attempting a revisionist history of Anabaptism. In explaining the Anabaptist movement in terms of its social and political context, these historians have added another dimension to our understanding of the many facets of the Reformation era. The insistence that Anabaptism had a multiplicity of beginnings, a position anticipated by A. H. Newman, Jan Kiwiet, and others, has been formalized as the polygenesis theory by James M. Stayer. Likewise, Bullinger's theory of the close relationship of Thomas Müntzer and the Great German Peasants' War to the rise of the Anabaptist movement has enjoyed a belated revival. The Münster fiasco has also once again become the focus of renewed interest. While we cannot dismiss as biased much of the work of social historians, many of whom have produced solid scholarship and careful research, we cannot allow certain assumptions underlying their work as well as some conclusions to remain unchallenged.

The assumption that confessional historians, even when searching for the roots of their own faith communities, are by virtue of their religious orientation disqualified from doing the work of a critical historian is surely unwarranted. Every responsible church historian recognizes, as Penrose St. Amant stated in the Holland Lectures, that faith has no power to create history nor to give a license to distort it. "It goes without saying that the historian must not allow any 'message' which he feels the past has for today to distort the effort to reconstruct the past objectively. He must remember, as Professor John Knox has reminded us, that 'faith has no power to create historical facts.'"[1] By the same token, the secular historian is not necessarily free of bias or of a "partisan" approach due to a lack of personal faith or of allegiance to a confession. Admittedly every historian has some bias, but all are constrained by the vocation to deal honestly with the historical data. Obviously some have not. Heinrich Bullinger is a case in point, but not Fritz Blanke, out of the same Swiss Reformed Church, whose *Brüder in Christo* is a model of a carefully researched monograph. Therefore, the fact that a historian may be a person of faith does not necessarily preclude the necessary objectivity of his craft.

In this revised edition of *The Anabaptist Story*, I will challenge a number of assumptions held by contemporary historians of sixteenth-century Anabaptism. For example, a basic assumption that the Anabaptist movement was simply a variant expression of the German Peasants' War fails to take into consideration the profound differences between the two movements, historically and theologically. To view the anticlericalism of the German peasants as of the same genus as that of

---

1. Penrose St. Amant, *Christian Faith and History* (Fort Worth, Tex.: Holland Foundation Lectures, 1954), p. 2.

Erasmus or the Swiss Brethren is once again to fail to understand or to appreciate the basic religious insights that drove the Anabaptists to lay down their lives rather than to betray their faith. Indeed, it was the difference between anarchy and the Lordship of Christ, but those who fail to understand this distinction may be ill-equipped to understand the essence of Anabaptism.

Purpose Restated

This book was first written from the conviction that a study of the sixteenth-century Anabaptists can be instructive for those of us who seek to follow Christ in obedient discipleship in this last decade of the twentieth century and for those who still search for a life with meaning and purpose. With Arnold Toynbee, I believe that the task of the historian is more than that of an antiquarian or of an academician who goes along just for the ride. Therefore, in this book I hope to impart something more than information. I dare to hope that through these pages the world of the sixteenth century may come alive, and the Anabaptists within it, with all their virtues and faults, their strengths and weaknesses, but above all with the faith and ideals that motivated them to witness in word and deed in life and in death for that truth which for them was worth the living and the dying.

The format of this book remains the same as in previous editions, but some sections have been enlarged. The notes accompanying each chapter will cite the most relevant recent sources while a select bibliography will include only those considered most helpful to the reader.

Preface to the Second Edition

FOUR HUNDRED AND FIFTY YEARS AGO THE ANABAPTIST MOVEMENT was launched with the inauguration of believers' baptism and the formation of the first congregation of the Swiss Brethren in Zürich, Switzerland. I am particularly gratified that upon the four hundred and fiftieth anniversary of this occasion this narrative history of the Anabaptist movement is allowed a new lease on life. This is the first completely revised edition since the book came out in 1963.

So much has happened in Anabaptist research during the past decade that the temptation to write a completely new history of the movement was exceedingly difficult to resist. However, the reception given *The Anabaptist Story* by so many different schools and churches has greatly affected the decision to stay with the original title and format. While the book remains very much the same in appearance, hopefully it is a much more accurate account of the Anabaptist movement and, therefore, a far better introduction to the subject than that provided by the first edition.

Many changes have been made. They will be most apparent to the careful student who takes advantage of the footnotes. It is here that technical discussions which would have encumbered the narrative are found. The reader will also discover within this documentation references to the major works on the Radical Reformation that have appeared during recent years. While some German and Dutch titles are included, most bibliographical notes refer to books readily available in

English. However, changes have also been introduced within the text itself. As a result no chapter has escaped untouched. An attempt has been made to correct all recognized errors of fact and interpretation. Additional material has been added either in order to round out the narrative or to correct an imbalance in the account. A studied attempt has been made to retain as much of the narrative style of the original edition as possible while making only the most necessary changes. How well the author has succeeded in achieving this goal the reader will have to judge.

Whatever success this revised work has achieved in accuracy and readability is due to a number of factors. A sabbatical year spent in Switzerland during 1967-68 opened up many doors for travel and research that increased the author's knowledge of the Reformation and the Anabaptists immeasurably. Seminars on the Reformation with Professor Fritz Büsser of the University of Zürich were particularly stimulating. On other occasions travel in Europe has brought face-to-face contact with such thorough and genial scholars as Professors J. A. Oosterbaan and Irvin B. Horst, both of the University of Amsterdam. During the past six years the author has been working, as time from his teaching and writing responsibilities would permit, on his own translation of the basic documents of Anabaptism during its first decade. This project received an extra boost as a result of skills sharpened by a course on sixteenth-century paleography ably conducted by Professor Arthur Carl Piepkorn in the Eighth Institute of Reformation Research at Concordia Theological Seminary, St. Louis, Missouri.

I am also indebted to many scholars for their encouragement and advice. I wish particularly to express my appreciation to Professors Jarold Knox Zeman, Acadia University, Wolfville, Nova Scotia; J. C. Wenger, Goshen College, Goshen, Indiana; John J. Kiwiet, Southwestern Baptist Theological Seminary, Fort Worth, Texas; John Howard Yoder, Associated Mennonite Biblical Seminaries, Elkhart, Indiana; Irvin B. Horst, University of Amsterdam; J. A. Oosterbaan, University of Amsterdam; and Franklin H. Littell, Temple University. My indebtedness to other scholars, living and dead, is beyond computation. Such a work as this is possible only because of the dedicated scholarship of countless others.

Many libraries have also permitted me the use of their facilities and holdings. They are the Zentralbibliothek, Zürich; the Harold and Wilma Good Library, Goshen College; the Menno Simons Historical Library and Archives of Eastern Mennonite College, Harrisonburg, Virginia; Concordia Theological Seminary Library, St. Louis, Missouri; the Mennonite Archives, Amsterdam; Bethel College Library, North Newton, Kansas; and the Fleming Library (now A. Webb Roberts Library), Southwestern Baptist Theological Seminary, Fort Worth, Texas.

Grateful as I am for all the help I have received in the production of this work, I realize that it is not a final word on the Anabaptists. It really was never intended to be other than a preliminary word. If it succeeds in awakening interest and stimulating serious study by the contemporary student of sixteenth-century Anabaptism, I will be grateful.

W. R. ESTEP

Introduction

THE HISTORY OF ANABAPTISM BELONGS TO THE CATEGORY OF "NOW it can be told" stories. Perhaps there is no group within Christian history that has been judged as unfairly as the Anabaptists of the sixteenth century. Theirs has been the lot of the widely misunderstood, deliberately misrepresented, or completely ignored. With the exception of the present generation all but a handful of competent historians have joined in a "thumbs-down treatment" of four centuries' duration.[1]

There are several factors which explain this otherwise baffling and inexcusable situation. The first of these is hostile polemics. Scholars of preceding generations have leaned heavily upon the highly partisan and quite unreliable accounts of sixteenth-century Anabaptism in the writings of Ulrich Zwingli, Justus Menius, Heinrich Bullinger, and Christoph Fischer, to say nothing of the milder but just as erroneous accounts of Martin Luther and Philip Melanchthon.[2] Other problems have been

1. Beginning with the works of C. A. Cornelius and Ludwig Keller in Europe, and John Horsch in America there has been a noticeable improvement in both materials available for study to students of the sixteenth-century Anabaptist movement and in treatment of Anabaptist history by non-Mennonite historians. Symbolic of this change is the publication of *The Recovery of the Anabaptist Vision,* ed. Guy F. Hershberger (Scottdale, Pa.: Herald Press, 1957), in which appear chapters by interested scholars of many different communions.

2. The most offensive of these were Heinrich Bullinger's *Der Widertäufferen*

1

unavailability of source materials, lack of interest by European scholars, and unwillingness by American historians (with notable exceptions) to deal with materials which were available.[3]

Ursprung, fürgang, Secten, wäsen, fürneme und gemeine jrer leer Artickel, published in 1561, and Christoph Andreas Fischer's *Von der Wiedertauffer verfluchtem Ursprung, gottlosen Lehre und derselben gründliche Widerlegung* of 1603.

3. The more important sources of Anabaptistica, either recently discovered or made available for the first time in centuries, are as follows:

(1) In 1923, Rudolf Wolkan edited and published the *Geschicht-Buch der Hutterischen Brüder* (Wien: S. Fromme). For years it had been presumed lost. Beck was not able to locate a copy of it. It was found in one of the Hutterite colonies in Paraguay and made available by Wolkan once again to the world. In 1943, an American edition was published.

(2) In 1947, A. J. F. Zieglschmid published *Das Klein-Geschichtsbüch der Hutterischen Brüder* (Philadelphia: Carl Schurz Memorial Foundation). It is almost as large as the *Large Chronicle (Die älteste Chronik der Hutterischen Brüder).* In addition to a nearly exhaustive bibliography of the Anabaptists, it contains a heretofore unknown *Gemeinde Ordnungen* and a history of the Hutterian Brethren from 1802 to 1947.

(3) In 1939, Claus Felbinger's *Confession* of 1560 was published in both German and English by the Society of Brothers, Primavera, Alto, Paraguay in their magazine *Plough and Pflug.* The manuscript, formerly unknown, was found in the Zentralbibliothek of Zürich, Switzerland. It has since been made available to the English reader by Robert Friedmann, "Claus Felbinger's Confession of 1560," *The Mennonite Quarterly Review* 29 (April 1955): 141-61. Hereafter *The Mennonite Quarterly Review* is cited as MQR.

(4) In 1946, an undated codex owned in 1737 by "Claus Wüterich *in der varderen Noremat Un Trub*" in the Emmenthal, Bern Canton, Switzerland, was found in the attic of a Mennonite farmhouse near Langnau, Switzerland, by Samuel Geiser. It was transcribed in 1955, making a manuscript of 156 typewritten pages. It contains thirteen hymns, some of which are as early as 1530, and five doctrinal writings dating from 1529 to 1583.

(5) In 1949, Peter Riedemann's *Rechenschaft* was translated and published for the first time in English.

(6) In 1954, Robert Friedmann discovered a manuscript, *Offenbarung Johannis,* an exposition of the book of Revelation, in twenty-two chapters — 162 leaves copied by Elias Walter in 1883. It turned out to be a commentary on Revelation written by a Spiritual Franciscan by the name of Petrus Johannis Olivi (1248-98), first published a year after his death in 1299 and evidently in the possession of the Hutterites since 1573.

(7) In 1955, Heinold Fast discovered in the Bürgerbibliothek at Bern,

In 1534 a group of fanatics at Münster attempted to set up the kingdom of God by force. Before they were overthrown, many atrocities were committed in the name of religion. This fiasco, the most serious aberration of sixteenth-century Anabaptism, has long been exaggerated out of all proportion to its true importance.[4] It strengthened the posi-

Switzerland, a manuscript codex of 740 pages dated September 21, 1561, by Jörg Maler of Augsburg, editor and copyist. It contained the *Kunstbuch,* some minor items, and forty-two letters and documents of 1527-55, largely from the Pilgram Marpeck circle of South German Anabaptists. A short time later Fast wrote a detailed description of the *Kunstbuch* and a commentary on sections of this significant document. See William Klassen, "Pilgram Marpeck in Recent Research," MQR 32 (July 1958): 211-14 for more information concerning this discovery.

(8) In the same year, 1955, Fast and Gerhard Goeters discovered two additional codices of lesser significance.

(9) Also in 1955, twenty-two Hutterite codices formerly at Schloss Mittersill, Austria (three are missing), were located in the City Library at Bratislova (Pressburg), Czechoslovakia.

(10) In 1957 a new volume of selected English translations of Anabaptist and Spiritual writers came off the press. The volume, which is entitled *Spiritual and Anabaptist Writers* (Philadelphia: Westminster Press, 1957), is edited by George Huntston Williams and Angel Mergal and contains selections from works of George Blaurock, Thomas Müntzer, John [Hans] Denck, Balthasar Hubmaier, Melchior Hofmann, Obbe Philips, Dietrich Philips, Menno Simons, Ulrich Stadler, Sebastian Franck, and Casper Schwenckfeld. Approximately one hundred pages are given to a translation of selections from the works of Juan de Valdés. In addition, this work contains a rather complete bibliography of English translations representative of the Radical Reformation (1524-75).

(11) Harold Bender writes: "The only comprehensive treatment of Anabaptist historiography to date is that by Christian Hege in his article 'Geschichtsschreibung' in *Mennonitisches Lexikon,* Vol. II, 96-101," MQR 31 (April 1957): 100. Subsequently, Hans Joachim Hillerbrand compiled the most extensive bibliography on Anabaptism yet published under the title *A Bibliography of Anabaptism, 1520-1630* (Elkhart, Ind.: Institute of Mennonite Studies, 1962). In 1975, the Center for Reformation Research published in its *Sixteenth Century Bibliography* series *A Sequel — 1962-1974* to Hillerbrand's previous *A Bibliography of Anabaptism, 1520-1630.*

(12) In 1958, Robert Friedmann was allowed access by the Hutterites of Canada to a hitherto unknown collection of letters of sixteenth-century Anabaptist origin. The value of this new material is unknown at present.

4. Too much has been said of Münster. It belongs on the fringe of Anabaptist life, which was completely divorced from the evangelical, biblical heart of the

tion of those who persecuted the Anabaptists and left the name Anabaptist in odious repute. To an extent not true before, the term Anabaptist became equated with such epithets as *Schwärmer* (fanatic), *Bolsheviki,* and "stepchildren of the Reformation."[5]

At times, the nature of the Anabaptist Reformation has been misunderstood because of confusion in the use of the terms Anabaptists, inspirationists *(Spiritualisten),* rationalists (antitrinitarians), and libertines. The Lutherans consistently associated the radical inspirationists, such as the Zwickau prophets and Thomas Müntzer, with the Swiss Brethren. The Calvinists often linked them with the rationalists and libertines. Deliberate or not, such careless treatment did not help the Anabaptist cause or encourage history to judge them properly. Modern research, however, coupled with a less heated and more objective approach to the subject, has moderated the situation.[6]

---

movement. One should interpret Münster in the light of the whole movement and not the movement in the light of Münster. Cornelius Krahn in his *History of Dutch Anabaptism, Origin, Spread, Life and Thought (1450-1600)* (The Hague: Martinus Nijhoff, 1968) does an excellent job of placing the whole Münster episode in proper perspective.

5. Luther called them *Schwärmer,* which literally translated means enthusiasts. Preserved Smith uses the term *Bolsheviki* in *The Age of the Reformation* (New York: Henry Holt, 1920), p. 154. Williams points out that J. Lindeboom, *Stiefkinderen van het Christendom,* uses the term "step-children of the Reformation." See Williams and Mergal, *Spiritual and Anabaptist Writers,* p. 26. See also Leonard Verduin, *The Reformers and Their Stepchildren* (Grand Rapids: William B. Eerdmans Publishing Company, 1964), for an incisive theological study of sixteenth-century Anabaptism utilizing the terms of reproach hurled against the Anabaptists as chapter headings.

6. There is no excuse today in light of materials now available for the informed student of the Reformation to confuse the various groups within the Radical Reformation with one another. The "left wing of the Reformation" is a term used by Bainton to characterize the inspirationists, Anabaptists, and rationalists, but Williams prefers "the Radical Reformation." "All three groupings within the Radical Reformation," he suggests, "agreed in cutting back to that root and in freeing church and creed of what they regarded as the suffocating growth of ecclesiastical tradition and magisterial prerogative. Precisely this makes theirs a 'Radical Reformation'" (Williams and Mergal, *Spiritual and Anabaptist Writers,* p. 22). Williams is not the first to make use of this terminology, but he explains why such usage is to be preferred. In fact, a similar technical distinction has been

Anabaptist Historiography

C. A. Cornelius, a Roman Catholic scholar, was one of the first historians to take a new look at the Anabaptist movement. He turned to sources rather than the perverted accounts of antagonistic writers. From his work, *Die Geschichte des Münsterischen Aufruhrs* (1855), modern Anabaptist historiography may be dated. This pioneering effort encouraged Ludwig Keller to continue studies in a similar vein. He published three books on the subject. Ernst Troeltsch and Max Weber in their "religio-sociological works" made invaluable contributions to Anabaptist historiography.[7] Excellent treatments of the historiography of sixteenth-century Anabaptists are now readily available in English.[8]

To those able scholars of many different communions, all students of the Anabaptist movement are indebted. Indeed, such a work as this would have been greatly altered, if possible at all, without the fruits of their dedicated scholarship.

made by some scholars for half a century. As early as 1531, William Barlow, an English student of the continental Anabaptist movement, referred to it as "the thyrd faccyon" of the Reformation. See Irvin B. Horst, "England," *Mennonite Encyclopaedia*, 2:220. Hereafter *Mennonite Encyclopaedia* is cited as ME.

7. See Hershberger, *Recovery of Anabaptist Vision*, pp. 4-5, for titles by Keller, Troeltsch, and Weber.

8. See Franklin Hamlin Littell, *The Anabaptist View of the Church* (Boston: Starr King Press, 1958). The first edition was published in 1952 as the Prize Essay of the Frank S. Brewer Fund of the American Society of Church History. It presents an Anabaptist historiography and relative problems, pp. 5-18. This section is revised and brought up to date in the second edition, 1958. Two articles, "Historiography of the Anabaptists," MQR 31 (April 1957): 88-104, and "Historiography" by Harold S. Bender and Cornelius Krahn in ME, 2:51-69, are of real value. See also George Huntston Williams, "Studies in the Radical Reformation (1517-1618): A Bibliographical Survey of Research Since 1939," *Church History* 27 (April 1958): 124-60. In the Introduction to Williams and Mergal, *Spiritual and Anabaptist Writers*, Williams gives a splendid bibliographical survey of the Radical Reformation along with many stimulating suggestions for interpreting the movement. The third edition of George Huntston Williams's *The Radical Reformation* (Kirksville, Mo.: Sixteenth Century Journal Publishers, Inc., 1992) remains the most comprehensive detailed historical treatment of the entire Radical Reformation. No serious student of Anabaptism can neglect this most significant work.

New Interest in the Anabaptists

The revival of interest in the Anabaptists has been sparked by factors other than those thus far mentioned.[9] Among these is the amazing growth of the free church movement. This growth and the crystallization of Marxian concepts present new challenges to the age-old state-church concepts from widely divergent ideological standpoints.

Since the state-church system has been threatened by communism in the Western world, those who have considered this form of ecclesiastical institutionalism *sacrosanct* have been forced to reexamine for the first time the merits of the free church idea. Denominations in the United States have been successful in operating without the support of the state. By contrast, the state-church system shows serious failings on the continent of its birth. Such facts have led many to a realization that a religious monopoly with the support of the state may not be an unmixed blessing.[10]

The critique of the established church of Denmark by Søren Kierkegaard did not ignite a flame which threatened to consume "the system" in his day. His judgment, however, is vindicated by the fact that such a flame is burning fiercely today. For this situation within Protestant Christianity, the theologians of the neoorthodox circles are to a great degree responsible. Karl Barth and Emil Brunner have stoked the fires of critical analysis of state-church systems. They have done it at the points where sixteenth-century Anabaptism challenged the Roman Catholic, Lutheran, and Reformed Church establishments alike. Barth's *Die Kirchliche Lehre von der Taufe*[11] was a stunning blow against some age-old baptismal errors. Oscar Cullmann, T. F. Torrance, and John Baillie have tried valiantly to meet it.[12] Yet responsible criti-

9. Factors already mentioned are new discoveries of source materials and the emergence of recent treatments of sixteenth-century Anabaptism.

10. Two modern works on the free church movement are indicative of increased interest in this direction: Franklin Hamlin Littell, *The Free Church* (Boston: Starr King Press, 1957), and Gunnar Westin, *The Free Church Through the Ages*, trans. Virgil Olson (Nashville: Broadman Press, 1958).

11. (Zürich: Evangelischer Verlag AG, 1953). See Ernest A. Payne's translation, *The Teaching of the Church regarding Baptism* (London: SCM Press, 1954).

12. For an able discussion of the issues in the current controversy see

cism of infant baptism and other outward appendages of a medieval theology continues. Such discussion has helped to throw the spotlight of historical investigation upon those who led in the free church movement, the once-despised Anabaptists.[13]

Purpose of This Work

Who were the sixteenth-century Anabaptists? Were they heretics, fanatics, or saints? Where did the movement originate? What was its relationship to the Reformation? Does Anabaptism comprise a distinct type of Reformation development? What were the motivations of the movement? What did the Anabaptists believe about God, man, the church, baptism, the Christian life? What kind of people were they? These and other questions find their answers in the following pages, which attempt to tell the story of the Anabaptists.

Today is a particularly opportune time to retell the story of this little-known movement. The importance of a new study of the Anabaptists will become increasingly apparent as the narrative unfolds. This is true because of the historical legacy to which many modern denominations are indebted. It is also true because of the problems that confront evangelical Christianity in the contemporary world.

Do the Anabaptists have anything to say to the present generation?

Robert G. Bratcher, "The Church of Scotland's Report on Baptism," *The Review and Expositor* 54 (April 1957): 205-22. The most able defense of infant baptism thus far presented is by Oscar Cullmann, *Die Tauflehre des Neuen Testament* (Zürich: Zwingli-Verlag, 1948). J. K. S. Reid has translated this as *Baptism in the New Testament* (Chicago: Henry Regnery Company, 1950). It is Cullmann's declared intention to repulse Barth's attack on infant baptism. He considers it fallacious but significant; "His study is in fact the most serious challenge to infant baptism which has ever been offered" (pp. 7-8).

13. See Karl Barth, *Die Taufe als Begründung des christlichen Lebens* (Zürich: EVZ-Verlag, 1967); Athol Gill, *A Bibliography of Baptist Writings on Baptism, 1900-1968* (Rüschlikon-Zürich: Baptist Theological Seminary, 1969); *The Review and Expositor* 65, no. 1 (Louisville, 1968) for a symposium of articles on baptism in this issue; see also *The Anvil* 1, no. 4 (Melbourne, June 4, 1969), which is also largely devoted to the contemporary dialogue on baptism.

The author's conviction that they do has called forth this effort to pen their history for a twentieth-century audience.

The narrative begins with the rise of the Anabaptists in Switzerland and follows their trek across Europe in search of freedom. Interspersed with biographical sketches of the early leaders and theologians, the story moves from Holland to England and finally to the colonies of the New World. An attempt is made to examine the relationship of continental Anabaptism and early English Baptists and to measure the influence of Anabaptism upon English and American separatism. It is hoped that this treatment of the sixteenth-century Anabaptists will prove a satisfactory introduction to the movement. Clearly, Anabaptism deserves serious attention in its own right, regardless of possible historical relation with other groups.

I

๚   ๚

The Birth of Anabaptism

O N A CRISP OCTOBER NIGHT IN 1517, THE THIRTY-FIRST TO BE EXACT, a black-garbed Augustinian monk made his way undetected to the castle church. The place was an insignificant medieval German town named Wittenberg. With swift, determined strokes he nailed one of the most inflammable documents of the age to the church door, which served as the village bulletin board. Within a fortnight all Europe was echoing the sound of that inauspicious hammer. A month later the hardly audible taps had become sledgehammer blows assailing the very citadel of the Roman Catholic Church.[1] For the Austin friar of that October night was Martin Luther and the apparently innocent Latin manuscript was his first fusillade against Rome, the Ninety-five Theses.

The Sixteenth Century, Religious and Otherwise

Whether Luther recognized the fact or not, the Reformation was launched. Pope Leo X was soon to find the church going to pieces under his pontifical feet and the roof falling in around his jewel-studded tiara. This was the time of epoch-making events, only one of which was the publication of the Ninety-five Theses.

1. Roland H. Bainton, *Here I Stand* (New York: Abingdon Press, 1950), pp. 79ff.

Less than a hundred years before the papal schism had come to an end. The memory of the ludicrous spectacle of two and, at times, three popes anathematizing one another still haunted the papacy. It sparked popular skepticism that mocked papal claims of infallibility. The vindictive execution of John Huss and the senseless posthumous burning of John Wycliffe upon orders of the Council of Constance served as grim reminders of the diabolical power of a secularized church. Torquemada's blood purge set a new pattern for inquisitorial procedures, an ill omen, indeed, for the remainder of Europe.[2] The Renaissance, with its peculiar mingling of pagan and religious attributes, led to an exposé of medieval ecclesiastical forgeries such as the pseudo-Isidorian decretals and the Donation of Constantine. It became most pagan in its Italian manifestation and most religious in its German development.

Simultaneously with the Renaissance and its developing book culture, Europe was undergoing a number of profound economic and political changes. Feudalism was gradually giving way to a monetary economy. Great banking houses were founded in Florence, Genoa, Augsburg, and Antwerp. The new economy impoverished many a feudal lord while it enriched some and gave rise to a new class of merchants and artisans. Peasants found themselves caught in a "squeeze play" between the demands of the lords and the bare necessities of life, for the embattled nobility began to take away their traditional grazing, hunting, and fishing rights. Life, which had always been marginal for serfs and peasants, now became unbearable. Those who could, fled the manors for the rapidly growing towns and cities. Others rebelled. From the 1350s, peasants organized and protested their increasingly difficult lot, sometimes violently, but always invoking religion in justification of their actions.

Politically, on the eve of the Reformation the face of Europe was changing. England and the continent witnessed the birth of both new cities and nations in the making. Among these, sixteenth-century Ger-

---

2. Thomas M. Lindsay, *A History of the Reformation* (Edinburgh: T. and T. Clark, 1907), 2:599-600. Lindsay writes: "Llorente has calculated that during the eighteen years of Torquemada's presidency 114,000 persons were accused, of whom 10,220 were burnt alive, and 97,000 were condemned to perpetual imprisonment or to public penitence."

many, although far from achieving nation status, still was experiencing a growing spirit of nationalism to which Luther did not hesitate to appeal. With the discovery of new trade routes to the Far East and the continents of the Western hemisphere, Europeans suddenly found themselves in a strange new world, much of which was unknown. But that which was known was enough to raise questions about age-old assumptions regarding the world, the universe, and God. It was an unsettling time.

The preceding paragraphs do little more than allude to some facets of a society that provided the backdrop for possibly the most upsetting force of all, the sixteenth-century Reformation. Once begun, the Reformation spread with an incredible speed. Books and Bibles, tracts and pamphlets came forth from nondescript presses all over Europe in an ever increasing stream. Without the printing press it would have been difficult, if not impossible, for the Reformation to have crystallized into a highly articulate movement.[3] Before Luther's day some twenty editions of the German Bible had come from the press. The ink was hardly dry on the first edition of Erasmus's Greek New Testament when Luther found himself thrust into the forefront of the developing controversy as champion of Reformation truth.[4]

The Zürich Reformer

In that eventful year, 1517, another German-speaking priest was wrestling with the tantalizing new Greek text. Born high in the Toggenburg Valley of the Swiss Alps seven weeks after the birth of Martin Luther, Ulrich Zwingli had already become a thoroughgoing humanist and a great admirer of Erasmus. At Einsiedeln, where he was then serving as people's priest, Zwingli first began to apply himself seriously to the study of the New Testament. The young priest found it increasingly difficult to resist its truth. By the time Zwingli had accepted the call to Zürich as people's priest of the Grossmünster, he had resolved to preach nothing but the gospel. By 1522 the Reformation in Zürich

3. *Ibid.,* 1:45.
4. See Kenneth A. Strand, *German Bibles Before Luther* (Grand Rapids: William B. Eerdmans Publishing Company, 1966), pp. 15-32.

had quickened its pace. Zwingli was indisputably in control. This came in spite of his admitted immorality before coming to Zürich and the open opposition of some Zürichers to his call. During the brief span of three years he succeeded in overcoming opposition and endearing the people to himself and his cause.

Zwingli's Leadership

The Reformation in Zürich was not a haphazard development. Rather, under Zwingli's guidance, it proceeded along clearly defined lines. The Swiss reformer well knew that pulpit eloquence alone could not accomplish the task of reform. Thus, to preaching he added teaching and the disputation. Finally, he sought legal support from the ruling authorities of Zürich, the city council.[5]

In Zwingli, the scholar, the humanist, and the evangelical reformer were blended into an attractive and forceful personality. Consequently, there were drawn to him a number of gifted young intellectuals primarily interested in study of the Greek classics. Into this group by November, 1521, had come a youthful vagabond scholar by the name of Conrad Grebel. Grebel's father was a member of the Great Council of the city of Zürich. This new association gave Grebel an opportunity to continue his studies of the Greek language and literature into which he had been initiated a few years before in Paris.[6]

Love of learning and admiration for Erasmus characterized the young humanists. Taking advantage of this, Zwingli soon introduced them to the Greek New Testament. By 1522 they, too, had become zealous for reform, particularly Grebel. But less than three years later their convictions had driven them far beyond Zwingli. The public break between Zwingli and his erstwhile disciples came with evident finality at a fateful disputation in January, 1525. The council proclaimed Zwingli the victor and denounced the radicals. The alternatives were

5. Samuel Macauley Jackson, *Huldreich Zwingli* (New York: G. P. Putnam's Sons, 1900), pp. 200-205.

6. Harold Bender, *Conrad Grebel* (Goshen, Ind.: The Mennonite Historical Society, 1950), pp. 56-57. Hereafter cited as *Grebel*.

quite clear. The little group could conform, leave Zürich, or face imprisonment. It chose the last.[7]

The Birth of Anabaptism

A few days later, January 21, 1525, a dozen or so men slowly trudged through the snow. Quietly but resolutely, singly or in pairs they came by night to the home of Felix Manz, near the Grossmünster.[8] The chill of the winter wind blowing off the lake did not match the chill of disappointment that gripped the little band that fateful night.

The dramatic events of the unforgettable gathering have been preserved in *The Large Chronicle of the Hutterian Brethren*. The account bears the earmarks of an eyewitness, who was probably Jörg Cajakob, called George Blaurock, a priest who had recently come to Zürich from Chur.

And it came to pass that they were together until anxiety [*angst*] came upon them, yes, they were so pressed within their hearts. Thereupon they began to bow their knees to the Most High [*hochstenn*] God in heaven and called upon him as the Informer of Hearts [*Hertzenkundiger*], and they prayed that he would give to them his divine [*götlichen*] will and that he would show his mercy unto them. For flesh and blood and human forwardness did not drive them, since they well knew what they would have to suffer on account of it.

After the prayer, George of the House of Jacob stood up and

---

7. *Ibid.,* pp. 81-82.

8. *Ibid.,* p. 137. Fritz Blanke of the University of Zürich holds that January 30 rather than 25 is the date of this gathering. He follows the dating given to the Egli manuscripts M. 636.1, entitled *Bekenntnis der Täufer,* which is now in the state archives of Zürich and reproduced by Leonhard von Muralt and Walter Schmid in *Quellen zur Geschichte der Täufer in der Schweiz* (Zürich: S. Hirzel Verlag, 1952), vol. 1, no. 30, pp. 39-40; hereafter cited as *Quellen.* In spite of the two dates suggested here — January 30 or February 7 — Bender seems to be more nearly correct when he suggests that the first baptism could not have taken place later than January 23 and almost certainly had to be on the night of January 21, 1525. See *Grebel,* p. 264, n. 3, for Bender's viewpoint.

besought [*gebeeten*] Conrad Grebel for God's sake to baptize him with the true [*recht*] Christian baptism upon his faith and knowledge [*erkanndtnus*]. And when he knelt down with such a request and desire, Conrad baptized him, since at that time there was no ordained minister [*dienner*] to perform such work.[9]

After his baptism at the hands of Grebel, Blaurock proceeded to baptize all the others present. The newly baptized then pledged themselves as true disciples of Christ to live lives separated from the world and to teach the gospel and hold the faith.

Anabaptism was born. With this first baptism, the earliest church of the Swiss Brethren was constituted. This was clearly the most revolutionary act of the Reformation. No other event so completely symbolized the break with Rome. Here, for the first time in the course of the Reformation, a group of Christians dared to form a church after what was conceived to be the New Testament pattern. The Brethren emphasized the absolute necessity of a personal commitment to Christ as essential to salvation and a prerequisite to baptism.[10]

9. A. J. F. Zieglschmid, *Die älteste Chronik der Hutterischen Brüder* (New York: Carl Schurz Memorial Foundation, 1943), p. 47. The full account is also given in *Das Klein-Geschichtsbüch der Hutterischen Brüder,* ed. Zieglschmid. Joseph Beck, in his edition of *Die Geschichte-Bücher der Wiedertaufer in Oesterreich — Ungarn* (Vienna: Carl Gerald's Son, 1883), pp. 19-20, gives essentially the same account. English translations of this first baptism are given by John Christian Wenger, *Glimpses of Mennonite History and Doctrine* (Scottdale, Pa.: Herald Press, 1947), pp. 24-25, *Grebel,* p. 137, and Williams and Mergal, *Spiritual and Anabaptist Writers,* pp. 41-46. *Die älteste Chronik* will henceforth be indicated by an English designation, the *Large Chronicle.* In 1987, the Hutterian Brethren published an English translation of *Das grosse Geschichtsbuch der Hutterischen Brüder.* For the account of the first baptisms among the Swiss Brethren in the Hutterian translation, see p. 45.

10. Fritz Blanke is undoubtedly correct when he writes: "It has been ascertained that Conrad Grebel and his circle, viz., the Zürich opponents of infant baptism had already in 1524 reached the conviction on the basis of the New Testament that baptism must be preceded by repentance; impenitent persons must not be baptized. It was a necessary condition that the person to be baptized should have reached an age at which he or she would be capable of repentance. Thus only responsible persons could be baptized." See Fritz Blanke, "The First Anabaptist Congregation: Zollikon, 1525," MQR 27 (January 1953): 28. See Fritz

The introduction of believers' baptism was not an unpremeditated act. Even though its revolutionary character might well have struck the hearts of those assembled on that January night with fear, it was no spur-of-the-moment decision. Rather, it was a culmination of convictions derived from an earnest study of the Scriptures and a series of disappointing events. After failing to convince Zwingli of an alternate program of reform, they proceeded to act out their convictions by withholding their children from the traditional infant baptism still administered by Zwingli and the Reformed preachers with "blowing, driving out the devil, crossing, moistening with saliva, and anointing with oil."[11]

The October Disputation

As early as December, 1523, there is evidence that dissatisfaction had developed among some of Zwingli's most dedicated followers. There is no mistaking the tone of Conrad Grebel's letter of December 18. He was writing to his brother-in-law and former teacher, Vadian, pastor of the Reformed Church at St. Gall. Among other things, he implied that he had lost confidence in Zwingli and was taking a "dim" view of the future of the Reformation in Zürich. In a disputation in October, he had opposed Zwingli's appeal to the council to settle questions pertaining to the mass and images. Evidently, this had placed him in bad light in Zwingli's eyes. He wrote to Vadian, "if you can believe a suspected person as I" *(si tamen suspecto magis quam mendaci credas)*.[12] Five days after Grebel's letter, December 23, Simon Stumpf was banished from Zürich. Along with Grebel he had taken an active part in the October disputation and had continued his agitation against the mass.

In two short months the relationship between Zwingli and Grebel had deteriorated rapidly. The cause, however, is not difficult to discover. Grebel and Stumpf seem to have taken a position somewhat more ad-

---

Blanke, *Brüder in Christo* (Zürich: Zwingli-Verlag, 1955), for a fuller account of early Anabaptism in Zürich (E.T. *Brothers in Christ*, trans. Joseph Nordenhaug [Scottdale, Pa.: Herald Press, 1961]).

11. Fritz Blanke, *Brothers in Christ*, p. 23.
12. *Quellen*, 1, no. 8, p. 8.

vanced than Zwingli's in the October disputation. According to the record, however, Zwingli had agreed with the younger men that the Word of God and not the Zürich council should determine the disposition of the mass and the use of images.[13] Yet following the disputation, Zwingli seemed to submit to the decision of the council. He was unwilling to alter observance of the Lord's Supper to conform to the Scriptures and his earlier promises. This became the point of contention between him and Grebel.

On the first day of the disputation, October 26, the use of images was discussed and roundly denounced by all participants. On the second day the mass was repeatedly described as an abomination before God. At this juncture in the disputation Grebel, Stumpf, and possibly others had expected some explicit directions from Zwingli to the council on the abolition of the mass. Prior to the debate Zwingli and his young disciples apparently agreed to follow the Bible explicitly in their program of reform. Throughout the October disputation the common appeal of the speakers had been to the Word of God.[14] Undoubtedly Zwingli and his followers had dared to hope that the disputation would prepare the way for changing the mass into an observance of the Lord's Supper. But the close of the debate on the mass brought forth no instructions concerning its abolition.

The burgomaster had already announced that the disputation would move on the next day from further consideration of the mass to a discussion of purgatory. Whereupon Grebel arose to request that the present subject not be forsaken until other abuses of the mass had been discussed and instructions given as to the means of its abolition. To this suggestion Zwingli replied, "My lords will decide whatever regulations are to be adopted in the future in regard to the Mass."

This unexpected and rather curt statement from Zwingli provoked Simon Stumpf to exclaim, "Master Ulrich, you do not have the right to place the decision on this matter in the hands of my lords, for the decision has already been made, the Spirit of God decides."

---

13. See John Howard Yoder, "The Turning Point in the Zwinglian Reformation," MQR 32 (April 1958): 128-40 for a thorough discussion of the disagreement between Grebel and Zwingli on issues of the October disputation.

14. See the account of the second disputation of Zürich in *Huldreich Zwingli's Werke,* ed. Melchior Schuler and Joh. Schulthess (Zürich: Friedrich Schulthess, 1828), 1:459-540. Hereafter cited as *Zwingli.*

Zwingli next delineated the difference between truth as determined from study of the Scriptures and the implementation of truth by the council. The closing remarks of Stumpf indicate that to him implementation of that which was so clearly enunciated in the New Testament was not the prerogative of the council. "If my lords adopt and decide on some other course that would be against the decision of God, I will ask Christ for his Spirit, and I will preach and act against it."[15]

Zwingli immediately responded to Stumpf's statement with a ringing affirmation. *"Das ist recht,"* he replied. "I will also preach and act against it if they decide otherwise. I am not putting the decision in their hand. They are not over the Word of God, and this goes not only for them but for the whole world [*ja ouch alle welt nit*]."[16] Then once again Zwingli differentiated the diverse functions of the disputation and the implementation of its judgments by the council.

Purgatory had been previously announced as the topic for discussion on the third day. However, the heated exchange between Zwingli and his youthful disciples the previous day had derailed the discussion. Thus, the mass and not purgatory demanded the attention of the assembly throughout the day. Grebel spoke first, followed by Balthasar Hubmaier, a priest from Waldshut on the Rhine. Much of the time the disputation became a dialogue between Grebel and Zwingli. Finally Grebel grew quiet and Zwingli turned his attention to those who represented an even more moderate position than his. Apparently, Grebel's silence toward the close of the October disputation was not induced by assent. But he, at least, held his peace until some two months later when all hope of abolition of the mass in the foreseeable future was gone.

As far as Grebel was concerned, Zwingli had abandoned his avowed position of no compromise where the Word of God had spoken. At least, he had openly bowed to the will of the council and abandoned his previously announced plans to abolish the mass on Christmas Day, 1523. Looking back to the October disputation, Grebel was able to

15. *Grebel,* p. 98.

16. See *Zwingli,* 1:459-540, for the entire text of the minutes of the disputation as recorded by Ludwig Haetzer. For Yoder's position more fully stated see his *Täufertum und Reformation in der Schweiz,* I: *Die Gespräch zwischen Täufern und Reformatoren, 1523-1538* (Karlsruhe: H. Schneider, 1962).

mark this occasion as the historical divide between himself and Zwingli. The events of the disputation were reviewed afresh with the publication of its minutes on, or about, December 8. New outbursts against the mass and images two days later emphasized popular discontent with the slowness of the Zwinglian reform.

But the demonstrations were without their desired effect. By December 19, Zwingli had completely capitulated to the judgment and authority of the council, arriving at an impossible position as far as Grebel was concerned. In the eyes of the Brethren he had compromised revealed truth in deference to constituted political authority. The authority of the Word of God had been sacrificed on the altar of human expediency.[17] The Brethren felt themselves to have been betrayed.

Harold Bender detects in the break between Zwingli and his youthful critics the beginning of the free church movement. "The decision of Conrad Grebel to refuse to accept the jurisdiction of the Zürich council over the Zürich church is one of the high moments of history, for however obscure it was, it marked the beginning of the modern 'free church' movement."[18] Other historians date the cleavage between Zwingli and his former disciples sometime later. Regardless of the exact date, it is evident that almost a year later, when the Zürich radicals were attempting to establish contact with Thomas Müntzer, they had formulated a rather complete program of reform based upon their understanding of the New Testament.

17. *Grebel,* pp. 106-7. An excerpt from Grebel's letter to Vadian, December 18, indicates just how keenly he felt this cleavage with his former compatriot. "Nec aliud temere, quam pessime rem evangelicam hic habere (si tamen suspecto magis quam mendaci credas) et tunc coepisse, cum tu providentia senatoria praesidentem ageres, cum celebraretur, concilium; tunc (deus videt et in auribus eius est) cum verbum a doctissimis eius praeconibus inverteretur, retruderetur et alligaretur. Nunc dicam, quomodo super missa tractantes utergue ordo senatorius nodum hunc enodandum tradiderunt octo senatoribus, Zinlio, commendatori, abbati Capellano, praeposito Imbriacensi et nescio, quibus monstris rasis." *Quellen,* 1, no. 8, p. 8.

18. *Grebel,* pp. 99-100. Yoder sees the turning point in Grebel's attitude between December 10 and 19, when Zwingli worked out his compromise in order to appease the council ("Turning Point," pp. 128-40). The evidence for Bender's position is not conclusive. Yoder seems to have the edge, yet one cannot dismiss Grebel's probing questions and obvious dissatisfaction on the third day of the October disputation.

Crystallizing Conviction

The following year was one of importance for the embryonic Anabaptist movement. Grebel emerged as the leader and spokesman of the group of young radicals that included Simon Stumpf and Felix Manz. By the end of the year their number totaled seven.[19] Many attempts were made by Stumpf, Manz, and Grebel to present a more biblical program of reform to Zwingli and Leo Jud, but without success. Failing in a last-ditch effort to win the Zürich Reformers to their position, the radicals began to meet quietly in the homes of sympathetic friends. One favorite meeting place was the home of Felix Manz on a street called Neustadt. Bible study included expositions given by Manz and Hottinger. Correspondence with Luther, Müntzer, Carlstadt, and others, along with the distribution of Carlstadt's tracts, occupied time and energy during the closing months of 1524.[20]

Within the movement there soon developed a serious question regarding the validity of infant baptism. Wilhelm Reublin, pastor at Wytikon, a neighboring village to Zürich, seems to have been the first among the Swiss Brethren to preach against infant baptism. Within the year, three fathers at Zollikon withheld their children from baptism with the support of a former priest, Johannes Brötli. Retaliation was quick to follow. Reublin was imprisoned in August and not long afterward was forced to leave Zürich. It was the insistence on believers' baptism by Reublin, Brötli, Grebel, and others that precipitated the crisis which led to the disputation of January, 1525.[21]

Even though believers' baptism was not initiated in Zürich until January, 1525, Grebel had heard as early as a year and a half before that some were claiming that infants should not be baptized.[22] But he was not aroused by the issue until after Reublin and others had taken

19. *Quellen*, p. 21. *"Konrad Grebel und Genossen an Thomas Müntzer,"* no. 14, pp. 13-21. The names ascribed to the Müntzer letters are: Conrad Grebel, Andress Castelberg, Felix Manz, Heinrich Aberli, Joannes Panicellus, Hanss Oggenfuss, and Hanss Huiuf.

20. *Grebel*, pp. 103, 107, 109-24.

21. *Ibid.*, pp. 124, 132-33.

22. *Ibid.*, p. 125. Bender cites at this point a letter from Benedict Burgauer to Grebel dated July 21, 1523, a portion of which is cited in the Notes on p. 260.

their stand. Once aroused, he became completely committed. Although Grebel's disillusionment with the Swiss Reformation began with Zwingli's failure to follow through on plans to observe the Lord's Supper in a simple apostolic pattern on Christmas day, 1523, by 1525 the protest movement involved much more than the mass, or even believers' baptism — it involved the nature of the church. The concept of a church of committed believers had taken the place of a church made up of the mixed multitude. This new church, like that of the apostles, was to be made up only of those confessing Christ as Lord followed by believers' baptism, instead of everyone born in a given parish. The Lord's Supper would then be observed by the baptized in a simple manner, shorn of its medieval trappings, as a pledge of brotherly love in remembrance of the one, all-sufficient sacrifice of Christ.

Fritz Blanke has asserted that the characteristics of the church described above "were not to be found any where else at that time." Then he asked, "What is the source of this new view of the Christian church?" Grebel answers: "We were listeners to Zwingli's sermons and readers of his writings, but one day we took the Bible itself in hand and were taught better."[23]

Zwingli, Oecolampadius, Jud, Grossman, and others had expressed doubt concerning the validity of infant baptism. And, of course, it is not startling news that the Zwickau prophets had questioned the scriptural-ness of the practice as early as 1521.[24] There were some significant differences in these earlier doubts regarding the validity of infant baptism and the baptism inaugurated by Grebel and Blaurock. First, there is no documentary evidence that those on record opposing infant baptism moved from theory to practice. Second, for these first Anabaptists, believers' baptism became an integral part of both the concept of disciple-ship and of the church. Third, the authority upon which they based their action was neither dreams nor visions, but the New Testament.[25]

---

23. Blanke, *Brothers in Christ*, p. 14. Blanke has reconstructed the development of the first Anabaptist congregation with its unique features from the sources as published in the *Quellen*.

24. Albert Henry Newman, *A History of Anti-Pedobaptism* (Philadelphia: American Baptist Publication Society, 1896), p. 70.

25. *Quellen*, 1, 14.

It is also evident that these bold pioneers of the free church movement did not at first part with Zwingli because of a difference of opinion over baptism but over the Lord's Supper and ecclesial authority. The questions regarding baptism apparently first arose during their studies of the New Testament with Zwingli but did not become an issue until the nature of the church demanded their attention. If this is an accurate account of the formation of convictions within the Grebel-led group, the act of baptism clearly set the emerging Anabaptist movement apart from Thomas Müntzer and the Zwickau prophets, as well as from Zwingli, who had also at one time, according to former colleagues, questioned the validity of infant baptism. Thus, within the context of the Zwingli-led Swiss Reformation the Anabaptist movement began to take shape. Stepchildren or not, the Anabaptists were offspring of the Reformation.[26]

Anabaptists, Inspirationists, and Rationalists

Failure to distinguish between the Anabaptists, inspirationists *(Spiritualisten)*, and rationalists (antitrinitarians) has led to gross misunderstanding of the entire Radical Reformation.[27] These were three broad categories of somewhat diverse groups. The Anabaptists frequently found themselves theologically closer to the magisterial Reformers than to other "radicals." In addition, some individuals would gravitate from one group to the other or take on characteristics of more than one group, defying

26. Until believers' baptism was instituted and a church formed by the Brethren, their movement differed in few essential respects from those of other radicals, their emphasis upon the Scriptures making the greatest degree of difference. I believe Bender is only partially correct when he sees the rise of the free church movement in Conrad Grebel's disagreement with Zwingli over the issue of church and state relations *(Grebel,* pp. 99-100). Without a doubt the free church movement does stem from the Swiss Brethren, but this was by no means launched until believers' baptism had been inaugurated by the Brethren and a church was formed after what was conceived to be the New Testament pattern. See Blanke, *Brothers in Christ,* pp. 7-27.

27. Alfred Hegler (1863-1902), through original research, first began to make use of distinctions and terms which are generally followed today in any serious treatment of the Anabaptists. Troeltsch, Payne, Bainton, Littell, and most recently George Huntston Williams make essentially the same distinctions.

facile identification. That which makes the concept of a Radical Reformation useful, however, is the recognition it gives to free church origins as distinguished from state-church Protestantism, for all groups within the Radical Reformation denied the state's authority in matters of faith and order. Almost all also rejected infant baptism without necessarily adopting believers' baptism. All three of the groups composed elements in what has been termed the "Radical Reformation." They were all antipedobaptists, but at this point the comparison ceases.

The attitude toward authority both united and divided the radicals. They were agreed in rejecting the role of the state in matters of religion but they were not agreed regarding the ultimate authority in matters of faith and the Christian life. The concept of the ultimate spiritual authority shaped to a large extent the nature of the groups within the three main categories of the Radical Reformation.

For the Swiss and south German Anabaptists, the final authority for the Christian life and the faith and order of the church was the New Testament, in particular the life and teachings of Christ. While they tended to interpret the Scriptures in a literal sense, they were Christocentric. It was Christ who in the actual formulation of the faith became the ultimate authority to which they appealed. Although they did not reject the Old Testament in a Marcionite fashion, it was never allowed to take precedence over the New Testament or to become normative for the Christian faith. Theirs was a New Testament hermeneutic that assumed a progression in the biblical revelation that culminated in the Christ-event. Therefore the Old Testament, although useful and often quoted, could never stand alone, unqualified by the New Testament.[28]

For the inspirationists, the Spirit took precedence over the Bible. Thus the immediate illumination of the Spirit became the norm for the inspirationist's program of reform. The Zwickau prophets, Nicolaus Storch and Thomas Müntzer, claimed special revelation, as did later inspirationists.[29] The inspirationists were not primarily concerned with the visible church. With the Anabaptists, they shared antipathy to reformation by civil authority. They did not, however, share the Ana-

28. *Grebel*, p. 100. Also see Hershberger, *Recovery of Anabaptist Vision*, p. 58.
29. Newman, *History of Anti-Pedobaptism*, pp. 67ff., and Chapter VII, "Thomas Müntzer and the Peasant's War," pp. 77-87.

baptists' emphasis on restoration of the New Testament church or believers' baptism.[30]

The rationalists, as the term implies, put primary emphasis on the place of reason in interpreting the Scriptures. For the most part the evangelical rationalists were antitrinitarian, but they were antitrinitarian because they were rationalists and not the reverse. Reason, therefore, and not Scripture or special revelation became for them the source of ultimate authority.[31] Such disparate leaders as Michael Servetus, Juan de Valdés, Sebastian Castellio, George Biandrata, and Faustus Socinus are to be listed in this category.[32] Some remained within the Roman Catholic Church, and others attempted a restoration of what they conceived to be New Testament Christianity in separated churches.[33] All were much more evangelical than they have at times been represented.[34]

The value of the above distinctions is to recognize that there were fundamental differences between parties and movements within the Radical Reformation. However, it is not always an easy task to identify or to separate the strands. For example, Melchiorite Anabaptism, which

30. Williams and Mergal, *Spiritual and Anabaptist Writers,* p. 21.

31. Earl Morse Wilbur, *A History of Unitarianism: Socinianism and its Antecedents* (Cambridge, Mass.: Harvard University Press, 1945), p. 5.

32. See Roland Bainton, *The Travail of Religious Liberty* (New York: Harper & Brothers, 1958), for informative biographical sketches of Servetus and Castellio. See Wilbur, *History of Unitarianism,* for a more detailed treatment of Servetus, pp. 49-185, and Socinianism.

33. *The Racovian Cathechism,* published in 1605, is particularly illuminating at this point. Cited by Newman, *History of Anti-Pedobaptism,* pp. 337-39.

34. Newman, *History of Anti-Pedobaptism,* p. 338. In the following excerpt Newman delineates some of the more salient features of the rationalist theology. "'The Lord Jesus' is said to have 'been conceived of the Holy Spirit and born of a virgin, without the intervention of any human being.' He is spoken of as 'from his earliest origin the only begotten Son of God.' He is said to have 'been sent by the Father, with supreme authority, on an embassy to mankind.' 'He was raised from the dead by God and thus as it were begotten a second time. . . . By this event he became like God immortal.' It is recognized that he possesses 'dominion and supreme authority over all things.' He is said to have been 'not merely the only begotten Son of God, on account of the divine power and authority which he displayed even while he was yet mortal; much more may he be so denominated now, that he has received all power in heaven and earth, and that all things, God himself alone excepted, have been put under his feet.'"

characterized the movement in the Netherlands and north Germany, reflected a heady mix of apocalypticism and inspirationism in which visions and dreams appeared to have taken precedence over the Scriptures. The New Testament hermeneutic that was basic to other Anabaptists was noticeably lacking in Melchior Hofmann's version of Anabaptism. As a Lutheran, the self-taught furrier proclaimed the gospel with a heavy emphasis upon eschatological expectations, which became both more detailed and pronounced upon uniting with Strasbourg Anabaptists in 1530. Therefore, Hofmann concocted a strange mixture of spiritualism, Christology (derived from Caspar Schwenckfeld), and elements of Anabaptism that was to have disastrous consequences for himself and the Münsterites. Hofmann is only one example of those who might better be termed "marginal Anabaptists" or simply "Melchorites." Nevertheless, for want of a less confusing scheme of classification, in this book the term "Radical Reformation," suggested by George Huntston Williams, is used with the three major categories, albeit with the inevitable qualifications.

Anabaptism and Medieval Evangelicals

If the origin of the inspirationists is to be found in medieval mysticism and that of the rationalists in Renaissance humanism, what can be said about the roots of Anabaptism? Almost everything that could be said has, at one time or another, been said — and by competent scholars at that.

Albrecht Ritschl viewed Anabaptism as a continuation of medieval Franciscan *Tertiarii,* which manifested itself in the form of Anabaptism in the sixteenth century and in the form of Pietism in the seventeenth. Ludwig Keller developed the theory that held the Anabaptists to be an outgrowth of the Waldenses, Bohemian Brethren, and other groups which he labeled "the old-evangelical brotherhoods."[35] This position is essentially that of Thomas M. Lindsay: "For the whole Anabaptist movement was medieval to the core; and, like most of the medieval religious awakenings, produced an infinite variety of opinions and

35. Hershberger, *Recovery of Anabaptist Vision,* p. 36. See Robert Friedmann, "Conception of the Anabaptists," *Church History* 9 (October 1940): 351-52.

practices."[36] Smithson, Whitley, and Vedder, Baptist historians of another generation, favored with some reservations, such a view.[37]

To project Waldensian antecedents for the Anabaptists, as some have done, has long been a temptation difficult to resist. Van Braght of *Martyr's Mirror* fame held tenaciously to this view, as have John T. Christian and some other Baptist and Mennonite historians. Henry Elias Dosker as early as 1921 rejected the theory of Waldensian origin of the Dutch Anabaptists as completely unsupported by the known facts.[38] A similar position is taken in relation to Anabaptist origins in general by such accomplished Anabaptist scholars as Harold Bender, Robert Friedmann, and Fritz Blanke. A lone exception is the Mennonite scholar Delbert L. Grätz, who cautiously advanced the theory of a dual origin for the Bernese Anabaptist movement.[39]

Other contemporary scholars are just as positive that sixteenth-century Anabaptism had medieval roots.[40] Rufus Jones classed the Ana-

36. Lindsay, *History of Reformation*, 2:441.

37. R. J. Smithson, *The Anabaptists* (London: James Clarke & Co., Ltd., 1935), pp. 29ff.; W. T. Whitley, *A History of British Baptists* (London: Charles Griffin and Co., Ltd., 1923), p. 2; Henry C. Vedder, *A Short History of the Baptists* (Philadelphia: The American Baptist Publication Society, 1907), p. 130. Vedder stated his position in these words: "The utmost that can be said in the present state of historical research is that a moral certainty exists of a connection between the Swiss Anabaptists and their Waldensian and Petrobrusian predecessors, sustained by many significant facts, but not absolutely proved by historical evidence."

38. *The Dutch Anabaptists* (Philadelphia: Judson Press, 1921), p. 20. "There is not a scintilla of proof for the whole Waldensian theory." Thus writes Dosker on the claims of a Waldensian origin for the Dutch Anabaptists. What he says of the Dutch Anabaptists can also be said for the Swiss Brethren. Even though this was written over seventy years ago and much new material has been discovered, his thesis still stands.

39. *Bernese Anabaptists* (Scottdale, Pa.: Herald Press, 1953), p. 7. Grätz maintains that the Anabaptists of Switzerland are of two separate origins: the earlier segment from Waldensian influence and the later from the Swiss Brethren of Zürich.

40. Even though there is much to be said in favor of this view, not one of the Swiss Anabaptist leaders came from a Waldensian background. To the contrary, some have been mistakenly identified as Waldenses who actually were Roman Catholics. See Williams and Mergal, *Spiritual and Anabaptist Writers*, p. 141. In fact, all of the early Anabaptist leaders came originally from the Roman Church and to Anabaptism through the influence of the Swiss Reformation, or directly out of Catholicism into Anabaptist life. Too, as Friedmann has pointed out, the

baptists with the mystics and put them directly in line with medieval mysticism. Walther Köhler and Paul Peachey held that there were direct connections with the evangelical humanists.[41] Köhler also referred to Erasmus as the "profound spiritual father of the Anabaptists."[42] While in basic agreement with Köhler, Davis wrote that Erasmus "mediated not so much humanism as the spirit of the *devotio moderna* to the Anabaptist leaders."[43] This is essentially the same position advocated by Torsten Bergsten.[44]

A more inclusive approach to the questions of the origins of Anabaptism is the polygenesis theory vigorously advocated by James M. Stayer, Werner O. Packull, and Klaus Deppermann.[45] While the theory

---

differences between the Waldenses and the Anabaptists are greater than their similarities: "It is a fact that there are immediate links between the Waldenses and the Bohemian Brethren; but one must not confuse the Bohemian movement with that of the Anabaptists. The Bohemians had sacraments, hierarchy, confessions and Lent, like the Waldenses or the Donatists, while the Anabaptists lived according to a more Protestant pattern. Therefore, there was never any serious approach or important disputation between these groups. They went on untouched by one another, and it is obviously wrong to speak so generally of 'evangelical brotherhoods without finer distinction'" ("Conception of the Anabaptists," p. 353). See Jarold Knox Zeman, *The Anabaptists and the Czech Brethren in Moravia, 1526-1628* (The Hague: Mouton, 1969), pp. 27-30 for a concise yet thorough discussion of the relationship between the Bohemian Brethren and the Anabaptists.

The Waldenses themselves differ from time to time and place to place, as A. H. Newman has pointed out: "The early Waldenses, as we have seen had scarcely anything in common with Baptists. Of the later Waldenses some, probably not a large proportion, came to reject infant baptism" (*History of Anti-Pedobaptism*, p. 61).

Even though there are similarities between some Waldensian ideas and Anabaptist tenets of faith and the general geographical location of strong Waldensian communities and early Anabaptist agitation coincide, one must be exceedingly careful not to build a family tree without the connecting trunk. Almost the same thing could be said for the Bohemian Brethren in relation to the Anabaptists or of the Spiritual Franciscans for that matter.

41. Friedmann, "Conception of Anabaptists," p. 354.

42. Kenneth Ronald Davis, *Anabaptism and Asceticism: A Study in Intellectual Origins* (Scottdale, Pa.: Herald Press, 1974), p. 24.

43. *Ibid.*

44. Torsten Bergsten, *Balthasar Hübmaier: Seine Stellung zu Reformation und Täufertum* (Kassel: J. G. Oncken Verlag, 1961), pp. 23-30.

45. See the article authored by the three scholars titled "From Monogenesis

has received wide acceptance among historians of the Radical Reformation, this has not been unanimous. Its advocates have frequently taken a polemical stance in arguing vehemently for a position reminiscent of that of Karl Holl and earlier of Heinrich Bullinger. In this scenario, if the Zwickau prophets, and particularly Thomas Müntzer, were not the actual founders of the Anabaptist movement, they precipitated its rise by providing an ideological base upon which the Anabaptist leaders built. Hence, Anabaptism was portrayed in its Swiss and south German expressions as an integral part of the Great German Peasants' War.

While Stayer and his collaborators have provided insights that help in understanding certain social aspects of the Radical Reformation, their conclusions at times seem to be based on something other than historical evidence. For example, to treat the Anabaptist movement as simply one aspect of the social upheaval of sixteenth-century Europe is to ignore the profound intellectual and religious motivation that provided its driving force, of which the evidence was not only written in ink but also in blood. Again, to ascribe to Thomas Müntzer the role of founder of the Anabaptist movement is to ignore all the evidence to the contrary and to champion an untenable position.

Apparently, among social historians there has been a failure to understand or to appreciate the biblical and theological principles that provided the dynamic of Swiss and south German Anabaptism. No responsible historian can deny that sixteenth-century Anabaptism had a variety of expressions nor that the sources that contributed to the religious milieu in that century were also varied. But neither sources nor later developments can be understood apart from the "Anabaptist Vision" of those who first caught and shared it in the critical first decade of the movement. Contrary to what Stayer has written about being "preoccupied with the essentially sterile question of where Anabaptism began,"[46] for the historian the question of Anabaptism's beginning is as necessary as it is inescapable — no less so than the study of Luther's religious pilgrimage for the understanding of the Reformation as in the study of the beginnings of any other religious phenomenon.

---

to Polygenesis: The Historical Discussion of Anabaptist Origins," MQR 49 (April 1975): 83-121.
    46. *Ibid.*, p. 85.

There is little doubt that the Swiss Brethren were influenced to some degree by certain aspects of medieval spirituality through Erasmus, if through no other medium.[47] The influence of Zwingli is undeniable and that of Luther only less so. But the most determinative influence was that of the Bible, the sourcebook of the Christian faith, to which Zwingli and Luther also appealed.[48]

47. See Davis, *Anabaptism and Asceticism*, for a thorough and balanced study of possible medieval sources of Anabaptist spirituality.

48. Perhaps Marxist historians' interest in Thomas Müntzer and the Great German Peasants' War has led to an inordinate amount of attention to the social and economic aspects of the sixteenth-century Reformation. As a result, a veritable industry has busied itself with publishing articles and books on "the prophet of God's wrath" and his peasant partisans. A few of the more recent and significant books are as follows:

Friesen, Abraham. *Reformation and Utopia: The Marxist Interpretation of the Reformation and its Antecedents.* Wiesbaden: Franz Steiner Verlag GMBH, 1974.

———. *Thomas Muentzer, A Destroyer of the Godless: The Making of a Sixteenth-Century Religious Revolutionary.* Berkeley: University of California Press, 1990.

——— and Hans-Jürgen Goertz. *Thomas Müntzer.* Darmstadt, Germany: Wissenschaftliche Buchgesellschaft, 1978.

Gritsch, Eric W. *Reformer without a Church: The Life and Thought of Thomas Müntzer (1488?-1525).* Philadelphia: Fortress Press, 1967.

———. *Thomas Müntzer: A Tragedy of Errors.* Minneapolis: Augsburg Fortress, 1989.

Stayer, James M. *The German Peasants' War and Anabaptist Community of Goods.* Montreal: McGill-Queen's University Press, 1991.

II

꙳   ꙳

Meteors against the Night

THE HARVEST WHICH THE ANABAPTISTS REAPED DID NOT ALWAYS conform to the seed sown. Like that of the early church, the Anabaptist witness was accompanied by persecution unto death. One explanation for the treatment which the Anabaptists received from Catholic, Lutheran, and Reformed alike was the darkness of the age. The sixteenth century was dark because it was the product of previous centuries. Civilization had become increasingly oblivious to human suffering and the value of the individual. Piety was evaluated by the amount of accumulated external acts. Hypocrisy became the hallmark of the age. In the darkness the Anabaptists shone like so many meteors against the night.

Church and state were considered indivisible in both Catholic and Protestant areas. Any deviation from the established churches was considered a crime of treason. Rebaptism, sedition, anarchy, blasphemy, sacrilege, and hypocrisy were lumped together indiscriminately under the label of treason. Often there was not the slightest symbol of justice in the treatment of the accused. Frequently an accusation of Anabaptism was tantamount to condemnation. Imprisonment and torture were normally followed by death. Drowning, sword, and stake were all used to exterminate the hated movement.

The first Anabaptist known to have died for his faith was Eberli Bolt, a preacher, who was burned at the stake in Schwyz, Switzerland, at the hands of Roman Catholic authorities on May 29, 1525.[1] With

1. Wenger, *Glimpses,* p. 37.

29

the death of Bolt began a period of martyrdom for the Anabaptists that was to continue to a greater or lesser degree of intensity through three centuries or more. The number of the executed will never be completely known. In some countries the records were not kept and in others the records are incomplete. However, from the minutes of the various trials, from eyewitness accounts, and from the Anabaptists themselves there is an abundance of material.[2]

Conrad Grebel

Little more than a year after Conrad Grebel had instituted believers' baptism among the Swiss Brethren, he was dead. Actually his ministry as an Anabaptist preacher extended no longer than a year and eight months.[3] In spite of long periods of imprisonment and poor health, Grebel's brief ministry was little short of phenomenal. The vagabond humanist scholar had become a flaming evangelist possessed by a crusading zeal that knew no rest until death. Grebel had not always been so motivated.

2. Those whose biographies are sketched herein are representative of others whose lives in some respects may have been nobler or for other reasons may be considered more worthy but who were not quite as influential in the development of the movement as those selected. A study of the Anabaptist movement which gives considerable attention to persecution is Claus-Peter Clasen, *Anabaptism: A Social History, 1525-1618* (Ithaca, N.Y.: Cornell University Press, 1972). The author claims that his work is based on facts. However, it is quite obvious that the author's use of "facts" is highly selective. As a result a certain imbalance persists throughout the work. While the author is a much more responsible historian than the early antagonists of the Anabaptists, such as Fischer and Bullinger, the impact of his narrative is often just as prejudicial.

His chapter on persecution is the best of the lot. Clasen's treatment of persecution is limited, as is his entire book, to German-speaking areas of Europe. It would appear from Clasen's study that the Roman Catholic governments were responsible for eighty-four percent of the executions whereas Protestant governments, or those with Protestant leanings, were responsible for only sixteen percent.

3. *Grebel*, p. 162. The author is greatly indebted to Harold Bender in his monumental work on Conrad Grebel for much of the factual material relating to Grebel's life used in this sketch.

Conrad was one of two sons in a family of six children born to Jacob and Dorothea Fries Grebel. The Grebels were a prominent and wealthy Swiss family. Junker Jacob Grebel during Conrad's boyhood served as magistrate in Grüningen, just east of Zürich. Later, he was a member of the Council of Zürich. To this fact Conrad owed his educational advantages.

After having attended the Carolina School of the Grossmünster in Zürich for six years, Conrad became one of the eighty-one students at the University of Basel during the winter term of 1514. At Basel he lived in a *bursa*[4] under the management of Basel's outstanding humanist scholar, Heinrich Loriti, better known as Glarean. Here Grebel's intellectual appetite was whetted by his first taste of humanist thought. The Basel humanism was no pagan Italian license, with its exaggerated worship of form in literature and art. Rather it was an Erasmian type of humanism. In Glarean the evangelical humanism of Erasmus found a champion. Even though at times rude and proud, Glarean challenged his students to a thorough scholarship, high moral standards, and to a discipleship of Christ rather than of Catullus or Porphyry.

The next year Grebel left Basel for the University of Vienna in the company of his cousin, John Leopold Grebel, and two other students from Zürich. He may have transferred from the small University of Basel to the much larger and more prestigious university upon the advice of Zwingli, who was chaplain of the Chapel of the Virgin of Meinrod in Einsiedeln at the time. More likely it was a scholarship provided by Emperor Maximillian I, to which Grebel refers in a letter to Zwingli, that induced Jacob Grebel to send his son to Vienna. His father was always looking for such financial advantages. The fact that Joachim von Watt of St. Gall (Vadian), a physician and professor of geography, was already making his mark at Vienna was further incentive for Swiss students to look favorably upon the university. At Vienna, Grebel missed the thorough scholarship of Glarean, but this was more than offset by his personal appreciation for Vadian. This is evident from a letter Grebel wrote to Zwingli, September 8, 1517: "You desire to

_____

4. A *bursa* was a combination boardinghouse and college under the management of an accomplished scholar. Here the students lived and studied while enrolled in the university.

hear, I presume, the trend of my fortune or some news. Vadian I have as a teacher, a man singularly deserving of all titles of honor; by him I am loved as a brother, while he is himself loved and cherished and respected by me as a most devoted father."[5]

This was the beginning of a lifelong friendship, the evidence of which is preserved in fifty-seven extant letters of Grebel to Vadian. For three years Grebel was associated with Vadian in Vienna. He spoke of other teachers with some degree of appreciation; but Vadian, in his estimation, excelled them all. The esteem of the student for his teacher was matched by the high regard in which Vadian held Grebel. He dedicated the first edition of his *Commentary on Pomponious Mela* (a Roman geographer of the first century) to Grebel and selected him to write the introduction to the second edition. Vadian married Grebel's sister in 1519.

The standard curriculum for the baccalaureate degree in all medieval universities consisted of the *Trivium* and the *Quadrivium*. However, Grebel's interests did not coincide with this curriculum. He loved the Latin classics and was particularly intrigued by the new subject of geography.[6] The humanism in vogue at Vienna was of the Italian variety with little emphasis upon what was called the Renaissance of Christianity and none at all upon morals. Grebel spent three years in the University of Vienna but did not receive a degree. However, he thoroughly imbibed the humanism of the Italian Renaissance during his residence there.

Vienna, itself, was a beautiful but immoral city. The presence of the five thousand students of the university did not improve the moral

5. *Grebel,* p. 19. Later in the letter to Zwingli, Grebel also wrote: "I have cherished the aforementioned study of literature in Vienna, just as I will continue to cherish it. And though I might be enjoying some advantages here more than there, I would still prefer to be enrolled among the French students of Glarean." Leland Harder, ed., *The Sources of Swiss Anabaptism: The Grebel Letters and Related Documents* (Scottdale, Pa.: Herald Press, 1985), p. 56.

6. Grammar, rhetoric, and logic composed the *Trivium* and arithmetic, geometry, music, and astronomy, the *Quadrivium*. See T. Walter Wallbank and Alastair M. Taylor, *Civilization Past and Present* (New York: Scott, Foresman and Co., 1942), pp. 371-75, for a brief but informative discussion of medieval university life.

situation. Drunkenness among the students was scandalous. Brawls were frequent and sexual promiscuity common. Grebel's extracurricular activities included both brawls and women. From a brawl he had been painfully wounded in the hand. To his immoral relations with women he attributed a disease from which he suffered the remainder of his life. "Deservedly so," he writes, "since oft have I consorted with females carnally."[7] All in all Vienna for Grebel may have been a stimulating experience intellectually but it was spiritually and morally debilitating. It is not surprising that he left Vienna without securing a degree.

September 30, 1518, found Grebel in the company of two other students on the road to Paris. His disappointment in not being permitted to return to Vienna was mitigated somewhat by the anticipation of resuming studies with Glarean, his friend and teacher of Basel days. For this purpose his father had secured a rather adequate French pension with which to finance his stay in Paris. So, Grebel was off to Paris for his last sustained attempt at formal university study.

Whatever anticipation Grebel may have felt at the thoughts of study in Paris with his old teacher was short-lived. Glarean had not changed, but Grebel had. In less than three months his escapades were sufficient cause for him to be dismissed from the *bursa*. International brawls were among the most popular forms of recreation in which the students of the university engaged. Things grew progressively worse. Grebel became implicated in a brawl which brought death to two Frenchmen. Consequently he smarted terribly under the severe reprimands and censures of his father and his friends, Vadian and Myconius.

Grebel had other problems also, one of which was his health. He was so ill at times from his "old trouble" that he despaired of life. The ravages of the plague added to his anxiety. In addition, the Sorbonne was anything but a community of scholars. The professors were characterized by Valentin Tschudi in a letter to Zwingli as filled with "barbarity," "wild beasts devoid of human nature," and "the most stupid of all men."[8] This description was written before the Royal Lecturers were brought to the university by Francis I in 1530.

7. *Grebel*, p. 233.

8. *Ibid.*, pp. 36-37. "Sorbonne" was used then to refer to the theological faculty of the University of Paris.

The twenty months that Grebel spent in Paris were frustrating months indeed. His father had taken a "cut" from the benefice which amounted to two-thirds of the total amount appropriated. Due to the "short change," as well as his own undisciplined desires, he was soon penniless. His pleas for money produced no favorable response, only rebuke. Finally, a messenger came with an ultimatum from his father to return home. Sometime in July, 1520, the prodigal returned to his father's house.

At the end of a year and eight months that seemed only to increase his despair and frustration, Grebel's only possible accomplishment was in the realm of language study. At Paris he had begun the study of Greek and possibly Hebrew. There is some indication that he attended the lectures of the more outstanding professors at the university. Why he never saw fit to enroll for a course is not known. Perhaps he just never got around to it. It was a very crestfallen young humanist, indeed, who had not yet begun to learn of Christ that reentered his native land early in July, 1520.

The next two years were to become the most meaningful of Grebel's life. For months, however, he accomplished nothing. Trying to decide whether to go to Pisa upon the insistence of a papal legate or to return to Basel for more study consumed anxious hours of indecision. He did return to Basel but not for long. In ten weeks he was home again, having found in the scholarship of Zwingli and others of like mind, such as Simon Stumpf and George Binder, that which he had failed to find in Vienna, Paris, or Basel.

Under Zwingli's leadership Grebel and others began the study of the Greek classics. By November, 1521, they were reading Plato. By this time two old friends of Grebel, Valentin Tschudi and J. J. Ammann, had joined the study group. Early in 1522 Felix Manz became the tenth man. Their concern in the beginning was not primarily religious but typically humanistic. However, they did study the biblical languages, Greek and Hebrew, together. This was obviously Zwingli's method of attracting able young men to himself in order to gain their support for his program of reform. These periods of study eventually became known as prophecy meetings. Beginning with the Latin text of a particular passage of Scripture, Zwingli would lead his eager students to an examination of the same passage in a biblical language. After further study and exegesis in German, one of the number would then bring an expository sermon in the local dialect. It is hard to imagine a more thorough approach to Bible study.

The year 1522 was one of crisis for Grebel. In February of the previous year he was still a very miserable young man, frustrated on every side. Temporarily, at least, he found happiness and joy almost incapable of expression in a love affair with a girl by the name of Barbara, whom he called his *Holokosme* (whole world). Writing to his brother-in-law Vadian from Basel, where he had journeyed in the hopes of finding work with a printer, he exclaimed: "at last the heart of your poor Grebel is enraptured, hence rejoice with me if you love me."[9] His flight to Basel only proved to be another in a series of disappointing experiences. The expected finances with which he had hoped to establish a household proved inadequate for his plans, and his health was poor. After two brief months he was back in Zürich, resolved never to leave again. In spite of his financial straits and the disapproval of his parents, marriage could not wait. So, taking advantage of the absence of his father, Conrad was united in marriage with his *Holokosme* by Heinrich Engelhart, parish priest of the Fraumünster, on February 6, 1522.

The marriage was not without its problems. The bride was from a lower social class. For this and other reasons, Grebel's parents refused to be reconciled to the new state of affairs. Conrad's mother wept unceasingly. The tension mounted. "Against me she is godless and against my wife she rages," he confided in a letter to Vadian some months later.[10] Increasing indebtedness added to his already overburdened condition. Marriage, it seems, instead of solving his problems had added immeasurably to them.

What marriage could not do for Grebel, conversion did. The details of this experience are not given, but there is no mistaking its occurrence. Everything in Grebel's subsequent years points with unmistakable certainty to such an inner transformation. His letters were no longer embellished with allusions to the pagan Greek and Roman gods. Instead they were filled with references to Christ, the Word of

9. *Ibid.,* p. 61.
10. *Ibid.,* p. 76.

God, and scriptural admonitions. The flowery and verbose *eloquentia* of the humanist was supplanted with a style characterized by simplicity, purpose, and integrity. His problems had by no means disappeared, but he was now on top of, not under them. His children received biblical names.

The month following Grebel's marriage, the Zwingli-led reform movement shifted gears. After three years of sermons, prophecy meetings, and pamphleteering, the Reformation in Zürich moved from theory to action. During Lent, when the printer Christopher Froschauer and his workers had just finished running off a cheap edition of Paul's epistles for the Frankfurt book fair, Froschauer decided to celebrate the event by serving sausages instead of fish. For the occasion, he had invited several guests, including three priests and a few ardent lay supporters of Zwingli. All ate the *Wurst*, except Zwingli, in the full knowledge that they were violating canon law and long-standing traditions of the Roman Church. Instead of a precipitous action of enthusiasts, as it first appeared, it was evidently the result of a prearranged plan, either with Zwingli's compliance or with the knowledge that he would not disapprove. Nor did he. On March 29, Zwingli preached a sermon on freedom in the choice of food and drink that was later published in a pamphlet on April 16. Grebel could hardly have escaped knowing of these events. At least three friends with whom he later would be associated were numbered among those who broke the Lenten fast on March 6; however, Grebel was not among them.[11] Grebel's absence may be explained by his preoccupation with his marriage and the problems it had exacerbated in the Grebel household or by the fact that at the time he had not yet "put on Christ."

However, on July 7, Grebel with Heinrich Aberli, Bartlime Pur, and Claus Hottinger were accused before the city council of taking over the pulpits in the Dominican monastery and denouncing their teachings. In this episode, the actions of the accused appeared a prelude to

---

11. G. R. Potter, *Zwingli* (Cambridge: Cambridge University Press, 1976), p. 75. As Potter points out, accounts of those present in Froschauer's house the night of March 6 vary. In addition to Zwingli, Leo Jud, Heinrich Aberli, and Bartlime Pur seem certain; George Binder, Hans Utinger, Hans Hottinger, Wolf Ininger, Lorenz Hochrutiner, and Hans Ochenfuss are probables.

Zwingli's orchestrated assault on the cloisters of Zürich. Five days later, Francis Lambert, a Franciscan monk from Avignon, while preaching a series of four sermons (in Latin) in the *Fraumünster*, was interrupted twice by Zwingli himself. This led to a debate between Zwingli and Lambert in the Chapter House of the canons of the *Grossmünster*, in which Lambert professed to have been converted. When the matter was brought before the city council, Wyss reported that "Mayor Roist admonished all concerned to work together in peace and to take further questions of this kind to the provost and chapter in Zürich."[12] This conciliatory statement provoked Zwingli to exclaim: *"Ich bin in diser statt Zürich bishof und pfarrer."* (It is I who am bishop and priest in this city of Zürich.)

This is further evidence that at this stage of the reform movement in Zürich, Grebel and his friends were acting in tandem with Zwingli in pushing for the changes the Reformer envisioned for the Zürich church. In July, 1522, he publicly defended the gospel and even expressed the desire to become a minister of the gospel. Plainly Grebel had been converted sometime prior to this. The weak, vacillating young humanist had become a soldier of the cross. The Word of God from henceforth was to be his marching orders.

Zwingli's preaching and teaching were effective. Heinrich Engelhart, Simon Stumpf, and Felix Manz, as well as Grebel, were soon numbered among the ranks of the Reformers. But their devotion to the Word of God was to take precedence over their loyalty to Ulrich Zwingli. To Zwingli they owed much, but to the Bible, more. These two loyalties were not to come into conflict until late in the year 1523.

The first evidence of a cleavage between Grebel and his mentor, according to the minutes of the Second Disputation in Zürich, was over the Lord's Supper. Even though by the end of the dialogue upon that occasion, Grebel seemed satisfied, by December 19 it was clear that Zwingli was unwilling to proceed with any change in the mass in face of the hardened opposition in the Small and Large Councils. The restoration of the sacrament to apostolic simplicity would have to wait — and Grebel was clearly disappointed. In a letter to his brother-in-law and confidant, he expressed his disgust with Zwingli and dated the

12. Harder, *Sources of Swiss Anabaptism*, pp. 174-75.

failure of the Reformation to the Second Disputation, when Zwingli bowed to the concilior authority of the city the previous October. "On that occasion," he wrote, "the Word was overthrown, set back, and bound by its most learned heralds."[13]

Grebel was not the first to break with Zwingli, nor was he the first to question infant baptism in the Zollikon-Zürich area. But by 1524 he was clearly at odds with Zwingli, and it was Grebel who initiated believers' baptism on that historic night in January, 1525. Thus, Conrad Grebel emerged as a champion of the Anabaptist reformation, along with Blaurock and Manz.[14]

Only one year and eight months were granted Grebel as an Anabaptist preacher. In spite of imprisonments and increasingly poor health, the accomplishments of those last twenty months were little short of phenomenal.

In February Grebel and Manz went from house to house witnessing, baptizing, and conducting the Lord's Supper after the new order of the Swiss Brethren. During February Grebel baptized Gabriel Giger of St. Gall at the home of Felix Manz. He also probably baptized Anna Manz. Sometime during the month, near Schaffhausen, he baptized Wolfgang Ulimann, a former monk, by immersion in the Rhine River. Ulimann prior to his baptism had reached Anabaptist convictions, which led him to request baptism at the hands of Grebel, but not out of a platter *(nit wolt mit ainer schussel mit wasser allain begossen)!* Whereupon Grebel and Ulimann promptly went down into the Rhine where Grebel, according to Kessler, "put him under the waters of the river and covered him over" *(in dem Rhin von dem Grebel under getruckt und bedeckt werden).*[15]

---

13. Letter of Grebel to Vadian, dated December 18, 1523, in *ibid.,* p. 276.

14. From Zwingli's viewpoint, Grebel was clearly the most important man among the Anabaptist leaders. See *Grebel,* p. 136. However, this does not necessarily indicate that Grebel was the founder of the Anabaptists. One is hardly justified in speaking of "a founder" of the Anabaptists. Emil Egli, in *Die Züricher Wiedertäufer zur Reformationszeit* (Zürich: Friedrich Schulthess, 1878), p. 19, names Blaurock, Grebel, and Manz the three major leaders of the Anabaptist movement in Zürich. He also refers to Zwingli's designation of Grebel as the "Koryphäender Wiedertäufer."

15. Johannes Kessler, *Sabbata mit Kleineren Schriften und Briefen,* ed. Emil Egli and Rudolf Schoch (St. Gallen: Hubor, 1902), p. 144.

Two months were spent in Schaffhausen in an attempt to advance the cause of the Brethren among the leading ministers of the city. Here he, Wilhelm Reublin, and Johannes Brötli met with some degree of success. Grebel continued to labor in Schaffhausen until his return to Zürich sometime prior to March 21.

In the meantime two of Grebel's converts, Ulimann and Gabriel Giger, joined Lorenz Hochrutiner, who had been expelled from Zürich in 1523. They began to witness in and around St. Gall with marked success. The fruitful activities of Giger and especially of Ulimann led Grebel to join them. He also hoped that he might win his brother-in-law, Vadian, to his cause. At St. Gall he preached to an exceedingly responsive congregation, which had been prepared to receive the Anabaptist message through the zealous efforts of Ulimann. The climax came on April 9, 1525, when Grebel baptized a huge throng in the Sitter River. Some five hundred persons are said to have been baptized by the Brethren during the initial stages of the movement in St. Gall. Back once again in Zürich, Grebel kept up a writing campaign on behalf of the Brethren. First he corresponded with the city council, then with the Brethren and Vadian, but his efforts were in vain. St. Gall, following the lead of Zürich, took measures to repress the promising movement.

From the latter part of April until June, Grebel was forced into hiding in Zürich. Fearing imprisonment at the hands of Zwingli, he became extremely cautious about his movements. He kept in contact with the Brethren through correspondence, only occasionally daring to meet with them. While in hiding he was continually plagued by two old enemies, poor health and poverty. His poverty became so acute that he made arrangements to sell his library. Then quite suddenly he appeared back in the forefront of the movement, apparently finding it impossible to remain inactive any longer.

Grüningen, the boyhood home of Grebel, was east of Zürich. Here his father had previously served for twelve years as magistrate, and here were to come Grebel's greatest triumph and severest trial. Here he worked with extraordinary success from the end of June until his arrest on October 8, 1525. For the better part of the four months, Grebel visited from house to house, witnessing to one or two, or preaching to small groups. His messages emphasized the necessity of repentance and faith upon the authority of the Scriptures. The point of departure from the standing order always seemed to have been the issue of baptism. The Brethren from Zollikon, Chur, and Waldshut often worked together in an intensive effort to spread the gospel of Anabaptism. One such occasion took place on October 8. As Grebel, Manz, and Blaurock were preparing for a service in a nearby field, Grebel and Blaurock were arrested by Magistrate Berger and imprisoned in the castle at Grüningen. Three weeks later Manz, who had escaped the clutches of the magistrate on the eighth, was seized and incarcerated in the same prison.

Grebel and Blaurock, after more than a month in confinement, were finally brought to trial and sentenced along with Manz to an indefinite term of imprisonment on November 18, 1525. They were condemned "because of their anabaptism and their unbecoming conduct to lie in the tower on a diet of bread and water, and no one was permitted to visit them except the guards."[16]

The case against the Anabaptists was extremely weak. Upon rather dubious evidence, Zwingli accused the Brethren of sedition. Actually the charges were based upon perverted accounts of what the Brethren taught. Instead of denying the magistracy, as one Dr. Hofmeister had charged, Felix Manz stated his opinion: "No Christian could be a magistrate, nor could he use the sword to punish or to kill anyone, for he had no Scripture for such a thing."[17]

The Brethren denied that they taught a community of goods as the Christian way of life but insisted that a Christian ought to share with those who were in need. Manz and Grebel asserted that infant baptism was wrong and affirmed their conviction that believers' baptism was the sign of membership in the true church.

Many other Anabaptists were imprisoned. During the long winter months the Zürich tower rang with the hymns and prayers of the indomitable prisoners. Grebel used his time to prepare a manuscript on baptism, as he had promised his followers at Grüningen. One witness testified that Grebel had said before his imprisonment, "If they would permit his writing to be printed, then he would be ready to dispute with Master Ulrich Zwingli, and if Master Ulrich would win out, he,

16. *Grebel,* p. 155.
17. *Ibid.,* p. 159.

Conrad, would be willing to be burned, whereas if he, Conrad, would win out, he would not demand that Zwingli should be burned."[18]

Grebel appears to have been the major writer among the Brethren. Although Andreas Castelberger wrote Karlstadt, Luther's former colleague, it was Grebel who wrote Luther and Karlstadt, and, on behalf of the radicals in Zürich, Thomas Müntzer as well. Grebel's letters to Luther and Karlstadt are not extant, but because the letter and an 850-word postscript never reached Müntzer, they provide valuable insights into the Anabaptist movement in the process of formation.

The letter to Müntzer reveals that his would-be Swiss disciples knew little of Müntzer's actual teachings. They had read a few tracts from his pen and thought his position on infant baptism and his anti-Luther stance were analogous to theirs in Zürich. News of his sermon before Duke John and his son (Electoral Saxony) in Weimar on July 13, 1524, had just reached them, and was quite disconcerting.[19] It is clear that in spite of wishful thinking regarding their identification with Müntzer, these young men, sure of their interpretation of the Scriptures, were telling him — not asking.

According to the letter, they were critical of his German mass, benefices, and the stone tablets upon which he had engraved the ten commandments and placed in his church. They also expressed the hope that he was not, in spite of what he had written against infant baptism, baptizing little children. Grebel even wrote: "If you or Carlstadt do not write sufficiently against infant baptism, and all that is associated with it, how and why one is to baptize, etc., I (Conrad Grebel) will try my hand at it."[20] Twice, Grebel admonishes Müntzer against the use of the sword in defense of the faith. "One should also not protect the gospel and its adherents with the sword, nor themselves." Then he invokes the cross principle: "True believing Christians are sheep among wolves, sheep for the slaughter. They must be baptized in anxiety, distress, affliction, persecution, suffering, and death." Then he explains: "They [true disciples of Christ] employ neither worldly sword nor war, since

---

18. *Ibid.*, p. 151.

19. Williams and Mergal, *Spiritual and Anabaptist Writers*, pp. 47-70.

20. J. C. Wenger, ed. and trans., *Conrad Grebel's Programmatic Letters of 1524* (Scottdale, Pa.: Herald Press, 1970), ll. 231-32.

with them killing is absolutely renounced."[21] Evidently the priority of the New Testament over the Old, characteristic of the movement (with few exceptions), was already being employed by the Brethren, for in rejecting the tablets, Grebel wrote: "the New Testament teaches nothing of the kind, neither by text or example. In the Old Testament, to be sure, the writing was indeed outward, but now in the New the writing is to be on the fleshly tablets of the heart."[22]

Since Müntzer was soon involved in the battle of Frankenhausen and executed and Karlstadt failed to write as expected, Grebel, as he had promised, wrote a pamphlet on baptism. No copies of this treatise are extant. However, as Samuel Macauley Jackson points out, the major outline of the work can be reconstructed from Zwingli's attempted refutation of Grebel's tract and the Schleitheim Confession, titled *Refutation of the Tricks of the Baptists* of 1527.[23] Apparently, Grebel and his colleagues had a rather fully developed theology of baptism by the fall of 1524. This is not surprising, since some time before, possibly as early as 1522 and certainly by October of 1523, Zwingli himself had said that according to the New Testament no one should be baptized who had not reached the age of moral responsibility.[24] Because believers' baptism had the potential of dividing the fledgling Reformation in Zürich, the cautious Reformer refused to follow his own convictions. This may be one reason why baptism became such a flash point between Zwingli and his former disciples. By the time Zwingli brought out his *Refutation*, Grebel was dead.

21. *Ibid.*, ll. 185-92.
22. *Ibid.*, ll. 152-54.
23. Samuel Macauley Jackson, ed., *Ulrich Zwingli (1484-1531): Selected Works* (Philadelphia: University of Pennsylvania Press, 1901 and 1972), pp. 123-258. Unfortunately, the translators of this work, Henry Preble and George W. Gilmore, translated the title *In catabaptistarum strophas elenchus* as indicated in the text, thus lending to the persistent confusion between Baptists of the seventeenth century and the Anabaptists of the sixteenth.
24. See Verduin, *Reformers and Their Stepchildren*, pp. 199-200. After quoting Zwingli on believers' baptism, Verduin asked why Zwingli dragged his feet and why he allowed himself to be party to the perpetuation of a practice which, "as he saw things lacked Biblical warrant." He suggests, "It is again the matter of offence. He adds specifically: 'But on account of the possibility of offence I omit preaching this; it is better not to preach it until the world is ready to take it.'"

After five months of imprisonment, the dauntless Grebel asked permission to have his prison manuscript printed. Such exasperating audacity provoked an aggravated response. The rebuff to Grebel's request came on the heels of a second trial, which was held on March 5 and 6, 1526. The day following a sentence of life imprisonment was passed upon all the defendants. On the same day a new mandate made the act of performing baptism a crime punishable by death. But the life imprisonment was of short duration. Fourteen days later some unknown benefactors helped the prisoners to escape.

Harassed and hounded by the authorities of his native canton, Grebel continued an itinerant ministry in the company of Felix Manz in the cantons of Appenzell and Graubunden. Alone, Grebel turned his face toward Maienfield in the Oberland where, overtaken by the plague, he died. Never strong physically, Grebel became a victim of the ever recurrent plague in the summer of 1526, probably in August.[25]

A year and eight months or less encompasses the whole ministry of Conrad Grebel as an Anabaptist preacher. A few sermons, numerous letters, many imprisonments, one pamphlet, a few baptisms, much poverty, misunderstanding in his home, and dishonor in his native canton mark the tragically brief career of the earnest would-be Reformer. And, yet, in the movement of which he was a vital part, his life and influence still continue.

Felix Manz

If Grebel was the "Coryphaeus of the Anabaptists," as Zwingli contended, Manz was the "Apollo" and Blaurock the "Hercules." Next to Grebel in importance in the early life of the Anabaptist movement, Manz surpassed him in eloquence and popularity. It was Manz who became the first Anabaptist martyr to die at the hands of Protestants and the first to die in Zürich.

Felix Manz was born in Zürich, possibly in the year 1498.[26] Like

---

25. Kessler, *Sabbata mit Kleineren Schriften und Briefen.* Grebel, Manz, and Blaurock are called "Arch-Anabaptists." See pp. 142, 143, 148, 314.

26. Christian Neff, "Felix Manz," trans. Harold Bender, ME, 3:472.

Erasmus, Leo Jud, and Heinrich Bullinger, Manz was an illegitimate son of a Roman Catholic priest. His father was a Canon of the Grossmünster in Zürich. Manz evidently had the educational advantage of the privileged classes, for he was well trained in Latin, Greek, and Hebrew. He early gained recognition as an accomplished Hebraist.[27] By 1522 he had joined the enthusiastic circle of young Greek scholars studying the New Testament with Zwingli. Later he, as well as Grebel, was numbered among Zwingli's converts.

However, possibly by the summer of 1523 and certainly after the disputation in October of that year, Manz became dissatisfied with Zwingli's program of reform. His dissatisfaction became increasingly vocal during the following year. Two years later Zwingli reported that Manz, Grebel, and Stumpf had each presented an alternate program of reform to him.[28] It is clear that Manz was one of the leaders of the opposition party from the beginning. His name follows that of Castelberger in Grebel's letter of September 5, 1524, to Thomas Müntzer.[29] Sometime before, the small band of earnest Christians had begun to meet regularly in the home of Felix Manz on Neustadt Street, near the Grossmünster. In these meetings Manz took a prominent part, occasionally teaching the Bible from the Hebrew Scriptures. It was here that the first believers' baptism among the Brethren would be administered in 1525.

A month to six weeks before that first baptism, Manz made a final effort to explain to the Small and Large Councils his position and that of his brethren on believers' baptism. Undated and unsigned, according to Herder, it was written sometime between December 13 and 28.[30] Among the reasons that Manz gave for writing was that he had been charged by some as "a revolutionary and a brute."[31] He also wrote that

27. Ekkehard Krajewski, *Leben und Sterben des Zürcher Täuferführers, Felix Mantz* (Kassel: J. G. Oncken, 1957), pp. 22-23. Krajewski's work is the definitive biography of Felix Manz. It is a careful and detailed account of one of the more important leaders in early Anabaptism.

28. *Grebel*, pp. 103-5. Evidently the presentation of the suggested program of reform took place before Stumpf's expulsion from Zürich, December 23, 1523.

29. *Quellen*, no. 14, p. 19.

30. Harder, *Sources of Swiss Anabaptism*, pp. 311-15.

31. William R. Estep, *Anabaptist Beginnings (1523-1533)* (Nieuwkoop:

when he had tried to explain his position on baptism, he was not even permitted to read the supporting Scriptures but Zwingli overwhelmed him with words to the extent that he could not speak. Hence, he explained, he determined to express his thoughts in the form of a letter.

First, Manz denied that he was a disturber of the peace. "All those with whom I have had anything to do will testify that I have never desired nor caused an insurrection nor have I taught or spoken anything which has or would incite one."[32] To the contrary, he argued that a change in the traditional baptism of infants would in no way threaten the stability of the government. These were peripheral concerns. The major thrust of his letter was given to an explanation of the necessity and nature of believers' baptism. Beginning with Matthew 28:19, 20, he cites several passages related to baptism in the New Testament. In referring to Paul's baptism by Ananias, he wrote, "From these words we clearly see what baptism is and when it should be practiced. One should be baptized who has been converted through God's Word, who has changed his heart, and now henceforth desires to live in newness of life."[33] He argued that the nature of baptism precluded the baptism of infants. So convinced was he of the truth of his conviction that in Pauline fashion, he wrote: "Even an angel from heaven can't teach other than what has been mentioned above. The eternally true Word of God will sing in every man's heart whether he works against it or not; it remains the truth of God."[34]

Immediately after the formation of the first Anabaptist church, the Brethren began a house-to-house visitation in Zürich and Zollikon. Baptisms were frequent, and the Lord's Supper was observed in the simplest manner upon several occasions. Manz and Blaurock spearheaded the drive for converts in the Zürich area. In the early days of the movement Grebel attempted to carry the Anabaptist message to the leaders of the Reformation in Schaffhausen. Manz and Blaurock, meanwhile, continued their efforts among the farmers and artisans of

---

B. De Graaf, 1976), p. 56. The translation of "A Declaration and Defense" in this sourcebook is that of John David Hopper of Rüschlikon, Switzerland.

32. *Ibid.*

33. *Ibid.*, p. 57.

34. *Ibid.*, pp. 57-58.

Zollikon. This division of labor was not rigidly followed. Manz did attempt to witness to Dr. Hofmeister on one occasion, as Hofmeister testified at the trial of 1526.[35] When Grebel turned his attention toward Grüningen, Manz and Blaurock were laboring in Chur and Appenzell. However, Manz and Blaurock were both with Grebel on October 8, 1525, at Hinwil in Grüningen when Blaurock and Grebel were arrested and imprisoned. At the time Manz escaped but was apprehended a few weeks later, on the thirty-first. He was incarcerated with Grebel and Blaurock in the castle at Grüningen. Later all three were imprisoned together in the Witch's Tower in Zürich.

Fourteen days after their escape from the Witch's Tower, Manz is reported to have baptized a woman at Embrach. Two months later Manz and Blaurock, this time without Grebel, returned to Grüningen. Almost on the very anniversary of his arrest in Grüningen the year before, Manz was arrested in St. Gall on October 12, but soon afterward released. However, he was arrested again with Blaurock in a Grüningen forest two months later. This was to be his last imprisonment. Hardly a prison in the vicinity of Manz's labors escaped being honored by his presence.[36]

> On January 5, 1527, he was sentenced to death, "because contrary to Christian order and custom he had become involved in Anabaptism, . . . because he confessed having said that he wanted to gather those who wanted to accept Christ and follow Him, and unite himself with them through baptism, . . . so that he and his followers separated themselves from the Christian Church and were about to raise up and prepare a sect of their own . . . because he had condemned capital punishment, . . . since such doctrine is harmful to the unified usage of all Christendom, and leads to offense, insurrection, and sedition against the government, . . . Manz shall be delivered to the executioner, who shall tie his hands, put him into a boat, take him to the lower hut, there strip his bound hands down over his knees, place a stick between his knees and arms, and thus

35. *Grebel,* p. 142.
36. He was imprisoned in Chur, St. Gall, Grüningen, the Witch's Tower in Zürich, and the Wellenberg prison in Zürich.

push him into the water and let him perish in the water; thereby he shall have atoned to the law and justice. . . . His property shall also be confiscated by my lords."[37]

Since Grebel was dead, Manz was clearly the foremost leader among the Swiss Brethren. His noble life, eloquence, education, and enthusiasm made him extremely popular with the masses. To the same degree he was a dangerous seditionist as far as Zwingli was concerned. It was a foregone conclusion that if the Swiss Reformation were to continue within the context of a state church, Manz must go. The mandate demanding the death penalty for rebaptizing had been issued the previous March, but it had not as yet been enforced. The time had come for the crucial test, and the first victim was to be Felix Manz.

Manz, according to the sentence, was taken bound from the Wellenberg prison past the fish market to the boat. All along the way he witnessed to the members of the dismal procession and to those standing on the banks of the Limmat River, praising God that even though a sinner he would die for the truth. Further, he declared that believers' baptism was the true baptism according to the Word of God and the teachings of Christ. His mother's voice could be heard above the subdued throng and the ripple of the swift-flowing stream, entreating him to remain true to Christ in the hour of temptation. After the sentence was pronounced, he was placed into a boat, just below the Rathaus, which moved downstream to a fish hut that was anchored in the middle of the Limmat. As his arms and legs were being bound, he sang out with a loud voice, *"In manus tuas, Domine, commendo spiritum meum"* (Into thy hands, O Lord, I commend my spirit). A few moments later the cold waters of the river closed in over the head of Felix Manz. According to the Zürich chronicler Bernhard Wyss, Manz's execution took place January 5, 1527, at 3 o'clock Saturday afternoon.

Even though Manz wrote little, he did leave a written testimony to his faith and a hymn of eighteen stanzas. It now appears that Manz was also the author of a defense of the Anabaptist position presented to the Zürich Council some two years before, entitled *Protestation und Schutzschrift.* In these works his witness still rings across the centuries.

37. ME, 3:473.

Love to God through Christ, shall alone avail and subsist; but boasting, reviling, and threatening, shall fail. Charity alone is pleasing to God; he that cannot show charity, has no part with God. The unadulterated love of Christ puts to flight the enemy. It is incumbent upon him that will be an heir of Christ, to be merciful, as the Father in heaven is merciful. . . . Christ hated no man; his true disciples are likewise devoid of hatred, thus following Christ in the true way, as he went before them. . . . I will now conclude my memorial. . . . I hereby resolve that I will remain faithful to Christ, and put my trust in him who knows my every distress, and is mighty to deliver. Amen.[38]

Amish Mennonites and Hutterites still sing in the German from the *Ausbund*, their sixteenth-century hymnal. It includes a hymn written by Felix Manz, the first stanza of which reads:

With gladness will I sing now;
My heart delights in God,
Who showed me such forbearance,
That I from death was saved
Which never hath an end.
I praise thee, Christ in heaven
Who all my sorrow changed.[39]

---

38. Thieleman J. Van Braght, *The Bloody Theatre or Martyrs' Mirror of the Defenseless Christians,* trans. I. Daniel Rupp (Lancaster, Pa.: David Miller, 1837), p. 344. Hereafter referred to as *Mirror.*

39. A. J. Ramaker, "Hymns and Hymn Writers Among the Anabaptists of the Sixteenth Century," MQR 3 (April 1929): 114. See the complete hymn of eighteen stanzas in the *Ausbund* (Lancaster, Pa.: Press, Inc., 1955), p. 41. The first stanza as it appears in the *Ausbund* reads:

Mit Lust so will ich singen,
  Mein Herz freut sich in Gott,
Der mir viel Kunst thut bringen,
  Dasz ich entrinn dem Tod
Der ewiglich nimmet kein End.
  Ich preiz dich Christ vom Himreel,
Der mir mein Kummer wend.

George Blaurock

George Blaurock, the Hercules of the Anabaptists, surpassed both Grebel and Manz in the extent and effectiveness of his ministry. Severely beaten with rods on the day Felix Manz was put to death, he spread the Anabaptist faith for two and a half more years before his own execution for heresy. He was burned at the stake on September 6, 1529, near Klausen in the Tyrol.

Blaurock was born Georg Cajacob (Jorg vom Haus Jacob) in the village of Bonaduz in Grisons, Switzerland, around 1491. Even though his parents were peasants, he managed to attend the University of Leipzig for a short time. It is not surprising that university studies did not appeal to him, least of all at Leipzig. By 1516, he had become a priest and a vicar in Trins in the diocese of Chur, which he gave up two years later. In 1524 he came into historical focus as a vagabond ex-priest seeking to learn more about the Swiss Reformation at its center.

When Blaurock came to Zürich, he was already married. He was described as a "tall, powerful figure with fiery eyes, black hair and a small bald spot." His aggressiveness won for him the nickname "strong George" *(der starke Jörg)*. Zwingli called him "a fool, who in his presumption counted no one a child of God unless he was a 'madman' like himself."[40] The nickname that stuck, however, was that of "Bluecoat" *(Blaurock)*. The Hutterite *Large Chronicle* records the incident, which was the occasion for the new appellation.

> At this point it came to pass that a person from Chur came to them, namely, a priest named George of the House of Jacob, commonly called Bluecoat *(Blaurock)* because one time when they were having a discussion of matters of belief in a meeting this George of the house of Jacob presented his view also. Then someone asked who it was that had just spoken. Thereupon someone said: "The one in the blue coat has spoken." Thus he received the name, Blaurock, for he had worn a blue coat.[41]

40. ME, 1:356.
41. Zieglschmid, *Large Chronicle*, p. 46.

Blaurock impressed no one with his learning but everyone with his zeal. With characteristic earnestness he set out on a pilgrimage to Zürich, the center of the Swiss Reformation, seeking an audience with the most zealous of its leaders. Upon being told that there were men more zealous than Zwingli, he immediately sought them out. Satisfied that his search was ended, he cast his lot with the handful of young Swiss radicals, and in zeal excelled them all. It was he who asked and received baptism at the hands of Grebel and then baptized the others on that eventful night in January, 1525.

Like that of the first English Quakers, Blaurock's zeal sometimes exceeded his judgment. He even disrupted the worship services of the Reformed churches. An event that took place on January 29, 1525, in the village church in Zollikon reveals the sincere but impetuous nature of Blaurock. As the minister was making his way to the pulpit, George asked him what he intended to do. "Preach the word of God," was the reply. "You were not sent to preach, it was I," declared Blaurock. Thereupon he proceeded to the pulpit and preached.[42]

On the next day, January 30, Blaurock, Manz, and twenty-four of those who had been baptized in Zollikon, and one other not yet baptized, were arrested and imprisoned in the old Augustinian monastery in Zürich. Upon his release Blaurock, driven by a sense of urgency, promptly accelerated the pace of his activities. A glimpse of Blaurock in action is given by Rüdi Thomann, in whose home an Anabaptist meeting took place.

> After much conversation and reading, Hans Bruggbach stood up weeping and crying out that he was a great sinner and asking that they pray God for him. Then Blaurock asked him whether he desired the grace of God. He said he did. Then Manz rose and said, "Who will forbid that I should baptize him?" Blaurock answered, "No one." Then Manz took a dipper with water and baptized him in the name of the Father, Son and Holy Spirit.[43]

Blaurock and Manz spent the night in the house of their host, Rüdi Thomann, and before they departed the following morning succeeded

42. Wenger, *Glimpses,* p. 29.
43. Newman, *History of Anti-Pedobaptism,* p. 107.

in winning to Christ and baptizing all that were in the house, with the exception of Heinrich Thomann, Rüdi's brother.

Later, after being released from prison, Blaurock, this time alone since Manz was not released, continued his itinerant person-to-person evangelism, first in Zürich and then in Zollikon. On his last day in the Zürich-Zollikon area, a Sunday, he was reported to have baptized eight women and two men. After his departure, Jörg Schad, a Zollikon layman, baptized some forty or so in the village church.

The renewed activity on the part of the Zollikon Anabaptists did not sit well with Zwingli and the city council. By March 16, nineteen men were apprehended and imprisoned once again along with Blaurock. Fifteen of those from Zollikon were fined, warned, and released. A so-called disputation in which each of the remaining defendants appeared one at a time before Zwingli, two other pastors of the city, two schoolteachers, the burgomaster, and some members of the city council began on March 20 and lasted three days. As usual, Zwingli declared that he had vanquished the Anabaptists, and the Zürich authorities agreed. Blaurock and his wife along with four others were banished from the canton.

The following July Blaurock and Manz were in trouble again — this time for preaching and baptizing in Chur where they were apparently enjoying considerable success. Manz was sent back to Zürich, and Blaurock, after his release through the intervention of friends, continued his evangelistic activities in Appenzell. In October, he returned to the Canton of Zürich where he joined Grebel and Manz in the Grüningen district. Impatient for results, once again he attempted to commandeer the pulpit of a village church — this time in Hinwil. Arrested again, he was taken into custody and imprisoned. Although admittedly the most effective evangelist among the Swiss Brethren, Blaurock may have done the movement in the Canton of Zürich more harm than good. His crude imprecations upon Zürich and its "false prophets" must have "turned off" even some who were in sympathy with the movement.

The tragedy of Manz's execution was compounded by the shameful treatment of George Blaurock. As troublesome as he must have been to Zwingli and the city fathers, there is no justification for the beating he received at the hands of the executioner. On the same day that Manz was drowned (January 5, 1527), Blaurock was stripped to the waist and beaten with rods until the blood ran down his back, from the site of the execution to the Niederdorf Gate. Once through the gate, the indomitable Anabaptist preacher shook the dust of the city from his clothing and shoes in a farewell act of apostolic scorn.[44]

From Zürich Blaurock turned his steps toward Bern. Here a disputation was held. Zwingli faced the banished Blaurock and the Bernese Anabaptists in an attempt to convince them of their error. The learned doctors of the Reformed church were as unsuccessful in their mission at Bern as Zwingli had been in Zürich. As a result Blaurock and all the others, except one who recanted, were expelled. From Bern the battle-weary evangelist turned toward Biel. Here a large congregation of Anabaptists, which owed its origin to his own labors, had worshiped for some time. Driven from Biel by the authorities, Blaurock labored for a time in Grisons and again at Appenzell. He was arrested and later banished on April 21. After the fourth banishment in as many months, Blaurock left Switzerland for good.

Turning to the Austrian Tyrol, the zealous Anabaptist disciple began what was to become his last and most fruitful ministry. An Anabaptist Church in the Adige Valley had lost its pastor, Michael Kürschner, by burning at the stake on June 2, 1529. In answer to a request for help from the orphaned congregation, Blaurock became its pastor. In the meantime, from Klausen to Neumarkt his preaching was accompanied by great crowds. Believers were baptized and congregations were formed up and down the Inn and Etsch river valleys.[45] The numbers increased steadily. Secrecy became increasingly difficult.

44. Blaurock's sentence as translated by John Allen Moore, *Anabaptist Portraits* (Scottdale, Pa.: Herald Press, 1984), p. 87, reads: "That he be turned over to the executioner, who should strip him to the waist, bind his hands and, along the way from the Fishmarket to the Lower Gate, beat him with a rod so that the blood flows." There he should be required to take an oath not to return to Zürich territory. "Then if he should afterwards return, be it for a short time or long, he would receive the now well-known sentence of drowning without mercy as had Felix Mantz."

45. In his monograph on Blaurock, Moore wrote in 1955, "Wir finden Spuren seines Wirkens in Vels, in Triers am Breitenberg und am Ritten, in Leifers und am vielen anderen Orten. In Klasen versammelten sich die Brüder von den Bergen auf beiden Seiten des Flusses, der den kleinen malerischen Ort durchstromt." Moore, *Der Starke Jörg* (Kassel: J. G. Onken Verlag, 1955), p. 55.

On August 14, 1529, Blaurock and Hans Langegger, a layman, were taken into custody by the Innsbruck authorities. They were cruelly tortured, for the authorities wanted information concerning the number of Anabaptists in the area and the importance of their captives, for Ferdinand was determined to exterminate every remnant of Anabaptism in his territory. Three weeks later, on September 6, 1529, Blaurock and Langegger were burned at the stake near Klausen (now Chiusu, Italy).

Since the location of Blaurock's last sustained labors was in Hapsburg territory, the charges brought against him reflect a Roman Catholic understanding of his "heresy." Because he was a former priest, he was viewed as a traitor to the faith as well. The charges, as recorded in the *Martyrs' Mirror*, were:

> Because he had abandoned the office of papist priest; because he did not maintain infant-baptism, and preached a new baptism to the people; because he had rejected mass and confession as instituted by the priests; because he disallowed of invoking or worshiping the mother of Christ. For these reasons he was executed, and gave his life for them, as becomes a soldier and hero of faith. On his way to the place of execution, he earnestly addressed the people, and referred them to the Scriptures.[46]

Blaurock's last will and testament was in the form of a prison epistle, a brief sermon, and two hymns. From the prison cell in the Guffidaun castle came the epistle and his final admonition. These give the contemporary student a glimpse into the earnest martyr's devotional emphasis and a sample of his preaching. In psalmlike tones Blaurock exclaimed:

> I will therefore sing praises in my heart to thy holy name, and for ever proclaim the grace I have experienced. I entreat thee, O God! in behalf of all thy children, preserve all for ever from all the enemies of souls; I will not build upon flesh, for it passes away, and is of no duration, but I will place my trust in thy word; . . . Our latter end is at hand. Blessed Lord! enable us to bear the cross to the destined

46. *Mirror*, p. 357.

place; and incline thyself to us in mercy, that we may commit our spirits into thy hand.[47]

Blaurock was not content to bequeath only a devotional epistle for the edification of the Brethren. He also left a brief admonition written in sermonic form in which the eschatological element is dominant. In spite of much suffering and impending death, his faith in the final judgment of God remained unshaken. In the light of this inevitable judgment, he warned the ungodly to turn to God in repentance and faith while there was yet time.

"But when the Lord comes in glory to judgment, then will the sinner repent; it is then too late to acquire forgiveness; he here publishes his divine word, and teaches men that they shall forsake their sinful lives, believe in Christ, be baptized on faith, and render obedience to the gospel. Therefore, sons of men," he pleads, "forsake your sins, and continue no longer in your hardness, sickness, blindness and ungodliness, when you can have a physican [sic] who can heal all your infirmities, and who will afford his services gratis (Matt. ix.12)."[48]

Two hymns by Blaurock are preserved in the *Ausbund.* The first, *Gott Fuerht ein recht Gericht,* has thirty-three stanzas and the second, *Gott, dich will ich loben,* has thirteen. The first hymn is one that sets forth the conditions of salvation, emphasizing the inevitability of judgment and the way of hope. The second is a beautiful hymn setting forth in personal terms the author's faith in God. The first and sixth stanzas breathe the spirit of an unconquerable faith.

Lord God, how do I praise thee
From hence and evermore,
That thou real faith didst give me
By which I thee may know.

Forget me not, O Father,
Be near me evermore;

47. *Ibid.,* p. 358.
48. *Ibid.,* p. 359.

Thy spirit shield and teach me,
That in afflictions great
Thy comfort I may ever prove,
And valiantly may attain
The victory in this right.[49]

Although Blaurock was no profound theologian, his was a major contribution to the Anabaptist movement in the early years of its development. It was he who first asked for baptism at the hands of Grebel and who joined Manz and Grebel in carrying the message of the Swiss Brethren to the neighboring towns and villages. While his zeal at times ran ahead of his judgment, Blaurock was largely responsible for the formation of the Anabaptist congregation in Zollikon. Unquestionably sincere, his unflinching commitment to the Anabaptist understanding of the faith and his effectiveness in sharing it cost him his life.

49. Ramaker, *Hymns and Hymn Writers,* pp. 115-16.

III

ᴄ᷾ᴤ ᴄ᷾ᴤ

A Superlative Witness

ARTYRDOM BECAME AN ANABAPTIST HALLMARK. AMONG THOSE
who died at the hands of the authorities for their faith were
countless worthy, often unknown, unforgettable witnesses.
However, there were none who surpassed Michael Sattler in the hour
of death. His superlative witness became a symbol of Anabaptist fidelity
in the eyes of the sixteenth-century world wherever the story of his
heroic martyrdom found an audience.

On a spring day in May, 1527, Michael Sattler was sentenced to
death at the imperial city of Rottenburg on the Neckar River. The
sentence read:

> Michael Sattler shall be committed to the executioner. The latter
> shall take him to the square and there first cut out his tongue, and
> then forge him fast to a wagon and there with glowing iron tongs
> twice tear pieces from his body, then on the way to the site of
> execution five times more as above and then burn his body to powder
> as an arch-heretic.[1]

---

1. There are four extant accounts of the trial and death of Michael Sattler.
Wilhelm Reublin's account is found on pp. 250-53 of *Quellen*. Klaus von
Graveneck's account is in the Wolfenbuttel library. An original German account
is edited by W. J. Köhler in *Flugschriften aus den ersten Jahren der Reformation*
(1908), vol. 2, no. 3. Another account is found in the Hutterite *Large Chronicle*

Who was this condemned man? What had he done to bring down upon his head the unmitigated wrath of the judges? The answer is to be found, in part at least, in a study of Sattler's life.

Michael Sattler was born at Stauffen in the Breisgau, near Freiburg, Germany, around 1490. Little is known for certain about Sattler's life prior to his appearance in Zürich. He was apparently a prior in St. Peter's monastery, a Benedictine cloister in the Black Forest northeast of Freiburg, when he left the order. Freiburg was a university town. Johannes Eck, Luther's antagonist, once headed a *bursa* in the city and also taught in the university. Freiburg was also a city known for its vigorous defense of Catholic orthodoxy and heavy-handed repression of Protestant dissent. Sattler may have attended lectures here before becoming a monk, although there is no record of his matriculation in the university. Somehow, he was rumored to have a knowledge of Greek, Hebrew, and Latin.[2] Apparently, he was fluent in Latin but it is less certain that he knew the biblical languages, although it is not impossible. What is also strange is that there is no record of his stay at St. Peter's or mention of his position as a prior. However, two fires at the monastery could account for the missing records; or, since he became an Anabaptist and was executed as a heretic, all traces of his name could have been eradicated as was the case with some former Catholic prelates who had become "heretics" in other Catholic strongholds of Europe.[3] During his stay in the monastery, Sattler had begun the study of the Pauline epistles. This increased his dissatisfaction with the vice and hypocrisy of his fellow monks. Sattler's new-found evangelical faith finally precipitated a crisis which was only resolved with a severance of all ties with the monastery and the Church of Rome.

Much more is known about the history of St. Peter's than about

---

which differs in some slight detail from the others. It is this last account from which the *Mirror* version is taken.

2. Hutterian Brethren, trans. and eds., *The Chronicle of the Hutterian Brethren* (Rifton, N.Y.: Plough Publishing House, 1987), 1:51-52.

3. See C. Arnold Snyder, *The Life and Thought of Michael Sattler* (Scottdale, Pa.: Herald Press, 1984), pp. 23-65. Snyder has made an exhaustive search to verify the little information given by other authors and has drawn a blank. His monograph is the latest and most thorough study of the celebrated martyr.

Sattler before he severed his ties with the Benedictines. The monastery had become subject to a tug of war between Margrave Ernst and Austrian authorities. The margrave claimed when his troops were quartered in the convent that he was protecting the peasants from the heavy taxation levied by Abbot Jodocus. There is no doubt that the peasants were unhappy with the increasingly heavy tax burden and other injustices at the hands of feudal lords, including the abbot and his monks. As elsewhere, the peasants generally viewed the monks as parasites living high off the sweat of peasant brows. Luther called monks "fleas on God Almighty's fur coat."[4] It is doubtful that the peasants viewed the margrave as a savior, however, for later they took over his castles and he was forced to take refuge in Freiburg. The peasants' rebellion in southwest Germany reached its peak about the time Sattler took his leave of St. Peter's. Abbot Jodocus had forsaken his post some time before, leaving Sattler in charge. Moore dated Sattler's departure on the day the peasants occupied the monastery, May 12, 1525. The peasants were beginning to press their claims for justice by laying siege to Freiburg. Some of the peasants who took over the monastery were, according to Snyder and Moore, Anabaptists from Waldshut and Hallau.[5]

---

4. Cited by Bainton, *Here I Stand.*

5. See Moore, *Anabaptist Portraits*, p. 98, and Snyder, *Michael Sattler,* p. 64. Although Snyder has based his conclusions regarding the life and work of Michael Sattler upon thorough research, at times his conclusions are too general and open to serious question. His statement about the south German peasant uprising and Anabaptism being indistinguishable is a case in point. If he had made this statement in reference to the Lutheran Reformation and the peasant movement, he would have been closer to the truth of the matter. It is true that from 1522 to 1525, the peasant protests became increasingly anticlerical and proevangelical. But it was a nondescript evangelicalism that apparently took its inspiration from Luther's teachings on the authority of the Bible and the priesthood of believers that provided the religious justification for the south German Peasants' War. Christoph Schappeler and Sebastian Lotzer figure prominently in this development. They were more Lutheran than anything else and actively involved in the peasants' demands for a reformation of society. It was Lotzer, the military secretary of the largest of the Swabian peasant armies, that put these demands in the form of the Twelve Articles of the Peasants. Barbara Bettina Gerber wrote: "The Twelve Articles broke the dams between the evangelical and the social movement." See

It is possible, as Moore has suggested, that through the Anabaptist peasants Sattler made contact with Hans Kuenzi, an Anabaptist of Oberglatt who took him in and taught him the weaver's craft. Oberglatt was located on the Swiss border with Germany between Schaffhausen and Waldshut. Although historians disagree, solid documentary evidence does not place Sattler in Zürich in the company of the Swiss Brethren until November, 1525. The last major Anabaptist disputation took place over a three-day period, November 6-8. Although Zwingli promised that everyone would be permitted to discuss freely at length the issue of infant baptism versus believers' baptism, this was hardly the case since several of the Anabaptist participants were already in custody. Among these was Michael Sattler.

Sattler had probably accompanied Ulrich Teck of Waldshut and Marty Ling of Schaffhausen to Grüningen where Grebel, Manz, and Blaurock were enjoying much success in the community of Grebel's boyhood. While here, they were arrested and turned over to the Zürich authorities. In order to give the popular trio a semblance of a fair hearing, Zwingli had decided to stage a disputation. His proposed agenda was that of his just finished reply to Balthasar Hubmaier's *Von der christlichen Tauf der Glaubigen (On the Christian Baptism of Believers)*. Since Austrian designs against Hubmaier prevented his appearance, the local Anabaptists defended their position as best they could. The presence of peasants from the countryside, who also took part sometimes rudely and crudely, did not help the Anabaptist cause. Zwingli was declared the victor as usual. Charges of "rebaptizing and improper conduct etc." were brought against Grebel, Manz, and Blaurock, who

---

her essay "Sebastian Lotzer," in Hans-Jurgen Goertz, ed., *Profiles of Radical Reformers* (Kitchener, Ont.: Herald Press, 1982), p. 82.

The above remarks are not intended to deny that Anabaptists were in sympathy with the demands of the peasants nor that some Anabaptists from Waldshut and Hallau were involved in the South German peasant uprising. Rather, my intent is to emphasize that the Anabaptist movement in Switzerland and southwest Germany was a deeply religious movement with social implications, not a social movement with religious overtones. To fail to recognize this distinction is to fail to recognize the distinctive nature of the Anabaptist movement, not only after Schleitheim but before as well.

were sentenced to be held in the New Tower on bread, water, and mush as long as it "pleases God and seems good to my lords etc."[6]

On the same day, November 18, Teck, Ling, and Sattler were banished from the canton after paying court costs and taking an oath not to return. Teck was to be imprisoned if he refused to take the oath. Nothing is said regarding similar treatment of Sattler and Ling.[7] It could be that neither had been baptized as yet or had not baptized anyone in the canton. And of course neither was from Waldshut, Hubmaier's city.

Whether Sattler and Ling were in Grüningen is an open question, since the Zürich documents do not so indicate. In fact, Sattler's activities are difficult to follow immediately before and after his appearance in Zürich in November. Sometime after leaving St. Peter's, he married "Margaretha," who was reported to have been a member of the Beguines and "a talented and clever little woman."[8] She proved to be a faithful Christian and a courageous wife.

Just when Sattler was baptized is not known. Apparently from May, 1525, to August, 1526, he made his home near Schaffhausen in the Swiss *Unterland*. Living only a short distance from Waldshut, he was familiar with the work of Hubmaier and Wilhelm Reublin, who preached and baptized in the area, as well as Johannes Brötli, who was at work in Hallau. It is probable that Sattler was baptized by Reublin, a fellow German from the Black Forest. His personal contacts with Grebel, Manz, and Blaurock, as well, gave him ample opportunity to observe the nature of the movement and its varied expressions in Switzerland and southwest Germany. A year or so after he was banished from Zürich he surfaced in Strasbourg, one of the more tolerant cities in Europe.

Like a magnet, Strasbourg drew a variety of religious radicals to

6. *Quellen*, p. 136. For the English translation of the court document see Leland Harder, *Sources of Swiss Anabaptism*, p. 442.

7. *Ibid.*

8. The Beguines were comprised of groups of devout women living in community for the purposes of cultivating the spiritual life and serving the sick and the poor. Chastity and a high moral standard characterized their lifestyle. They were suspected of heresy ever since their founding in the Netherlands in the twelfth century.

its environs. At the time Sattler was there both Hans Denck and Ludwig Haetzer were in the city. Although Haetzer was frequently in the company of Anabaptists, he was never baptized. While both Haetzer and Denck were university educated and able linguists, they were not appreciated by Martin Bucer and Wolfgang Capito, the leading Reformers of the area. Not so with Sattler, who was highly esteemed by both Reformers. After Sattler's execution, they wrote:

> Thus we do not doubt that Michael Sattler, who was burned at Rottenburg, was a dear friend of God, even though he was a leader in the baptism order; yet much more qualified and honorable than some others. He also spoke concerning baptism, in such a way that you can see that he only rejected infant baptism, through which one thinks to be saved. For as a printed booklet concerning him reports, he proved his point by arguing that faith alone can save. Furthermore he pled for instruction from biblical Scripture and offered to accept the same.[9]

Evidently, Sattler's theological position as well as his irenic spirit endeared him to the Strasbourg reformers. Although both Denck and Haetzer were asked to leave the city, Sattler left on his own accord. After leaving he wrote a letter "to his beloved brothers in God Capito and Bucer and others who love and confess Christ from the heart." In this letter he set forth a statement regarding the nonnegotiable core of his faith, which prompted him to break off the dialogue. With characteristic clarity, he delineated in twenty points his position on faith, baptism, the church, discipleship, and separation from the world. He concluded his letter by stating that his conscience would not allow him to remain longer in Strasbourg and with a plea for the release of the imprisoned Anabaptists.[10] There is nothing in the letter that had not surfaced before in the Anabaptist movement with the exception of the attitude toward the Reformers. The acceptance of Bucer and Capito as "brothers in God," in spite of their worldly state church, infant baptism, and complicity in the imprisonment of Anabaptists, was in marked

9. Quoted in John Howard Yoder, trans. and ed., *The Legacy of Michael Sattler* (Scottdale, Pa.: Herald Press, 1973), p. 19.
10. See *ibid.*, pp. 21-24, for an English translation of the entire letter.

contrast with the attitude of Grebel and his colleagues toward Zwingli and Leo Jud in Zürich.

Apparently, Sattler never questioned the sincerity of Bucer and Capito when they insisted that 1 Timothy 1:5 made acceptance of infant baptism mandatory since "love was the end of the law." Zwingli and Jud had used this same argument effectively against Hubmaier a few months earlier, which persuaded him for "the sake of love" to agree to give up his insistence on believers' baptism. It had no such effect on Sattler, who had probably come to Strasbourg to seek the release of the imprisoned Anabaptists, among whom was Jakob Gross from Waldshut.

Moving to Germany on the invitation of Reublin, Sattler began to work north of Rottenburg, making Horb the center of his activities.[11] In the environs of Horb and Rottenburg, Sattler succeeded in winning a number of converts and gathering them into house churches. He apparently also wrote five tracts for the edification and instruction of new converts.

Although the five tracts were anonymous, T. J. van Braght (1625-64) attributed them to Sattler. According to Moore, the content and style are those of Sattler. This was also the opinion of Wenger. Another bit of evidence that the first of the tracts, *On the Satisfaction of Christ (Gnugthuung Christi)*, was Sattler's is that it is the fourth item of nine in a German collection of tracts published around 1600 called *Sammelband*. It follows an account of Sattler's martyrdom.[12] Within the tract itself, the author did not reject justification by faith but in typical Anabaptist fashion insisted that the faith that saves is also the faith that produces works of righteousness. If this tract did not come from Sattler's hand it must have come from the Sattler circle in or around Horb; in either case it testifies to his influence in the area.

The second of the tracts contrasted two different kinds of obedience: servile and filial. According to the author, filial obedience is rooted in the love of the Father whereas servile is a legal obedience that

---

11. Gustav Bossert, Jr., "Michael Sattler's Trial and Martyrdom in 1527," trans. Elizabeth Bender, MQR 25 (July 1951): 202-3.

12. See John C. Wenger, "Concerning the Satisfaction of Christ, An Anabaptist Tract on True Christianity," MQR 20 (October 1946): 243-54. An English translation of the tract is given with an extensive introduction by Wenger.

only does what is required by the law. Herein is revealed an Anabaptist application of Luther's contrast between Law and Gospel. The author wrote: "The filial is not contrary to the servile, as it might appear, but is better and higher. And therefore let him who is servile seek for the better, the filial; he dare not be servile at all."[13]

The three other tracts, *On Divorce, Concerning Evil Overseers,* and *The Hearing of False Prophets or Antichrists,* attributed to Sattler, reflect Anabaptist insistence upon the higher revelation in the New Testament than that of the Old, and the necessity of separation from "false Prophets," both Catholic and Protestant. Conceivably, all five tracts could have been written by Michael Sattler or someone in the Sattler circle. They certainly reflect the strong christological center of Anabaptist worship and life. Absent are tracts on the sword and the oath. These issues would be addressed in the first group "confession" of the movement at Schleitheim.

Whatever else may be said about the Schleitheim Confession, it represents a turning point in early Swiss and south German Anabaptism. It is also indicative of the growing influence of Sattler, who was, without reasonable doubt, its major architect. Anabaptism stood at the crossroads. On January 5, 1527, Felix Manz had been executed by drowning in Zürich, the first martyrdom of an Anabaptist at the hands of a Protestant government, an ill omen indeed for Reformed Christianity as well as for the Anabaptists. Many Anabaptists had only recently received believers' baptism with a modicum of instruction, and some, apparently, had been involved in the south German peasant rebellion. It would have been strange, indeed, if some had not cried for vengeance or determined to defend themselves with the sword. Since the peasants had been so decisively defeated in their attempt to claim what they considered their just rights, others feared that Anabaptism would suffer a similar fate. These fears were not groundless. There was a vacuum in leadership. Grebel and Manz were dead. Blaurock was in the Tyrol and Hubmaier in Moravia. Reublin and Brötli evidently lacked the ability to lead a movement that demanded a leader with the depth of conviction, clarity of thought, and unflinching courage that characterized Michael Sattler.

13. J. C. Wenger, trans., "Two Kinds of Obedience: An Anabaptist Tract on Christian Freedom," MQR 21 (January 1947): 20.

Sattler recognized the crisis: it was time to regroup. The call went out. Secretly, the Brethren decided to assemble at Schlaten am Randen, near Schaffhausen, to consider the future of the movement. For this purpose, Sattler had drawn up, and possibly circulated before the meeting, seven articles that constituted in his mind the basic principles of faith and order that would henceforth distinguish the movement from all others. Snyder held that Schleitheim marked the beginning of sectarian Anabaptism.[14] Yoder wrote that "early 1527 must be recognized as the coming-of-age of a distinct, visible fellowship taking long-range responsibility for its order and its faith."[15] Schleitheim was indeed significant, yet it was not the beginning of the movement. It may best be seen as a restatement of the distinctive faith and order of the Anabaptists that set the movement apart not only from the Reformed Church of Switzerland but from others as well.

The Schleitheim Confession was not intended to be a doctrinal formulation. There are no strictly theological concepts directly asserted in it. Such topics as God, man, the Bible, salvation, the church, and eschatology are not discussed. The articles are concerned with order and discipline within congregations. Baptism, excommunication, the Lord's Supper, separation from the world, pastors, the sword, and the oath are the subjects to which attention is given. The articles are in the nature of a church manual, such as the *Didache* of the second century.

An implied theology is present in this work. There is a clarity of thought regarding baptism and the Lord's Supper which defies any sacramental interpretation. The articles concerning discipline, the sword, and swearing indicate a fundamental fidelity to the faith and practice of the Swiss Brethren. The precarious existence of the small Anabaptist congregations scattered across southern Germany is revealed in selections from the section on pastors.

> The pastor *of the flock should be* . . . some one who has good testimony from those who are outside the faith. Let his office be . . . in all things that pertain to the body of Christ to watch how it may be sustained and increased, that the name of God may be honored

---

14. Snyder, *Michael Sattler,* pp. 198-202.
15. Yoder, *Legacy of Michael Sattler,* p. 29.

and praised through us, but the mouth of *blasphemy* may be stopped. But know that a support, if he is in need of it, ought to be supplied by the church which elects him. . . . But if a pastor be either *expelled* or led to the Lord through the cross another ought to succeed him at once that the people or flock of God be not scattered but preserved through exhortation and may receive consolation.[16]

While the Schleitheim meeting was in progress, the Anabaptists were discovered by the authorities of Rottenburg. Upon returning to Horb, Sattler and his wife, Reublin's wife, Matthias Hiller, Veit Veringer of Rottenburg, and a number of other men and women from Horb were arrested. The importance of Sattler was immediately apparent to the government officials. They had found in his possession the Schleitheim Confession and documents relating to the strength and activities of the Anabaptists. Due to this fact and the presence of many Anabaptists and sympathizers in the city, the prisoners were moved from Horb to Binsdorf.

From the tower of Binsdorf, Sattler wrote a touching letter of consolation to his beloved congregation at Horb. Typical of Anabaptist prison epistles, it abounds in Scripture references, emphasizes love to all, and is completely devoid of bitterness. He opens the letter with a trinitarian salutation: "Beloved companions in the Lord; the grace and mercy of God, our Heavenly Father, through Jesus Christ our Lord, and the power of their Spirit, be with you, brethren and sisters, beloved of God."

The emphasis upon love as the undergirding motivation of the Christian life finds characteristic prominence in the admonition of Sattler.

---

16. W. J. McGlothlin, *Baptist Confessions of Faith* (Philadelphia: American Baptist Publication Society, 1911), pp. 5-6. Yoder, in *Legacy of Michael Sattler,* pp. 28ff., provides a new translation of the Schleitheim Confession. He also translated many Sattler letters in this first publication of the "Classics of the Radical Reformation" series. See also Beatrice Jenny, "Das Schleitheimer Täuferbekenntnis, 1527," in *Schaffhauser Beiträge zur väterlandischen Geschichte,* ed. *Historischen Verein des Kantons Schaffhausen* (Thayngen: Verlag Karl Augustin, 1951). For the serious student who can handle the German, Jenny's work is well worth careful study. The title of the Confession in German is *Brüderlich Vereinigung etzlicher Kinder Gottes.*

If you have love for your neighbor, you will not be envious in punishing or excommunicating, will not seek your own, will think no evil, will not be ambitious, and finally will not be puffed up; but will be merciful, just, mild in all things, submissive and compassionate towards the weak and infirm. I Corinthians XIII.15. Galatians V. Tab. IV.5. Romans XV.8. I Corinthians VIII.32.

Like a faithful shepherd whose primary consideration, even at the prospects of his own death, is the welfare of the sheep, Sattler attempted in the final paragraphs of the letter to prepare his followers for the inevitable.

And let no man take away from you the foundation which is laid by the letter of the holy Scriptures, and sealed with the blood of Christ and many witnesses of Jesus. . . . The brethren have doubtless informed you, that some of us are in prison; and the brethren being apprehended at Horb, we were afterwards brought to Binsdorf. At this time numerous accusations were preferred against us by our adversaries; at one time they threatened us with the gallows; at another with fire and sword. In this extremity, I surrendered myself, entirely to the Lord's will, and prepared myself, together with all my brethren and my wife, to die for his testimony's sake . . . hence I deemed it necessary to animate you with this exhortation, to follow us in the contest of God, that you may console yourselves with it, and not faint under the chastening of the Lord. . . .

In short, beloved brethren and sisters, this letter shall be a valedictory to you all who love God in truth, and follow him. . . .

Beware of false brethren; for the Lord will probably call me to him, so take warning. I wait for my God; pray without ceasing for all that are in bonds; God be with you all. Amen.[17]

The prisoner's apprehension of execution was fully justified. He was in the hands of Austrian authorities, who had the jurisdiction of Rottenburg. Ferdinand, the Catholic king of Austria, had declared "the third baptism" (drowning) to be the best antidote to Anabaptism. Because of Sattler's importance to the movement, Ferdinand suggested

17. *Mirror,* pp. 346-48.

that he be drowned immediately. Authorities headed by Count Joachim, however, wanted to give this "ecclesiastical case" some semblance of justice. The delay in securing theological representatives from the Roman Catholic universities made it necessary to postpone the trial until May 15. Finally, two doctors from the university did agree to take part in the trial. They were not doctors of law, as had been requested, but doctors of the arts. Two representatives also came from Ensisheim, a city notorious for its bad government and heresy trials.

On May 15, the court convened with twenty-four judges. The chairman of this imposing body was the *Landeshauptmann,* Count Joachim of Zollern. The attorney for the defense was the Mayor of Rottenburg, Jakob Halbmayer, hardly a sympathetic advocate. Sattler felt that Halbmayer was responsible for the outcome of the trial.[18]

The trial actually began on May 17. There were fourteen defendants on the bench of the accused. At first they were given their choice of attorney. Sattler, who acted as spokesman for the group, declined the offer upon the basis that this was not a legal matter. According to the Word of God, he said, they had no right to go to law over religious affairs. His manner was courteous but definite. In this reply Sattler wisely addressed the judges as the servants of God, recognizing their authority but denying their jurisdiction. He also questioned the competence of the court.

Count Joachim then proceeded to have the charges read against the defendant. The first seven were against all the accused, and two additional charges were brought against Sattler alone.

> 1. That he and his adherents acted contrary to the decree of the emperor. 2. He taught, maintained, and believed, that the body and blood of Christ were not present in his sacrament. 3. He taught and believed, that infant-baptism was not promotive of salvation. 4. They rejected the sacrament of unction. 5. They despised and reviled the Mother of God, and condemned the saints. 6. He declared, that men should not swear before a magistrate. 7. He has commenced a new and unheard of custom in regard to the Lord's Supper, placing the bread and wine on a plate, eating and drinking the same. 8. Contrary

18. Bossert, *Sattler's Trial and Martyrdom,* p. 206.

to the rule, he has married a wife. 9. He said if the Turks invaded the country, we ought not to resist them, and if he approved of war, he would rather take the field against the Christians than against the Turks, notwithstanding, it is an important matter to set the greatest enemies of our faith against us.[19]

These charges revealed a gross misunderstanding of the Anabaptist teachings and no sympathy for the teachings which were understood. The fifth charge was clearly a caricature of Anabaptist views and the seventh, a baseless rumor. Charges one, six, and nine were grounds for a civil case. The first charge was based upon the premise that "the emperor is the protector of the church, this was the premise and conclusion of the medieval church and the church is the Roman Catholic Church. The church, its doctrine, its organization, its law were alone valid on Austrian soil."[20] The ninth charge was the most damaging. No other power on earth struck fear in the hearts of Austrians like that of the Turks. Conscious or not of misstating Sattler's position, the authorities intended to use this as a final blow to condemn him before the world.

After the reading of the charges and discussion of them, Sattler asked that the articles be reread. At this the secretary, who was from Ensisheim, tauntingly sneered, "he has boasted of the Holy Ghost. Now if this boast is true, it seems to me, it is unnecessary to grant him this; for, if he has the Holy Ghost, as he boasts, the same will tell him what has been done here."[21] Unperturbed, Sattler renewed his request, which was begrudgingly granted.[22]

Sattler's defense was both skillful and courageous. In answer to the first charge he pointed out that the imperial mandates were against the Lutherans. They directed that Lutheran doctrine and error not be followed but rather the gospel and the Word of God. "This we have observed," he stated, "for I am not aware, that we have acted contrary to the gospel and word of God; I appeal to the word of Christ." He

---

19. *Ibid.,* 209-10.

20. *Ibid.*

21. Williams and Mergal, *Spiritual and Anabaptist Writers,* p. 139.

22. Bossert asserts that the articles were not read even then but rather only their substance given; see *Sattler's Trial and Martyrdom,* p. 209.

accepted the second charge as valid, defending the Anabaptist position with numerous Scripture references. The third charge he did not deny, but used the opportunity to affirm believers' baptism. In speaking to the fourth article, he distinguished between oil as a creation of God which is good and the oil of extreme unction, which is no better. "What God has made, is good, and not to be rejected; but that the pope with his bishops, monks, and priests, has made it better, we deny; for the pope has never made anything good." Concerning the Virgin Mary, he said:

> We never reviled the mother of God, and the saints; but the mother of Christ should be esteemed above all women; for she had the favor of giving birth to the Savior of the world; but that she shall be an intercessor, is not known in Scripture. . . . As to the saints, we say, that we who live and believe are the saints; in evidence of this I appeal to the epistle of Paul to the Romans, Corinthians, Ephesians, etc. He always writes: To the beloved saints. We, therefore, who believe, are the saints: those who die in the faith, we consider the "blessed."[23]

Sattler accepted the sixth charge as justified and defended the Anabaptist position with Matthew 5:34, 37. The seventh charge was ignored. He evidently felt it unworthy of consideration.

Next, Sattler turned his attention to the last two charges brought against him personally. He defended his action in taking a wife on two grounds: first, the gross immorality among priests and monks, and second, that marriage is an ordinance of God. Regarding his teaching about the Turks, Sattler asserted the Anabaptist principle of nonresistance. He then proceeded to restate his position with complete candor.

> If the Turks should make an invasion, they should not be resisted; for it is written: Thou shalt not kill. We ought not to defend ourselves against the Turks and our persecutors; but earnestly entreat God in our prayers, that he would repel and withstand them. For my saying, that if I approved of war, I would rather march forth against the so

23. *Mirror,* p. 345.

named Christians who persecute, imprison, and put to death, the pious Christians, I assign this reason: The Turk is a true Turk, knows nothing of the Christian faith, and is a Turk according to the flesh; but you, wishing to be Christian, and making your boast of Christ, persecute the pious witnesses of Christ, and are Turks according to the Spirit. Exodus XX.30. Matthew VII.7. Titus I.16.[24]

In his closing appeal Sattler established the legitimacy of the office of magistrate, defining its jurisdiction, limitations, and responsibilities. His final plea was for an opportunity to discuss the Scriptures with the judges in any language of their choice. He expressed fervent hope that the judges would "repent and receive instruction."

The response according to the account, reminiscent of apostolic days, was indicative of the spirit of the court.

> The judges laughed at the discourse, and after consultation, the town clerk of Ensisheim said: Oh you infamous, desperate villain and monk, you would have us engage with you in a discussion! the executioner will dispute with you, we think for a certainty. Sattler exclaimed: Let the will of God be done.[25]

Much more of the same followed. The town clerk of Ensisheim became more and more violent. Caught up in an emotional frenzy he threatened to take Sattler's life on the spot. The prisoner's patience and composure were obviously exasperating to his would-be judges.

During the hour and a half while the judges deliberated, Sattler was alternately threatened and ridiculed. Some cried out, "When I see you get away, I will believe in you." Another seized his sword and said, "See, with this we will dispute with you."[26] A voice from the crowd asked why he had not remained a lord in the monastery. Sattler replied, "I was a lord according to the flesh, but it is better thus."[27] Seemingly nothing could destroy Michael Sattler's calm self-composure. Even the sentence, to which reference has already been made, failed to shake him.

24. *Ibid.*
25. *Ibid.,* p. 346.
26. Bossert, *Sattler's Trial and Martyrdom*, p. 214.
27. *Mirror,* p. 346.

Klaus von Graveneck, an eyewitness, wrote of Sattler's conduct, "All this I saw myself. May God grant us also to testify of Him so bravely and patiently."[28] The events recorded above took place over a two-day period. The sentence was read on May 18. Two days later, on May 20, Sattler was executed.[29]

The torture, a prelude to the execution, began at the marketplace, where a piece was cut from Sattler's tongue. Pieces of flesh were torn from his body twice with red-hot tongs. He was then forged to a cart. On the way to the scene of the execution the tongs were applied five times again. In the marketplace and at the site of the execution, still able to speak, the unshakable Sattler prayed for his persecutors. After being bound to a ladder with ropes and pushed into the fire, he admonished the people, the judges, and the mayor to repent and be converted. Then he prayed, "Almighty, eternal God, Thou art the way and the truth: because I have not been shown to be in error, I will with thy help to this day testify to the truth and seal it with my blood."

As soon as the ropes on his wrists were burned, Sattler raised the two forefingers of his hands, giving the promised signal to the brethren that a martyr's death was bearable. Then the assembled crowd heard coming from his seared lips, "Father, I commend my spirit into Thy hands."[30]

Three others were then executed. After every attempt to secure a recantation from Sattler's faithful wife had failed, she was drowned eight days later in the Neckar.

Perhaps no other execution of an Anabaptist had such far-reaching influence. Wilhelm Reublin's booklet containing an account of Sattler's execution found its way throughout Germany, Austria, and Switzerland. Lutheran, Reformed, and even Catholic witnesses were never quite able to get away from the scene of that infamous day in Rottenburg. Bucer and Capito were grieved at the news of the execution. The impact of Sattler's superlative witness is felt to this day. To this fact Gustav Bossert,

---

28. Bossert, *Sattler's Trial and Martyrdom,* p. 214.

29. A difference of opinion about the date of Sattler's execution exists. It was either on Monday, May 20, 1527, or Tuesday, May 21. See *ibid.,* p. 215, for a rather detailed discussion of the problem.

30. *Ibid.,* p. 216.

Jr., a contemporary Lutheran pastor and Anabaptist scholar of Wurttemberg, testifies. He writes, "Sattler's character lies clearly before us. He was not a highly educated divine and not an intellectual; but his entire life was noble and pure, true and unadulterated."[31]

Others, Witnesses Too

What Bossert has written of Sattler could serve as an accurate characterization of the rank and file of the movement. Many, like Sattler, sealed their faith with their blood. A casual turning of the pages of the *Martyrs' Mirror* will reveal the severity of persecution which increasingly became the lot of these harassed people. As far as the sixteenth-century world was concerned, the Anabaptists were nobodies. What difference did it make that another Elizabeth, Melchior, Hans, Leopold, Leonhard, or Anna was dead?

A typical entry in the *Martyrs' Mirror* reads:

> In this year 1538, in the month of August, ten, or seventeen persons, male and female, were apprehended in the town, who were accused of rebaptism. These were principally of the poorer class, except one, a goldsmith, called Paul von Drusnen, of whom it is reported that he was their teacher. Paul, and three others, were put to death at Vucht, in the theatre, then afterwards burnt on the 9th of September.

The account continues with a description of an attempt on the part of the Dominicans to break down the women in an effort to secure proper recantations.

> Paul's wife said: O Lord! enlighten these who inflict such sufferings upon us, that they may see what they are doing. I thank thee, O God! that thou didst think me worthy to suffer for thy name's sake.
>
> The dominican said to another woman: Will you not stay with the holy church? She replied: I will remain with God; is this not a sufficient holy church?
>
> Then spoke the dominican to a man, John von Capelle: Pray that he may forgive you, because you have set us a bad example. He

31. *Ibid.,* p. 217.

replied: I did not err, but I have been engaged in the word of God and I am sorry that I remained so long in darkness. I entreat you, brothers, read the gospel, and live according to its precepts, and leave off your debauchery, roguery, and cursing, and the crossing of yourselves, etc.

The third woman said: O, Almighty God! lay no greater burden upon me than I can bear, etc. Thus they died cheerfully.[32]

Other accounts like the one quoted above often give the number, date, and place of execution but rarely a complete list of the names. The following examples illustrate this fact: "Wolfgang Brand-Huber, Hans Niedermaier, and about seventy others, A.D. 1529."[33] "Wolfgang Ulimann . . . was burnt at Waltzen, together with his brother and seven others, all testifying to their faith with their death, A.D. 1528." Mass executions were common. However, the execution of "three hundred and fifty . . . at Altzey" upon the emperor's command in 1529 was out of the ordinary.[34]

In 1529 a death decree was issued against the Anabaptists by the Second Diet of Speiers. This greatly accelerated the program of extermination already in progress.[35] At times the customary efforts of oppression proved inadequate to stem the tide of the growing movement. Other methods were then tried. The most atrocious application of this policy was made in Swabia. Four hundred special police were hired to hunt down Anabaptists and execute them on the spot. The group proved too small and was increased to one thousand.[36]

The severe persecution was not without effect. However, the effect was not always what those in authority might have wished. Untold thousands must have died. The extant records preserved in the *Geschichts-Buch*, the *Martyrs' Mirror*, and court records are fragmentary and at times

32. *Mirror*, p. 374.

33. *Ibid.*, p. 360.

34. *Ibid.*, p. 354.

35. Philip of Hesse was one of the few rulers in Europe who refused to put Anabaptists to death. Regardless of one's opinion concerning his immoral escapades, one cannot but marvel at the degree of his leniency in this regard in contrast with that of the Reformers. See Littell, *Landgraf Philipp und die Toleranz* (Bad Nauheim: Im Christian-Verlag, 1957), for a discussion of toleration under Philip.

36. Hershberger, *Recovery of Anabaptist Vision*, p. 33.

inaccurate. Nevertheless, they indicate that thousands of Anabaptists fell victim to one of the most widely spread persecutions in Christian history. The Count of Altzey was dismayed at the increase of Anabaptists after mass executions failed to halt their spread. He is reported to have said, "What shall I do, the more I execute, the more they increase."[37]

Persecution was so intensive and thorough in some areas that the Anabaptist movement was effectively stamped out. In other sections where persecution was less thorough the testimony of the martyrs led to phenomenal growth. Persecuted in one country, those dispossessed and threatened fled to another, hoping for respite in one of Europe's vanishing islands of freedom. It was a vain hope. Nowhere did the Anabaptists escape. Burning fagots and smoldering stakes marked their trek across Europe. Even a century and a half later, Anabaptists were the objects of court procedure in Bern, Switzerland.[38]

Such is the sordid story that stains the history of the established state churches of the Continent. Against the darkness of Europe's long night of death, the Anabaptist's "meteors" shine even more brightly. The darkness, while extinguishing the meteors, could not put out the light. The Anabaptists they killed, but the truth they could not quench. "Truth is immortal."[39]

37. *Mirror*, p. 364.
38. Grätz, *Bernese Anabaptists*, pp. 34-37.
39. Clasen, *Anabaptism*, has made a detailed study of the number of executions of Anabaptists in Switzerland, south and central Germany, Austria, Bohemia, and Moravia from 1525 to 1618. As a result he comes up with the figure of 715 executions that can be documented. To these he adds 130 "probable executions." However, he does not include the 600 alleged executions at Ensisheim or 350 at Heidelberg. Zieglschmid lists, according to Clasen, 1,195. From his study Clasen concludes: "Once again it is clear that Anabaptism in our area was already largely destroyed in 1528 and 1529, several years before the Kingdom of Münster. In 1530 the death toll was again high, with 80 executions, but in the following years the number of executions decreased, and from 1540 onward it decreased still more sharply. In Bavaria, the Tirol, and Switzerland, however, executions continued to take place until the early seventeenth century" (p. 371). In evaluating Clasen's conclusions one must remember that his is a very limited study. For example, he makes no attempt to write the history of the Anabaptists in North Germany, the Netherlands, Poland, or England. His work is also limited chronologically. Therefore, his conclusions are often subject to serious question.

IV

❧   ❧

Truth Is Immortal

U NDOUBTEDLY, DR. BALTHASAR HUBMAIER WAS ONE OF THE MOST brilliant stars in the Anabaptist firmament. A creative theologian, he was well trained in scholastic theology and patristics. Both his eloquent tongue and prolific pen were turned to the advancement of the faith, which finally cost him his life. He was the Simon Peter of the early Anabaptist disciples. Impetuous and outspoken, at forty-five years of age he became an Anabaptist. Compromise and denial marred his otherwise splendid testimony, but repentance led to renewed faith and a courageous death. One is reminded by Hubmaier's death of his most characteristic expression, "Truth is immortal." This chapter, and to some degree the entire book, is a vindication of that statement.

Little is known about Hubmaier's birth. It is believed that he was born about 1480-81 of unknown peasant parentage.[1] His native town was Friedberg, five miles east of Augsburg. He attended the Latin school at Augsburg. Much older than the average first-year university student,

---

1. Johann Loserth, "Balthasar Hübmaier," ME, 2:826. For many years Loserth's *Doctor Balthasar Hübmaier und die Anfänge der Wiedertaufer in Mähren,* published in 1893, was the finest biographical treatment of Hubmaier. However, it was superseded by Torsten Bergsten's *Balthasar Hübmaier: Seine Stellung zu Reformation und Täufertum, 1521-1528* (Kassel: J. G. Oncken, 1961). Bergsten's monumental work of 550 pages is an invaluable tool and an indispensable aid in Hubmaier research.

Hubmaier matriculated at the University of Freiburg on May 1, 1503.[2] The lack of sufficient funds with which to continue his education forced him to withdraw from the university. For a short time he taught school at Schaffhausen until he became financially able to return to the university.

Upon his return from Schaffhausen (1507) Hubmaier applied himself to his university studies with fresh enthusiasm, receiving his *baccalaureus biblicus* on August 1, 1511. Prior to earning this degree, the protégé of Dr. John Eck had taken his B.A. after only a year in the university and succeeded his teacher as rector of a *bursa* known as the *Pfauenburse* in the fall of 1510.

Hubmaier received the master's degree before leaving Freiburg again. Upon receiving this degree, the gifted student was eulogized in the most flattering terms by his teacher, the renowned Dr. John Eck:

> It is wonderful to say with what circumspection and eagerness he acquired the doctrines of philosophy, how he hung upon the lips of his teacher and zealously wrote down the lectures — a diligent reader, an unwearied hearer and an industrious repetitor of other hearers. So he obtained the Master's degree with the greatest honour.[3]

The admiration of the teacher for his student was matched, if not surpassed, by that of the student for his teacher. In Latin verse Hubmaier extravagantly lauded his mentor in a manner which must have fed Eck's insatiable ego sufficiently, for the time at least.

> A rare theologian, skilled in law and wisdom, he often sows the good seed among the people. A knotty logician, a master of sentences, whatever mathematician or astronomer teaches, all that orator, historian, or poet knows — I'll be hanged if this single man does not know it all![4]

Hubmaier's devotion to his teacher was such that, after Eck left Freiburg for the University of Ingolstadt less than a year and a half later, he

---

2. Henry C. Vedder, *Balthasar Hübmaier* (New York: G. P. Putnam's Sons, 1905), p. 27.

3. *Ibid.*, p. 28. "Repetitor" was the term applied to a teaching fellow who repeated the lectures of the teachers in the university for the benefit of other students.

4. *Ibid.*, p. 30.

followed him there. A short time later Balthasar became Dr. Balthasar Hubmaier, receiving the doctorate in theology on September 29, 1512.

Hubmaier, already ordained to the priesthood, was appointed as university preacher and chaplain of the Church of the Virgin, the university church. His advance in the Roman Catholic Church and in the affairs of the university was most rapid. Three years later at Easter, 1515, he became vice-rector of the university. The nominal rector was the Margrave Friedrich von Brandenburg. Hence Hubmaier's new position actually involved all the administrative duties and responsibilities of the rector. But Hubmaier's administration, due to a number of factors, was short-lived. He was not particularly successful as an administrator. Besides, his fame as a pulpiteer had grown to the extent that less than a year later he received a call to become chief preacher at the new cathedral of Regensburg. The call, when it came, proved irresistible. Therefore, Hubmaier left Ingolstadt for Regensburg on January 25, 1516.

Regensburg was easily the most prominent city and its cathedral the most outstanding in the area. Upon his arrival the new preacher found the town in an uproarious anti-Semitic campaign to rid the city of the Jews. He immediately championed the cause, evidently without a qualm of conscience. Hubmaier obviously shared the prejudices of the people of his day and probably the moral standards of his fellow ecclesiastics. With the Jews out of the way, the books were wiped clean. The city fathers found themselves free of debts and in possession of a synagogue building. Under Hubmaier's leadership the deserted synagogue was transformed into a Catholic chapel dedicated "to the beauteous Mary" *(zur Schönen Maria).*[5]

Immediately the renovated chapel was a success. Miracles took place daily. News traveled rapidly over the countryside, and the city was soon filled with credulous pilgrims. Hubmaier listed fifty-four miracles which he testified had taken place since its inauguration. But there was a fly in the ointment. Offerings of pilgrims to the shrine aroused the hostility of local monks, who suffered from the loss of income and prestige. All efforts of Hubmaier to mediate between city authorities and the irate inmates of the impoverished monastery failed.

5. *Ibid.,* p. 44.

The jealousy of the Dominicans was probably a major factor in Hubmaier's decision to leave Regensburg for the more secluded but smaller town of Waldshut on the Rhine. At any rate, discretion dictated a move, and Hubmaier left Regensburg much against the will of his parishioners. The city fathers, whose gratitude he well deserved, presented him with forty gulden in appreciation of his efforts for city and cathedral.

In 1521 at Waldshut he could look back over the past seven years at Ingolstadt and Regensburg with some degree of satisfaction. As a zealous son of the Roman Church he had served the university and cathedral well. He was successful in ridding Regensburg of its Jewish population. While incurring the wrath of the Jews and their friends, he had gained many friends and left highly respected.

During his first year at Waldshut, Hubmaier conscientiously performed the duties of a typical medieval parish priest. During thunderstorms he stationed himself at the church door with the Host and blessed the clouds. At Easter and on other occasions, as when the Host was carried to the sick, he saw that everything was done with much pomp and ceremony. In fact, Waldshut had never before witnessed such elaborate processions or such impressive ritual. The reverend doctor reverenced Mary and all the saints and was in turn revered by the citizens of Waldshut.

But all of this was destined to change. However, it may not have been apparent to anyone but Hubmaier in 1522. This was the year of decision for him. Sometime before, perhaps from the beginning of his days at Waldshut, he had begun to study the Scriptures, giving special attention to the Pauline epistles. In June, 1522, he journeyed to Basel, where he made the acquaintance of Glarean, Grebel's old teacher, and Erasmus. After visiting other Swiss cities and noting the progress of the Reformation, he returned to Waldshut. He was more intent than ever on a study of the New Testament, which became increasingly the sourcebook of his theology.[6]

Later in 1522, a new call came from Regensburg — evidence that the people had not forgotten the eloquence or zeal of their former

6. *Ibid.,* pp. 53-54.

people's priest. But this time, whether they knew it or not, it was not the same Dr. Hubmaier that they had known a short time before. The old Hubmaier, the popular but superficial cleric of Regensburg days, had given way to the new Hubmaier, the evangelical preacher of Waldshut. He reopened his ministry with a message from the Gospel of Luke and announced a series of the same. It should have been clear to his listeners that Dr. Balthasar was now committed to the Reformation and personally to Christ. He was, indeed, a "captive to the Word of God."

The shock was too great, the change too abrupt. Regensburg was not ready for such preaching. About three months later, on March 1, Hubmaier left Regensburg for Waldshut. Although friends tried to induce him to return upon two other occasions, he remained in Waldshut determined to reform the churches of the city much after the pattern of the Swiss Reformation in Zürich.

Like Zwingli, Hubmaier introduced changes in the traditional liturgy gradually. Although his initial conversion was due to Lutheran influence, he never considered himself a disciple of Luther. He found himself much closer to Zwingli and the Swiss Reformation. It is not surprising, therefore, that after contacting Zwingli, he participated in the second Zürich disputation as an ally of the Swiss reformer. En route to Zürich, Hubmaier met Vadian and preached at St. Gall and in Appenzell. During the disputation, he conferred with Zwingli on matters of common interest, including the lack of scriptural support for infant baptism. He also distinguished himself as an eloquent defender of Zwingli's position on the Lord's Supper. It is evident that by this time the Bible had taken the place of "the old church teaching" in providing the guidelines in matters of faith and order for the vicar of the Church of St. Marien in Waldshut. This much is clear from the following statement he made at the October disputation.

> Dear devout Christians, this is my conviction which I have learned from the Scriptures, namely, about images and the mass. Wherein my teaching is not right and Christian I ask you all through Jesus Christ, our only Savior, I ask and beseech you, to correct my judgment in a brotherly and Christian way with the Scriptures. I may err, I am a man; but a heretic I cannot be. I will (and desire from

my heart) receive correction and give many thanks to those who make known my error for I will follow God's Word willingly and in all obedience come under its judgment for you and all of us to be truly Christ's disciples and follow after Him.[7]

After the Zürich disputation Hubmaier returned to Waldshut to launch a program of reform for the whole area. His initial move was to invite all the clergy of the district to participate in a disputation. For the proposed disputation he prepared eighteen articles *(Schlussreden)*. These articles were in print by April or May, 1524. The *Achtzehn Schlussreden* became Hubmaier's first published work. The articles were probably finished by March while the memories of the October Zürich disputation were still fresh in his mind. It is evident from their content that he had completely overhauled the scholastic theology characteristic of his Freiburg and Ingolstadt days. The thrust of his thought is reflected in the articles which follow:

1. Faith alone makes us holy *(Frumm)* before God.

2. This faith is the acknowledgment of the mercy of God which he has shown us in the offering of his only begotten son. This excludes all sham Christians, who have nothing more than an historical faith in God.

3. Such faith can not remain passive but must break out *(aussbrechen)* to God in thanksgiving and to mankind in all kinds of works of brotherly love. Hence all vain religious acts, such as candles, palm branches, and holy water will be rejected.

4. Those works alone are good which God has commanded us and those alone are evil which he has forbidden. Hence fall away fish, flesh, cowls, and tonsures.

5. The mass is not a sacrifice but a remembrance of the death of Christ. Therefore, it is not an offering for the dead nor for the living. Hence fall to the ground weekly, monthly, and yearly masses for the dead.

---

7. This is the author's translation of a part of Hubmaier's address before the assembled delegates at the October disputation taken from the minutes recorded by Ludwig Haetzer. The entire proceedings, as recorded, may be found in *Huldreich Zwingli's Werke,* ed. Melchior Schuler and Johann Schulthess (Zürich: Friedrich Schulthess, 1828), 1:459-540, hereafter referred to as ZW.

6. As often as the memorial is observed should the death of the Lord be preached in the language of the people. Hence, all private masses fall together in a heap.

8. As every Christian believes for himself and is baptized, so each individual should see and judge by the Scriptures if he is rightly provided food and drink [the Lord's Supper] by his pastor.

13. The members of the church are obliged to support with adequate food and clothing those who teach them the word of God purely, clearly, and sincerely. Hence fall to the ground courtiers, pensioners, incorporators, absentees, repeaters of false legends, and dream babblers.

16. To promise chastity in the strength of men is nothing other than to promise to fly over the sea without wings.[8]

Hubmaier now became a man of action in implementing the principles set forth in these articles. All pictures and images were removed from the church by the end of the year. With action, his convictions were strengthened. Marriage followed rapidly the decision to begin the reform in earnest at Waldshut. Elizabeth Hügline, the daughter of a citizen of Reichenau, became Hubmaier's bride. She proved to be a faithful and courageous wife. And all of these revolutionary events had taken place over a two-year period, as indicated in one of Hubmaier's letters to some close friends of Regensburg days.

Further, I hear with great sadness how in your city of Regensburg more men preach vanity than the pure Word of God, that makes my heart ache; for what does not flow forth from the living word is dead before God. Therefore says Christ, Search the Scriptures. He does not say, Follow the old customs — though I did nothing else when I was the first time with you. However, I did it ignorantly. Like others, I was blinded and possessed by the doctrine of men. Therefore I openly confess before God and all men, that I then became a Doctor and preached some years among you and elsewhere, and yet had not known the way unto eternal life. Within two years has Christ for the first time come into my heart to thrive. I have

8. Gunnar Westin and Torsten Bergsten, *Balthasar Hübmaier Schriften* (Gütersloher: Verlagshaus Gerd Mohn, 1962), pp. 72-74. Hereafter referred to as *Schriften*.

never dared to preach him so boldly as now, by the grace of God. I lament before God that I so long lay ill of this sickness. I pray him truly for pardon; I did this unwittingly, wherefore I write this. I wonder if your preachers now will say, I am now of another disposition than formerly, that I confess[,] and condemn all doctrine and preaching, such as were mine among you and elsewhere, that is not grounded in the divine word.[9]

From the time of the Zürich disputation, Ferdinand I kept a watchful eye on Waldshut and the activities of its preacher. Soon afterward, two commissioners were sent from Ensisheim, the fanatical Catholic Austrian "command post" in Breisgau, to the city council of Waldshut demanding that Hubmaier be dismissed as the chief priest of the city and turned over to the bishop of Constance. The commissioners' request was bluntly rejected by the city council, which was loyal to Hubmaier. The following April a letter came from the Austrian government. It asked the city to dismiss "the said Doctor and preacher from the city, and choose in his place another suitable and pious preacher, who does not hold Luther's condemned doctrines." The bishop of Constance joined the government of Austria in calling for the dismissal of the "heretical preacher."

Hubmaier was summoned to stand trial before the episcopal court but refused, saying, "It was none of his duty to appear before that hypocrite."[10] The pressure mounted, but Waldshut stood firm in the support of its chief minister. Hubmaier, however, in order to spare the city the danger of armed intervention, decided to leave. On the first of September, 1524, he began the life of a fugitive as he prepared to take refuge in Schaffhausen. (Although Schaffhausen was in Swiss territory, it was within the diocese of the bishop of Constance.)

The Austrian government pursued him there. Even though Schaffhausen refused to surrender the hated heretic, Hubmaier's position was a precarious one. While there, uncertain of the future and separated from his beloved church and town, he wrote several treatises. One of these, a pamphlet on religious liberty, was destined to take its place

9. Vedder, *Hübmaier*, p. 78.
10. *Ibid.*, p. 80.

among the most significant in all Reformation literature. Entitled *Concerning Heretics and Those Who Burn Them (Von Ketzern und ihren Verbrennern)*, it enunciated in graphic and eloquent terms concepts of freedom and limitations of the magistrates' power to which the whole Anabaptist movement was to give prominence.

At the outset, Hubmaier redefines the term "heretics" as those who "deceitfully undermine the Holy Scriptures." In the second article he becomes even more specific. "The same are also heretics who conceal the Scriptures and interpret them other than the Holy Spirit demands, such as, those that everywhere proclaim a wife as a benefice; ruling for pastoring; stones for the rock; Rome for the Church, and compelling us to believe this prattle." Hubmaier claims: "the inquisitors are the biggest heretics of all since against the teaching and example of Christ they have condemned heretics to the flames and before the time of the harvest root up the wheat together with the tares."

Hubmaier's conviction that faith cannot be coerced is based primarily on his understanding of the gospel. "Therefore," he writes, "to burn a heretic is in appearance to confess Christ. Tit. 1. But in reality to deny him and to be more detestable than Joachim, the King of Judah. Jeremiah 36." This truth is stated repeatedly in various articles. Perhaps the thirtieth article contains the fullest statement. "Hence, the greatest deception of the people is in their zeal for God in that without scriptural support they wish to gain the salvation of the soul, honor of the church, love of truth, a good reputation, good custom or habit, the episcopal decrees, and all in order to instruct the reason which is an inheritance of natural light. Therefore, these are deadly darts when they are not grounded in the Scriptures and corrected thereby."

Since faith is not subject to coercion, Hubmaier hastens to remind his readers that this does not mean that the Christian has no obligation toward unbelievers. To the contrary, he writes: "However, this word does not bring us ease but a conflict in that we without letting up fight, indeed, not against men but their godless teachings." The true heretic or unbeliever, it is affirmed again and again, must be won by spiritual means, that is, by the careful use of Scripture, patience, prayer, and a credible witness. Even the state has no right to use force against someone because of religious differences, even when that person is an atheist. It is at this point that Hubmaier's thought is both most logical and most radical. "Therefore, it is well and good that the secular authority puts to death the criminals who do physical harm to the defenseless, Romans 13. But no one may injure the enemy of God [gotssfind] who wishes nothing for himself other than to forsake the gospel."

The sovereignty of God is a theme that recurs throughout *Von Ketzern.* It is Hubmaier's profound conviction that God alone can determine the difference between wheat and tares. Therefore, God has not placed in the hands of man the right to burn a heretic, be he truly a heretic or not. He has set definite limits on the jurisdiction of secular authorities and clearly prescribed the methods of evangelism for Christians. Hubmaier brings his remarkable tract to a close with article thirty-six. "Now it is apparent to everyone, even the blind, that the law which demands the burning of heretics is an invention of the Devil." Then follows his characteristic motto, which adorned everything he ever published: *Die warhait ist untödlich* (Truth is Immortal).[11]

From Schaffhausen, Hubmaier, "the fly of Friedberg," issued a challenge to his old friend and teacher Dr. John Eck, "the elephant of Ingolstadt." For debate he proposed twenty-six articles of evangelical faith which he had drawn up while in Schaffhausen. His attitude at this time reflected anything but admiration for his former teacher. The new-found knowledge of Christ had enabled Hubmaier to see through his erstwhile friend, the pompous and verbose champion of Catholic orthodoxy.

In his theses against his former mentor and "doctor father," entitled *Axiomata,* Hubmaier called for a disputation upon the basis of the principles of his new-found faith set forth in twenty-six articles.[12] In matters of conduct, he conceded that the functioning church had the authority to discipline. But in matters of faith, he declared, the Bible alone, specifically the words of Christ, was the final authority. Therefore he recommended that his former teacher search the Scrip-

11. *Schriften,* pp. 96-100.

12. The critical German text is found in *Schriften,* pp. 85-90, and an English translation of the *Axiomata* in H. Wayne Pipkin and John H. Yoder, eds., *Balthasar Hübmaier, Theologian of Anabaptism* (Scottdale, Pa.: Herald Press, 1989), pp. 49-57. Unless otherwise indicated, the translations or paraphrases of selections of Hubmaier's treatises are my own.

tures, not papal law, nor councils, fathers, or schools, "for it is Christ and what he has spoken that shall judge all things. Christ himself (IPSE) is the truth, the planting [plantatio], and the vine" (IX). Then he admonishes Eck to search the Scriptures like the "noble Thessalonians to see whether things [Hubmaier's teachings?] are so" (XI).

In the twelfth article Hubmaier makes what is possibly an unflattering allusion to Eck's manner of debate when he recommends his own method of Bible study, where understanding "does not come with useless chatter or in a battle of words with a loud hoarse voice but in comparing the more obscure passages with the clearer" (VII).[13]

By October, according to an unfriendly witness, Hubmaier was back once again in Waldshut, welcomed by its citizens as if he were a returning hero or emperor. The reception ended at the market house with a feast in his honor. He was reestablished as chief preacher and pastor and his salary set at two hundred gulden a year. At once he entered into the preparation then in progress to protect the city against invasion by the Austrian government. The presence of numerous peasants nearby gave the city a sense of security. Yet there is little evidence that Hubmaier's relation to these peasants was any more than one of sympathetic concern for their grievances. He was primarily concerned with the gospel; the issue between him and Austria was freedom — freedom to preach and evangelize. The program of reform and proposed armed resistance to Ferdinand and his forces called forth moral support in Zürich and Schaffhausen but very little else. Few cantons could afford to risk war with the forces of Ferdinand.

While the party of Conrad Grebel was in the process of crystallizing its convictions, Hubmaier was moving in the same direction. The principles set forth in his Eighteen Articles and especially in *Concerning Heretics and Those Who Burn Them* indicate that he was rapidly moving in the direction of Anabaptism.[14] Just how far his thinking on baptism had progressed is revealed in a letter to Oecolampadius of January 16, 1525: "The meaning of this sign and symbol [baptism], the pledge of faith until death, in hope of the resurrection to the life to come, is to

---

13. *Schriften*, p. 89. Admittedly my translation of articles from the *Axiomata* is not literal but an attempt to translate meaning, not words.

be considered more than a sign. This meaning has nothing to do with babes, therefore infant baptism is without reality."[15]

Hubmaier confessed that he still, upon parents' insistence, baptized infants, but of his preaching he wrote: "As to the word, however, I do not yield to them in the least point. I have written twenty-two theses with sixty-four remarks, which you will soon see." By February 2, he published a tract called "The Open Appeal of Balthazar of Friedberg to All Christian Believers." In this he was even more definite about rejecting infant baptism. After issuing the challenge to anyone to prove on the basis of the Scriptures that infants ought to be baptized, he indicated what he was prepared to do: "Balthazar of Friedberg pledges himself, on the other hand, to prove that the baptism of infants is a work without any ground in the divine word, and that he will do this in German with plain, clear, simple Scriptures relating to baptism, without any addition."[16]

Two months later, in April, 1525, Wilhelm Reublin, who had been driven out of Zürich, sought refuge in Waldshut. Here he baptized Hubmaier and about sixty others. On Easter Sunday, Hubmaier himself baptized over three hundred people out of a milk pail. The Monday after Easter witnessed the observance of the Lord's Supper in a simple apostolic manner. In the following days many others were baptized, and foot washing was engaged in by the newly baptized.[17] In every way possible Hubmaier sought to reproduce the pattern of what he considered the New Testament faith and practice.

On May 28, Zwingli's pamphlet entitled "On Baptism, Anabaptism, and Infant Baptism" came from the press. It was an attack on the Anabaptist view of believers' baptism. Hubmaier's response was thorough and biblical. It appeared the following July under the title *The Christian Baptism of Believers*. In this book Hubmaier was at his best. The Catholic historian Loserth writes: *"Vom christlichen Tauf der Glaubigen . . .* is correctly regarded as the classic presentation of his

14. See article 8.
15. Vedder, *Hübmaier,* p. 108.
16. *Ibid.,* pp. 109-12.
17. Vedder holds that foot washing was practiced by Hubmaier even before believers' baptism was introduced.

teaching on baptism and as one of the best defenses of adult baptism ever written."[18]

Excerpts from this work reveal something of the style, logic, and use of the Scriptures which characterized Hubmaier's presentation of the Anabaptist view of baptism.

> Every pious Christian can see and comprehend that he who wants to purify himself with water must previously have a good understanding of the Word of God, and a good conscience toward God; that is, he must be sure that he has a gracious kindly God, through the intercession of Christ. . . .
>
> Therefore baptism in water is not what cleanses the soul, but the "yes," [of] a good conscience toward God, given inwardly by faith.
>
> Therefore the baptism in water is called a baptism *in Remissionem Peccatorum* (Acts second chapter), that is, for the pardon of sins. Not that through it or by it sins are forgiven, but by virtue of the inward "yes" of the heart, which a man outwardly testifies to on submitting to water baptism, saying that he believes and is sure in his heart that his sins are forgiven through Jesus Christ.[19]

As his numerous references to the matter affirm, Hubmaier denies that baptism is necessary to salvation. He insists, however, that it is essential to the life of the church.

> Where baptism in water does not exist, there is no Church, no brother, no sister, no fraternal discipline, exclusion or restoration. I speak here of the visible Church as Christ said (Matt. 18). For there must be some outward sign of testimony by which brothers and sisters can know one another, though faith be in the heart alone. By receiving baptism, the candidate testifies publicly that . . . he has submitted himself to his brothers and sisters . . . that is, to the Church.[20]

---

18. Loserth, "Hübmaier," p. 827.

19. Balthasar Hubmaier, "Concerning Christian Baptism of Believers," trans. G. D. Davidson, pp. 98-99. Pagination is that of the Davidson translation, in unpublished manuscript. See also this passage in Pipkin and Yoder, pp. 117, 118.

20. *Ibid.,* p. 111.

For Hubmaier baptism was not only essential to the life of the church but also to Christian discipleship. According to his viewpoint baptism was the sign of committed discipleship. It symbolizes one's commitment to Christ and submission to his fellow believers in the church.

On the other hand, he denounces infant baptism as a sign without meaning. Those who practice infant baptism "rob us of the true baptism, and show us a sign before an inn in which is not wine." To the charge "that there is nowhere in the Scriptures a clear word to the effect that one must not baptize infants," Hubmaier, in inimical style, answered:

> It is clear enough for him who has eyes to see it, but it is not expressed in so many words, literally: "do not baptize infants." May one then baptize them? To that I answer: "if so I may baptize my dog or my donkey, or I may circumcise girls. . . . I may make idols out of St. Paul and St. Peter, I may bring infants to the Lord's Supper, bless palm branches, vegetables, salt, land and water, sell the Mass for an offering. For it is nowhere said in express words that we must not do these things."[21]

Hubmaier thus uses logic, humor, the Scriptures, and the fathers to show that infant baptism is unnecessary, useless, and an abomination before God. He asserts that infant baptism is not of New Testament origin. Cyprian, Augustine, and the archives of the Vatican are cited as containing proof of his position.

In the chapter entitled "Order of Christian Godliness," Hubmaier suggests that baptism be preceded by hearing the word, repentance, faith, and confession. "Then he [the convert] must be baptized in water by which means he publicly professes his faith and purpose."[22] Baptism is then followed by a life of Christian profession and public testimony. The life of the Christian is a life of gratitude. This gratitude finds symbolic expression in the Lord's Supper. Baptism for Hubmaier was not a part of the saving process but an act in which the new disciple confessed his allegiance to Jesus Christ.

21. *Ibid.*, p. 121.
22. *Ibid.*, pp. 132-33.

Baptism in the name of the Father and of the Son and of the Holy Ghost is when a man first confesses his sins, and pleads guilty; then believes in the forgiveness of his sins through Jesus Christ, and turns to live according to the rule of Christ, by the grace and strength given him from God the Father, the Son and the Holy Ghost. Then he professes this publicly, in the eyes of men, by the outward baptism of water. He is then truly baptized, even if the baptizer did not speak these words over him.[23]

Evidently Hubmaier's book on baptism was widely circulated among the Anabaptists. Its effect among non-Anabaptists must have been quite alarming, for Zwingli rushed into print by November 5 a reply entitled "A True, Thorough Reply to Dr. Balthasar's Little Book of Baptism." Zwingli's style is caustic and bitter. He adds very little to his previous arguments. The main point is that Anabaptists were schismatics and would ultimately destroy the existing order in Switzerland if allowed to continue unmolested.[24]

This particular controversy between Zwingli and Hubmaier was brought to a halt with Hubmaier's response, "A Dialogue Between Balthasar Hubmaier of Friedberg and Master Ulrich Zwingli, of Zürich, on Infant Baptism." Even though written at once, it was not published until the following year, after Hubmaier had gone to Nikolsburg. This was the last work which Hubmaier wrote at Waldshut.

After defeating the peasants, the Austrian government at the insistence of Ferdinand turned its attention to Waldshut. Hubmaier knew that the slender resources of the isolated town of Waldshut were no match for the mighty forces of Ferdinand, so he fled. After a tearful farewell in which he took leave of Waldshut on December 5, Austrian soldiers were in the city the next day. Hubmaier had no time to plan an orderly escape. According to his own testimony he would like to have gone to Basel or Strasbourg, but the presence of Austrian troops prohibited this. Since Schaffhausen and Constance were out of the question at the time, Hubmaier, who was ill and terribly depressed, headed for Zürich. His presence in the city was soon known, and on the orders of the

23. *Ibid.*, p. 128.
24. Vedder, *Hübmaier*, pp. 118-19.

city council both he and his wife were seized and imprisoned. According to Zwingli, Hubmaier was arrested to keep him from fomenting an insurrection. Bullinger admitted it was really because Hubmaier was so highly regarded by the Anabaptists. Since Zwingli felt himself already under siege by the local *Wiedertäufer,* the action was, in this case, not surprising. While a prisoner, Hubmaier renewed his request for a disputation, which was granted. This led to a wholly unexpected result.

The meeting did not follow the pattern of the previous Zürich disputations. Present for this discussion were Zwingli, Leo Jud, Oswald Myconius, Komtur Schmid, Sebastian Hofmeister, four members of the city council, and a Zürich schoolteacher by the name of George Binder. Zwingli, Myconius, Jud, and Hofmeister were mentioned in Hubmaier's request (July 10) for a disputation on the baptismal question. Binder, doubtless reflecting Zwingli's true feelings and attempting to impress his mentor with his fidelity, took a pugilistic stance, calling Hubmaier, among other things, a *Filzhut* (a miser) and a Swabian frog. Hubmaier did not answer in kind but proceeded to quote Zwingli, place and time, when he asserted children should not be baptized until they could be instructed in the faith. Zwingli claimed he had been misunderstood. Hubmaier was dumbfounded. The upshot of it all was that he did agree to recant, but before making a final statement requested the privilege of talking with Jud, Myconius, and Hofmeister alone. He well knew that in former days they, too, had questioned the scriptural validity of infant baptism. In fact, Hofmeister had openly, according to Hoschek, so expressed himself before the city council of Schaffhausen. After the conference Hubmaier agreed to write out his recantation, which he read before the Small Council and before the Council of Two Hundred the next day. He then was asked to read the recantation before the congregation of the Fraumünster after Zwingli's sermon on Friday, December 29, and later at Grüningen.

Once Hubmaier was in the pulpit of the Fraumünster, instead of recanting, he began, "Oh what anguish and travail I have suffered this night over the statements which I myself have made. So I say here and now, I can and I will not recant."[25] He then proceeded to defend

---

25. Emil Egli and Rudolph Schoch, eds., *Johannes Kesslers Sabbata mit kleineren Schriften und Briefen* (St. Gallen: Fehrsche Buchhandlung, 1902), p. 151. Hereafter referred to as *Sabbata.*

believers' baptism. Zwingli entered the other pulpit and silenced the people. Hubmaier was reminded of his previous recantation and accused of being devil-possessed, which was obviously the reason for his conduct at the moment.[26] Refusing to back down, he was seized and placed in the Wellenberg prison, known as the "Wasserturm" since it stood in the Limmat, just a short distance from the Fraumünster.

During this imprisonment Hubmaier wrote *Twelve Articles of Christian Belief,* which was not printed until a year later in Nikolsburg. Full of theological implications which will be considered later, it closed with these pathetically prophetic words:

> O holy God, O mighty God, O immortal God, that is my belief, which I confess with heart and mouth and have witnessed before the Church in water-baptism. Faithfully, graciously, keep me in that till my end, I pray thee. And though I be driven from it by human fear and terror, by tyranny, pangs, sword, fire or water, yet hereby I cry to thee, O my merciful Father: Raise me up again by the grace of thy Holy Spirit, and let me not depart in death without this faith. This I pray thee from the bottom of my heart, through Jesus Christ, thy best-beloved Son, our Lord and Saviour. For in thee, O Father, I hope; let me not be put to shame in eternity. Amen.[27]

With his second Zürich imprisonment Hubmaier was subjected to torture. While stretched on the rack, he uttered the required recantation and afterward committed it to writing as demanded by Zwingli. Although far less damaging than it might have been, the recantation satisfied Zwingli and demonstrated the weakness of Hubmaier. Subsequently it became the occasion for deep repentance and confession. In this confession, which was given the title *Short Apology,* the note of pride and arrogance that at times marked his earlier works had disappeared. In its place, we find here the cry of Hubmaier's soul over the weakness of the flesh.

> I may err — I am a man — but a heretic I cannot be, because I ask constantly for instruction in the word of God. But never has any

26. *Ibid.,* p. 129.
27. *Ibid.,* p. 136.

one come to me and pointed out a single word, but one single man and his followers — against his own previous preaching, word and print, whose name I spare for the sake of God's word — who against common justice and appeal in behalf of his own government, the confederacy, and also the Emperor, by capture, imprisonment, sufferings and the hangman, tried to teach me the faith. But faith is a work of God and not of the heretic's tower, in which one sees neither sun nor moon, and lives on nothing but water and bread. . . . O God, pardon me my weakness. It is good for me (as David says) that thou hast humbled me.[28]

Like Grebel, Blaurock, and Sattler before him, the disappointed Hubmaier left Zürich and its memories behind. For the man who failed to defeat him in debate resorted to the base tactics of an inquisitor. Discredited before the followers of Zwingli and disgraced in the eyes of the Anabaptists, Hubmaier quietly slipped out of the city. The secrecy surrounding his departure from Zürich continues to enshroud in mystery his journey to Nikolsburg.

Nikolsburg, under the jurisdiction of Moravian noblemen, was one of the most tolerant cities in Europe in 1526. The influence of Huss was still felt in the area. The Moravian evangelicals received Hubmaier gladly and listened to his message sympathetically. Converts were rapidly made. Among them was a Moravian baron, Leonhard von Lichtenstein, who was baptized by Hubmaier.[29] This marked the beginning of one of the most fruitful periods in Anabaptist history.

It has been conservatively estimated that at least six thousand were baptized in the one brief year of Hubmaier's incredible ministry at Nikolsburg. Besides his preaching and teaching ministry, Hubmaier was busily engaged in writing. Froschauer (Simprecht Sorg), a printer

28. *Ibid.*, p. 141.
29. Zieglschmid, *Large Chronicle*, p. 50. "Aug welches hat er den Herren Leonhart von Liechtenstain auff Nicolspurg wonende welcher dazumal ach getaufft unnd ein Breuder ist genennt worden Desgleichen Seinem Breudern Herr Hunsen mit Sampt Irem Predicanntem." See also Jerold Knox Zeman, *The Anabaptists and the Czech Brethren in Moravia, 1526-1628* (The Hague: Mouton, 1969), for a thorough account of the relationship of Hubmaier to the Lichtenstein barons and the Moravian evangelicals.

from Zürich who had been forced to flee the city because of his Anabaptist views, became the publisher of Hubmaier's numerous tracts. No less than seventeen of his pamphlets bear the imprint of Nikolsburg during the years 1526 and 1527.[30]

Hubmaier took advantage of the window of opportunity that his Nikolsburg stay made possible to construct a literary defense of Anabaptism as he understood it. For the first time in his brief reformatory career, all the conditions — a printer, a patron, and time — were present to assure the publication of the products of his pen. His fellow ministers, Hans Spittelmaier, Oswald Glaidt, and Martin Goschel, doubtless relieved Hubmaier of many pastoral duties, freeing him for his specific responsibility of teaching the distinctive Anabaptist beliefs, the major tenets of which are found in his Nikolsburg treatises.

The Nikolsburg writings were largely concerned with matters of church order, such as baptism, the Lord's Supper, and discipline. However, the two treatises on the freedom of the will, one on the sword and one on the catechism, and *A Brief Apologia* present Hubmaier's basic theological concepts in differing formats. In *Freedom of the Will I* and *Freedom of the Will II* Hubmaier sets forth his anthropology and soteriology, arguing that man, although fallen with Adam, still has the capacity to believe in Christ, who alone can save. There is no other way, for this is God's revealed will, according to Scripture. Therefore, the new birth *(Wiedergeburt)* is a divine necessity if one is to see God. Repeatedly, he declares that it is God's will that all might be saved, but whether or not a person is saved depends upon that person's acceptance of the grace of God offered in Christ. This grace is not of man but of God. When it is accepted by faith in Jesus Christ, one is saved, redeemed, and born again. Henceforth the Christian's life, although not sinless, is characterized by obedient discipleship that finds its highest expression in love of God and neighbor.

30. Loserth, "Hübmaier," p. 829, suggests the number was "no fewer than 18 works" while Hubmaier was at Nikolsburg. Vedder catalogues the Nikolsburg works: "Of these Nikolsburg writings eleven are concerned with the Christian sacraments, or the . . . ordinance of baptism; four are apologetic and polemic; while two are contributions to systematic theology." Vedder, *Hübmaier,* pp. 154-55. Simprecht Sorg should not be confused with his uncle Christopher Froschauer, who was Zwingli's printer.

Hubmaier's understanding of the New Testament's teaching that grace, faith, and love are contingent upon a person's ability to accept or reject the proffered salvation in Christ was confirmed in his own experience. As a popular but superficial cleric, he had led Regensburg to drive out the Jews. Six years later in his pamphlet *On the Christian Ban,* he contrasts the treatment of members of the church who are under the ban with that of one's "enemies, Jews, and pagans." These, like the banned member, should be given food, drink, shelter, and "works of necessity," but Jews and pagans, unlike the banned person, are to be the objects of friendship "so that they might be drawn by a Christian example to faith in Christ, Gal. 5:23."[31] Such a change in attitude toward the Jews is reflected elsewhere in his writings and can only be explained by the transformation of life Hubmaier experienced in his own personal conversion, to which he alludes repeatedly in his writings.

A Christian Catechism (Eine christliche Lehrtafel) sets forth in the format of a dialogue between Leonhard and Hans the basic features of the Anabaptist faith in the form of a catechism. It antedates Luther's catechisms by two or three years. While it touches upon every distinctive teaching of the Anabaptists, it also finds common ground with both Catholics and Protestants in affirming the traditional teachings of the church on the trinity, as set forth at Chalcedon. It is clear, however, that the Bible, not Augustine, councils, nor the "schoolmen" of the church, is the "plumb line" of Christian doctrine for Hubmaier. In his capacity as teacher of the Anabaptist church of Nikolsburg, he succeeded in producing a most useful book of instruction, not only for the youth, as he says in the introduction, but also for those who like himself and the Lichtenstein barons had been so long in error.

The Nikolsburg writings, as well as those written before 1526, provide the modern reader with a number of insights into the life and thought of Hubmaier as an Anabaptist theologian. A product of the universities of Freiburg and Ingolstadt in the nominalist tradition of his mentor, Dr. Johannes Eck, he admitted that he had never read Paul's epistles and knew next to nothing about the Bible before he left Regensburg. Even though he apparently had a knowledge of Greek and

---

31. Pipkin and Yoder, *Hübmaier,* p. 419.

Hebrew, he did not begin to study his Bible, which was that of the Latin Vulgate, seriously until he had arrived in Waldshut. Within a relatively brief time, he had become, pretty much on his own, thoroughly acquainted with the Scriptures in German as well as in Latin, and this was before publication of both the Froschauer Bible of Zwingli's initiative and the complete Luther translation.

Although Hubmaier lacked the tools of a modern textual critic, he did honestly attempt to discover what the Scriptures taught and to exegete them faithfully. It is also evident that the New Testament became for him the sole authority for the Christian life and the life of the church. Therefore, he became a severe critic of the moral laxity that marked the Lutheran reform. His own moral and ethical sensitivity led him to champion the freedom of the will, for without it he saw no basis for Christian responsibility. Neither the sovereignty of God nor the grace of God nullified for Hubmaier the necessity of an uncoerced response to the gospel. It was the Word and the Spirit that God used to bring salvation to fallen humanity. Once a person through faith had accepted Christ, life could never be the same again. He or she was born again and consequently committed to a life of obedient discipleship. This was not an isolated laissez-faire experience but involved a community of faith, the church. It was within the context of the church that Hubmaier understood the role of both baptism and the Lord's Supper. Although in the weakness of the flesh Hubmaier sought to avoid torture and martyrdom, he knew and taught that suffering was an essential element in discipleship and that baptism was in its most profound meaning a commitment to live and to die for Christ.

Hubmaier always demonstrated a willingness to accept new insights of truth even from those who would burn him. A lover of the academic debate and frequently caught up in the heat of a controversial issue, he never became bitterly caustic. He steadfastly refused to engage in personal innuendoes. He did not refer to Zwingli by name in any of his tracts written against his position until after he had been imprisoned and tortured at his hands. Even then, in the polemical pamphlet on infant baptism, Hubmaier did little more than mention the methods used by Zwingli against him and other Anabaptists.[32]

---

32. *Ein Gespräch auf Zwinglis Taufbüchlein, 1525-1526, Schriften*, pp. 164-214.

Open-mindedness and devotion to truth, wherever it may be found, help to explain Hubmaier's conduct in Zürich and again in Vienna. Hubmaier never moved beyond the position, "I may err — I am a man — but a heretic I cannot be, because I ask constantly for instruction of the Word of God."

An appeal to the Word of God was the method which Hubmaier used in dealing with difficulties which threatened the Anabaptist fellowship. Hans Hut, an erstwhile follower of Thomas Müntzer, had been baptized by Hans Denck in 1526. Shortly thereafter he arrived in Nikolsburg. He still championed chiliastic ideas and insisted on use of the sword by the godly "against the ungodly, in setting up the kingdom of God."[33]

Hut was not long in securing a following among the refugees in Nikolsburg. Jacob Wiedemann, an Anabaptist preacher who held that community of goods should be a cardinal principle among New Testament Christians, joined forces with Hut. Their common ground was their opposition to Hubmaier. Wiedemann and his group held to an extreme form of nonresistance, even to the point of refusing to pay taxes. Yet they evidently "found little difficulty in grafting Hut's doctrine of the sword, as the exclusive perquisite of the saints, upon their previous tenet of non-resistance."[34]

Against the vagaries of Hut and the convictions of Wiedemann, Hubmaier took a positive stand. He upheld the legitimacy of the state.

---

33. Vedder, *Hübmaier,* pp. 160-61.

34. *Ibid.,* p. 163. A sample of Hut's preaching is given on p. 166. "Then (shortly before the end of the age) all the godless will be destroyed, and that by true Christians; if their number (the true Christians) shall be sufficient, they will go from Germany to Switzerland, and to Hungary, and have no regard to princes and lords. Then some thousands of them shall assemble, and every one shall sell his goods and take the money with him, so as to be sure, meantime, of food; then they shall wait until the Turk comes. If the Turk fails to strike down any of the princes, monks, priests, nobles, or knights, they will then be stricken and slain by the little company of true Christians. But if the godless shall march against the Turks, then the true Christians shall remain at home; but if many of the princes or many of the lords remain at home too, and do not march against the Turks, they shall be struck down a little while afterwards. Then it will come to pass that the true Christians will have no one, but God alone, and God himself will be and remain their lord."

For the state alone he affirmed the right to bear the sword, and to the church alone he ascribed authority in spiritual matters. Thus, in rejecting the anarchistic principles of Hut, he departed from the nonresistant principle of earlier Anabaptists, but to a much less serious degree than had Hut.

When confronting Wiedemann's communism, he affirmed the position of Felix Manz and the Swiss Brethren. He rejected the community of goods but held to the principle that the Brethren ought to share what they have with those in need.[35]

Hubmaier's position on the magistracy was never accepted by any sizeable group of Anabaptists. Wiedemann and his followers became known as the people of the staff *(Stäbler),* for they continued to hold to nonresistance as well as the community of goods. Therefore, Hubmaier's Nikolsburg ministry, as fruitful as it might appear, was not all sweetness and light. However, the controversy did provide the occasion for the last and one of the most important works of his Nikolsburg stay. It was entitled *On the Sword (Von dem Schwert).*[36]

Before Hubmaier aligned himself with the Anabaptist movement, he introduced the Reformation into Waldshut, where he was the leading priest of the city and the vicar of the Church of St. Marien. While he was indebted to Luther for some of his insights, after an intensive study of the Bible, he found himself closer to Zwingli in his understanding of the nature of the reforms he envisioned for Waldshut. Therefore the pattern of the Hubmaier-led reformation was Zwinglian. It is not surprising that when he returned from his self-imposed exile in Schaffhausen in October, 1524, he stood his watch on the wall with the

---

35. The term "communism" here must not be confused with the Russian experiment founded upon the dialectical materialism of Karl Marx. The term "communal" is to be preferred but does not always fit.

36. See James M. Stayer, *Anabaptists and the Sword* (Lawrence, Kans.: Coronado Press, 1972), pp. 141-45. Stayer classifies Hubmaier's position as *real politic* but concludes, "Thus Hubmaier could accept the nonresistants' premise, that 'there is a higher standard in the New Testament than in the Old', without accepting their conclusion that a Christian could not use the Sword." Stayer believes Hubmaier is much closer to Zwingli's position than he is to the nonresistant Anabaptists. He also gives in brief fashion a digest of Hubmaier's *Von dem Schwert.* Vedder, in his *Hubmaier,* translates the entire work (pp. 273-310).

citizen defenders of the little town against the threatened invasion by the Austrians. After becoming an Anabaptist, he appears never to have accepted the Schleitheim dictum on the sword. It was the only major point with which he disagreed with those Anabaptists who followed Michael Sattler and the Swiss Brethren. Yet his position as set forth in his treatise *On the Sword* also differed from that of Zwingli. Although close to that of Erasmus, as George Huntston Williams observes, it was not identical. At Nikolsburg, the Hubmaier-led Anabaptists were known as the *Schwertler,* and the Wiedemann-led opposition as the *Stäbler. On the Sword* was written against the *Stäbler* but conceivably against others of his "dear brothers" who held a similar position.

Positively, *Von dem Schwert* was written to set forth what Hubmaier held to be the scriptural position on the legitimacy of governments and the relationship of Christians to earthly kingdoms. There is something more than simple biblicism here. He cites numerous passages, mostly from the New Testament, for he held that "there is a higher standard *[Stuffel=Stufe]* in the New Testament than in the Old," to support his position that a Christian can serve as a magistrate when called upon to do so.[37] Besides, he argued, all things being equal, a Christian would make a better ruler than a non-Christian. Since governments are necessary for the sake of peace and justice, Christians have not only a moral responsibility to support and pray for rulers but to serve as judges, mayors, and the like when chosen for those offices. This inevitably involves the use of the sword, which no one should take upon his own initiative but only upon the authority of a just government.

While the magistracy is ordained of God and, therefore, Christians may serve in various capacities in government, Hubmaier argued, there are certain limitations to the use of the "temporal" sword. It is forbidden those "who would preach the gospel," for they are not to be entangled in secular affairs. Nor is the sword to be used to further one's own ambitions or to launch adventurous warfare, for "to attempt to conquer land and people with the sword and force is against God." Hubmaier concludes in his commentary on Romans 13:1 that magistrates should not desire "to be saluted as gracious lords, like secular kings, princes,

37. *Schriften,* p. 445.

and lords, for the magistracy is not for the purpose of lording it over people like a knight with sword in hand, but servanthood, according to the ordinance of God."[38]

Hubmaier also raised the question of a Christian's options when forced to live under an unjust or tyrannical government. He suggested that a Christian has three options. If the government can be changed without violence, it should be. However, if this is not possible, the Christian is permitted to flee to a more hospitable land. But if this is no longer an option, he must suffer even as Christ our Lord suffered, "for the servant is not above his master." In any case, he implied that armed insurrection is forbidden a disciple of Christ. In the end, Hubmaier embraced a position of personal pacifism which he was called upon to exemplify sooner than he had thought.

While Hubmaier defended his position upon scriptural grounds, so did the *Stäbler*. It appears that Hubmaier's past experiences with magistrates of one kind or another conditioned him for taking a more positive attitude toward the state than did Sattler and the majority of Anabaptists. While he envisioned a day when governments would limit themselves to secular ends for which they were ordained of God, he realized that suffering and death were more likely the results of faithful discipleship. But unlike Hut, he refused to advocate the use of the sword even in preparation for the second advent of Christ. He became and remained personally a pacifist.

Hubmaier's pamphlets and books enjoyed a circulation far beyond the borders of Moravia. Ferdinand I, Hubmaier's old enemy, made no attempt to hide his alarm at the rapid progress of the Anabaptists in his territories. Moravia had come under his jurisdiction as part of the hereditary lands of Austria upon the death of King Louis of Hungary. As soon as the affairs of state would permit, he directed his attention to the eradication of every vestige of heresy in Moravia. The relative independence which the Moravian nobles had formerly enjoyed was no more. The Lichtenstein barons found it increasingly difficult to resist the designs of Ferdinand against their esteemed preacher.

Under a general edict of August 28, 1527, which required instant and strict enforcement of the decree of the Diet of Worms, Hubmaier was taken prisoner. In obedience to Ferdinand's decree the Lichtenstein

38. *Ibid.*, p. 453.

nobles and their chaplains accompanied their pastor to Vienna. Here Hubmaier and his wife were imprisoned. After a preliminary hearing they were taken from Vienna to the castle of Kreuzenstein on the Danube.[39]

Until March, 1528, Hubmaier was held in custody at Kreuzenstein. Ferdinand used the time to assemble all possible evidence against the accused in order to strengthen the state's case of sedition against him. The prisoner took advantage of the delay to request a visit from John Faber, his friend of former years and rapidly rising vicar-general of the bishop of Constance. Faber responded favorably to the request and hastened to win what he anticipated would be an easy victory. But the resultant discussions on theology, which lasted over a period of several days, proved fruitless.

Hubmaier, under the pressures of ill health, the inevitable death sentence, and his characteristic openness to the truth, succeeded in seriously compromising his former position at several points. But he refused to back down on baptism, the Lord's Supper, and his previous denial of the existence of purgatory.

At most points Hubmaier's position as stated in the *Rechenschaft seines Glaubens,* which he sent to Ferdinand in the vain hope that his life might be spared, could be interpreted in various ways. At two points the broken man affirmed Roman Catholic dogmas which he had forsaken at Waldshut five years before.[40] Doubtless he considered these points matters of little consequence. His *Rechenschaft* went unheeded. It was not the recantation that was desired, but it represented the last degree of compromise Hubmaier was willing to make.[41] To the Austrian authorities it was not enough.

39. Zieglschmid, *Large Chronicle,* pp. 50-51. Zieglschmid adds this footnote to alleviate confusion over the place of Hubmaier's imprisonment: *"Graitzenstain, jetzt Kreuzenstein, eine in Niederosterreich liegende Burgruine, nordlich von Korneuburg; Zeitweise und so auch 1527 Staatsgefängnis"* (pp. 50-51).

40. "10. Mary is the Mother of God" and "21. On the fast days one should eat no meat." Vedder offers a translation of the *Rechenschaft* on pp. 230-35 of his *Hübmaier.* See Pipkin and Yoder, pp. 524-62, for a complete translation in contemporary English.

41. Hubmaier seems to have sent a second letter to Ferdinand further explaining his obstinacy, but it has been lost. See Leo T. Crismon, "The Interview Between John Faber and Balthasar Hübmaier, Vienna, December, 1527-January, 1528," *The Review and Expositor* 46, no. 1 (January 1949): 38-42.

On March 3, the condemned man was taken to Vienna and once again tortured on the rack; but this time no recantation was forthcoming. The weaknesses that had been his at Zürich, and to a lesser degree at Kreuzenstein, had been replaced by a hitherto unknown fortitude. When urged to confess to a priest and receive the last rites of the church before his execution, he refused. Seven days after returning to Vienna and tribulations known only to God, Dr. Balthasar Hubmaier was led forth to his death on March 10, 1528.

An eyewitness account of Hubmaier's execution was given by Stephen Sprügel, dean of the philosophical faculty at the University of Vienna. Hubmaier, he said, was "fixed like an immovable rock in his heresy." With his wife exhorting him to fortitude, he was taken to the place of execution. When the company reached the pile of fagots, he cried in the Swiss dialect:

"O gracious God, forgive my sins in my great torment. . . ."
To the people he said, "O dear brothers, if I have injured any, in word or deed, may he forgive me for the sake of my merciful God. I forgive all those that have done me harm."
While his clothes were being removed: "From thee also, O Lord, were the clothes stripped. My clothes will I gladly leave here, only preserve my spirit and my soul, I beseech thee!" Then he added in Latin: "O Lord, into thy hands I commit my spirit," and spoke no more in Latin.
As they rubbed sulphur and gunpowder into his beard, which he wore rather long, he said, "Oh salt me well, salt me well." And raising his head, he called out: "O dear brothers, pray God that he will give me patience in this my suffering."[42]

As his beard and hair caught fire, he cried out, "O Jesus, Jesus." Suffocating from the smoke, he died. Three days later the execution of his wife by drowning in the Danube followed.

Having put the leading Anabaptist preacher to death, the Catholic authorities now had to reckon with the truth for which he died. His works were burned whenever discovered by the authorities. How-

---

42. Vedder, *Hübmaier,* p. 243. Vedder and Loserth both draw upon Stephen Sprügel's account, which seems to be fair and objective.

ever, almost a hundred years later they were still in circulation. In 1619 they were felt to be such a threat that they were placed on the Index of Prohibited Books *(Index Librorum Prohibitorum)* drawn up for the Spanish Inquisition. Hubmaier is mentioned four times in this seventeenth-century document. "His name stands forth among the *hereticorum capita aut duces,* preceded only by those of Luther, Zwingli, and Calvin. Schwenckfeld is the only other heretic named."43

Hubmaier's death left the more constructive Anabaptist party of Nikolsburg without strong leadership. Agitation for community of goods and the doctrine of nonresistance were continued by Jacob Wiedemann and the *Stäbler.* The ill-will aroused by the growing division finally compelled the Lichtenstein barons to expel Wiedemann and his party from their lands. From this group, with its peculiar emphasis upon communal life, the Hutterite expression of sixteenth-century Anabaptism developed.

Eventually, the Anabaptists of Nikolsburg ceased to exist. It is possible that at least some of those who remained may have joined the Hutterites or Philippites. At any rate, Hubmaier's works survived in the Hutterite community, whose major features he had opposed back in Nikolsburg in their nascent form.

Loserth points out that Peter Riedemann's *Rechenschaft* shows heavy dependence on Hubmaier. This opinion is substantiated by Franz Heimann, who has made a thorough study of the relationship of the works of Hubmaier and Riedemann.44 The *Large Chronicle* speaks of Hubmaier as one to whom the Hutterites owe a debt of gratitude for his teaching concerning baptism and the Lord's Supper.45 It also refers to two hymns which were attributed to Hubmaier. Vedder has translated one of those believed to be from Hubmaier's pen. The last two stanzas reecho the author's unquenchable faith in Christ, the Son of God, and in his Word, which "stands sure forever."

43. *Ibid.,* p. 247.
44. "The Hutterite Doctrine of Church and Common Life, A Study of Peter Riedemann's Confession of Faith of 1540," MQR 26 (two parts; January and April 1952). Cf. Zieglschmid, *Large Chronicle,* pp. 51-52, 143ff.
45. Zieglschmid, *Large Chronicle,* pp. 51-52.

O Jesus Christ, thou Son of God,
Let us not lack thy favour,
For what shall be our just reward
If the salt shall lose its savour?
With angry flame to efface thy name
In vain shall men endeavour;
Not for a day, the same for aye,
God's word stands sure for ever.

Praise God, praise God in unity,
Ye Christian people sweetly,
That he his word has spread abroad —
His word, his work completely.
No human hand can him withstand,
No name how high soever;
And sing we then our glad Amen!
God's word stands sure for ever.[46]

In this hymn is not Hubmaier still saying, lyrically at least, "truth is immortal"?

46. Vedder, *Hübmaier,* p. 321.

V

⚘   ⚘

From Zollikon to Augsburg

THE DAY FELIX MANZ WAS DROWNED AND GEORGE BLAUROCK WAS driven from Zürich was dark indeed for the Swiss Brethren. The movement which had begun only two brief years before found itself completely devoid of leadership. From that day on, Zürich Anabaptists never regained the momentum lost under the intolerant policy of Zwingli and the Great Council. Shortly afterward the center of Anabaptist activity in Switzerland became and remained the Canton of Bern, where Grebel had met with an eager response as early as 1526. Here the Anabaptist faith took deep root and produced a sturdy strain of Anabaptism. Three hundred years of subsequent persecution — characterized by imprisonment, deportation, and emigration — failed to stamp it out.

Driven from their native cantons as animals before a forest fire or as dust before a storm, the Brethren fled into south Germany and Moravia. From Moravia they went to Poland, North Germany, and the Netherlands. From Zollikon to Friesland the Swiss Brethren and their disciples left an indelible testimony in the minds and hearts of multitudes. That they were effective, contemporary witnesses were forced to admit. In 1527 Capito, a leading minister of the Reformed Church in Strasbourg, wrote:

> I frankly confess that in most [Anabaptists] there is in evidence piety and consecration and indeed a zeal which is beyond any sus-

picion of insincerity. For what earthly advantage could they hope to win by enduring exile, torture, and unspeakable punishment of the flesh. I testify before God that I cannot say that on account of the lack of wisdom they are somewhat indifferent toward earthly things, but rather from divine motives.

Franz Agricola, a Roman Catholic theologian, writing some fifty-five years later, testified regarding the Anabaptists:

> As concerns their outward public life they are irreproachable. No lying, deception, swearing, strife, harsh language, no intemperate eating and drinking, no outward personal display, is found among them, but humility, patience, uprightness, neatness, honesty, temperance, straightforwardness in such measure that one would suppose that they had the Holy Spirit of God.

Of course the witness to which Agricola testifies was not without its effect upon those who had a yearning for just such an expression of Christianity. To this fact Sebastian Franck was a contemporary, and not an altogether unsympathetic witness.

> The Anabaptists . . . soon gained a large following . . . drawing many sincere souls who had a zeal for God, for they taught nothing but love, faith, and the cross. They showed themselves humble, patient under much suffering; they brake bread with one another as an evidence of unity and love. They helped each other faithfully, and called each other brothers. . . . They died as martyrs, patiently and humbly enduring all persecution.[1]

From the beginning, the Anabaptist trek across Europe was a "martyr's pilgrimage," yet it was something more; it was a march — a march to Zion. Joining step with the condemned were numbered those of almost every tongue and nation of Europe.

---

1. Hershberger, *Recovery of Anabaptist Vision,* pp. 45-46.

Hans Denck

As early as 1525, Anabaptists were preaching the gospel in cities along the border of Switzerland and Germany. Wilhelm Reublin, Michael Sattler, and Hans Denck were among the first to labor extensively among the south Germans. Of these, Hans Denck was easily the most scholarly and at the same time the most controversial.

On the same day that believers' baptism was initiated by the Swiss Brethren in Zürich, Denck was expelled from the city of Nürnberg "forever." For almost two years he had served as headmaster of St. Sebald's School, which had been erected under the auspices of the humanists of the city. At first Denck was an honored member of the Nürnberg community of scholars. Increasingly, his critical evaluation of the Lutheran reform and his apparent radicalism caused alarm among reform leaders, leading first to Denck's dismissal and then to his exile.

There are striking similarities between the theological ideas of Denck at the time of his dismissal and those of the Zürich radicals. When asked to amplify his position on baptism and the Lord's Supper for the city fathers, Denck wrote:

> Water cannot wash away sin, even as one cannot wash away the red color from tile. Only the Word of God is powerful to pierce into the abyss of the heart. Whoever has accepted this Word and has been baptized unto the death of Christ, will receive the Spirit of Christ and will walk in newness of life.[2]

It was evidently Denck's position that the "sacraments" had no objective value in themselves. It is not amazing, then, that the Nürnberg preachers were not satisfied with Denck's statement and even somewhat confused. "We still cannot understand," they countered, "whether or not bread and wine is the blood and flesh of Christ according to Denck's conception, because one time he says yes, and other times no."

However, the position of the erstwhile Nürnberg humanist was clear enough that he was expelled from the city on grounds of heresy.

---

2. Jan J. Kiwiet, "The Life of Hans Denck (Ca 1500-1527)," MQR 31 (October 1957): 240. A concise biographical sketch of Hans Denck is given in Walter Fellmann, *Hans Denck Schriften* (Gütersloh: C. Bertelsmann Verlag, 1956).

His whereabouts during the next few months is in doubt. He probably embarked on a religious pilgrimage, seeking fellowship with some of like mind in the variegated milieu of the fast-breaking Reformation. It was rumored, but not verified, that Denck spent some time in Mühlhausen. If he did actually go to Mühlhausen, he did not stay for long. Undoubtedly he found himself just as much out of step with the radical Lutheran, Thomas Müntzer, and his frenzied militarism as he had been with the authorities of Nürnberg. In June, 1525, just after the disputation between the Anabaptists and the leaders of the Reformed Church, Denck arrived at St. Gall. He was not yet an Anabaptist, but here he came to be identified with them.

It was from the St. Gall sojourn and the impression that Denck made on Vadian (Joachim von Watt) and Johannes Kessler that his reputation for heresy became known. Of Denck during those days, Vadian wrote:

> Denck really was in every respect excellent, even so that he surpassed his age and seemed greater than he was. He, however, so misused his mind that he defended with all efforts the opinion of Origen concerning the liberation and salvation of those who are condemned. He could cite Scripture passages sharply and above understanding. The bountiful love of our God was praised so much — as he did for instance in a certain meeting — that he seemed to give hope even to the most wicked and most hopeless people that they would obtain salvation, which would be granted to them some day however distant it might be.[3]

Kessler's misunderstanding of Denck's soteriology was even more serious than that of Vadian, but his admiration of his ability was equally as great.

> Hans Denck, a Bavarian, was a learned, eloquent and humble man. . . . He was tall, very friendly, and of modest conduct. He was to be praised very much, had he not defiled himself and his teaching with terrible errors. . . . He was exceedingly trained in the word of the Scriptures and educated in the three main languages. . . . His

3. Kiwiet, "Life of Denck," p. 242.

opinion was that no man would go to hell nor would the devil be lost forever, but after a certain time all would be saved; for Paul said: God desires all men to be saved.

Actually, as Kiwiet, Denck's latest and most careful biographer, has demonstrated, Kessler misunderstood his position. Denck did not teach that all people would eventually be saved. Instead, he taught that Christ's death was an atonement sufficient for all humankind but efficacious only to the believer. His theology was not so much an echo of Origen as an anticipation of Jacobus Arminius.

It is beyond question that Denck was no blind follower of the scholastic theologians or even of Augustine. A graduate of the University of Ingolstadt with a recognized proficiency in Latin, Greek, and Hebrew, he was well equipped to pursue the theological inquiry pretty much on his own. A Lutheran since his Regensburg days, he was soon to find himself numbered with the Anabaptists due to the influence of Balthasar Hubmaier, also of Ingolstadt and Regensburg. It is entirely possible that Hubmaier was responsible for Denck's conversion to Lutheranism in the first place.[4]

In the autumn of 1525 Denck went to Augsburg to teach Greek and Latin. Here he was identified with a group of young radicals, among whom were Sebastian Franck, Casper Schwenckfeld, and Ludwig Haetzer. At the time the evangelical community was sharply divided over the Lord's Supper. Considering the argument as nothing more than needless bickering over inconsequential matters, Denck wrote with an obvious mystical slant: "What does it profit if you reject all external

---

4. *Ibid.,* pp. 243ff. Denck's soteriological heresy may have been nothing more than the position held by the author of the *Theologia Germanica* as revealed in the following passage which Denck probably quoted in full at St. Gall. "Insomuch that if the Evil Spirit himself could come into true obedience, he would become an angel again, and all his sin and wickedness would be healed and blotted out and forgiven at once. And could an angel fall into disobedience, he would straightway become an evil spirit although he did nothing afresh." Thomas S. Kepler, ed., *Theologia Germanica* (Cleveland: World Publishing Company, 1952), p. 73. From Denck's *Widerruf,* it is clear he was not a universalist. See Fellmann, *Hans Denck Schriften,* or Heinold Fast, *Der linke Flügel der Reformation* (Bremen: Carl Schünemann Verlag, 1962), pp. 196ff.; and Clarence Bauman, *The Spiritual Legacy of Hans Denck* (Leiden: E. J. Brill, 1991), p. 74.

ceremonies? What does it profit if you want to keep all of them? Teach each other to know God. . . . On both sides I see not only the people but also the pastors going astray."[5]

By the following year Denck's position had radically changed. The learned Bavarian humanist was formally identified with the Anabaptists. He was probably baptized by Dr. Balthasar Hubmaier, who spent some time in Augsburg on his way from Zürich to Nikolsburg. Immediately, Denck rose to a place of prominence among the south German Anabaptists. One of his first converts was the erratic Hans Hut, a one-time follower of Thomas Müntzer. Subdued and baptized, Hut set out on a missionary journey to Franconia, Austria, and Moravia, spreading his chiliastic hopes and baptizing many converts along the way.

Shortly after this, Denck felt it necessary to leave Augsburg. Differences had arisen between him and the leading Reformer of the city, Urbanus Rhegius. However, he had laid the groundwork for an Anabaptist congregation which would soon be formed by some of his and Hut's converts. The little congregation of five souls was formally established shortly before Easter, 1527. It soon began to exercise considerable influence in and around Augsburg. Sigmund Salminger, who had only recently come to Augsburg from München, was made elder. Jacob Dachser, a former Roman Catholic priest, was elected his assistant. Salminger and Dachser carried the burden of the work, preaching with much power and effect in and around Augsburg. They were faithfully supported by Eitelhans Langemantel, a wealthy convert of Hans Denck, and other members of the new church.

In the meantime, Denck had made his way to Strasbourg. An Anabaptist congregation had begun a rather precarious existence here as early as August of 1526. From the beginning of his brief respite in this unusually tolerant city, Denck was an unwelcome guest. Capito was dead set against him before he came. He had reached his opinion of Denck from the reports of Vadian and Kessler and prejudicial accounts of skirmishes with the authorities of Nürnberg.

Bucer was also highly suspicious of Denck. In order to get concrete evidence on which to accuse him, Bucer challenged him to debate. The

5. Kiwiet, "Life of Denck," p. 244, and "The Theology of Hans Denck," MQR 32 (January 1958): 278.

basis was Denck's earlier work, *Vom Gesetz Gottes (Concerning the Law of God)*. However, the disputation proved disappointing to its sponsors. It revealed no great heresy in the teaching of Denck. In fact, he declared that on major points of doctrine he was in substantial agreement with the Reformers, an assertion which Capito denied. Undoubtedly the real bone of contention was Denck's effectiveness as an advocate of the Anabaptists.

Therefore, Hans Denck was expelled from the city of Strasbourg on Christmas day, 1526. The day following Capito hastened to write a letter to Zwingli in which he declared:

> He [Denck] has disturbed our church exceedingly. His apparent sacrificial life, brilliance, and decent habits have wonderfully captivated the people. . . . He left yesterday. His going left some disturbance behind; but the remaining problems can be easily settled with diligence and caution. There is, however, about these people that which I cannot excuse; they certainly wish to appear to be fighting for the Scriptures which we profess as a testimony to the spiritual doctrine, which is given to us.[6]

It is significant that Michael Sattler was in Strasbourg during Denck's encounter with Bucer and was a welcome guest in the home of Capito. Only two months later Sattler penned the Schleitheim Confession as expressive of the faith and practice of south German Anabaptism in and around Horb. It is entirely possible that these articles were directed against some deviant teachings of Denck and Hut. These two were at variance with each other on the point of chiliasm. Apparently they stood together, however, in disagreeing with the Swiss Brethren on the role of the Bible in the life of the believer.[7]

Smarting under the treatment of the Strasbourg Reformers, Denck

---

6. Huldrici Zwingli, *Opera (Turici Apud Friedericum Schulthessium,* 1830), 7:579. See also Capito's letter of December 10, 1526, 7:572.

7. Kiwiet follows Fritz Blanke in holding the position that the Schleitheim Confession was written against the Denck and Hut emphasis. Some American scholars such as Wenger tend to reject this approach but admit that the south German Anabaptists had a different emphasis from that of the Swiss Brethren with whom Sattler is identified.

embarked on an extended missionary journey down the Rhine Valley. First, Bergzabern, where Denck publicly presented the gospel to the Jews of the city, and then Landau became scenes of his labors. By the first of February, 1527, he had entered Worms, whose walls were still ringing with the bold defiance of the young Luther of some six years before. Finally, the Reformation had actually come to Worms, and by the time Denck arrived two of the pastors had decided to do away with infant baptism. Apparently, the town was ripe for the Anabaptist message.

Ludwig Haetzer, a friend of Denck and an accomplished Hebrew scholar, was already at work in Worms on a translation of the Old Testament prophets and had completed his translation of Isaiah before Denck arrived. Within two months an exceedingly accurate translation of the prophets was made from the Hebrew into the German. Its popularity was immediate. The first edition was reprinted ten times in the space of two years. Several editions followed. Both Zwingli and Luther used this translation in their German Bibles. Denck also wrote his fifth and last work, *Of the True Love (Von der wahren Liebe)* during the stay in Worms.

On June 9, Kautz, the leading preacher of the city, posted seven theses on the cloister of the cathedral. The theses contained Anabaptist teachings on the Scriptures, baptism, the Lord's Supper, and redemption according to Denck's interpretation. By six o'clock Thursday morning, Denck, Haetzer, and Kautz were openly defending the new theses in the marketplace. But the Anabaptist teachings were evidently too radical for people still close to Catholicism. As an immediate aftermath of the market disputation, all four pastors of the city were dismissed. The proposed reform measures were unceremoniously rejected.

However, a few converts were made. In spite of severe reprisals by Ludwig V, elector of the Palatinate, and elaborate rebuttals by both Catholics and Lutherans, the seed took root. Subsequently, many a peasant from the rack and through prison bars continued to confess "Christ and his baptism."[8]

After Worms, Denck journeyed to Basel and from Basel via Zürich to Augsburg. Sometime in the later part of August, 1527, he and Hans

8. Kiwiet, "Life of Denck," p. 254. See also Bauman, pp. 16, 17.

Hut shared in a preaching service with the Augsburg congregation. At this time it numbered some sixty persons. The burden of Hut's preaching was the second coming of Christ, which he predicted would take place within two years. This bold pronouncement immediately provoked consternation and division.

A few days later the quieting influence of Denck upon Hut became apparent once again. The two brethren took a hasty recess to talk things over. In private conference they reached an agreement regarding the emphasis to be placed upon eschatology in relation to the other doctrines of the faith.

> Hut called this meeting a *concilium* and sent a letter to the brethren outside Augsburg about the agreement. Whenever a brother left on a missionary journey he would take a copy of this letter with him. In this letter Hut admonished all those who were initiated into the secrets of the kingdom not to take offense at other children of God who only proclaim a life according to Christ. With the congregation of Augsburg he had made the agreement not to preach about judgment, the end of the world, the resurrection, and about other eschatological subjects, unless he was requested to do so. Therefore all the brethren were admonished to act in the same spirit and to be steadfast in unity and love.[9]

After Augsburg, Denck — "the pope of the Anabaptists," as Bucer called him — labored for a while in Nürnberg and later in Ulm. Weakened by the rigors of the life of a refugee he wrote an old friend, Oecolampadius, for permission to enter Basel. Soon afterward he died there, a victim of the plague. Thus, the brief but intense ministry of the gifted Anabaptist leader seemingly came to an end in obscurity.

But this did not prove to be the case. Denck was not allowed to be silent even in death. Reminiscent of Jeremiah, whom he first made to speak in German, he wrote in the introduction to his first book.

> Does one want to give testimony of his faith to those who desire, then they say we want to sow dissension and rebellion among the people. Does one close one's ears to bad words, then they say we shun

9. *Ibid.*, p. 256.

the light. Well, God has drawn me from the shelter. I open my mouth against my will, but God urges me, I am not allowed to be silent.[10]

Denck had come to Basel to rest, but Oecolampadius pressured him into making a statement of his faith which was not made public until sometime after his death. The highly publicized *Hans Denck's Recantation* was not such at all. In ten points Denck drew up his confession of faith, which retracted nothing and differed in no essential respect from his earlier teachings as an Anabaptist. As Kiwiet has shown, only one point looks like a recantation and was possibly an interpolation by Oecolampadius himself. The style at this spot is not that of Denck. Keller had a copy of the *Recantation* in which this passage was in a different place from the copy publicized by Oecolampadius.

Often misunderstood and misinterpreted in life, Denck was not to escape such treatment in death. However, far from being a convert of Oecolampadius as his host had widely proclaimed, it is now quite evident that he died in the faith in which he had lived.

Evaluations of Denck's life and work vary in accordance with the position of those making such judgments. He has been claimed by the Unitarians, Quakers, and Baptists. Regardless of the final position which he may be given, few will disagree with Neff's judgment when he writes:

> Yet it should be noted that Denck stood somewhat apart from the main theological stream of Anabaptism, and that he cannot be regarded as the spokesman of the group in those areas where he held to his peculiar emphases. His major contribution lay in the earnestness with which he contended for Christianity as discipleship, and in the beauty of his sincere Christian spirit. He is one of the few personalities of the 16th century who never indulged in controversy except with a heavy heart; not a trace of abusiveness or unfairness is to be found in his writings.[11]

Denck was above all the apostle of Christian love. Love is the theme of his greatest work, *Of the True Love (Von der wahren Liebe)*.

---

10. *Ibid.,* p. 244. Bauman thinks it probable that Denck died in the home of Michael Bentinus, pp. 18, 19.
11. W. F. Neff, "Hans Denck," ME, 2:35.

The implementation of this virtue was the main thrust of his life. This truth is no more evident than in Denck's last work, his so-called *Widerruf.* In the introduction to this confession, Denck lays bare his heart.

> It gives my heart pain that I should stand in disunity with many men who I cannot help but consider my brethren because they pray to the same God to whom I pray and they give honor to the Father for the same reason I honor him, namely, because he has sent his son, the Saviour, into the world. Therefore, as God wills, and so much as in me is, I will not have my brother as an opponent and my Father as a judge but in the meantime will attempt to reconcile all my adversaries with me.[12]

Fellow Apostles

If Denck were the chief apostle of the Anabaptists as Keller claimed, there were others in southern Germany who could be termed fellow apostles. In the early advance of Anabaptism in this area Hans Hut, Michael Sattler, and Wilhelm Reublin were in the vanguard of the movement. Within a month of Denck's death Hut was also dead in his prison cell, and less than a year later Sattler had been burned at the stake in Rottenburg. Wilhelm Reublin alone remained as a living link between early south German Anabaptist leaders and Pilgram Marpeck,

---

12. Fellmann, *Hans Denck Schriften,* pp. 104-5. In Article VI, "Of Schism and Sects," Denck shows both his "ecumenicity" and his loyalty to the Anabaptist concept that faith cannot be coerced. He writes: "Where such hearts are [those that accept Christ and do not scorn the gift of God], these God holds high through Christ and they follow in his footsteps, which gives me joy and I have love for them in so far as I know them. But with those who may not hear me and still will not remain silent regarding matters which are in dispute, I cannot have much fellowship. For I do not perceive in such the spirit of Christ, but a perverted one that would drag me from my faith by force and compel me to do his will, may God help us right or not. And if the zealot really possessed the truth, it is conceivable that he wishes to do good but acts without wisdom. Then he should know that in matters of faith all should be left free and uncoerced. So, I separate myself from unity; . . ." (p. 107).

who would become southern Germany's most important Anabaptist theologian.

Hut, the book peddler turned evangelist, must have presented a very striking figure in his travels across the land. A warning against the Anabaptists issued by the Council of Nürnberg on March 26, 1527, announced: "The highest and chief leader of the Anabaptists is Johannes Hut, a well-educated, clever fellow, rather tall, a peasant with light brown cropped hair and a blond mustache. He is dressed in a gray, sometimes a black, riding coat, a broad gray hat, and gray pants."[13]

Such a warning could only serve to increase the curiosity of many for whom Anabaptism held an almost irresistible attraction. At some of their meetings the curiosity seekers outnumbered by far the baptized community. Sometimes a few would remain to become *bona fide* Anabaptists themselves. Perhaps no one among the early Anabaptist leaders was more successful in preaching and baptizing than was Hans Hut.

Hut was a Lutheran before becoming an Anabaptist. His point of departure from the Lutherans was over the question of infant baptism. He first began to question the practice as early as 1524. In the company of some friends at Weissenfels he sought to defend the Lutheran position but began to doubt the scriptural basis for infant baptism. He then sought help in Wittenberg, the stronghold of Lutheranism, but was not satisfied with the answers he received.

Upon returning to his home in Bibra, Hut refused to permit his newborn child to be baptized. The penalty for such action was immediate. He was forced to sell his property and leave town, which he did with his wife and five children. However, not too many months had passed until Hut returned to Bibra. He was seeking refuge, hoping to escape the consequences of his association with Thomas Müntzer, under whose spell he had fallen at Frankenhausen. After the final defeat of the peasants, he was forced to flee again. This time he made his way to Augsburg. Here the pacific influence of Denck soothed his disturbed spirit and won him for the Anabaptist movement. A few days after initiation into the fellowship by baptism, Hut began his meteoric career.

From the beginning of his ministry eschatological ideas formed the backdrop for his fervent evangelism. Driven by the conviction of

13. Loserth, "Hans Hut," ME, 2:846.

the imminent return of Christ, he preached divine retribution on the wicked and vindication for the saints. Dates were set for the return of Christ. When Christ did not return on the second anniversary of the beginning of the peasants' war at Frankenhausen, he did not hesitate to set another date. Hut's pronounced chiliasm, with its strange mixture of nonresistance and revolution, both heightened his preaching and left confusion in its wake. It certainly did not lessen his effectiveness as an evangelist. However, it did bring division among the Anabaptists and was a source of disappointment to Denck and bitterness to Hubmaier.

The labors of Hans Hut came to an end with his death in a prison cell in Augsburg. Imprisoned and tortured over a period of almost four months, he died of asphyxiation from a fire of unknown origin which had been ignited near his wasted form. But even death itself did not keep him from human judgment. "The officials took the dead body to court on a chair, tied the chair to the executioner's cart, sentenced it to die, and burned it at the stake on December 7."[14]

Hans Hut left behind a significant legacy. It included four tracts and several hymns, some of which, ironically enough, later found their way into Lutheran and Reformed hymnals. Of greater significance by far was the vigorous Anabaptist movement of central and southern Germany. It had a chiliastic accent for which Hans Hut was largely responsible.[15] From northern Franconia to Austria his was a familiar figure among the Anabaptists. Wherever he wandered, the newly baptized formed churches to continue his work and to prepare the people for the day of the Lord. The visitation of the Turks, which he had prophesied, did come, but the righteous were not vindicated. Martyrdom continued to be their lot.

Hans Hut was not a great organizer nor a thorough teacher, but he was unexcelled as an evangelist. Fortunately the influence of Denck, Sattler, Hubmaier, and Reublin tended to offset the chiliastic extremism

14. *Ibid.,* p. 849. One of the basic differences between Hut's apocalypticism and that of Müntzer was his apparent willingness to let God take the initiative in ushering in his millennial kingdom, whereas Müntzer identified his own impatience and resultant violent activism as God's divine will.

15. John S. Oyer, "Anabaptism in Central Germany," MQR 35 (January 1961): 37.

of Hut. At least, it never completely captivated south German Anabaptists.

Sattler's influence was, indeed, great. Even though he was executed some months before Hut died, his influence was still strong in southern Germany, and it remained so for many years. His death was mourned by both Capito and Bucer, who held him in high esteem as an earnest minister of the gospel. The effect of his death, as reported by Wilhelm Reublin, was so great that the Austrian authorities considered making a counter report. Their better judgment, however, prevailed. The manner of interrogating Anabaptists was changed after Sattler's execution. In some cities the authorities put forth a great deal of effort to persuade the recalcitrant victims to recant. "One consequence of the enormous excitement caused by Sattler's execution can be observed. In Württemberg the authorities now had the Anabaptists indoctrinated by clergymen . . . to persuade them to recant."[16] Sattler's labors had been confined to Horb and its vicinity. Yet his heroic death undoubtedly gave him and the Schleitheim Confession wide publicity in the whole of south Germany, Austria, and Moravia.

Hubmaier's contribution to south German Anabaptism was more indirect than personal. The influence of his thought is seen in the writings of Pilgram Marpeck, Hans Denck, and Peter Riedemann. His writings also found their way into every nook and cranny of south Germany, Moravia, and Switzerland. The impact of his theology was so great that many years later his books were placed on the Index of Prohibited Books by Roman Catholic authorities.

However, the living link between the early Anabaptist leaders of Switzerland and south Germany and Pilgram Marpeck was the ubiquitous Wilhelm Reublin. Reublin, a native of Rottenburg, was the first in the environs of Zürich to preach against infant baptism. He was also the first among the followers of Zwingli to take a wife in marriage. Before coming to Wytikon, he had attended the University of Freiburg. Among other positions he served as people's priest at St. Alban's Church in Basel. It was at St. Alban's that he began to preach Reformation doctrine, denouncing the mass with all the vehemence at his command. Eventually, Reublin's bold stand led to the loss of his position and

16. Bossert, "Michael Sattler," ME, 4:433-34.

expulsion from the city. Arriving in Zürich in the autumn of 1522, he rapidly became the most radical of Zwingli's followers.

After the debate on January 17, 1525, Reublin was among those who were expelled from the city of Zürich for practicing rebaptism. During his exodus journey, he preached at Schaffhausen, baptized Dr. Balthasar Hubmaier and sixty of his members at Waldshut, and debated with Capito on baptism in Strasbourg. Finally, he came to labor in the vicinity of his hometown of Rottenburg. The death of Michael Sattler was the occasion for his next period of wandering. From Reutlingen, where he took refuge in the home of a married sister, he wrote the widely publicized account of Sattler's trial and execution. He and Denck labored together for a while at Esslingen, where he calmed irate Anabaptists and kept them from taking up arms in retaliation for the death of Sattler. From this city Reublin was expelled with lash in 1528. Once again he turned to Strasbourg in hopes of securing a brief respite from the ever-present persecution.

The Anabaptist movement in Strasbourg had become increasingly vigorous and vocal. The presence of Kautz and Reublin only served to increase agitation against the Reformed Church and its ministers. On October 22, 1528, an Anabaptist meeting was interrupted by police, and Reublin was arrested. In an ensuing pen-and-paper debate Reublin and Kautz gave an account of their faith:

> Water baptism is the enrollment of the believers in the visible church of God. If [a believer] desires it he shall not be refused, if he has heard the word of penitence and consented to it in his heart. A confessed faith . . . must precede and not follow baptism. Thus it is clear that infant baptism is contrary to the command of Christ. . . . Again, we know from experience that your preachers are comparable to poor carpenters, who have, to be sure, torn down the church of the pope, but have not yet built a church of Christian order; thus their call is not of God, not divine, but earthly.[17]

The results of the debate were inconclusive. Nevertheless, Reublin and Kautz were released from prison and driven from the city, being warned on threat of drowning not to return. From Strasbourg, Reublin

---

17. Bossert, "Wilhelm Reublin," ME, 4:305-6.

now turned with his wife and children to Moravia and the Anabaptist communities of Austerlitz and Auspitz.

His ministry among the Hutterites met with a mixed response. Schism in the Austerlitz group was the result. With three hundred followers, Reublin set out to join the Auspitz colony from which he was later expelled as an Ananias.[18] Returning to Esslingen, he succeeded in gathering some three hundred Anabaptists together, only to be dispersed by the Swabian League. His last days are somewhat obscure. He ceased to be an active leader among the Anabaptists of south Germany sometime in the thirties. But another had arisen to take his place. His name was Pilgram Marpeck.

Pilgram Marpeck

Within a few months after the death of Michael Sattler, a prominent citizen of Rattenberg on the Inn River in Austria's Tyrol became an Anabaptist. At the time of his conversion, Pilgram Marpeck was the highly respected city mining engineer. His decision to join the Anabaptists initiated a series of events which were to reduce Marpeck to a "wandering citizen of heaven." On January 28, 1528, he lost his position. Three months later, on April 1, his possessions were confiscated on the pretext of raising funds for the care of the three orphans who had been in his home. If Marpeck had not been a prominent man from an outstanding family, he undoubtedly would have been dealt with more severely than he was.

Strasbourg, to which Denck, Kautz, Sattler, and Reublin had fled, became a refuge for him and his family after a brief residence south of the city. Succeeding Reublin as leader of the Strasbourg Anabaptists, he soon gained the ire of the Reformed preachers of the city. Bucer found it difficult to say anything complimentary about the new arrival.

> Concerning Pilgram, know that he is nothing but a stubborn heretic. He has forsaken much but can never forsake himself. He accused him of rejecting God's temporal gifts and of possessing

---

18. Cf. Zieglschmid, *Large Chronicle*, p. 98. See also *The Hutterian Brethren*, trans. and eds., *The Chronicle of the Hutterian Brethren* (Rifton, N.Y.: Plough Publishing House, 1987), 1:90, 91. Afterward referred to as *Hutterian Chronicle*.

conceited forwardness. Otherwise he and his wife are of fine irreproachable character.[19]

Marpeck's pamphlets were banned by the authorities as quickly as they appeared, and soon he was arrested. The imprisoned Marpeck was permitted to debate with Bucer. The *colloquium* took place in the presence of the city council and lasted three days. Bucer was declared the winner; and Marpeck, along with other leading Anabaptists, was expelled from the city on December 18. During the disputation Marpeck had argued for the separation of church and state. He set forth believers' baptism as an act of obedience of a committed disciple in contrast to those who held it to be a means of grace.

A third and final disputation was held on January 18, 1532, after which Bucer characterized Marpeck as "the worst sort of heretic." But in his denunciation he revealed that by this time the former Lutheran is without question the undisputed leader among the Strasbourg Anabaptists: "You see in what manner the ungodly audacity of these men [Anabaptists] breaks forth; and in the meantime they look up to him and honor him like a little god, — as many so ever as there are Anabaptists anywhere."[20]

The next twelve years Marpeck lived the life of a wanderer. His exact whereabouts are not fully known. He spent some time in the Tyrol, and in 1540 he made his way to Austerlitz, Moravia. The following year he tried his hand at uniting the various Anabaptist groups but met a stubborn wall of resistance. When he attempted to discuss the matter with the Hutterites, they would not listen but prayed instead while he talked. Such a stubborn spirit embittered Marpeck; he declared, according to Braitmichel, that he would rather unite with the Turks and the pope than with this congregation.

Fortunately, Pilgram was far more successful with the pen than he had been with the olive branch. The remaining years of his life were by all odds the most fruitful.

Prior to 1542 the only product of his pen was a confession of

19. Wenger, "The Life and Work of Pilgram Marpeck," MQR 12 (July 1938): 147.
20. *Ibid.* The quotation here is taken from *Schiess Bündnerisches Monatsblätt* 15, no. 3 (Mar. 1916): 315.

faith which had been forged in the fires of controversy with Bucer ten years before.[21] During the next eight years his most significant writing would be done in collaboration with Leopold Scharnschlager, leader of the Anabaptists in the Grisons, and other compatriots. A treatise on baptism and the Lord's Supper, known as the *Taufbüchlein* or *Vermanung*, was the first of these works to be completed. It now appears that a major part of this work was a revision and translation of Bernd Rothmann's *Bekentnisse von beyden Sacramentum*.[22] The *Vermanung* reveals Marpeck's genius, which is seen in his ability to draw on other sources and add creatively to the older concepts. In the *Vermanung* Marpeck attacked the Hofmannite view of the incarnation, community of goods, the Münsterites, and all use of force. There is also the addition of an alternate form of baptism. Immersion was the preferred form in the *Bekentnisse*.

Casper Schwenckfeld von Ossig was a Silesian nobleman and leader among the inspirationists of south Germany. On appearance of *Vermanung*, he hurriedly published a bitter attack entitled *Judicium*. Marpeck and Scharnschlager arose to the fray, publishing in 1544 the first part of the Anabaptist answer entitled *Vindication (Verantwortung)*. The second part was slow in coming from the press, for Marpeck had begun work on a massive concordance. The concordance *(Testaments-erläuterung)* was ready for publication by 1550. The second part of the *Vindication* bore the names of six co-authors and may have been completed by Scharnschlager.[23]

The last eleven years of Marpeck's life were spent in Augsburg. He was employed by the city as engineer on May 12, 1545, and held this position till his death in December, 1556. That he was an active

21. The full text of Marpeck's confession of faith is transcribed and edited by Wenger in MQR 12 (July 1938): 167-202.

22. Frank Wray has made the discovery that the *Vermanung* is actually a revision and translation of the *Bekentnisse von beyden Sacramentum* published by Bernd Rothmann in 1533. Klassen, "Pilgram Marpeck," p. 214, points out that Marpeck and Scharnschlager admitted using other sources. The *Vermanung* is considerably larger than the *Bekentnisse*.

23. The date and authorship of *Verantwortung*, part 2, and even that of the *Testamentserläuterung* are subject to debate. See Klassen, "Pilgram Marpeck," pp. 221-22, for a brief discussion of the problem.

Anabaptist was known to the council and the cause of frequent reprimands. Apparently, he was too valuable a man for the city to lose. The council, it seems, did nothing more than protest his activities as complaints arose.

Marpeck became the most influential theologian among the south German Anabaptists. His theology was both biblical and practical. In fact, theology for Marpeck was the exposition of the Scriptures. Since he was not a trained theologian, his approach to theology was neither blessed nor hampered by the traditional stances of Augustine, Lombard, or the scholastics. He was a layman's theologian. In a plausible and simple manner he explained what he understood to be the meaning of the Trinity, the gospel, the church, the ordinances, discipleship, and eschatology. He occasionally quoted the Apocrypha and was somewhat nonplused over the problem of predestination. Yet he made a solid contribution by his sane approach to scriptural authority and the relation between the Old and New Testaments. Through equally voluminous writings, he almost equated Menno Simons in influence. For south Germany he was, to a lesser degree, what Menno was to north Germany and the Netherlands.

The importance of Marpeck to the Anabaptist movement in south Germany is not as obscure as it once was. More information about him has come from the *Kunstbuch,* a collection of early Anabaptist documents.[24] His influence among Hutterites was nil. After their experience with Reublin, they were probably more reluctant than ever to give an

---

24. In the *Archiv für Reformationsgeschichte,* 47, part 2 (1956), two articles were published which are of inestimable value for Marpeck research. The first of these deals with the discovery of the *Kunstbuch,* an early Anabaptist codex of 16 unpaginated and 354 paginated leaves, by Heinold Fast and Gerhard Goeters in a Bern library *(Bürgerbibliothek)* in July, 1955. It is a glowing testimony to Heinold Fast's scholarship that he could publish such a full description of the contents of the codex within such a short time after its discovery, and could also supply an authoritative commentary on the contents of the various writings, grouping them in a quite ingenious way. All of the forty-two tracts and epistles contained in the codex are described and fitted into the article under the headings, "Martyr Witnesses from the Beginning," "Concerning the Unity of the Church of Christ (Spread of the Marpeck Circle)," "The Building up of the Body of Christ (About the Teaching and Order of the Churches of the Marpeck Circle)," and finally "On the Place of the Marpeck Circle in its Historical Context and the Preservation of the *Kunstbuch."* Klassen, "Pilgram Marpeck," p. 211.

audience to an outsider. Marpeck succeeded, however, in bringing a higher degree of unity to the discordant groups of Anabaptists in and around Augsburg. As a theologian his influence has continually increased well beyond his own group and generation. It is Kiwiet's opinion that Marpeck is the only one who has given the free church movement a thorough theology.[25]

Marpeck's most creative contribution to Anabaptist thought was his view of the Scriptures. While holding the Scriptures to be the Word of God, he made a distinction between the purpose of the Old Testament and that of the New. As the foundation must be distinguished from the house, the Old Testament must be distinguished from the New. The New Testament was centered in Jesus Christ and alone was authoritative for the Brethren. To hold that the Old Testament was equally authoritative for the Christian was to abolish the distinction between the two. Failure to distinguish between the Old and New Testaments leads to the most dire consequences. Marpeck attributed the peasants' revolt, Zwingli's death, and the excesses of the Münsterites to this cause. Making the Old Testament normative for the Christian life is to follow the Scriptures only in part. In Marpeck's eyes the pope, Luther, Zwingli, and the "false Anabaptists" were all guilty of this fundamental error.[26] Though Marpeck did not include Calvin in his list, was it not at this same point that the renowned reformer of Geneva made his most serious blunder? If Marpeck had made no other contribution to Anabaptist theology than this one insight, would it not be sufficient to make him worthy of recognition?

25. Jan J. Kiwiet, *Pilgram Marbeck* (Kassel: J. G. Oncken Verlag, 1957), pp. 94-122. Kiwiet summarizes Marpeck's hermeneutics in the following terms. "Marbeck fasst dann den Unterschied in folgenden Totalbegriffen zusammen: Der Alte Bund war eine Zeit des Suchens und des Dürstens und erst der Neue Bund eine Zeit des Findens und des Stillens. Die Verheissung an die Alten geht im Neuen Bund in Erfüllung. Die Finsternis wird zu Licht und der tod zu Leben. Es ist wie der Unterschied zwischen gestern und heute; das Alte ist vorbeigegangen, und das Neue ist gekommen. Gestern ist das ware liecht ewigs lebens nit vorhanden gewest/welchs liecht erst heut durch die leibliche zukunft Christi in dise welt/die menschen erleuchte" (pp. 101-2).

26. Wenger, "The Theology of Pilgram Marpeck," MQR 12 (July 1938): 207ff. See also William Klassen and Walter Klaasen, trans. and eds., *The Writings of Pilgram Marpeck* (Scottdale, Pa.: Herald Press, 1978), pp. 159-302.

VI

錄　　錄

Of Moravia and the Community of Goods

U
NDER THE LEADERSHIP OF HUBMAIER AND THE TOLERANCE OF the Lichtenstein barons, Moravia became the most influential center of Anabaptist activity on the Continent. An endless stream of refugees continued to pour into the region as the heavy hand of persecution fell alternately upon one country and then another. From the Tyrol, south Germany, Bavaria, Württemberg, Hesse, and even from Switzerland they came.

As one might suspect, such a heterogeneous gathering of bold apostles of a new faith was not always a harmonious one. However, until Hubmaier's arrest some degree of order had been preserved. With his execution and the seizure of his distinguished colleague, a former bishop named Goschel, only Hans Spitalmaier, the chaplain of the Lichtensteins, remained to defend his position. Increasingly, vocal opposition came from Jacob Wiedemann and his followers.[1]

"One-eyed Jacob," as Wiedemann was known, followed the eschatological teachings of Hans Hut and the nonresistant principles of the Swiss Brethren. To these he added the doctrine of the community of goods. Wiedemann based his teaching on the example of the primitive church at Jerusalem. Against Wiedemann, the Hubmaier group

1. Newman, *History of Anti-Pedobaptism,* p. 185.

maintained that the principle of sharing with brethren in need was the actual teaching of the New Testament. In this position Hubmaier's followers, the men of the sword *(Schwertler)*, were closer to the Swiss Brethren than the people of the staff *(Stäbler)*, their antagonists.

Wiedemann was adamant. For the *Stäbler*, the doctrine of the community of goods soon overshadowed all others and became the indispensable mark of the true church. The divisive tendencies already present became increasingly articulate. The *Stäbler* withdrew from the other Anabaptists of the city to worship separately under the guidance of Wiedemann and Philip Jäger.[2]

The endless wrangling was too much for the lords of Nikolsburg. When the Wiedemann party refused to live peacefully with the other Anabaptists, they were invited to look elsewhere for a permanent abode. Apparently, Leonhard von Lichtenstein had not quite caught the significance of the teachings of Hubmaier and the Swiss Brethren regarding the state. If he had, he was at least unwilling to take the risk involved in their complete implementation. Leonhard had attempted earlier to silence Hans Hut and had delivered his own pastor into the hands of Ferdinand. He now escorted Wiedemann and his followers to the borders of his territory.[3]

The Anabaptists who remained in Nikolsburg received the patronage of Lord Leonhard until his death in 1552. Afterward they maintained an existence in spite of the Counter Reformation until the early years of the seventeenth century.[4] In the intervening years their numbers were greatly depleted by the constant removal of individuals and groups to neighboring Anabaptist communities, which proved to be the more durable in the time of travail.

Until their dismissal from Nikolsburg, the community of goods was purely an academic doctrine among the *Stäbler*. Now a decision was clearly before them. Should they stay together or go their separate

2. ME, 4:941.

3. John Horsch, *The Hutterian Brethren* (Goshen, Ind.: The Mennonite Historical Society, 1931), pp. 7-8.

4. See Henry A. DeWind, "A Sixteenth Century Description of Religious Sects in Austerlitz, Moravia," MQR 29 (January 1955): 44-53, and Robert Friedmann, "Christian Sectarians in Thessalonica and their Relationship to the Anabaptists," pp. 54ff.

ways to become once again refugees in a hostile world? While encamped in the abandoned village of Bogenitz, they reached the decision to stay together. There were many widows and orphans among them but little food, fewer clothes, and less money.

In view of their desperate straits they decided to follow the example of the Jerusalem church and pool all their earthly possessions. They then chose ministers of temporal needs *(Diener der Notdurft)*, who proceeded to spread a cloak upon the ground. Everyone "laid down on it his earthly possessions unconstrained and with a willing mind for the maintenance of the needy after the reading of the prophets and apostles. Isaiah 23. Acts 2, 4, 5."[5] Thus, a way of life which was to become characteristic of the Hutterite expression of Anabaptism was first implemented.

The first communal Anabaptist settlement *(Brüderhof)* was established shortly thereafter at Austerlitz on the manorial estates of the lords of Kaunitz. The four Kaunitz brothers held to the toleration which characterized many Moravian noblemen. Here the Hussites had been known and protected for almost a century. In the years to come they were to defend their quasi-independent status, as well as their Anabaptist citizens, against all encroachments of the Austrian authorities with varying degrees of success.

Communal life among the Anabaptists almost failed to get off the ground. The admittedly delicate experiment in practicing the community of goods ran into some severe difficulties early in its history. *"Grosse unordnung,"* to use Wiedemann's terminology, began to characterize the fellowship at Austerlitz.

Reublin, who joined the *Brüderhof* early in 1530, found much mumbling and grumbling in Zion. Old Jacob, as Reublin unflatteringly referred to Wiedemann, seems to have dominated the *Brüderhof* in a rather high-handed manner. He directed the young women of the *Brüderhof* to marry the eligible young men available, threatening to secure heathen wives for them if they failed to follow his admonition.[6] He attempted to silence Wilhelm Reublin, who had become quite popular as a preacher. Reublin was a substitute rather than one of the

5. Zieglschmid, *Large Chronicle*, p. 87.
6. ME, 4:306.

duly elected elders *(Diener des Wortes)* among the brethren. A public hearing before all the brethren was finally held. Reublin brought several serious charges against Wiedemann and the leaders of the Austerlitz congregation. Among other things, he accused the elders of unequal distribution of goods and hypocrisy in their vacillating attitude toward payment of the war tax. Also, they coerced the young women to marry "without the knowledge and consent of their heart." He also accused Wiedemann of false doctrine:

> Fourthly, they taught that water baptism is a work of righteousness, whereas that should be faith; this, I have heard from their own mouth, from the elder Jacob, which I also reproved him for in the presence of his brethren at the time, for he said that his comfort and salvation rested on water.[7]

That Wiedemann was actually guilty of holding this position on baptism is open to doubt. It is quite clear that Reublin's attitude toward the envious *Vorsteher* (chief minister) was acrimonious. This may well have colored the interpretation of the rumors which he had heard. At any rate, an open schism was inevitable. It came seven days later.

On January 26, after having reached Auspitz, Wilhelm Reublin sat down to write a full account of the cause of division between the Brethren at Austerlitz. He wanted his old friends in the Strasbourg congregation to have his side of the story. The Reublin version has been corroborated by other witnesses as being substantially correct. Perhaps he was guilty of exaggerating the hardships involved in making the transfer from Austerlitz to Auspitz. Undoubtedly it was not an easy experience. "Therefore trusting in God and His grace," he wrote, "and for the sake of the truth, we left Austerlitz on the eighth day of January, departing from the false brethren and shaking the dust off our shoes against them." He continued:

> Oh how richly and powerfully God manifested His power to the blind, the lame, the lepers, and the cripples, and showed Himself faithful. They held up their heads to testify to God's truth as they

---

7. Wenger, trans. and ed., "A Letter from Wilhelm Reublin to Pilgram Marpeck, 1531," MQR 23 (April 1949): 70-73.

departed with us. We numbered two hundred fifty apart from children as we departed on a single day.[8]

Some forty sick persons in addition were lodged in a cottage and supplied with food from the meager store until the Brethren could make a fresh start at Auspitz.

Soon, however, Reublin had organized a new *Brüderhof* along the same lines as the Austerlitz community with himself as the *Vorsteher*. Johanna von Boskowitz was a noblewoman and abbess of Mariasaal near Brno. She invited them to establish their community in a village by the name of Steuroqwitz, putting the parsonage at their disposal. The new beginning in the middle of a rich agricultural region of Moravia gave every promise of success.

Internal dissension soon returned to plague the Brethren and continued until the arrival of Jacob Hutter from the Tyrol. Hutter had been in contact with the Austerlitz Anabaptists. He had joined them in the name of his congregation in the Tyrol but was absent when the division took place. However, his sentiments were with the Auspitz group. So it was to this community he turned, seeking refuge for himself and his congregation.

The Hutterites

What John Calvin was to the Reformed Church, Jacob Hutter was to the Anabaptists of Moravia. It is from the beginning of his work with the Auspitz *Brüderhof* that the movement which bears his name actually began.

Hutter was a native of the Puster Valley in the Tyrol. Since educational advantages were extremely limited for all but the clergy and nobility, he was sent to Prague to learn the trade of hat making. His business forced him to travel widely until he finally settled in Carinthia. While here he came in contact with Anabaptists in a neighboring village, becoming an Anabaptist preacher in 1529. His first church was in the Puster Valley. From a rather inauspicious beginning, Hutter soon

8. *Ibid.*, p. 74.

emerged as the most energetic and successful evangelist among the Anabaptists of the Tyrol.

As their numbers increased, so did the persecution. Tyrolese authorities, writing to Ferdinand in Vienna, told the story. Hardly a day had passed in two years in which Anabaptist matters had not come up in the council. "More than 700 persons have been in part executed, in part expelled, in part have fled into misery, who left their property as well as their children behind." The exasperated authorities continued: "These people not only have no horror of punishment but even report themselves; rarely is one converted; nearly all only wish to die for their faith."9

From the beginning of his work Hutter had sent many harassed Anabaptists to Moravia. Finally, the tempo of persecution increased to the point of making his work virtually impossible. He also left the Tyrol for Moravia. He arrived in Auspitz on August 11, 1533, with one companion. After surveying the situation, Hutter announced in his first sermon delivered before the assembled brethren that a reform of the *Brüderhof* was a dire necessity. Reorganization, he said, would be instituted immediately.

Hutter's assumption of authority and proposed reform went against Philipp, Schützinger, and Gabriel, the duly elected elders. There is little doubt that communal life among the Anabaptists up to this point had been something less than an overwhelming success. The inability of the Brethren to arrive at a *modus operandi* threatened the new development with extinction. All of this the erstwhile hat maker, now completely committed to the communal way of life, clearly saw. Consequently, he resolved to put the *Brüderhof* on firm footing.

With great difficulty Hutter secured recognition as chief administrator *(Vorsteher)* of the *Brüderhof* at Auspitz. He promptly reorganized it, establishing the community of goods in both production and consumption. The dissatisfaction of the former elders led to the formation of other *Brüderhofe,* which were designated by the names of their pastors. The Philippites, followers of Philipp Plenner, remained in Auspitz. The Gabrielites, followers of Gabriel Ascherham, moved to Rossitz. The mother congregation at Auspitz was soon augmented with fresh refugees from the Tyrol. At the time of Hutter's death, it took his name for its own, thus becoming known as Hutterites.

9. ME, 2:851.

Hutter's leadership among Moravian Anabaptists was of short duration. The Münster episode crystallized Ferdinand's determination to rid Europe of every vestige of Anabaptism. In order to implement his plans, he attended the Moravian Diet of 1535. He demanded that the Moravian nobles expel the Brethren from the land.

All appeals of the Brethren and their Moravian landlords were fruitless:

> They were thus driven into the field like a herd of sheep. Nowhere were they permitted to camp until they reached the village of Tracht in the possessions of the lord of Liechtenstein. There they lay down on the wide heath under the open sky with many wretched widows and children, sick and infants.[10]

In a letter eloquent with pathos, Hutter wrote to the governor, Kuna von Kunstadt:

> Now we are camping on the heath, without disadvantage to any man. We do not want to wrong or harm any human being, not even our worst enemy. Our walk of life is to live in truth and righteousness of God, in peace and unity. We do not hesitate to give an account of our conduct to anyone. But whoever says that we have camped on a field with so many thousands, as if we wanted war or the like, talks like a liar and a rascal. If all the world were like us there would be no war and no injustice. We can go nowhere; may God in heaven show us where we shall go. We cannot be prohibited from the earth, for the earth is the heavenly Father's; may He do with us what He will.[11]

The letter only served to make Hutter an increasingly heavy liability to the disheartened refugees. Therefore, the Tyrol once again became the field of his labors. His evangelistic endeavors were accompanied by growing interest and some converts. Such success could not hope to continue undetected, nor did it. In the latter part of November, 1535, Hutter and his pregnant wife were captured in the home of Hans Steiner of Clausen. They were immediately taken to the episcopal

10. *Ibid.,* p. 852.
11. *Ibid.,* pp. 852-53.

fortress of Brandzell. Shortly thereafter Hutter was removed to Innsbruck where numerous attempts were made to secure a recantation. Neither the logic of Dr. Gallus Müller, the stabbing pain of the rack, nor the bruises from the brutal whippings to which he was subjected moved him to betray the faith. On February 25, 1536, some three months after his arrest, he was burned at the stake.

Upon hearing of his death and heroic conduct under fire, the bereaved *Brüderhof* of Auspitz took his name for its own. Hans Amon was chosen as the new *Vorsteher.* Gradually, the Brethren were able to re-establish themselves on various estates of sympathetic Moravian noblemen. Scarcely had the forests and caves given up their refugees when the Hutterites began missionary endeavors. They were to carry the gospel to every part of German-speaking Europe. The burden of the missionary witness, according to the *Geschichts-Buch* cited by Horsch, was thoroughly evangelical.

> They spoke with power of the kingdom of God showing how all men must repent, be converted, and turn from the vanity of this world and its unrighteousness, from a sinful, vile and wanton life to God, their Creator, and Jesus Christ, their Savior and Redeemer. To all such work God gave his blessing and grace, so that it was carried on with joy.[12]

The Hutterite missionary effort was a costly enterprise. It is estimated that 80 percent of the missionaries *(Sendboten)* died a martyr's death. Typical of these martyr missionaries was Claus Felbinger. Felbinger, a locksmith by trade, was arrested with another Hutterite, Hans Leutner, near Neumarkt in Bavaria. He was immediately placed in chains and imprisoned in the village of Landshut. While in prison he was tortured unmercifully on the rack. He remained steadfast, and resolved not to divulge any information that would bring added sorrow upon the heads of his brethren.

During the two months of his imprisonment hardly a day passed in which he escaped interrogation. Priests, monks, and theologians visited his cell. Upon one occasion Felbinger was questioned about

---

12. Horsch, *Hutterian Brethren,* p. 28. See also the *Hutterian Chronicle* account of the martyrdom of Hans Schmidt and Heinrich Adams, pp. 354-61.

recanting. He replied that they (he and his fellow prisoners) would abide in the "simplicity of Christ." The chancellor was aroused to ask: "Are you simple? I do not believe it . . . not one of a hundred could defend himself, and maintain his position as fairly as you have done."[13]

Felbinger's prison manuscript, setting forth his convictions about the faith and practice of the Hutterites, shows that the interrogator was correct. The prisoner before him was no simpleton. He proved himself to be well versed in the Scriptures and a man of deep convictions, sincerely devout and mentally alert. He addressed his prison treatise to the authorities, whom he calls "my lords" and "servants of God." This reflects both his position in regard to constituted authority and his courteous demeanor. Along with other doctrines of the Anabaptists, Felbinger discussed baptism, the Lord's Supper, and the church in a vigorous and fresh style. He showed both a very intimate knowledge of Peter Riedemann's *Rechenschaft* and an ability to set forth his own position effectively. A few excerpts will help one to catch something of the spirit of Hutterite life and faith in the face of certain martyrdom.

> We are accused also of condemning all who are not of our mind and who act not as we do. That we deny. We condemn no man, but we show to men their reprobate life and warn them of condemnation, and this we do in accordance with the Word of God that cannot lie. . . . No human being can condemn another. Judgment is in the hand of the Lord; but sinful, evil works are what condemn man, when he has not left them in accordance with the Word of God and brought forth honest fruits of repentance. . . .
>
> Further I was asked with regard to *baptism,* how often I was baptized. I said, "Once, as God has commanded." They then asked if I had not also been baptized by the brothers. I answered, "The devout brothers who baptized me in accordance with the command of Christ first taught me repentance and faith in the name of Jesus Christ. Then, at my request, they baptized me on confession of my faith; which faith, God, according to His promise, also sealed and strengthened with His Holy Spirit, who has until now kept me in the way of truth. And it is my hope in God that He take Him not from me until my end."

13. *Mirror,* p. 567.

Infant baptism is next examined and denounced.

> Infant baptism I regard as simply nothing. It is conceived by men
> for the sake of money, that the parsons may by its means enrich
> themselves. . . . For they find not a single word in the Old or in the
> New Testament about infant baptism. . . . On the contrary, [Christ
> and his disciples] held to the one and only true baptism. And that
> is when those who, having reached years of discretion, join the faith
> . . . and . . . let themselves be united by the covenant of grace of
> true Christian baptism. . . . The devil strives through his messengers
> to hinder at all costs the revelation of the true Christian baptism.
> Therefore has the antichrist, the abomination of desolation, the
> pope, placed such emphasis on the accursed infant baptism. . . .
> Baptism is a covenant of a good conscience with God (I Peter 3:21)
> and a certain declaration that the man has been accepted as a light
> to the inheritance of all saints. Now what does a young child know
> of a "good conscience with God"? It is mere trumpery! . . .
> To sum up, [infant baptism] is a foolish and blind affair. Through
> it all manner of evil and infamous men get the precious name, in
> that they call themselves Christians, which thus but becomes a cloak
> for their knavery. For a Christian has not received his name from
> baptism, but from the conduct of his whole life.

After denying the real presence of Christ in the mass, Felbinger
proceeded to set forth the Hutterite view of the ordinance.

> "But," they say, "He has clearly said, This is my body and my
> blood." Yes. We know also, praise be to God, the interpretation of
> this high mystery . . . namely, by means of bread and wine He has
> shown the community of His body. Even as natural bread is com-
> posed by the coming together of many grains, ground under the
> millstones, and . . . wine is composed of many grapes, each sharing
> its juice with the rest in the wine press, so that they become one
> drink. Even so are we also, in that we become completely one nature
> with Him, in life and death, and are all one in Christ: He is the vine
> and we His branches, He the head and we His members.[14]

14. Friedmann, "Felbinger's Confession," pp. 151-53.

With an exposition of the doctrine of the true church, Felbinger brought his confession to a close. This forthright and able defense of his faith may have well evoked respect but not mercy. Unceremoniously, far away from home, he and Hans Leutner were beheaded on July 10, 1560.

Peter Riedemann

Peter Riedemann, even though an active and effective missionary of the Hutterites, escaped the fate of Claus Felbinger. In fact, he lived to become a *Vorsteher* among the Moravian Hutterites and their most influential theologian.

Riedemann, a native of Silesia in Germany, found himself imprisoned at Gmünd by his twenty-third year for alleged Anabaptist activities. The year of his imprisonment, 1529, was also the year of his ordination as a minister of the word *(Diener des Wortes)*. The following three years were spent in prison. But they were not wasted years. Here he wrote his first *Confession*.[15] A second *Confession* was written while in prison at Hesse in 1540-41. It is this *Confession* which has been preserved through the centuries by the Hutterian Brethren.

In the following year Riedemann began a most eventful and fruitful period of missionary labors as a Hutterite missionary. En route to Franconia he visited the scattered Anabaptist congregations in upper Austria, inviting them to join the Hutterites. After arriving in the vicinity of Nürnberg, he was imprisoned but was released two years later on promising not to preach in the city.

In 1539, we find him again on the road. This time his destination was Hesse and his mission was reconciliation. He had been commissioned

15. The title is *Rechenschaft unseres Glaubens geschrieben zu Gmunden im Land ob der Enns im Gefencknus*. The *Rechenschaft* is still printed and bound by the Hutterites in the United States and Canada. I purchased a copy in 1965 from *Vorsteher* David Waldner which was printed in Alberta, Canada, and bound in the colony near Mitchell, South Dakota. The title reads *Rechenschaft unserer Religion, Lehre und Glaubens* (Alberta: Verlag der Hutterischen Brüder Gemeine., 1962).

to attempt the reconciliation of two estranged brethren. As an evangelist his success was remarkable, and perhaps it was not less so as a peacemaker. Once again the results of his labors brought him to the attention of the authorities. He was put in chains and imprisoned in Marburg.[16]

Riedemann's situation was soon eased, and he was allowed to assist the jailer in making shoes. Shortly thereafter the prisoner was moved to the nearby castle of Wolkersdorf. Due to the kindness of the administrator, he was given free run of the palace. His prison epistles continued to strengthen the Brethren in half a dozen different centers. It was at Wolkersdorf that he wrote his second *Confession*, a book of 183 pages. It was published by the Hutterites in 1565 and has remained the major doctrinal formulation of their faith.

Riedemann was a prisoner of Philip of Hesse. The chief purpose of this second *Rechenschaft* was to acquaint Philip with the nature of Anabaptist faith as practiced by the Hutterites. Even though Philip was not mentioned in the Foreword, he must have been in mind when Riedemann wrote:

> In order that no man, including the authorities — who, perhaps at the instigation of others, have already stretched out and laid their hand upon the Lord's people of peace — may bring further guilt upon themselves by violating the apple of the Lord's eye, we desire to give an account of our faith, doctrine, and life as much in sequence as is possible, through which we believe every man should see and recognize sufficiently that we are not heretics and seducers, as we are blasphemously called.[17]

The *Rechenschaft*, as Helmann has pointed out, is not a theological work but a simple confession of faith.[18] It is divided into two parts. The first is a confession of faith organized along the traditional lines of The Apostles' Creed. The second is something of an appendix to the first. A remarkable feature of this extremely influential Hutterite work is that so little space is given to the doctrine of the community of goods.

16. Friedmann, "Riedemann," ME, 4:326-27.
17. Peter Rideman, *Account of our Religion, Doctrine, and Faith*, trans. Kathleen E. Hasenberg (London: Hodder & Stoughton, Ltd., 1950), p. 9.
18. Heimann, "Hutterite Doctrine," part 1, p. 35.

After a lengthy discussion of baptism and the Lord's Supper, there follows a comparatively brief treatment of the community of goods. It is with obvious conviction that Riedemann presents an apologetic for the practice. The concern for personal gain, which finds expression in the desire to possess things, was not true of the primeval or sinless state of man. Such a desire, therefore, Riedemann insisted, is an expression of man's depraved, unregenerate nature. Man was not created to appropriate God's creation to his own private needs. This is the way of the world, and the true disciple of Christ cannot conform to the world. Therefore, he who will not forsake private property cannot be a disciple of Christ. The example of the Jerusalem church is marshaled to clinch the argument for the position of the Hutterites. Thus, from the nature of the creation, of Christian discipleship, and of the church, the community of goods is held to be a necessity.[19]

The *Rechenschaft* was destined to become one of the most influential of all Anabaptist prison manuscripts. It met with immediate acceptance among the Moravian Anabaptists. Its author was so respected by the Hutterites that, upon the death of Hans Amon, they requested his speedy return, "if he could do so in good conscience."

By the end of February, 1542, Riedemann was back in Moravia where he assumed a position of leadership along with Leonhard Lanzenstiel, who had been chosen *Vorsteher* upon the death of Amon. It was a fortunate arrangement. Lanzenstiel was the more practical of the two. Riedemann's interest was directed toward supplying the spiritual needs of the people. He became their undisputed spiritual leader, a position he held until his death in 1556.

By that time Riedemann had succeeded in restoring some of the Philippites and a majority of the Gabrielites to the Hutterite fold. The pastor's heart within him was deeply touched by the plight of these scattered brethren "as sheep without a shepherd." His earliest attempts to reach an understanding with the Philippites were frustrated by Austrian authorities. On December 6, 1539, they seized some 150 Hutterites and Philippites at Steinabrunn, assembled for a conference under Riedemann's leadership.

Riedemann arrived a week later. He found women and children

19. See Rideman, *Account,* pp. 88-91.

grief-stricken over the fate of the men, who had been incarcerated in the Falkenstein Castle. Ferdinand sent many priests, his executioner, and some theologians to interrogate and convert the imprisoned Anabaptists. The anticipated harvest was not forthcoming. Even torture on the rack failed to produce one recantation. The decision was finally made to send the prisoners to Trieste, where they were to become galley slaves.

Ninety of the able-bodied brethren were then chained two by two with iron collars about their necks. Just before setting out on the long journey by foot to Trieste, they knelt together in prayer. Their families and friends had come to Falkenstein for one last farewell before the final separation. The parting was so touching that even the royal provost and his aids could not restrain their tears. All along the way the brethren witnessed to the curious bystanders.

After twelve nights in prison the prisoners escaped, letting themselves down over the wall with the chain by which they had been bound. However, twelve of the brethren were recaptured at Laibach in Carinthia and returned to Trieste. The other seventy-eight of the original ninety who had been sentenced returned to their homeland with much rejoicing. However, three died soon after their arrival.[20]

Upon becoming a *Vorsteher* of the Hutterites, Riedemann renewed correspondence with the Philippites. A fraternal relationship with the Philippite Brethren continued as long as they maintained an organizational life. By mid-century this expression of sixteenth-century Anabaptism had virtually disappeared. Some reunited with the Hutterites, others with the Swiss Brethren, and still others, to use the terminology of the *Geschichts-Buch,* "went back into world."[21] Thus, a Hutterite type of Anabaptism disintegrated due to the failure to secure the quality of leadership which characterized the Hutterites.

While internal weakness undoubtedly contributed to the demise of the Philippites, a second great wave of persecution came at about the same time, threatening the life of the Hutterite movement itself.

20. Zieglschmid, *Large Chronicle,* pp. 202ff., and Horsch, *Hutterian Brethren,* pp. 44-47.
21. See Friedmann, "The Philippite Brethren," MQR 32 (October 1958): 272ff.

In fact, the whole movement was driven from Moravia. Abandoning their twenty-six thriving colonies, the Brethren fled to Hungary in 1548 where some Hutterites had set up a *Brüderhof* two years before. However, the Hungarian refuge was an insecure one. Ferdinand, flushed with victory over the Smalkaldian League and expulsion of the Anabaptists from Moravia, pursued them to Hungary. The Hungarian nobles put up some resistance, which proved futile. Finally their benefactor, Baron Franz von Prantsch, was forced to evict them from Sabatisch. He accompanied them to the border in order to protect them from the robbers who often dealt the Hutterites much misery.

The persecution lasted four years. A part of this time the Brethren were again forced to live in the forests and caves. They suffered much from the magistrates of Hungary and Moravia, being driven alternately back and forth across the border. The robbers, who sometimes stripped the fugitives of the clothes on their backs, inflicted much damage. Some of the men were able to secure work. In spite of much defection the movement not only survived, but the stalwart witness of the majority under such conditions caused many to be "added to the church." Eventually, as the waves of persecution subsided, the harassed victims gradually slipped back to form new settlements in Moravia. Intermittent persecution continued for another ten years but had practically ceased by 1563. It did not rise again in force until some thirty years later.

Life and Work in the *Brüderhof*

Forty years of comparative peace in Moravia gave the Hutterites opportunity to develop their way of life. Life in the *Brüderhofe* is portrayed by the chronicler in the *Geschichts-Buch* as idyllic.[22] The first among the many blessings of such life listed was freedom to practice their religion. "They gathered for worship in peace and unity and taught and preached the Gospel and the Word of God openly. Twice each week and sometimes oftener they held public religious meetings."

Casper Braitmichel, the chronicler, continued:

22. Quotations are from the translation by Horsch, *Hutterian Brethren*, pp. 21-23.

Christian community of goods was practiced according to the teaching of Christ. . . . All shared alike . . . there being, of course, special provisions for the sick and for the children. . . .

Swords were forged into pruning hooks, saws, and other useful implements. . . . Every one was his fellowman's brother and all lived together in harmony. . . . Revenge was forever done away. Patience was their only weapon in all difficulties. . . .

They were subject to the authorities and obedient in all good works, in all things that are not contrary to God, the faith, and conscience. What was due the government in the form of taxes or customs was paid . . . , since the government is ordained by God and is an institution as necessary in this evil world as the daily bread. . . .

No cursing nor swearing was heard . . . there was no betting, no dancing and card-playing, no carousing nor drinking. They did not make for themselves fashion, immodest, proud and unsuitable clothes. . . . There was no singing of shameful songs . . . but Christian and spiritual songs, and songs of Bible stories.

In a concluding summary, the *Geschichts-Buch* asserts: "In short, no one was idle; each did what was required of him and what he was able to do, whether he had been poor or rich, noble or commoner, before. Even the priests who joined the Church learned to labor and work."

When most of Europe was still illiterate, the Hutterites had established a system of primary schools. Among them education was compulsory. They believed that their movement depended on an educated people who could practice discipleship in light of New Testament teachings. Of course, the state churches felt no such need. Their religion was primarily in the hands of religious professionals. The layman's chief function in such ecclesiastical systems was to obey. For this purpose ignorance served as well as, if not better than, knowledge. For the Hutterites the educational process began very early. The Hutterite child entered school at the age of two and attended all day, the year round. At about five or six years, children were transferred from nursery school to work under a schoolmaster. Here they would learn to read and, after a very rudimentary education, to practice a trade. Religion was by far the most important element in the Hutterite school. Anabaptist doctrines were inculcated from the very earliest days of formal instruction.

In succinct fashion Riedemann outlined the curriculum and characterized Hutterite education:

> As soon as the mother hath weaned the child she giveth it to the school. Here there are sisters, appointed by the Church . . . ; and, as soon as they can speak, they lay the word of God's testimony in their mouths and . . . tell them of prayer and such things as children can understand. With them children remain until their fifth or sixth year, that is, until they are able to learn to read and write. . . .
>
> When they are thus far they are entrusted to the schoolmaster, who teacheth them the same and thereby instructeth them more and more in the knowledge of God, that they learn to know God and his will and strive to keep the same. He observeth the following order with them: when they all come together in the morning to school he teacheth them to thank the Lord together, and to pray to him. Then he preacheth to them as children for the space of half an hour, telling them how they ought to obey . . . their parents. . . .
>
> From such obedience to parents he teacheth them obedience to God and the keeping of his will . . . and [to] serve and cleave to him alone, as him from whom they have all that is good. Thus we teach our children from babyhood to seek not what is temporal but what is eternal.[23]

The teachers were not ordinarily graduates of the universities. However, from time to time, priests were converted and served the Brethren as schoolmasters. At least, this was the case of a former priest, Jeronimous Pael, who was put to death for his faith at Vienna in 1536. All of the teachers, regardless of educational attainments, were well instructed in the laws of sanitation. High standards of medical practice were developed early in the Hutterite communities.

Hutterite Physicians

Since the Renaissance the medical profession had been divided into three classes in Europe: the physician, the surgeon, and the barber-

23. Rideman, *Account,* pp. 130-31.

surgeon.[24] The physician was the theorist, the barber-surgeon actually the practicing physician. The surgeon was somewhat between the physician and the barber-surgeon in the medieval hierarchy. Among the Brethren no such distinctions existed. The traditional differentiating terms were used but without the distinctions.

Even though the Hutterite barber-surgeons lacked traditional training, they became very efficient in their profession. They became the most sought-after practitioners in Moravia, some even gaining international recognition. George Zobel, Balthasar Goller, and Hans Zwickelberger were three of their most notable physicians. Of these, Zobel was easily the most famous.

Through his medical practice Zobel gained reputation for himself and goodwill for the brotherhood. In 1581 he was called upon to help Emperor Rudolph II in Prague. The emperor was successfully treated and, after a six-month stay at his court, Zobel was sent back to Moravia. Upon numerous other occasions his skills were utilized by the nobility. Prague once again became indebted to Zobel. His services helped to stem the tide of disease in the plague-embattled capital, eighteen years after his visit to care for the ill monarch.

The practice of medicine among the Hutterites was a demanding one. Brotherhood members strove for excellence in this field of human endeavor as they did in all the trades in which they engaged. A physician among them was required to keep himself abreast of the best knowledge available. He had to be diligent about the gathering of herbs and giving proper care to the sick in the *Brüderhofe*. Certain of the physicians among the Brethren were quite familiar with the writings of Paracelsus, the famous sixteenth-century physician and philosopher. In fact, Paracelsus himself probably visited the early *Brüderhofe* of the Brethren. He may even have inspired their highly successful venture in the practice of medicine.

24. See John L. Sommer, "Hutterite Medicine and Physicians in Moravia in the Sixteenth Century and After," MQR 27 (April 1953): 119ff.

The Last Moravian Persecution

The excellent reputation which the Hutterites were winning in many pursuits became a matter of grave concern to their Roman Catholic antagonists. Christoph Fischer wrote three vindictive volumes against the Hutterites. The last appeared on the eve of the Thirty Years' War.[25] Among many baseless and highly prejudicial matters to appear in these works, Fischer had some very illuminating things to say about the Brethren. In his book, *Of the Cursed Beginnings of the Anabaptists,* Fischer wrote:

> Among all the heresies and sects which have their origin from Luther, . . . not a one has a better appearance and greater external holiness than the Anabaptists. Other sects are for the most part riotous, bloodthirsty and given over to carnal lusts; not so the Anabaptists. They call each other brothers and sisters; they use no profanity nor unkind language; they use no weapons of defence. . . . They own nothing in private but have everything in common. They do not go to law before judicial courts but bear everything patiently, as they say, in the Holy Spirit. Who should suppose that under this sheep's clothing only ravening wolves are hidden?[26]

Fischer vented his spleen against the popularity of the Hutterites in another tirade entitled *Fifty-four Important Reasons Why the Anabaptists Should Not Be Tolerated in the Land.*

> Anabaptists who come to the lords in Moravia are preferred before others. The lords do not desire to read or even to see the certificates of their previous training being satisfied to know that the elders of the church considered them qualified to fill the position in question. . . . Is this not blindness? Never do they promote Christians

25. *Von der Wiedertauffer Verfluchtem Ursprung, Gottlosen Lehre und derselben Gründliche Widerlegung* (Bruck a.d. Teya, 1603); *Vier und funfftzig Erhebliche Ursachen Warumb die Widertauffer nicht sein im Land zu leyden* (Ingolstadt, 1607); and *Der Hutterischen Widertauffer Taubenkobel. In welchem all ihr Wust, Mist, Kott und Unflat, das ist ihre falsche, stinckende unflaetige und abscheuliche Lehren werden erzahlet* (Ingolstadt, 1607).

26. Horsch, *Hutterian Brethren,* p. 32.

without definite knowledge concerning them, and yet such favors do they show the Anabaptists.

The Anabaptists have the greatest favor among the nobility. They have the preference as managers of estates, be it dairy or wheat farms, mills, tile yards, gardens, or anything else. They are appointed by them to high positions in the castles, such as manager, steward, and keeper. . . .

The lords must pay the Anabaptists larger salaries and wages than the Christians who have formerly held the same positions. This can be proved by the account books of some of the lords. The lords give the Anabaptists such great freedom that in certain offices they do not even require an account from them. . . .

It is displeasing to God that the lords do tolerate them and entrust their estates to them. It is contrary to Christian love. For if a Jew helps another Jew and heathen favor each other, why should not Christians also help each other? To this some one may reply, "It is true, it would be more just, but the Christians are not so faithful and reliable as the Anabaptists; therefore it is right that the lords employ the latter.[27]

The intolerant policy advocated by Fischer was soon to find realization. Great persecution fell on the heads of the Moravian Anabaptists in the opening days of the Thirty Years' War. For twenty-five years the brotherhood experienced many tribulations. First, Austrian soldiers encamped among them during the war between Austria and Turkey. Later the intruders were Turks, Tartars, and Hungarians. From the invasion of the Turks and their allies the Brethren suffered much. They lost sixteen colonies, eighty-one members were murdered, and two hundred and forty were carried off as slaves into Turkey. The victorious Catholic armies wreaked havoc with the remaining *Brüderhofe*. They plundered and destroyed, murdered and raped. From the *Geschichts-Buch* comes a graphic account of those terrible days of suffering.

It was stated above that the year 1621 began with much tribulation. . . . I cannot tell what awful devilish things were perpetrated

27. *Ibid.,* p. 30.

on many good, pious and honorable sisters . . . , yea, on children, both boys and girls. Women with child and mothers on their deathbed as well as virgins were most outrageously attacked. The men were burned with glowing irons and red-hot pans; their feet were held in the fire until their toes were burned off; wounds were cut into which powder was poured and then set afire; . . . eyes forced out by inhuman torture; men were hung up by the neck like thieves. . . . Such things were openly practised by the imperial soldiery who believed themselves to be the best of Christians. . . . One would suppose that the devil himself would have been more fearful of the might, power, glory and majesty of God than these shameless men. May God lead them to realize it, to whom and to whose righteous judgment we commit everything.[28]

Under the persecuting zeal of Cardinal von Dietrichstein the Brethren were robbed of all their savings and driven out of Moravia. Once again deprived of houses and land, cattle and household goods, they became wanderers upon the face of the earth. Their history in subsequent centuries is filled with all the pathos of a people universally despised and persecuted. Here and there, on the fringe of European civilization, they sought brief respite from the relentless hounds of persecution.

Persecution in Hungary and Transylvania

The hounds of persecution would not rest. To Hungary and Transylvania the Brethren had fled. Through the diabolical designs of the Jesuits a century and a half later, these areas became an inferno of hate, intrigue, and torment in which the Anabaptist movement was virtually consumed.

Upon the authority of the Empress Maria Theresa, the Jesuits proceeded in 1759-62 to make Roman Catholics out of the Hutterites. Their plans were carefully made. They decided on a *Blitzkrieg* type of simultaneous attack against all four *Brüderhofe* in Hungary. The object

28. *Ibid.,* pp. 54-55. This section is taken from the *Geschichts-Buch* (Wolkan), p. 565, and translated by Horsch. Compare with the *Hutterian Chronicle,* pp. 521-761.

of this first effort was to confiscate all the Hutterite books. The objective was only partially achieved. Priests were then stationed in the *Brüderhofe* and the people were forced to listen to their sermons. When these tactics proved fruitless, the leaders among them were seized and imprisoned in nearby towns and monasteries. Zacharias Walter, elder at Sabatisch, was imprisoned in the Jesuit monastery at Ofen, and Heinrich Müller, elder at Levar, in the monastery at Gran in upper Hungary. Müller, after a particularly hot debate with his captors, reportedly was put to death and his body was dumped into the Danube.

The remaining Hutterite men deserted the shops to live in the forests and caves. Some months later they were apprehended. The results are a sad commentary upon religious intolerance. After inhuman treatment incapable of description, those who were not killed turned Catholic. Thus there arose a group of apostate Hutterites in Hungary who are known today as *Habaner.*

Likewise, the Hutterites of Transylvania did not escape the lash of the tyrant's whip. Near the end of the persecution in Hungary, Delpini, the Jesuit in charge, reported to the Empress that the Anabaptists there had been exterminated. He offered his services to accomplish the same great mission in Transylvania — of course, only if her Highness approved. She did. So Father Delpini was off to Transylvania to what he had anticipated would be an easy victory. News of the brutality of the authorities and the final capitulation of the Hutterites in Hungary had undoubtedly preceded him. However, he soon discovered that his visions of victory were somewhat ill-advised.

He was careful to secure the approval of the secular authorities — not difficult, of course, with the backing of the Empress. He would then proceed with his work. His first proselyting efforts were expended at Alwintz. Horsch relates that he came here and demanded to preach. He

> took his place in the pulpit, while the ministers sat beside him on the bench and listened, together with the congregation, to what this false prophet would bring forth. . . .
>
> The Jesuit took a text from the Gospel of John, Chapter 16; and dwelt especially on the verse where Christ said to his disciples, "I have yet much to say unto you, but ye are not able to bear it now." This he applied to the Brotherhood saying that they did not under-

stand the Gospel sufficiently. Then he went on further with the words of Christ where he said, "But when he, the Spirit of truth is come, he will guide you into all truth"; this he applied to himself. . . . Further he praised the Catholic faith, and told many stories of miracles and wonders performed by saints, especially one about a Jesuit, such as he, who had removed a mountain. . . . When he was finished he stepped down from the pulpit and asked the congregation how they liked his sermon. . . .

Thereupon Brother Joseph Kuhr arose, stepped to the pulpit and said to the Jesuit: "What you repeated from the Gospel, that I know as well as you; and what you said about your many saints, that I do not believe. And what you said further about a Jesuit who removed a mountain is a Jesuit lie."[29]

Eventually the Transylvania Anabaptists were subjugated much as the Hungarian Anabaptists had been. Yet there was a remnant that escaped both death and apostasy and became the seed for a renewed movement in Wallachia which later reached Russia. Thus, the last glimpse the eighteenth century gives of the Hutterites is essentially the same as that with which the seventeenth opens. It portrays the now-familiar story of the Hutterites, a harassed and hounded people. Their ranks depleted by persecution, they were still seeking some spot on earth where they might worship their God in peace.

29. *Ibid.*, pp. 90-91.

VII

꒰ᕤ   ꒰ᕤ

Menno Simons and
Dutch Anabaptism

FIVE YEARS AFTER RETURNING TO THE VILLAGE OF HIS BIRTH AS
parish priest, Menno Simons renounced the Catholic Church to
cast his lot with the Anabaptists. His position of respect, with its
comfortable living, was cast aside for the life of a hunted heretic. And
what is more remarkable is that the decision was made while the air
was still heavy with the odor of death from the Münster tragedy. In his
Reply to Gellius Faber, Menno writes of this experience with a pronounced Pauline accent.

> Then I, without constraint, of a sudden, renounced all my worldly
> reputation, name and fame, my unchristian abominations, my masses,
> infant baptism, and my easy life, and I willingly submitted to distress
> and poverty under the heavy cross of Christ. In my weakness I feared
> God; I sought out the pious and though they were few in number I
> found some who were zealous and maintained the truth.[1]

Once his hand was put to the plow, Menno never looked back.
Indeed, he had no use for those who did. His life became so inseparably

1. Leonard Verduin, trans., and John Wenger, ed., *The Complete Writings
of Menno Simons* (Scottdale, Pa.: Mennonite Publishing House, 1956), p. 671.
Hereafter referred to as *Complete Writings.*

linked with the history of Dutch Anabaptism that it is virtually impossible to treat one without the other. But there were Dutch Anabaptists before Menno. Hence, the history of Anabaptism in the Netherlands must begin before he became part of the movement.

The Anabaptist Ferment

To Melchior Hofmann goes the honor of having been the first to introduce the Anabaptist message publicly in the Netherlands. Hofmann, a furrier by trade and an erstwhile follower of Martin Luther, was one of the most interesting personalities of the entire Reformation era. Born in 1495, he early became an enthusiastic disciple of Luther, who gave him much support in the early stages of his career.[2] Evangelistic fervor led him to preach the gospel with holy abandon in most of the countries of northern Europe. While passing through Denmark en route back to Germany from Sweden, he was given the position of preacher at Nicolaikirche in Kiel along with the stated pastor. Upon hearing of this new venture by the former furrier, Luther wrote that Hofmann ought to be silenced, since he was neither competent nor called to preach.

However, Frederick X soon took care of the matter. Though enchanted at first by the earnest eloquence of the new preacher, he soon grew uneasy over the effect of his bold eschatology and asked Hofmann to leave. Hofmann left, and by 1530 he had shaken the dust from off his shoes upon the whole Lutheran camp. For a while he joined forces with the Zwinglians in Strasbourg, but his sojourn with them was of short duration. On April 23 of the same year he was baptized into the Strasbourg Anabaptist brotherhood. At last, he seems to have found a congenial fellowship and a cause to which he could give himself without reservation. At least no question was likely to arise about his credentials among his new brethren.

Less than two months after his baptism, Hofmann appeared in Emden. By some means he succeeded in ingratiating himself with the authorities, who gave him permission to use one of the churches of the

2. Christian Neff, "Melchior Hofmann," ME, 2:779-81.

city. Apparently the harvest was ripe for the Anabaptist message. Success was immediate and phenomenal. Obbe Philips, one of the earliest of the Dutch Anabaptist leaders, writing some twenty years after the event, recalled:

> Among these [Reformers and Anabaptist leaders whom he had named] Melchior Hofmann stood out. He came from upper Germany to Emden to baptize around three hundred persons publicly in the church in Emden, both burgher and peasant, lord and servant.[3]

The numerous baptisms brought Hofmann's success to the attention of the clergy, who were now thoroughly aroused. They soon forced his departure from the city. He left Jan Volkertszoon (Trijpmaker) in charge as pastor of the newly formed congregation and headed for Strasbourg. Here his wife and child awaited him. The journey carried him up the Rhine, where he continued an evangelistic ministry with his customary success. Somewhere along the way he found time to publish a pamphlet entitled "The Ordinance of God" *(Ordonnanz Gottes)*, setting forth his views concerning baptism and, to a lesser extent, the Lord's Supper.[4]

"The Ordinance of God" abounds in the typological use of the Old Testament. Analogies are constantly drawn from Old Testament events and teachings to support Hofmann's new views concerning baptism. However, there is a noticeable absence of chiliasm. Apparently, at this stage of his ministry, baptism was central, pushing the chiliastic emphasis to the periphery. But this was not to be the case for long.

---

3. Obbe Philips, *A Confession*, 1559, in Williams and Mergal, *Spiritual and Anabaptist Writers,* p. 208. See Dosker, *Dutch Anabaptists,* p. 99 for a discussion of the authenticity of *A Confession*.

4. The complete Dutch title is *Die Ordonnantie Godts, De welche hy, door zijnen Soone Christum Jesum, inghestelt ende bevesticht heeft, op die waerachtighe Discipulen des eewigen woort Godts.* First published in 1530 in German, it is found only in a Dutch version. The Dutch translation (Amsterdam, 1611) appears in the critical edition by S. Cramer and F. Pijper, *Bibliotheca Reformatoria Neerlandica* ('s Gravenhage: Martinus Nijhoff, 1909), 5:148-98. An English translation has been made by Williams and is published with an introduction and critical notes in Williams and Mergal, *Spiritual and Anabaptist Writers,* pp. 182-203.

Once back in Strasbourg, he let eschatological considerations return to the forefront. In fact, he became so enamored with his own interpretation of the Bible that he decided that no one else in Germany preached the truth.[5]

For the next three years Hofmann made several trips into the Netherlands and north Germany. Interspersed among these evangelistic sallies were some opportunities for rest. He seized these to extend his ministry through a number of books and pamphlets. The Strasbourg writings reveal a man of unusual native ability and deep devotion. They abound in fanciful interpretations of the Scriptures and almost constant chiliastic overtones. Hofmann, however, affirmed his faith in the Triune God. Though rejecting the bearing of arms, he recognized the legitimacy of the state and the necessity of obedience to constituted authority.

Hofmann spent much time in the Netherlands and north Germany, preaching the gospel at Amsterdam, Leeuwarden, Emden, and doubtless many other centers. By 1533 he became convinced that the return of Christ was near at hand. An old Frisian Anabaptist had prophesied that he would be imprisoned half a year but then would be released to perform the function of Elijah in the return of Christ.[6] This prophecy he accepted as of the Lord. It served to confirm his growing conviction that, indeed, he was the prophesied Elijah. It was now clear in his mind: Strasbourg had been chosen by God himself to be the New Jerusalem. Christ was to return just as he had preached to rain destruction on the wicked and vindicate the righteous.

At Hofmann's own instigation, therefore, he was arrested and imprisoned in Strasbourg. As Hofmann's imprisonment lengthened, the faithful in north Germany and Holland were caught up in fanaticism at Münster. Under the sway of two unscrupulous opportunists, Jan Matthys and Jan of Leyden, visions and revelations multiplied. To them the millennium was no futuristic hope but a present reality. The New Jerusalem was in the making. It was not to be Strasbourg but Münster.

The leading evangelical reformer of the city was Bernhard Rothman. Formerly a priest at St. Mauritz Church, just outside the city, he

5. Neff, "Hofmann," p. 782.

6. See Philips, *Confession,* in Williams and Mergal, *Spiritual and Anabaptist Writers,* p. 212.

went over to the Reformation side in 1531. After visiting Marburg, Wittenberg, and Strasbourg, Rothman returned to champion Reformation truth in Münster. By August 19, 1532, all the churches in the city, with the exception of the Cathedral, were manned by evangelical pastors. However, Rothman began to question the validity of infant baptism under the influence of Hendric Rol from Wassenberg. A disputation was held to decide the issue. The decision went against Rothman and his party. He was dismissed and all unbaptized children were commanded to be baptized.

The crisis precipitated one of the most influential Anabaptist works of the sixteenth century. Krahn writes of it:

> Rothman now wrote his first Anabaptist treatise, *Bekentnisse* . . . in which he advocated believer's baptism and a symbolic view of the Lord's supper. When it was published November 8, 1533, it bore also the signatures of a number of the Wassenberg *predikanten*. The *Bekentnisse* constitutes a milestone in the reformation history of Münster and Westphalia and a signpost for Anabaptism.[7]

The publication of Rothman's *Bekentnisse* became the signal for the apostles of the New Jerusalem to make their appearance. On January 5, 1534, Bartholomeus Boekbinder and William de Kuiper, disciples of Jan Matthys, arrived in Münster and initiated believers' baptism. Soon Jan van Leyden followed.

As Enoch (Jan Matthys) and King David (Jan of Leyden) took charge, Rothman was captivated by their bold dreams and Hofmann found himself more and more a forgotten man. Rejected by the Swiss

---

7. Cornelius Krahn, *Dutch Anabaptism: Origin, Spread, Life and Thought (1450-1600)* (The Hague: Martinus Nijhoff, 1968), p. 123. Krahn does a superlative job of placing the Münster episode in its proper perspective. See pp. 80-164 for a rather full account of the development of chiliastic Anabaptism and Melchior Hofmann's relation to this phenomenon. The Münster story has been told and retold in numerous works which are available in English. It need not be given here for this reason and due to the fact that it lies outside of the scope of this work. Two works which contain rather full accounts of Münster are: E. Belfort Bax, *Rise and Fall of the Anabaptists* (New York: Macmillan, 1903), pp. 95-331, and Dosker, *Dutch Anabaptists,* pp. 63-94. Newman gives a balanced account of this period in *History of Anti-Pedobaptism,* pp. 264-94.

Brethren and spurned by the builders of the New Jerusalem, his lot became increasingly bitter. Death finally released him from prison in 1543, ten long years after he had cheerfully entered to await the deliverance of the Lord within six months.

Hofmann was not responsible for Münster. His was a different spirit from that of the architects of the New Jerusalem. If his was the legacy of Hans Hut, theirs was that of Thomas Müntzer. Neff reminds us that "Hofmann was a man of extraordinary gifts, of a consuming selfless zeal for the cause of the Lord Jesus, of a rare eloquence, combined with moral earnestness and a genuinely truthful character."[8] An entirely different spirit motivated the two Jans. Their spirit of self-seeking opportunism manipulated a guileless people for their own ill-conceived designs. Thus the highly eschatological Hofmannite form of Anabaptism was transformed into the holocaust of Münster.[9] Yet it must be admitted that Hofmann's revelations and prophecies formed a stock on which Matthys could graft his sanguinary program.

But not all Dutch Anabaptism was caught up in the fanaticism of Münster. Those who remained steadfast became the remnant out of which Dutch Anabaptism would arise after 1536. Among these were two brothers from Leeuwarden, Obbe and Dirk Philips. They never permitted themselves to be engulfed by the Münsterite spirit, even though it covered the Lowlands like a flood.

As the situation of the New Jerusalem grew increasingly desperate, uprisings of sympathetic revolutionaries erupted all over the country. Amsterdam, Leyden, and the Old Cloister *(Het Oude Klooster)* each in turn became rallying points for the assembling of recruits. The Münster emissaries had done their work well, but the would-be reinforcements were rapidly apprehended and mercilessly crushed. At the same time, however, other Anabaptists, motivated by biblical ideas similar to those of the Swiss Brethren, held meetings. They clarified their position and excommunicated the Münsterites. Such assemblies were convened at Sparendam in January, 1535, and again in Westphalia in the summer

---

8. Neff, "Hofmann," p. 784.
9. Philips, *Confession,* in Williams and Mergal, *Spiritual and Anabaptist Writers,* pp. 214-15.

of 1536. At the Westphalia meeting, according to Brons, "the impure and riotous elements were thrown out."[10]

At the beginning of this protest against the Münsterites, Dirk and Obbe Philips stood pretty much alone. Of those early days, Obbe wrote: "But God knows, that Dietrich and I could never find it in our hearts that such onslaughts were right; we taught firmly against this, but it did us no good, for most of the folks were inclined to this."[11] Obbe was the first of the two brothers to accept baptism at the hands of apostles sent out by Jan Matthys. Willem Cuyper and Bartholomew Boekbinder assured Obbe and his fourteen or fifteen followers of the pacific nature of their message. They baptized them and the next day ordained Obbe and John Scheerder with the laying on of hands.[12]

Following his ordination, Obbe immediately set out on an itinerant ministry of preaching and baptizing. Eight days later Dirk, Obbe's brother, was baptized by another of the Amsterdam apostles, Peter Houtzagher. Shortly thereafter Obbe ordained Dirk in Amsterdam and Menno Simons in Groningen.

An extremely sensitive individual, Obbe became increasingly disillusioned with the Münsterites. From the beginning he had opposed them, yet he was to fall under the same condemnation as they. He had received a second baptism and bore the hated name, *Wederdooper* (Anabaptist). In the back of his mind there always seems to have been a

---

10. Dosker, *Dutch Anabaptists,* p. 92. Dosker quotes from A. Brons, *Taufgestinnten oder Mennoniten* (Amsterdam, 1912), p. 59.

11. Philips, *Confession,* in Williams and Mergal, *Spiritual and Anabaptist Writers,* pp. 222-23.

12. Philips, *Bekentenisse,* in Cramer and Pijper, *Bibliotheca Reformatoria Neerlandica,* 7:129-30. Obbe wrote of his ordination in the following vein: "Alsoo hebben wy ons op dien dach meest alle laten doopen: Des anderen daechs als sy nu reysen wouden, hebben sy ons met Hans Scheerder onbooden, door aengeuen van andere broeders, ende ons dat ampt der predickinghe opgheleyt, met oplegginge der handen, te Doopen, leeren ende die Ghemeente voor te staen &c. *Die oplegginge der Handen voelden wy wel,* oock alle woorden hoorden wy wel *maer wy en voelden noch hoorden geenen H. Geest,* noch vernamen geen cracht van bouen, maer veel loose woorden, die macht nochnaedruck . . . hadden, als wy naederhandt ghenoechsaem beuonden, ende naedat sy sullix met ons wtgherichtet harden, zijn sy terstont desseluen daechs voortghereyst."

question about the validity of his commission.[13] Evidently, it was never resolved to his satisfaction. Later, it appears to have been a major factor in his separation from the Anabaptists. Very little is known of his life after 1540, when he slipped from view in Hamburg, Germany. The Obbenites here had gained an excellent reputation as a law-abiding and nonrevolutionary people.[14] Obbe's importance for Dutch Anabaptists lay in the fact that he was among the first to champion the nonviolent, anti-Münsterite Anabaptist party in the Netherlands. He also was responsible for the ordination of his brother Dirk and Menno Simons. These two men were to become molders of a biblical Anabaptism that survived the destruction of Münster.

Dirk, the younger of the Philips brothers, proved to be the more valuable as far as Dutch Anabaptism is concerned. This was due in part to his training but more to the caliber of his witness. Along with Obbe he early registered his opposition to the Münsterites.[15] In his book *Concerning Spiritual Restitution,* he accused the revolutionaries of defending from the Old Testament that which they could not support from the New. He declared that such a procedure has given rise to all sorts of false religions and deplorable errors. Unlike Obbe, however, he apparently entertained no sense of shame over the Münster catastrophe, for which he felt no responsibility. Younger in years than Obbe, his more mature judgment and strong ecclesiology held him steadfast. The cause was under heavy indictment, and it was no meager talent which he brought to its service.

Dirk and Obbe were sons of a Dutch priest of Leeuwarden, Friesland, and therefore suffered from the bar sinister. This fact did not prevent their receiving a thorough education. Obbe was trained in medicine and Dirk in theology. There is some uncertainty about the place of Dirk's education. It is probable that he was reared in the Franciscan monastery near Leeuwarden. In any event, he received a

---

13. See Philips, *Confession,* in Williams and Mergal, *Spiritual and Anabaptist Writers,* p. 217 for an English translation by Christian Theodoor Lievestro; or the critical Dutch text in Cramer and Pijper, *Bibliotheca Reformatoria Neerlandica,* 7:135-36.

14. N. van der Zijpp, "Obbe Philips," ME, 4:10.

15. *Vande geestelijcke Restitution,* in Cramer and Pijper, *Bibliotheca Reformatoria Neerlandica,* 10:341.

better-than-average education and demonstrated considerable ability as a scholar. He may have even taken orders. A letter of Joachim Kukenbiter to Gerhard Herbordink states that Dirk was "out of the Franciscan rabble."[16]

What is far more certain is the extent of Dirk's educational attainments. His writings reveal a knowledge of Latin, Greek, Hebrew, and German. It is probable that he spoke Brabants, a peculiar dialect similar to French, and possibly French also. He must have been quite a linguist.

Dirk was also an influential theologian. Though he was not as influential as Menno Simons, his writings are not inferior to those of Menno. To the contrary, they are, in some respects, superior. Menno's greater influence was the result of the character of his personality and his administrative ability. Dirk was a typical Frisian by nature, somewhat cold and austere. He moved through life a somber shadow dressed in black, Calvinistic in temperament if not in theology. He wrote well but not voluminously. No Anabaptist work of the sixteenth century surpassed the influence of his *Enchiridion*.[17]

F. Pijper writes in his introduction to the critical Dutch edition published in the *Bibliotheca Reformatoria Neerlandica*, "What the *Loci Communes* of Melanchthon was for the Lutherans, the *Confession* of Beza was for the Calvinists *(Fransche)*, the *Layman's Guide (Leken wechwyser)* was for the Dutch Reformed Church, the *Enchiridion* was for the Mennonites."[18]

The *Enchiridion* was not published in one volume until near the end of Dirk Philips's life. It consists of a number of shorter monographs written during his lifetime on various doctrines of Anabaptism. "Concerning the Incarnation" sets forth essentially the same view as that of Menno. "Loving Admonition" is a discussion of the use of the ban. Another article is "Concerning the New Birth." First published in 1564, the *Enchiridion* was subsequently published in several Dutch editions and also in German, French, and English.

16. William Keeney, "Dirk Philips' Life," MQR 32 (July 1958): 172.
17. The title is *Enchiridion* Oft *Hantboecxken van de Christelijcke Leere ende Religion.*
18. Cramer and Pijper, *Bibliotheca Reformatoria Neerlandica,* 1:4.

The sections of the *Enchiridion* dealing with "Spiritual Restitution" and "The Church of God" reveal a strong ecclesiology, which helps to explain why Dirk stayed with the movement which failed to command the final loyalty of his brother. Together, the selections of the *Enchiridion* form one of the most systematic presentations of Anabaptist theology of the sixteenth century. These works also reveal Dirk's rather thorough knowledge of the writings of the Fathers and his apparent independence of Luther.

It is entirely possible that Dirk was more influential in death than in life. During his lifetime he was overshadowed by Menno Simons. Certainly Dirk's inferior in learning, Menno possessed leadership ability that the younger Philips brother could not command. Together they made an effective team which all kinds of adversities could not shatter. Doubtless the work of one would have been incomplete without the balance and strength of the other.

Menno Simons

It was not by accident that the Dutch Anabaptists became known as Mennonites. There is no greater name among Anabaptists of the sixteenth century than that of Menno Simons. In fact his influence was such that the history of the Anabaptist movement in the Lowlands could well be divided into three periods: before Menno, with Menno, and after Menno. His accession to Anabaptist ranks signaled the beginning of a new era in the history of Dutch Anabaptism. The former parish priest of Witmarsum could not remain in seclusion for long. The call had come through the Brethren, but there was no mistaking its origin. It was from God, and Menno answered.[19]

Menno had begun his service in the Roman Church inauspiciously enough. He was ordained a priest at Utrecht in 1524, his twenty-eighth year. He came from Frisian peasant stock, and his education was limited to the formal training for the priesthood of his day.[20] The Bible was

---

19. Simons, *Reply to Gellius Faber*, in *Complete Writings*, pp. 671-72.

20. Cornelius Krahn, "The Conversion of Menno Simons, a Quadricentennial Tribute," MQR 10 (January 1936): 46.

an unknown book to him and was to remain so for two or three years. Finally in desperation he dared to search its pages for an answer to his questions over the doctrine of transubstantiation. Thus began a pilgrimage which was eventually to lead the young man out of the Roman fold and subsequently to the Anabaptists.

In his *Reply to Gellius Faber,* Menno wrote of these early doubts in characteristically forthright manner.

> My reader, I write you the truth in Christ and lie not. In the year 1524, being then in my twenty-eighth year, I undertook the duties of a priest in my father's village, called Pingjum, in Friesland. Two other persons of about my age, also officiated in the same station. The one was my pastor, and was well learned in part; the other succeeded me; both had read the scriptures partially; but I had not touched them during my life, for I feared, if I should read them they would mislead me. Behold! such a stupid preacher was I, for nearly two years.
>
> In the first year thereafter a thought occurred to me, as often as I handled the bread and wine in the mass, that they were not the flesh and blood of the Lord. I thought that it was the suggestion of the devil, that he might lead me off from my faith. I confessed it often — sighed and prayed, yet I could not be freed from this thought.

Menno admitted that his knowledge of the Scriptures was so limited that he could not discuss biblical concepts intelligently. "I could not speak a word with them [his fellow priests] without being scoffed at, for I did not know what I was driving at, so concealed was the Word of God from my eyes."

Eventually, Menno felt compelled to resolve his doubts by turning to the Scriptures. "Finally, I got the idea to examine the New Testament diligently. I had not gone very far when I discovered that we were deceived, and my conscience, troubled on account of the aforementioned bread, was quickly relieved, even without any instructions."

The source of Menno's doubts regarding the Eucharist is not revealed. There may have been no other than that of his own thoughts on the matter. He certainly was not the first priest to doubt the alleged miracle of transubstantiation. Whether the writings of Luther had influenced him in this regard is not known. They did prove to be a source of help in the initial stages of the pilgrimage already begun.

That which Menno learned from the Scriptures, he began to use in his ministry, thereby gaining a reputation as an evangelical preacher. This was a false impression, he confessed, but it had its compensations: "Everyone sought and desired me; the world loved me and I loved the world. It was said that I preached the Word of God and was a good fellow."[21] At this stage it is doubtful that Menno was farther along the evangelical road than his renowned contemporary and fellow Dutchman, Erasmus. He described his life as empty and frivolous, full of gambling and drinking, and "diversions as, alas, is the fashion and usage of such useless people." Apparently, it had suffered not even the slightest alteration at this time.

Not realizing the full implication of his Protestant stance, Menno seems to have accepted the Scriptures as doctrinally authoritative in a strictly propositional sense. In an easygoing manner he had apparently arrived at the rather secure and respected position of an evangelical humanist. He knew much the same success as that of Zwingli at Einsiedeln and during his early Zürich years. However, Menno was shocked into a fresh examination of the Scriptures in 1531. He heard of the execution of an otherwise unknown Anabaptist in Leeuwarden. Of this experience he wrote in his *Reply to Gellius Faber:*

> Afterwards it happened, before I had ever heard of the existence of the brethren, that a God-fearing, pious hero named Sicke Snijder was beheaded at Leeuwarden for being rebaptized. It sounded very strange to me to hear of a second baptism. I examined the Scriptures diligently and pondered them earnestly, but could find no report of infant baptism.[22]

The new-found knowledge set off a whole chain of events. First, Menno discussed the problem of infant baptism with his pastor, his immediate superior in the church at Pingjum, but to no avail. The result was that "after much talk he had to admit that there was no basis for infant baptism in Scripture." Next, he turned to a study of the

21. Simons, *Reply,* in *Complete Writings,* 668.
22. *Ibid.*

Fathers, who, he related, "taught me that children are by baptism cleansed from their original sin. I compared this idea with the Scriptures and found that it did violence to the blood of Christ."

Menno's search in hope of finding some scriptural basis for infant baptism subsequently led him to the writings of Luther, of Bucer, and finally, of Bullinger. Once again his efforts to uncover a satisfactory reason for the practice of infant baptism were disappointing. He registered his disappointment with these words: "When I noticed from all these that writers varied so greatly among themselves, each following his own wisdom, then I realized that we were deceived in regard to infant baptism."

In such a state of mind Menno was transferred from Pingjum to Witmarsum, his native village, "led thither," he confessed, "by covetousness and the desire to obtain a great name." By this time he was a thoroughgoing evangelical humanist whose life was still quite unaffected by his commitment to biblical authority.

At Witmarsum he wrote, "I spoke much concerning the Word of the Lord, without spirituality or love, as all hypocrites do, and by this means I made disciples of my own kind, vain boasters and frivolous babblers, who, alas, like myself did not take these matters too seriously."[23]

Menno had not served in his native village for more than a year when some unknown Anabaptists came to Witmarsum, preaching and practicing adult baptism. Sometime later emissaries of Münster came. Menno quickly discerned that they possessed zeal without knowledge. He did what he could to stem the tide of fanaticism. "I conferred twice with one of their leaders, once in private, and once in public, but my admonitions did not help, because I myself still did that which I knew was not right."

Menno was gaining a new reputation as a defender of the faith against the Münsterites. Yet his own soul was becoming more deeply involved in an indissoluble paradox. "My soul was troubled and I reflected upon the outcome, that if I should gain the whole world and live a thousand years, and at last have to endure the wrath of God, what would I have gained?" The source of his struggle was increasingly

23. *Ibid.*, p. 669.

evident. He saw in the misled fanatics a devotion to the truth, as they understood it, that put to shame his own love of security, position, and luxury. Also, he felt an underlying sympathy for their views of the Scriptures, the church, and Christian discipleship — which only increased his suffering. It is true that he considered them misled but only in certain matters.

His agony of soul became intolerable with a tragedy at the Old Cloister. Some three hundred Anabaptists, who had sought refuge there from persecution, were put to death. Among the dead was Menno's own brother. This event more than any other intensified the inner conflict of his soul, which had been raging for at least four years. He wrote:

> After this had transpired, the blood of these people, although misled fell . . . hot on my heart. . . . I reflected upon my unclean, carnal life, also the hypocritical doctrine and idolatry which I still practiced daily in appearance of godliness, but without relish. I saw that these zealous children, although in error, willingly gave their lives and their estates for their doctrine and faith. And I was one of those who had disclosed to some of them the abominations of the papal system. But I myself . . . acknowledged abominations simply in order that I might enjoy physical comfort and escape the cross of Christ.[24]

It was in April, 1535, that the Old Cloister near Bolsward fell. Menno was to know no peace of mind or heart from that day until the day of his conversion. "Pondering these things my conscience tormented me so that I could no longer endure it," he confessed. Such thoughts drove him to throw himself on the mercy of God in Christ for forgiveness and cleansing. Then and then only was Menno converted. Until that moment his faith had been *assensus*, not *fides*. There was intellectual acceptance but no life commitment. But all of this was to change.

> My heart trembled within me. I prayed to God with sighs and tears that He would give to me, a sorrowing sinner, the gift of His

24. *Ibid.,* p. 670.

grace, create within me a clean heart, and graciously through the merits of the crimson blood of Christ forgive my unclean walk and frivolous easy life and bestow upon me wisdom, Spirit, courage, and a manly spirit so that I might preach His exalted and adorable name and holy Word in purity.[25]

The *Reply to Gellius Faber*, in which the above passage occurs, was written some eighteen years after Menno's conversion. An account of the same experience, but one which is far more revealing, occurs in his *Meditation on the Twenty-fifth Psalm*. This was written only two years after his fateful decision. The intensity of feeling had not yet subsided when he wrote:

> I, a miserable sinner, did not know my faults and shortcomings as long as Thy Spirit had not pointed them out to me. I considered myself a Christian, but when I looked upon myself, I found myself to be very worldly, fleshly and outside Thy Word. My light was darkness, my truth falsehood, my justice sin, my religion public idolatry and my life certain death.[26]

In the meditation of the eighth verse, the plaintive cry of the sinner has become the song of the redeemed. Menno had referred to the faithful prophets of the Old Testament. Their message was not received, and they were often put to death because of their fidelity. Menno then declared:

> Nor did this exhaust the springs of Thy mercy, but Thou didst send Thy beloved Son, the dearest pledge of Thy grace, who preached Thy Word, fulfilled Thy righteousness, accomplished Thy will, bore our sins, blotted them out with Thy Blood, stilled Thy wrath, conquered the devil, hell, sin, and death, and obtained grace, mercy, favor, and peace for all who truly believe on Him. . . . He sent out

---

25. *Ibid.*, p. 671.

26. This translation in the main is from p. 329 of the *Opera Sommarie* of 1646 as found in Nan Auke Brandsma, *The Transition of Menno Simons from Roman Catholicism to Anabaptism As Reflected in His Writings* (unpublished B.D. thesis, Baptist Theological Seminary, Rüschlikon-Zürich, 1955), p. 16. It is the best work on the conversion of Menno Simons this writer has seen.

His messengers preaching this peace, . . . so that they might lead me and all erring sinners into the right way. . . . Their words I love, their practices I follow. Thy dear Son, Christ Jesus, whom they preached to me, I believe. His will and way I seek.[27]

The will and way of Christ for Menno became the way of the cross. To this concept he already had alluded in the *Meditation:*

Although I resisted in former times Thy precious Word and Thy holy will with all my powers, . . . nevertheless Thy fatherly grace did not forsake me, a miserable sinner, but in love received me, . . . and taught me by the Holy Spirit until of my own choice I declared war upon the world, the flesh and the devil, . . . and willingly submitted to the heavy cross of my Lord Jesus Christ that I might inherit the promised kingdom.[28]

The deep sense of sin reflected in these passages from the *Meditation* did not come from one who had lived a life of sexual promiscuity. Menno's sensitive nature had come under the judgment of the Bible. He realized the sinfulness of the human heart in the light of the holiness of God. Specifically, Menno felt that his sins included several things. Among these were false pride, love of ease and security, an aimless existence, and a timidity that caused him to shrink from the unpleasant. Even after commitment had been made, however, the Rubicon remained to be crossed.

For nine months he attempted to preach the gospel in the old pulpit:

I began in the name of the Lord to preach publicly from the pulpit the word of true repentance, to point the people to the narrow path, and in the power of the Scripture openly to reprove all sin and wickedness, all idolatry and false worship, and to present the true worship; also the true baptism and the Lord's Supper, according to the doctrine of Christ, to the extent that I had at that time received from God the grace.

27. *Meditation on the Twenty-fifth Psalm,* in *Complete Writings,* pp. 70-71.
28. *Ibid.,* p. 69.

Finally, the sheer impossibility of Menno's course of action was thrust upon him. His timidity and cowardice were overcome. The new man in Christ Jesus contemplated the incongruity of an Anabaptist in a Roman Catholic pulpit. In a moment of decisive action he turned his back on Rome to cast his lot with a variegated movement which was everywhere spoken against: "Then I, without constraint, of a sudden, renounced all my worldly reputation, name and fame, my unchristian abominations, my masses, infant baptism, and poverty under the heavy cross of Christ."[29]

For more than eighteen years Menno had been bearing the "heavy cross of Christ" when he wrote these lines. He knew well the cost of discipleship. It may well have been that he waited nine months before identifying himself with the Brethren because he wished to count the cost before taking the cross.[30]

Immediately he sought out the Anabaptists in the area and began to admonish them, reclaiming not a few from the Münsterite errors. Longing for a time of peace and quiet in order to meditate more fully over his new relationship, Menno slipped away to eastern Friesland. Here, a year after his departure from the Roman Church, a delegation of seven or eight persons from among the biblical Anabaptists found him. Menno characterized them as

> men who sincerely abhorred not only the sect of Münster, but the cursed abominations of all other worldly sects. . . . They prayerfully requested me to make the great sufferings and need of the poor oppressed souls my concern. . . . They urged me to put to good use the talents which I, though unworthy, had received from the Lord.[31]

---

29. *Reply,* in *Complete Writings,* p. 671.

30. Krahn, *Dutch Anabaptism,* p. 52, criticizes Menno for delaying so long after reaching convictions which led him to doubt the validity of transubstantiation and infant baptism before leaving the Roman Catholic Church. This criticism is unfounded when one takes into consideration that Menno was not converted until 1535, as Brandsma, *Transition of Menno Simons,* has pointed out. Before this time, he was evangelical in head but not at heart. When one considers his relative freedom in his home village and his naturally timid and retiring nature, nine months appears to be a rather brief period in which to make such an awesome decision.

31. *Reply,* in *Complete Writings,* p. 671.

At this invitation of the Brethren, Menno confessed, "my heart was greatly troubled." The sources of his concern were analyzed with utmost frankness. "I was sensible of my limited talents, my unlearnedness, my weak nature, the timidity of my spirit, the exceedingly great wickedness, perversity, and tyranny of the world, the great and powerful sects, the subtlety of many minds, and the woefully heavy cross that would weigh on me."[32] But Menno complied. As Calvin heard the voice of God through William Farel, Menno was called to become an apostle of the Anabaptists through a handful of Frisian peasants.

When Menno was baptized into the Anabaptist fellowship is unknown. On October 24, 1536, Herman and Gerrit Jans were arrested. They were charged with having "given lodging to Mr. Menno Simons, recently parish priest at Witmarsum," who was reported to have "received the covenant of the Anabaptists."[33] By October, 1536, Menno's defection from the Roman Catholic Church and affiliation with the Anabaptists must have been well known to the authorities. Probably, he was baptized shortly after leaving Witmarsum early in 1536. A year or so later, he was ordained in Groningen. Ordination as an elder in the Anabaptist fellowship came to him by the laying on of hands by Obbe Philips. As this was done at the request of the brotherhood, Menno immediately began an active ministry among the nonresistant, biblical Anabaptists.

During the first four or five years of his ministry Menno lived and worked in Groningen and eastern Friesland. He was married to a certain Gertrude, probably in 1536. However, he maintained no one residence during these early years but traveled extensively. His lot soon became exceedingly difficult for the former priest.

The cross of persecution was an inescapable reality for Menno, and at times he chafed under its galling weight. In his *Reply to Gellius Faber* he drew the contrast between the life of the well-paid priest of the state church and that of the Anabaptist preacher.

I with my poor, weak wife and children have for eighteen years endured excessive anxiety, oppression, affliction, misery, and persecu-

32. *Ibid.*, p. 672.
33. Brandsma, *Transition of Menno Simons*, p. 36.

tion. . . . Yes, when the preachers repose on easy beds and soft pillows, we generally have to hide ourselves in out-of-the-way corners. . . . We have to be on our guard when a dog barks for fear the arresting officer has arrived. . . . In short, while they are gloriously rewarded for their services with large incomes and good times, our recompense and portion be but fire, sword, and death.[34]

That Menno's picture of the harassed life of an Anabaptist elder was not overdrawn, many witnesses abundantly testify. An edict was published in the province of Groningen on January 21, 1539, commanding all Anabaptists to get out. Menno fled to the Dutch province of Friesland, where he resumed his ministry. During a previous visit there, Menno had stayed in the home of a "very pious and God-fearing man" by the name of Tjard Reynders. Shortly afterward, on January 8, 1539, his benefactor was arrested, broken on the wheel, and executed. Plans were made in 1541 by the "counselors" of Leeuwarden to seize Menno himself. His success was so great that the authorities despaired of ever eradicating the hated Anabaptists as long as Menno was free. Pardon was offered to any Anabaptists then in confinement who would deliver Menno into their hands, but no Judas was forthcoming.

Placards spread throughout the province of Friesland brought no results. Charles V, emperor of the Holy Roman Empire, then published an edict against Menno and placed a price of a hundred gold guilders on his head. All persons were enjoined against giving Menno food or shelter. His followers were to be arrested immediately. Complete pardon for any crime committed was promised to anyone delivering the renowned heretic into the hands of the authorities.[35]

For the next two years Menno labored in and around Amsterdam with a measure of success. Executions as usual followed the baptisms, but Menno remained free. What is even more amazing, he found time to write. Three books came from his pen during the initial period of his ministry in north Holland. They were: *Christian Baptism*, 1539, *Foundation of Christian Doctrine*, 1540, and the *True Christian Faith*, 1541.

34. *Complete Writings*, p. 674.
35. The writer is largely dependent on Harold Bender, *Menno Simons* (Scottdale, Pa.: Herald Press, 1956), for pertinent facts of Simons's life. See also Cornelius Krahn, *Menno Simons* (Newton, Kans.: Faith and Life Press, 1982).

Menno's work in Amsterdam was a brief interlude between the ministry in north Holland and the beginning of work in north Germany. Late in 1543 he left Holland for the more tolerant climate of north Germany. Here, he would devote eighteen years, the rest of his life. About two years were spent in the bishopric of Cologne. The remainder of the time allotted to him, from 1546 to 1561, he labored in Holstein and the Baltic seacoast region.

After moving to north Germany, Menno's attention for several years was given to internal problems of Anabaptism in the area. By this time he had emerged as the chief exponent of the movement. Almost from the outset of his work as an Anabaptist, he was recognized as a foremost leader. Having distinguished himself as an enemy of the Münsterites before leaving the Church of Rome, he could not go unnoticed by either his enemies or his friends.

His position of leadership became more firmly established with the apostasy of Obbe Philips in 1540. It was further enhanced by the publication of his most popular work, *Foundation of Christian Doctrine*, which came from the press in the same year. It was widely distributed in the northern coastal regions of Holland and Germany, in whose dialect it first appeared. Subsequently, it was published in revised form in 1554, in Dutch in 1558, in German in 1575, and in many English editions. The *Foundation* had a twofold purpose: to clear the Anabaptists of Münster connotations and to state clearly for the brotherhood the doctrines of the Scriptures.

Typical of Menno's writings, the *Foundation* is a simple and forthright presentation of Anabaptist faith and practice as he held it. Somewhat repetitious and unsystematic, it abounds in scriptural concepts and references. Its homespun logic was backed by the exemplary and sacrificial life of its author. The book exerted a greater influence over the common people than that of the ancient Church Fathers and the scholastics combined. The *Foundation* revealed Menno's wide knowledge of the Bible and familiarity with the writings of the early Church Fathers and Eusebius, bishop of Caesarea. Timely and effective, it admirably fulfilled the purpose for which it was written.

It is not surprising, in view of Menno's rising influence among the north German and Dutch Anabaptists, to discover that the biblical Anabaptists came to be called Mennonites (Menists). In 1544 the term occurred in a letter of John à Lasco, a Reformed Minister, to Countess Anna. He asked for a more lenient policy toward the Mennonite party, which he distinguished from other groups, such as the Batenburgers and Davidians. These were generally lumped indiscriminately together with the followers of Menno Simons.

The Batenburgers, followers of one Jan van Batenburg, continued to advocate the disastrous doctrines of the Münsterites. However, this remnant of the Münster kingdom was a declining menace. Of far greater danger to the Mennonites was the movement of David Joris. At one time a Münsterite also, Joris was disowned in 1536 by the biblical Anabaptists. An extreme inspirationist, he claimed that the Scriptures were inadequate and, therefore, destined to be supplemented by his own inspired writings. A master of duplicity, he disappeared from history under the alias of John of Bruges in Basel, where he died an honored citizen.

Menno was successful in leading the Mennonites through the treacherous shoals of the Batenburgers and Davidians with the help of his fellow elder, Dirk Philips. After this, he was forced to face the problem of doctrinal dissension from within the ranks of the Brethren. Upon this occasion the issue was the deity of Christ, and the champion of the new view was one ordained by Menno and Dirk in 1542, Adam Pastor. Pastor taught that Christ did not exist before the incarnation and was to be considered divine only in the sense that God dwelled in him. Two meetings were held by the elders of the Dutch and north German Anabaptists in 1547 to deal with the problem — the first in Emden and the second in Goch. At the first meeting hope was expressed that Pastor could be saved from his heresy, but by the time of the second meeting all hope was given up. The erring elder was banned.

Menno was never quite able to shake off the memory of that unpleasant experience. Like himself, Pastor had been a priest before he became an Anabaptist and in other respects he was apparently a true Anabaptist. He believed the Scriptures to be authoritative in matters of faith and practice. Rationalism led him to doubt the deity of Christ, while maintaining that Christ was the only mediator between God and man. However, Menno felt that the threat to the faith was so grave that he wrote a small book to counteract Pastor's influence, *Confession of the Triune God*. Menno, like all biblical Anabaptists, was thoroughly trinitarian. Therefore, he considered an attack on the deity of Christ as an effort to crack the very foundation of the Christian faith.

Menno's own view of the incarnation, however, became a source of controversy among the Anabaptists. It was never accepted by the Swiss Brethren.[36] His view was similar to that of Hofmann. The crux of the problem to him was the origin of Christ's physical nature. He held that it was a new creation of the Holy Spirit within the body of Mary. Menno's position differed from the historic view in denying that Christ received his human body from Mary. He replaced the orthodox view, *"per Spiritum Sanctum ex Maria virginenatus,"* with *"per Spiritum Sanctum in Maria virgine conceptus, factus et natus."*

The thrust of his argument was that God was the author of life and not man. Christ, therefore, received his life, both human and divine, from God. Menno's adversaries never tired of accusing him of heresy on this point. He was forced to discuss the doctrine of the incarnation against his will and to give a disproportionate amount of time to defending his unique view. Contrary to much that has been written, however, Menno never denied the full humanity of Christ. Nor did he attempt to divide the human and the divine in Christ. He recognized that the incarnation involved a certain degree of mystery which defied rational analysis. He wanted to obviate the possibility that Christ inherited a sinful nature without deifying the virgin Mary.[37]

Even some of Menno's adversaries felt that his doctrine of the "celestial flesh" of Christ was the most satisfactory explanation of a difficult concept. Musculus, a Zwinglian of great influence, was accused of adhering to this position by Micron. Micron was well acquainted with Menno's view of the incarnation, for he had debated with him on the subject in Wismar during the winter of 1554.

36. See John Horsch, *Menno Simons* (Scottdale, Pa.: Mennonite Publishing House, 1916), pp. 194-203, 146-52, and Brandsma, *Transition of Menno Simons,* p. 37.

37. Is this not what Pius IX attempted to do in postulating the dogma of the immaculate conception of Mary? It is likely that the pope was not so much worried about the sinlessness of Christ as he was concerned with that of Mary. At least Menno's view never led anyone to deify Mary as "the Mother of the Eternal Father" as Louis de Montfort and others have done in this enlightened age.

The Wismar disputation was one of many theological discussions in which Menno constantly found himself engaged. Such meetings had to be held in the utmost secrecy under the ominous threat of great danger to the participants. In spite of these facts, Menno and his followers must have felt that the value of the meetings far outweighed the risk involved. Even though apparently few converts were made through this procedure, the discussions undoubtedly helped to clarify the position of the Brethren. They also spread Mennonite views through an evangelical underground. At times Menno is reported to have visited with priests and monks in their churches and monasteries for the purpose of winning them to his cause through theological dialogue.

Not long after the disputation with Micron, Menno was again involved in a theological discussion at Wismar. However, upon this occasion the circumstances were vastly different from those of the preceding winter. This time the subject was the ban and its use among the Brethren, and the conferees were seven elders from the Mennonite churches of north Germany and Holland. Among the participants were Dirk Philips, Leenaert Bouwens, and Gillis of Aachen. Following the lead of Menno, the conference adopted nine resolutions reflecting a rather strict position in the use of the ban. Henceforth the ban was to be an increasingly pestiferous problem, recurring with annoying frequency until Menno's death. Subsequently it was to lead to serious division among the Dutch Mennonites.

Evidently the disputations at Wismar had alerted the authorities to the growing strength and influence of the Mennonites. Before the summer of 1554 had come to a close, Menno was forced to move again. This time he established his residence near Hamburg at Oldesloe, only to move after a brief period to Wustenfelde, a village on the estate of Fresenburg. Since 1543 the baron of Fresenburg, Bartholomew von Ahlefeldt, had permitted Mennonites to live on his property and under his protection. As a youth he had been greatly affected by the Christian character of Anabaptist martyrs. He had witnessed their executions in Holland as an officer in the army. The baron possessed a reputation for harshness which stood the Mennonites in good stead, for few dared to cross him, even in pursuit of Mennonites.

Even though Menno's last years were spent in comparative safety, they were far from peaceful. His strict position on shunning an excommunicated church member soon became divisive. He found himself caught between two fires. Leenaert Bouwens and Dirk Philips took an extreme position. They demanded that shunning be practiced between married partners to the extent of denying the excommunicated member "bed and board." After oscillating between this position and a somewhat more moderate one, Menno finally came out on the side of the milder position. From the beginning the Swiss and south German Anabaptists were dissatisfied with the Dutch position on shunning. Meeting in Strasbourg in 1557, they rejected the practice of shunning married partners and petitioned the Mennonites to reconsider their position.

This criticism of the strict position caused Menno to defend it. Once again he stood with his "dear brethren," Dirk Philips and Leenaert Bouwens, against the more liberal view of their critics.[39] However, the apparent sternness of Menno's position was mitigated by the transparent sincerity and love with which he wrote. His was not the vindictive act of a bitter old man but fidelity to his understanding of the scriptural injunctions to keep the church holy. Writing less than three years before his death, Menno in his *Instruction of Excommunication* expressed two fears: first, that he might be misunderstood; and second, that the ban might be improperly applied.[40]

The divisions and bitterness concerning his teaching on the ban continued to trouble Menno to the day of his death. In his sixty-sixth year he laid down his Bible and pen. After a brief illness he took a turn for the worse on the exact day of the twenty-fifth anniversary of his renunciation of Catholicism. He died the next day, January 31, 1561. Death came in his own home, and he was buried in his own garden.

Humble and self-effacing to the end, Menno's greatest contribution to the Anabaptist movement was his character. As Bender suggests, this, coupled with two other factors, his writings and his message, does much to explain Menno's greatness. However, there remains an intangible element without which an explanation of his influence is incomplete. This may best be termed the providence of God.

38. Horsch, *Simons,* p. 217.
39. *Final Instruction on Marital Avoidance,* in *Complete Writings,* pp. 1060ff.
40. *Complete Writings,* p. 965.

The Waterlanders

After Menno's death the mantle of leadership fell upon his lifelong fellow elder and friend, Dirk Philips. During the next seven years Dirk continued to lead the majority of Dutch Mennonites through an increasingly turbulent atmosphere. But Dirk lacked the ability to hold divisive factions together. He was harsh in exercising discipline, particularly in the case of Leenaert Bouwens. He deposed Bouwens and six other elders in 1565, greatly accentuating a fragmentation of the movement that was already in progress.

Dirk died in 1568. Upon his death Leenaert Bouwens returned to the active ministry among the Frisians. Bouwens still proved himself an effective evangelist. Between 1568, the year of his restoration, and 1582, the year of his death, he baptized some 3,509 converts. A total of 10,252 baptisms were performed during his entire ministry.[41] It is questionable that any other Anabaptist minister excelled Bouwens's effectiveness as an evangelist. The strength of the north German and Dutch Mennonite movement probably was due as much to the work of Leenaert Bouwens as to that of any other man.

It is significant that a schism destined to leaven the whole Mennonite movement began in north Holland. The extreme position on the ban, so ardently advocated by Dirk Philips and Leenaert Bouwens, had produced much strife and unrest among the congregations of the area. The liberal schismatics, who had separated themselves from the more extreme brethren in 1555, became known as Waterlanders. The designation was a natural one, being derived from a region in north Holland where Mennonites had been numerous since 1534. The Waterlanders rejected the Mennonite name, since they felt it inappropriate to be called by a man's name. They preferred to be known simply as *Doopsgezinden* (Baptizers).

A relatively liberal spirit existed from the beginning among the *Doopsgezinden*. Therefore, it is not surprising that a number of innovations were soon introduced among their congregations. In 1568 a conference, the first of its kind among the Dutch Mennonites, convened at Emden for the consideration of matters of mutual concern. It set a

41. Karel Vos, "Leenaert Bouwens," ME, 3:305.

precedent for subsequent conferences and inaugurated a type of connectionalism that was to develop in the subsequent history of Dutch Anabaptism. Under the leadership of Hans de Ries, the most able early leader of the *Doopsgezinden,* public prayers gradually replaced silent prayers. The practice of observing the Lord's Supper around a table was also introduced.[42]

In 1568 the *Doopsgezinden* sent the Prince of Orange a considerable sum to help in the war then in progress between the Netherlands and the Spanish. The Waterlanders became the first of the Dutch Mennonites to draw up a confession of faith. The confession of 1577 was the work of Jacob Scheedemaker, Hans de Ries, and a few other ministers. This act set a precedent which was followed by de Ries in 1611. At that time, John Smyth and his congregation of English Separatists sought to unite with the Amsterdam congregation of the Waterlanders.

All in all, the Waterlanders brought a much-needed and refreshing emphasis to sixteenth-century Dutch Anabaptism. However, their liberalizing tendencies later carried them and the Dutch Mennonites, for good or ill, beyond the theological insights of the biblical Anabaptists of the sixteenth century.

42. Van der Zijpp, "Hans de Ries," ME, 4:330.

VIII

ᶿᴿ   ᶿᴿ

Anabaptism and Reformation Theology

NABAPTIST THEOLOGY OF THE SIXTEENTH CENTURY CAN BE viewed either within the context of the Reformation or as a separate movement. Too often the latter approach has been taken to the detriment of a historically valid account of its doctrinal development. Since Anabaptism originated in Switzerland, from within and in tension with the Swiss Reformation, it must first be considered as a Reformation phenomenon. Only then can the contrast between the Magisterial Reformation and the Anabaptist movement be clearly drawn.

Research in sixteenth-century Anabaptist materials presents difficulties not encountered in a similar study of Lutheranism or Calvinism. For example, in attempting to unravel Lutheran theology of the Reformation era, one is concerned primarily with the theology of Luther and to some extent with that of Melanchthon. In addition, the authoritative creeds of Lutheranism limit the scope of inquiry somewhat. On the other hand, the Anabaptists produced no one theologian whose system won the unanimous approval of Anabaptists generally. As a rule, Anabaptist theologians did not live very long, nor did they erect elaborate speculative systems of theology. The primacy of the Scriptures in Anabaptist life discouraged the formulation of creeds that would tend to take precedence over the Bible. Anabaptist confessions of faith

177

were also rare and without binding quality. They were nothing more than the term implies, confessions of individuals or small groups of the Brethren.

Typical of the spirit motivating the early confessions is the following sentence taken from the introductory section of a confession of 1528: "When, however, a brother or sister is able to produce a better *Ordnung* it shall be accepted from him at any time (I Corinthians 14)."[1] However, the early confessions, sermons, hymns, and other literary expressions of faith form an extensive body of material. The twentieth-century student is able to draw from them a picture of sixteenth-century Anabaptist theology. An effort has been made in this section to let the Anabaptists speak for themselves. While not ignoring the lesser known among the Brethren, we have given major attention to the more influential writers.

Heretics?

The charge of heresy has been brought against the Anabaptists repeatedly and is fully justified in the eyes of many. Such a charge is not difficult to substantiate, for the term is a relative one. However, if one means by heresy a denial of basic Christian doctrines, the Anabaptists have been falsely labeled. They accepted the teaching of the Apostles' Creed, the trinitarian concept of God, the incarnation, the atoning work of Christ, and the authority of the Scriptures. They may have been heretics in the eyes of some of their contemporaries but certainly were not in regard to the major tenets of the Christian faith.

It is true that their two oldest group confessions contain no articles pertaining to these concepts. In fact, the first article in the Schleitheim Confession of 1527 deals with the place of baptism in the Christian life.[2] Likewise, the second oldest "confession" of the Anabaptists, "The Discipline of the Church, How a Christian Ought to Live," bypasses

1. Friedmann, "The Oldest Church Discipline of the Anabaptists," MQR 29 (April 1955): 164.
2. Wenger, "The Schleitheim Confession of Faith," MQR 19 (October 1945): 248.

a discussion of the more theological concepts. It presents practical aspects of the Christian life.[3]

The silence of these oldest documents of the Anabaptists on such vital themes can be interpreted in different ways. Such an omission could indicate a lack of interest in doctrine per se. It might indicate that the emphasis of the movement was on the Christian life and related matters, such as discipleship and the relation of the Christian to the church. More likely, the failure of the Brethren to deal with theological topics in the early documents is due to basic agreement with the Reformers. Introductory sections to both of the early confessions tend to verify this inference. Further evidence comes from the early writings of Grebel and other Swiss Brethren.

"The Brotherly Union of a Number of Children of God Concerning Seven Articles" (Schleitheim Confession) opens with a reference to the Trinity. "May joy, peace and mercy from our Father through the atonement of the blood of Christ Jesus, together with the gifts of the Spirit — Who is sent from the Father to all believers for their strength and comfort and for their perseverance in all tribulation until the end, Amen."[4] The introduction of this confession also expressly states that the articles were agreed upon as a means of resolving certain difficulties which had arisen among the Brethren. Obviously, the problems did not involve the more distinctly theological issues. If the articles were concerned with Hans Denck's supposed antitrinitarianism, much more attention would have undoubtedly been given to a discussion of Christology.

What has been said about the Schleitheim Confession can also be said about the Church Discipline of the Tyrol Brethren. A passing reference is made to "almighty God" and "His eternal and all-powerful Word," but there is no discussion of these terms or of their meaning. The burden of the *Ordnung* (Discipline) is a more orderly life of the brotherhood.

In the letter of Conrad Grebel and his compatriots of September 5, 1524, to Thomas Müntzer, the trinitarian concept is clearly discernible. The doctrine of the Trinity and other basic theological issues were

3. Friedmann, "Oldest Discipline," pp. 162-66.
4. Wenger, "Schleitheim Confession," p. 247.

not at stake. This is true of the crisis between the Brethren and Zwingli and of the discussion between the inquisitive Swiss and the revolutionary Müntzer.[5]

The apparent affinity of the Anabaptist movement for the more basic doctrines of the Reformation is not difficult to explain. Early Anabaptist leadership was dependent on the Reformers. Grebel and Manz were intimately related to Zwingli during the initial stages of the Reformation in Zürich. As Bender has clearly shown, Grebel's dependence on Zwingli for three years is unquestionable.[6] It was due to the influence of the Lutheran Reformation that Hubmaier, Marpeck, Sattler, and to a lesser degree Menno Simons, all owed their conversions. All the more amazing in the light of such indebtedness, these men dared to blaze new trails beyond the well-trodden paths of the esteemed Reformers.

The Use of the Creeds

The use of the historic creeds of Christendom indicates that the Brethren considered themselves in the main stream of the Christian faith. While imprisoned in Zürich, Hubmaier penned the Twelve Articles of Christian Belief, using as his guide the Apostles' Creed with the controversial *filioque* clause of Western usage.[7] In the *Künstbuch* of the Pilgram Marpeck circle the Athanasian Creed is reproduced.[8] Peter Riedemann began his *Confession of Faith* with the Apostles' Creed, which he used as the outline for a major section of the work.[9]

The Dutch Anabaptists seemed less inclined to use the Apostles'

---

5. "Konrad Grebel und Genossen an Thomas Müntzer," *Quellen*, pp. 13-21. The role of Thomas Müntzer in the emergence of Anabaptism is still subject to debate. Müntzer literature continues to grow. For the student who wishes a brief overview, Hans Joachim Hillerbrand's "The Impatient Revolutionary" in his *A Fellowship of Discontent* (New York: Harper & Row, 1967) will meet the need admirably. For Müntzer's own writings one must turn to Günther Franz, *Thomas Müntzer Schriften und Briefe* (Gütersloh: Verlagshaus Gerd Mohn, 1968).

6. Bender, *Grebel*, pp. 76-88.

7. Vedder, *Hübmaier*, p. 134.

8. Klassen, *Pilgram Marpeck*, pp. 212-13.

9. Riedemann, *Account*, pp. 15-45.

Creed outright than the Swiss and southern German *Täufer*. Nevertheless, their witness shows a basic agreement with its theology, and at times the wording of their confessions is identical with that of the popular creed. Dirk Philips in his *Confession* of 1544 *(Bekenntniss Unseres Glaubens)*, which is placed first in his *Enchiridion*, is clearly dependent on the Apostles' Creed for the sequence and content of thought.[10] The Dutch martyr, Jaques d'Auchy, began his Confession *(Bekenntenisse des Gheloofs)* of 1559 with statements which are very close to, and at times identical with, the Apostles' Creed.[11] The nearest approach that Menno Simons makes to the Apostles' Creed is in his *Confession of the Triune God*. However, even here there is not much resemblance to any historic creed. The concept of the Trinity is clearly enunciated, but at this point the similarity ends.[12]

Could it be that Menno feared that even a reference to the Apostles' Creed might be misleading? The foundation of his theology was the Bible interpreted through Christ. Repeatedly he used the phrase, "For other foundation can no man lay than that is laid, which is Jesus Christ" (1 Cor. 3:11). Upon one occasion Menno wrote that if Tertullian, Cyprian, Origen, and Augustine could support their teaching "with the Word and command of God, we will admit that they are right. If not, then it is a doctrine of men and accursed according to the Scriptures (Galatians 1:8)."[13]

In a similar vein Menno reminded his readers, "Put your trust in Christ alone and in His Word, and in the sure ministration and practice of His holy apostles, and by the grace of God you will be safe from all false doctrine and the power of the devil, and will walk with a free and pious mind before God."[14] Menno evidently made a studious attempt to avoid any phraseology even slightly resembling a creed. He feared that a creed might take precedence over the Bible or become in time a test of faith among the Brethren. However, this does not mean that

10. Dietrich Philips, *Enchiridion oder handbuchlien von der Christlichen Lehre und Religion* (New-Berlin: Christian Moser, 1851), pp. 1-7.

11. Van der Zijpp, "Apostles' Creed," ME, 1:137.

12. *A Solemn Confession of the Triune, Eternal, and True God, Father, Son, and Holy Ghost*, in *Complete Writings*, pp. 489-98.

13. *Reply*, in *Complete Writings*, p. 695.

14. *Foundation*, in *ibid.*, p. 138.

his theology was not in basic agreement with that of the ecumenical creeds.

With the exception of Hubmaier, there is little evidence that the Anabaptists made liturgical use of the historic creeds. It is certain that they never considered the creeds binding. The creeds were never used as a test of faith among the Brethren. However, it does seem fair to infer that use of the Apostles' Creed suggests that they felt themselves in substantial agreement with its theology.

The Trinitarian Concept

Far more important than any possible use of the Apostles' Creed is the unanimous acceptance of a trinitarian concept of God by the biblical Anabaptists. From Conrad Grebel to Menno Simons there is an abundance of evidence which suggests that the Anabaptists found the Triune God an inescapable reality.

Very few of Grebel's limited writings are extant. In those which are still available there is no discussion of the nature of God. In the postscript of the letter to Thomas Müntzer there is a reference to the trinitarian formula in a simulated apostolic benediction. "God, our Captain, with his Son Jesus Christ, our Saviour, and with his spirit and word be with thee and us all."[15] There is no reason to believe that Grebel and the Zürich Brethren held any different concepts of the Trinity from those of Zwingli.

In the trial of Michael Sattler at Rottenburg in 1527, the doctrine of God was not an issue. However, his tormentors made light of the Holy Spirit and evidently completely misunderstood the Anabaptist position in this regard. In answering the fifth charge concerning blasphemy against the Virgin Mary, Sattler carefully denied that Mary is a mediatrix or advocatess.[16] His prison epistle from the tower of Binsdoff opens with a trinitarian benediction. Clearly, he and the Anabaptists were trinitarians and alert to the damage which medieval Mariolatry had done to the biblical view of God.

Balthasar Hubmaier, the first Anabaptist theologian of any con-

15. Williams and Mergal, *Spiritual and Anabaptist Writers,* p. 85.
16. *Ibid.,* p. 140.

sequence, was thoroughly trinitarian. One of his earliest Reformation tracts begins not with a formal declaration of faith in the Trinity but with an indirect reference to the Holy Spirit. In redefining the term "heretic," Hubmaier writes:

> Heretics are those who deceitfully undermine the Holy Scriptures, the first of whom was the Devil, when he spoke to Eve. You shall not surely die. Gen. 3, together with his disciples. . . .
>
> The same are also heretics who conceal the Scriptures and interpret them other than the Holy Spirit demands, . . .

Here as elsewhere in Anabaptist works, the Holy Spirit is directly related to the interpretation of the Scriptures. There follow numerous references to God the Father and to Jesus Christ the Son. In a rather pretentious challenge to his old teacher, Dr. John Eck, Hubmaier wrote: "In this conflict, every one must teach equipped with the armour of the Holy Spirit."[17]

In the Twelve Articles of Christian Belief of 1526, there is a more extended and systematic statement of the trinitarian concept according to the pattern of the Apostles' Creed. These articles are for the most part simple, nonspeculative statements of biblical truth.

> 1. I believe in God, Father Almighty, maker of heaven and earth, as my most precious Lord and most merciful Father, who for my sake hast created heaven and earth . . . and hast made me as thy loved child. . . . Though I confess that we men, by the disobedience of Adam, lost this sonship rich in grace, . . . nevertheless in thee as my most gracious Father I set all my . . . trust, and know surely and certainly that this fall will not be to me injurious or bring condemnation.
>
> 2. I believe also in Jesus Christ, thine only begotten Son, our Lord, that he for my sake has expiated (atoned) before thee for this fall. . . . I hope and trust him wholly that he will not let his saving and comforting name Jesus (for I believe he is Christ, true God and man) be lost on me, a miserable sinner, but that he will redeem me from all my sins.

17. Vedder, *Hübmaier*, pp. 84, 91. Pipkin and Yoder translate the term *"versonet hab"* as "has atoned" (p. 235). Compare Pipkin and Yoder, pp. 235-40, with *Schriften*, pp. 216-20.

3. I believe and confess, my Lord Jesus Christ, that thou wast conceived by the Holy Spirit, without any human seed, born from Mary, the pure and ever chaste virgin, that thou mightest bring again to me and all believing men, and mightest obtain from thy Heavenly Father the grace of the Holy Spirit, which was withdrawn from me by reason of my sin. . . . For thou, Son of the living God, didst become man, in order that through thee we might become children of God.

4. I believe and confess also that thou didst suffer under Pontius Pilate, wast crucified, dead and buried, and all that because of my sins, in order that thou mightest redeem and ransom . . . by the pouring out of thy rose-red blood, in which thy greatest and highest love to us poor men is recognized. . . . Therefore I will praise and thank thee, my gracious Lord Jesus Christ, for ever and ever. . . .

8. I believe also in the Holy Spirit, who proceedeth from the Father and the Son, and yet with them is the only and true God, who sanctifieth all things, and without him is nothing holy, in whom I set all my trust that he will teach me all truth, increase my faith and kindle the fire of love in my heart by his holy inspiration. . . . For that I pray thee from the heart, my God, my Lord, my Comforter.[18]

The question arises, did Hubmaier forsake at Nikolsburg the trinitarian concepts which so definitely characterized his early ministry? It has been claimed that he did, upon the assumption that he was the author of the so-called Nikolsburg Theses. However, the German Baptist scholar Wilhelm Wiswedel has demonstrated convincingly what had long been suspected: that Hubmaier had nothing to do with the document in question.[19]

Even though there is a paucity of references to the Holy Spirit in the writings of Hubmaier when compared with the references to God the Father, and Christ the Son, and the Word of God, there is no basis upon which to accuse Hubmaier of antitrinitarianism. Pilgram Marpeck and Peter Riedemann follow him in this trinitarian emphasis.

18. *Ibid.*, pp. 130-36.

19. See Wilbur, *History of Unitarianism*, p. 32; Friedmann, "The Encounter of Anabaptists and Mennonites with Anti-Trinitarianism," MQR 22 (July 1948): 145. Friedmann believes the Nikolsburg Theses to be a fraudulent work from the pen of Urbanus Rhegius.

Pilgram Marpeck is unequivocally trinitarian in his concept of God. However, he put much more emphasis on the person and work of the Holy Spirit than Hubmaier did. For Marpeck, as for Hubmaier, God is spatially located and comes to us through the Holy Spirit. Wenger spells out Marpeck's view of the Spirit most carefully.

> He [the Holy Spirit] is the One who applies redemption to the individual soul, accomplishing the new birth. In the Holy Spirit we have forgiveness of sins. He is active in the Christian's conscience, purifying the heart. He strengthens God's people. He is the Comforter. He is "the One who guides into all truth." (This is perhaps Marpeck's favorite expression.) He is the Spirit of love and patience. He personally dwells in the believer.

The Dutch Baptist scholar Kiwiet agrees with Wenger that Marpeck is thoroughly biblical in his doctrine of God. Innumerable passages in the writings of Marpeck can be cited to support this assertion. Marpeck insisted on baptism in the name of the Father, the Son, and the Holy Spirit. He declared that where there is genuine faith in Christ, there dwell God, Christ, and the Holy Spirit. Marpeck and his *Kreis* (circle) quoted Schwenckfeld approvingly on the Trinity. From this writing Wenger has translated the following excerpt.

> We believe that there is one God and one divine Essence, but in the same divine Essence three independent (separate) Persons, the Father, the Son and the Holy Spirit; that all three are one God and that each Person possesses in Himself, undivided, the fullness of the divine Essence, which is also common to all three. It is our Christian faith that there are not three Gods, but only one God in three Persons and that each Holy Person in the Godhead, the Son as well as the Father, and the Holy Spirit as well as the Son, is God in Essence, of like power, might, honor, glory and splendor.[20]

---

20. Wenger, "Theology of Marpeck," p. 214; cf. Kiwiet, *Marbeck,* p. 13. See also William Klassen, *Covenant and Community* (Grand Rapids: William B. Eerdmans Publishing Company, 1968), for a relatively recent study of Marpeck's theology with special attention given to his hermeneutics. He takes issue with Kiwiet at several points.

What has been said of Marpeck can be said with even more force of Riedemann. Many pages are given to a discussion of God the Father, Christ the Son, and the Holy Spirit in his *Confession* of 1565. In this work the divine attributes of love and grace which the Anabaptists emphasized so effectively find full expression. Here again the exposition of the doctrine of God is without speculative overtones or metaphysical profundity. The Scriptures are used to such a great extent that it is difficult to extract Riedemann from the Bible or at times to distinguish one from the other.

In discussing the incarnation, Riedemann was careful to make clear the manner by which Christ became flesh. He sought to obviate any question about the genuineness of the incarnation. "For through the mingling and coming together of the Holy Spirit with Mary's faith the Word was conceived and became man. He brought not his human nature with him from heaven, but received and took it from Mary."

In the next paragraph Riedemann emphasizes both the virgin purity of Mary and the humanity of the incarnate Christ.

> Thus we confess that Mary conceived and bore this her fruit, without loss of her virginity; that during and after his birth she was as much a virgin as she was before, completely untouched; and she, we confess, bore the Saviour of the World, the comfort and hope of all believers and the glory of God the Father; nor was he someone invented and imaginary, but a true and real man, who in all things (sin only excepted) was tempted and tested, proving himself thereby to be really man.[21]

Riedemann's *Confession* is not, strictly speaking, a work in the field of systematic theology. By its acceptance among the Hutterites, however, it represents the thinking of a large segment of sixteenth-century Anabaptism on basic doctrines. One thing is quite clear; on the Trinity there is no deviation from orthodox Christianity.

Menno Simons held to the trinitarian concepts of other biblical Anabaptists but approached the incarnation from quite a different viewpoint. In Hubmaier and Menno we have the two opposite extremes in this regard. Hubmaier upon occasion was not averse to referring to

21. Riedemann, *Account,* pp. 27-28.

the Virgin Mary as the mother of God. Evidently, he held to the concept of Mary's perpetual virginity.[22] This concept and its implications Menno wished to avoid at all costs. Consequently, he developed from Hofmannite materials a well-defined doctrine of the incarnation that continued to prejudice the Mennonite cause into the seventeenth century.

Menno's doctrine of the incarnation has long been debated. He has been accused of Unitarianism and also of Docetism. These accusations reflect misunderstanding of Menno's teaching and perhaps misuse of the terms in question.

Menno repeatedly affirmed his faith in the Trinity. Typical of such affirmations is that found in *A Solemn Confession of the Triune, Eternal, and True God, Father, Son, and Holy Ghost.*

> God, we believe and confess with the Scriptures to be the eternal, incomprehensible Father with His eternal, incomprehensible Son, and with His eternal, incomprehensible Holy Spirit; not physical and comprehensible but spiritual and incomprehensible. For Christ says, God is a Spirit. Inasmuch as God is such a Spirit, as it is written, therefore we also believe and confess the eternal, begetting heavenly Father and the eternally begotten Son, Christ Jesus. Brethren, understand my writing well, that they are spiritual and incomprehensible, as is also the Father who begat; for like begets like. This is incontrovertible.[23]

In the rather high Christology revealed in this passage can be detected two considerations which undergird Menno's doctrine of the incarnation. As Oosterbaan has pointed out, these two considerations are derived from a single basic concept:

> Jesus Christ is an inseparable unity. This meant in the first place that the eternal Word or the eternal Son of God, who according to

---

22. Vedder, *Hübmaier,* p. 231. Even though Hubmaier's last *Rechenschaft* was made under duress and cannot be considered normative, it is interesting to note that in this work there are two articles pertaining to Mary in which Hubmaier asserts that she "is, and always was, pure and unspotted," and "Mary is the mother of God."

23. *Complete Writings,* p. 491.

the prologue of John's Gospel was with God in the beginning and who created all things, was also the Jesus Christ who became flesh (John 1:14). The Christ of creation is the same as the Christ of the atonement.

The inseparable unity of the preincarnate Christ with the incarnate Christ led Menno, as Oosterbaan observes, to regard as biblical truth an unusual view of the manner in which the Word became flesh. "The Word did not take on flesh but himself *became* flesh. Jesus did not receive His body from Mary; He himself became a body which was received by Mary in faith and through the Holy Spirit, that she might nourish Him and bring Him into the world according to the way of nature."[24] For Menno there was no conflict between this view of Christ's conception and his full humanity.

After speaking of the preincarnate Christ, Menno affirms that he

did in the fullness of time become, according to the unchangeable purpose and faithful promise of the Father, a true visible, suffering, hungry, thirsty, and mortal man in Mary, the pure virgin, through the operation and overshadowing of the Holy Spirit, and so was born of her. We confess that He was like us in all things, sin excepted; that He grew up as do other men; that at the appointed time He was baptized and entered upon His preaching task, and office of grace and love.[25]

Nowhere did Menno deny the reality of the incarnation. He simply attempted, guided by biblical concepts, to solve unresolved problems created by the traditional view. The orthodox position has always had difficulty with the relation of Mary to the Holy Spirit. Was this a celestial marriage? Also, the Augustinian concept of original sin and the inescapable Adamic nature of all humankind raises the problem of how a sinful woman could give birth to a sinless man. All sorts of bizarre explanations have been attempted, such as the perpetual virgin-

---

24. J. A. Oosterbaan, "The Theology of Menno Simons," MQR 35 (July 1961): 191-92. Cf. Franklin Hamlin Littell, *A Tribute to Menno Simons* (Scottdale, Pa.: Herald Press, 1961), pp. 53ff.

25. *Complete Writings*, p. 492.

ity of Mary, which, of course, implies that Adamic sin is inherent in sexual intercourse. The dogma of the immaculate conception of Mary is simply another attempt to solve the problem of sinlessness not only of Christ but also of the "ever virgin Mother of God."

Menno cut through these problems with his doctrine of the incarnation. He viewed Christ as the "first-born of a new creation." Mary, as did all humankind, belonged to the old fallen creation. But in Mary, God, through the Holy Spirit, began his new creation. When through faith in Christ people are born again, they become new creatures in Christ Jesus made conformable to his incarnate state. Thus Mary simply becomes the passive instrument which God used to bring his Son into the world. Salvation, it follows, is wholly of grace. It is the gift of God alone.[26]

An understanding of Menno's doctrine of the incarnation is basic to any proper evaluation of his whole theological system. It is Christocentric and specifically a theology of the incarnate Christ. No other theologian of the sixteenth century so thoroughly divorced Reformation theology from Roman Catholic Mariolatry. Perhaps no other theologian before Barth so effectively wrestled with the doctrine of the incarnation within the context of the biblical revelation. Consequently, Barth has been subjected to much the same criticism from which Menno Simons suffered for strikingly similar views.[27]

An acceptance or rejection of Menno's view of the incarnation must not blind one to the facts in either case. Menno cannot justly be branded as antitrinitarian. His Anabaptist brethren who refused to accept his interpretation did not make such an accusation. Instead, they felt that his view was not a true expression of the biblical doctrine of the incarnation. Toward the close of the treatise on the Triune God, Menno once again set forth quite clearly his concept of the Trinity. This time he placed emphasis on the Holy Spirit.

> Dear brethren, from these plain Scriptures, . . . we believe the Holy Spirit to be the true, essential Holy Spirit of God, who adorns us with His heavenly and divine gifts, and through His influence,

26. Simons, *The Spiritual Resurrection,* in *Complete Writings,* pp. 58ff.
27. Oosterbaan, "Theology of Simons," p. 194.

according to the good pleasure of the Father, frees us from sin, gives us boldness, and makes us cheerful, peaceful, pious, and holy. And so we believe and confess before God . . . and before all the world, that . . . the Father, the Son, and the Holy Ghost (which the fathers called three persons, by which they meant the three, true, divine beings) are one incomprehensible, indescribable, Almighty, holy, only, eternal, and sovereign God. As John says, There are three that bear record in heaven, the Father, the Word, and the Holy Ghost; and these three are one.[28]

The unanimous witness of the biblical Anabaptists to the Trinity can leave no doubt. They were in basic agreement with one another and with the Reformers on this historic doctrine of the Christian faith. Even though a number of approaches were made to the doctrine of God by the Brethren, indicative of the freedom which they felt from the shackles of Scholasticism, the end result was the same. Hubmaier, Marpeck, Riedemann, Philips, and Menno were in essential agreement on the doctrine of God. There was no conscious denial of the Trinity within the ranks of the evangelical Anabaptists. To the contrary their avowed allegiance was unquestionably given to the Triune God.

Sola Scriptura

The one sure touchstone of the Reformation and clear line of demarcation between Roman Catholics and Reformers was the authority of the Scriptures. Within the Reformation no group took more seriously the principle of *sola Scriptura* in matters of doctrine and discipline than did the true Anabaptists. In this regard the Reformation stance of the Anabaptists is unequivocal. The authoritative position of the Scriptures among the sixteenth-century Anabaptists was apparent from the beginning. The Bible became and remained for them the supreme judicature by which all human opinions were to be tried.

By the end of 1523, the young radicals who were to become Anabaptists had decided that Zwingli had abrogated the *sola Scriptura*

---

28. *A Solemn Confession,* in *Complete Writings,* p. 496.

principle. Earlier he, too, had given it allegiance; but by "special revelation" he permitted the Zürich Council to decide the disposition of the mass. In their letter to Thomas Müntzer there is no mistaking the appeal to scriptural authority by the Brethren. They admonished him to do nothing on his own authority and in no way to compromise the truth. "And do thou drop singing," they wrote, "and the Mass, and act in all things according to the Word, and bring forth and establish by the Word the usages of the apostles." Doubtless alluding to their own situation, Grebel continued, "It is much better that a few be rightly taught through the Word of God, believing and walking aright in virtues and practices, than that many believe falsely and deceitfully through adulterated doctrine."[29]

The Schleitheim Confession reflects the common Reformation appeal to the Scriptures on the part of the south German Anabaptists. This early document contains no article concerning the Bible, which in itself is revealing. Obviously, the question of biblical authority was not an issue among the *Täufer.* However, there are many references to the Scriptures and several quotations from the Bible. Such phrases occur repeatedly: "Hear what the Scripture says" and "Observe the meaning of this Scripture."

Since the nature of the *Ordnung* of approximately the same date is essentially the same as that of the Schleitheim Confession, one would expect much the same use of the Bible. Examination verifies this expectation. However, many more passages are cited in the exceedingly brief *Ordnung* than in the longer Schleitheim document. In this early Anabaptist manual of discipline, the appeal to scriptural authority is even more apparent.[30]

At the Bern disputation of 1538, the Anabaptist participants presented a careful statement on the nature of biblical authority. In substance, they said:

> We believe in and consider ourselves under the authority of the Old Testament, in so far as it is a testimony of Christ; in so far as Jesus did not abolish it; and in so far as it serves the purpose of

29. Williams and Mergal, *Spiritual and Anabaptist Writers,* p. 77.
30. Friedmann, "Oldest Discipline," pp. 164-66.

Christian living. We believe in and consider ourselves under the authority of the Law in so far as it does not contradict the new law, which is the Gospel of Jesus Christ. We believe in and consider ourselves under the authority of the prophets in so far as they proclaim Christ.[31]

It is evident that the Bernese Anabaptists held no wooden view of Holy Scripture.

During the October disputation of 1523 in Zürich, Hubmaier set forth his view of biblical authority. Undoubtedly, Zwingli shared it at this period in the development of the Reformation in Switzerland. "Wherefore also, those errors that have sprung up concerning images and the mass should be examined and corrected by the sole rule of the word of God. Moreover, whatever shall be founded on this will endure forever; for the word of God is eternal and immortal."[32] Hubmaier's favorite designation for the Bible was, "the word of God." Again and again he challenged the readers of his various pamphlets to examine what he taught in the light of the Scriptures. His "Short Apology" again asserts his willingness to be taught new truth and to be led to a deeper understanding of spiritual concepts upon the basis of scriptural light.

"I may err — I am a man," he wrote, "but a heretic I cannot be, because I ask constantly for instruction in the word of God." The Hubmaier of the "Apology" held the same position in regard to the Bible as did the Hubmaier of pre-Anabaptist days. The earlier view may be seen in the notable challenge to Dr. Eck to debate on the basis of twenty-six "Fundamental Articles." Article sixteen states: "The church should be heard in things relating to strife and brotherly love; but in disagreement regarding the faith the Scripture is the only standard."[33] At the time of the writing of these articles, it is clear that Hubmaier considered the basic thesis of the articles not only his position but also that of Zwingli. In this assumption he was correct. Hubmaier and the Anabaptists came to feel, however, that Luther, Zwingli, and Müntzer had forsaken the principle of which they alone remained the consistent

31. Jan P. Matthijssen, "The Bern Disputation of 1538," MQR 22 (January 1948): 30.
32. Vedder, *Hübmaier,* p. 60.
33. *Ibid.,* p. 90.

advocates. The documentary proof of this assertion is not difficult to come by.

The remarkable Confession of Claus Felbinger, written during his imprisonment at Landshut, 1560, shortly before he was beheaded, is a case in point. In answer to a hypothetical charge that the Anabaptist way of life was an impossible one, he retorted: "To this we answer that we believe the Word of God utterly: the Word that stands and that cannot lie. It does not conform to the world. Men have only to act in accordance with the Word."[34]

In the same document Felbinger sought to explain why the Brethren would not take up arms but rather sought to show love to all men.

> Therefore we do nothing to promote bloodshed, for such does not befit a Christian who is taught of God in His Son, since we should be like young children, without resentment or bitterness, and like a dove, guileless. To the men of old it was indeed said, "Thou shalt hate thine enemy and love thy friend." "But I say unto you," said Christ, "love your enemies, do good to them that hate you, pray for them that despitefully use you, that ye may be children of your Father in heaven." Therefore one must distinguish between the Old and the New Testaments.[35]

It is clear from this Hutterite missionary that the Anabaptists, while holding to the Bible as the Word of God, made the New Testament alone normative for the Christian life.

The Anabaptist characteristic distinction between the Old and New Testaments is most clearly enunciated in the work of Pilgram Marpeck. He sought to set forth in systematic fashion a theology of biblical revelation. In fact, theology for Marpeck, as Kiwiet has pointed out, was nothing more or less than systematic exposition of the Scriptures. There is no question about Marpeck's allegiance to the Bible as the Word of God. Yet for Marpeck there was an absolute distinction between the Old Testament and the New. He drew some graphic contrasts which emphasize the transitory (zeitlich) nature of the Old

34. Friedmann, "Felbinger's Confession," p. 150.
35. Ibid., p. 147.

Testament when compared to the eternal *(ewig)* nature of the New. In the Old Testament there is symbol *(Figur);* in the New the essence *(Wesen)* of that which is symbolized. The Old Testament speaks of Adam, sin, death, and the law; the New Testament centers in the message of redemption through the risen Christ. He alone brings to us the new birth through the power of the Holy Spirit.[36]

Marpeck's interpretation of the Bible, like that of the Swiss Brethren, the Hutterites, and the Mennonites, was Christocentric. Revelation was viewed as progressive and partial before Christ. Only in Christ is the revelation of God complete. Thus, the New Testament alone became the rule of faith and practice for the Anabaptists. Marpeck saw all sorts of dire consequences for Christendom in the failure to interpret the Old Testament properly. The Münsterites as well as Calvin were to be blamed in this regard. They had mistaken the foundation of the house for the house itself. They had based their theocracies on a revelation which was only preparatory and never intended to be final. Marpeck was followed by a host of Anabaptists in this, his most creative contribution to Anabaptist theology.

Marpeck's theory of revelation was greatly dependent upon Paul's treatment of the relation between the two covenants in the epistle to the Galatians. The epistle to the Hebrews and his own experience of grace supplied two other sources out of which his ultimate position was drawn. Since Leupold Scharnschlager was of the Marpeck group, it is not surprising to find essentially the same position echoed by him in regard to the Scriptures. For Scharnschlager as for Marpeck the Scriptures are Holy because holy men of God were moved by the Holy Spirit to write as God willed. But the Bible is to the natural man simply

---

36. Kiwiet, *Marbeck,* pp. 94-102. It is possible that Marpeck was influenced greatly by Martin Luther's early emphasis on the utter difference between law and gospel in developing his covenant theology. At the Heidelberg Disputation Luther drew some graphic contrasts in the law, which "works wrath, kills, curses, makes guilty, judges and condemns," and the gospel which saves. Of course Zwingli's emphasis on the New Testament was very pronounced in both his teaching and preaching until January, 1525. On Luther see James Atkinson, *Luther: Early Theological Works* (Philadelphia: Westminster, 1962), pp. 274-78, 291-95. For Zwingli's program of preaching see Jean Rilliet, *Zwingli, Third Man of the Reformation,* trans. Harold Knight (Philadelphia: Westminster, 1959), pp. 57-60.

lifeless ink and paper until the Holy Spirit enters into his heart and quickens his understanding. Then and then only can he understand, according to Scharnschlager, the true meaning of the Scriptures.[37]

The nearest approach to an article dealing with scriptural authority as such in the *Confession* of Peter Riedemann is found in a section entitled "Concerning the Covenant of Grace Given to His People in Christ."[38] In this section Riedemann followed the familiar Anabaptist emphasis. He borrowed liberally from Pauline concepts set forth in Galatians, as well as the characteristic emphasis of Hebrews. Throughout the *Confession* the reader is constantly confronted with the final court of appeals for all teachings concerning the Christian life, the Bible.

The Riedemann *Confession* contains more than two thousand references to the canonical Scriptures. There are some forty-eight citations of the Apocrypha. Twenty of these are from the Book of Wisdom. Of course Riedemann was not the only Anabaptist who held a high view of the apocryphal books.[39] Even Hubmaier occasionally referred to the Apocrypha, as did Pilgram Marpeck. Apparently the German-speaking Anabaptists used German editions of the Scriptures which were based upon the Vulgate. There were many such translations of the Scriptures before Luther's *September Bibel.* Among the Bibles known to have been popular with the Brethren were the *Froschauer* or *Zuericher Bibel* and a translation of the Prophets by Haetzer and Denck.

In his *Reply to Gellius Faber,* Menno wrote of Faber: "His beginning is unscriptural and unscriptural will his end be. Observe, the Word of God shall be our judge."[40] As this statement reveals, for Menno there was one plumb line for all human opinions, the Scriptures. Menno was fond of the phrases "The Word of God," "His holy Word," "God's Word," "the Word of the Lord." It is difficult to find a paragraph in his works in which some reference to the Scriptures does not occur. No Anabaptist theologian tried more persistently and conscientiously

37. Gerhard Hein, ed., "Two Letters by Leupold Scharnschlager," MQR 17 (July 1943): 168.
38. Riedemann, *Account,* pp. 165ff.
39. *Ibid.,* p. 280.
40. *Complete Writings,* p. 683.

to build his theology upon the Bible than did Menno. As both Wenger and Oosterbaan have abundantly demonstrated, Menno's theology was a biblical theology interpreted christologically. The center and circumference of his theological system was the living Word of God, God incarnate, Jesus the Christ.

Even though there are differing emphases among the various Anabaptist writers in regard to the Scriptures and their use, there are significant areas of agreement. For all Anabaptists the Bible was the only rule of faith and practice for discipleship and the church. Biblical revelation was held to be progressive. The Old Testament was preparatory and partial, whereas the New Testament was final and complete. All of the Scriptures, they insisted, must be interpreted christologically, that is, through the mind of Christ. The Holy Spirit alone can illuminate the letter of the Bible and give it convicting power in the life of the seeker. The Bible is the Word of God, that is, the written Word which brings us to the living Word, who alone can give us new life in the power of the Spirit.

The Anabaptist view of the Bible was far from a static concept. On the contrary it became a dynamic center of a biblical and creative theology free from the entangling hindrances of tradition and scholasticism alike. At this point the Anabaptists were the most Protestant and yet the furthest removed from Protestantism. They took the principle *sola Scriptura* seriously and sought to make the biblical witness a contemporary phenomenon.

Justification by Faith

The Reformation text, "The just shall live by faith," became for the Anabaptists a vital truth. They attempted to interpret and implement it in the full light of the biblical revelation. Luther's battle cry, "Justification by faith," became his plumb line for interpreting the Bible. However, due to the persistent Roman Catholic appendages of his theology, he was never able to give this truth consistent expression.

41. See articles IV, "Of Justification," and IX, "Of Baptism," in *The Augsburg Confession (Confessio Augustana)*.

Consequently, in Lutheranism there has always been an irreconcilable contradiction between the theology of justification by faith and the theological support of infant baptism.[41]

The Anabaptists were critical of the Lutheran doctrine of justification by faith at this point. They accused the Lutherans of making this biblical truth a meaningless shibboleth. For them faith was the means of a new life in Christ Jesus, the new birth of the Holy Spirit. This concept was emphasized by every Anabaptist theologian. Hubmaier, in setting up the eighteen articles as the doctrinal basis of the Reformation in Waldshut, devoted the first three articles to the doctrine of justification by faith and its implications for the Christian life.

> 1. Faith alone makes us holy before God.
>
> 2. This faith is the acknowledgment of the mercy of God which he has shown us in the offering of his only begotten son. This excludes all sham Christians, who have nothing more than an historical faith in God.
>
> 3. Such faith can not remain passive but must break out *(aussbrechen)* to God in thanksgiving and to mankind in all kinds of works of brotherly love. Hence all vain religious acts, such as candles, palm branches, and holy water will be rejected.[42]

These articles reveal both an indebtedness to Luther and an independence of thought that is characteristic of all Anabaptists, to some degree. In the first article there is the familiar *sola fide* ring, but instead of using Luther's term for justification *(Gerechtigkeit)*, Hubmaier employs the word translated "holy" *(frumm=Fromm)*. By making this change in the familiar evangelical formula, Hubmaier is doubtless attempting to say that saving faith brings about more than a declared righteousness — it produces a new quality of holiness in life. Again, Hubmaier rejects the medieval concept that faith is only *assensus,* the intellectual acceptance of certain propositions proclaimed as true by the church. The object of faith for him is the grace of God made available through the incarnate Christ. The third article contains his most poignantly graphic expression. It is his conviction that Christian faith possesses an irrepressible quality about it, for it breaks out *(aussbre-*

---

42. Vedder, *Hübmaier,* pp. 69-70.

chen) to God in thanksgiving and to one's fellow man in works of brotherly love. This faith produces gratitude in the heart toward God while evoking goodwill toward man. Thus the perpendicular and horizontal aspects of the Christian life are encompassed in the act of faith.

Menno spells out clearly and carefully that which is only implied in Hubmaier's brief articles. In his *Foundation of Christian Doctrine,* Menno opens the discussion on faith with these words:

> We teach with Christ and say, Believe the Gospel. That Gospel is the blessed announcement of the favor and grace of God to us, and of forgiveness of sins through Christ Jesus. Faith accepts this Gospel through the Holy Ghost, and does not consider former righteousness or unrighteousness, but . . . with the whole heart casts itself upon the grace, Word and promises of the Lord, since it knows that God is true, and that His promises cannot fail. In this the heart is renewed, converted, justified, becomes pious, peaceable, and joyous, . . . and so becomes a joint heir of Christ and a possessor of eternal life.[43]

Clearly for the Anabaptists, if Hubmaier and Menno are reliable guides, faith was not simply an academic matter. It could never be mere *assensus* but always *fiducia*. Faith was, in Menno's thinking, a life commitment to Christ. And with the trusting experience of casting oneself upon the grace of God come justification, the new birth, and eternal life.

Peter Riedemann viewed faith as a gift of God which comes to those who seek after God. The means of this faith is hearing the Word of God proclaimed by a messenger of the Lord. Therefore faith for Riedemann became the source of good in the Christian life.

"Thus faith," Riedemann wrote, "is also given victorious strength, as it is written, 'And our faith is the victory that overcometh the world,' as indeed God doth in us through faith. Thus faith doeth and worketh all things, and maketh men pleasing to and loved by God."[44]

While the idea that faith is itself a gift of God is also enunciated by Claus Felbinger in his prison confession of 1560, he brought to

---

43. *Complete Writings,* p. 115.
44. Riedemann, *Account,* p. 47.

light another facet of faith. Faith, Felbinger insisted, must be the free and uncoerced response of people to God. "Now, does Christ compel people with the stocks to hear His teaching, as in the manner of those who think they are Christians? God wants no compulsory service. On the contrary, he loves a free, willing heart that serves Him with a joyful soul and does what is right joyfully."[45] The implication of Felbinger's insight is that, while faith can exist even in the face of the threat of reprisals, compulsion can never produce faith. Faith is not the product of coercion.

For Pilgram Marpeck faith meant an annulment of the consequences of the fall for the individual. It was also the means by which a person experienced, through the work of the Holy Spirit, the new birth. This new birth for Marpeck had definite ethical and moral implications. The new birth experience was to be followed immediately by baptism. Without it baptism would be meaningless.[46] Justification by faith for Marpeck was far more than a legal transaction in the heavenly court. It meant a new life, a life of discipleship in obedience to the risen Lord.

The treatment of the Reformation concept of justification by faith by the sixteenth-century Anabaptists was distinctive. There is no repudiation of the Lutheran doctrine of justification by faith, but rather a new interpretation which attempted to read into the term more biblical and ethical content than they felt Luther ever gave it, without resorting to a soteriology based on a works righteousness.

What has been said of the doctrine of justification by faith can be said of the other doctrines in which the Anabaptists shared some measure of agreement with the Reformers. But in every case, the Anabaptists were never content with simply parroting the Reformers. They were both critical and creative. In both their criticism and their creativity, they sought to be consistently biblical. This fidelity to the Scriptures was to lead them farther than, and in a different direction from that taken by, Luther or Schwenckfeld, Zwingli or Calvin.

45. Friedmann, "Felbinger's Confession," p. 148.
46. Horst Quiring, "The Anthropology of Pilgram Marpeck," MQR 9 (October 1935): 162-63.

IX

❧ ❧

Baptism and Discipleship

IF THE MOST OBVIOUS DEMARCATION BETWEEN THE REFORMERS AND the Roman Catholics was biblical authority, that between the Reformers and the Anabaptists was believers' baptism. Believers' baptism was for the Anabaptists the logical implementation of the Reformation principle of *sola Scriptura*. Almost as soon as the Anabaptist movement could be distinguished within the context of the Reformation itself, believers' baptism became the major issue.

Early Anabaptist leaders without exception recognized the importance of the baptismal question. Felix Manz penned an important pamphlet on baptism. Hubmaier produced six books or pamphlets on the subject. Pilgram Marpeck, Menno Simons, and Dirk Philips wrote monographs on baptism and referred repeatedly to the ordinance in their other works. Riedemann, Denck, Scharnschlager, and Felbinger gave a considerable amount of attention to a discussion of baptism in their extant works. Early Anabaptist disputations and confessions were often preoccupied with believers' baptism.

Therefore, to ignore the role of baptism or to minimize its place in sixteenth-century Anabaptist life is historically unjustifiable. Indeed, understanding the place of baptism in Anabaptist life may well be the key to interpreting the Anabaptist views of discipleship and the church.

Probably, the most revolutionary act of the Reformation was the institution of believers' baptism by a handful of Swiss Brethren in Zürich. Of course, believers' baptism had been practiced before, but

201

after the apostolic period only spasmodically by various dissenting groups. Outside of the early period, rarely, if ever, had believers' baptism been practiced so consistently under such adverse circumstances. Yet, its reinauguration was a premeditated act by a little band of dedicated disciples. Their theological convictions demanded action in spite of clear knowledge of its bitter consequences. Immediately, baptism became the burning issue of the hour. And this symbol of Anabaptist discipleship became the occasion of severe oppression. Out of the fires of the resultant persecution wrote Menno Simons:

> Since we, for the sake of baptism, are so miserably abused, . . . we say and testify in Christ Jesus . . . that we are driven only by a God-fearing faith which we have in the Word of God to baptize and to be baptized, and by nothing else; nor will it be found otherwise, neither in this life nor in death, nor in the last judgment of God.[1]

Baptism among the Swiss Brethren

The earliest literary exposition of the Anabaptist position on baptism is found in the letter of the Brethren to Thomas Müntzer. After commending Müntzer for his rejection of infant baptism, Grebel proceeded, in an apostolic vein, to instruct his correspondent more perfectly in the faith.

At the outset Grebel indicated that the authority to which he appealed was nothing other than that of the Scriptures. Baptism signifies the forgiveness of sins, an inner transformation of mind and heart, and a pledge of a life of discipleship. He affirmed that the "water does not confirm or increase faith, as the scholars at Wittenberg say." In the next sentence he was even more unequivocal in his rejection of the sacramental nature of baptism: "Also baptism does not save, as Augustine, Tertullian, Theophylact, and Cyprian have taught, dishonoring faith and the suffering of Christ in the case of the old and adult, and dishonoring the suffering of Christ in the case of the unbaptized infants."

Grebel then proceeded to deny both the validity of infant baptism and its necessity from the viewpoint of the New Testament. "Infant

---

1. Simons, *Christian Baptism*, in *Complete Writings*, p. 236.

baptism is a senseless, blasphemous abomination, contrary to all Scripture," he declared. He expressed his hope that Müntzer was "not acting against the eternal word, wisdom, and commandment of God, according to which only believers are to be baptized, and [was] not baptizing children."[2] In spite of the certain prospect of persecution, he admonished Müntzer and Carlstadt to remain faithful to the truth which he believed them to share with him.

Four months later it was undoubtedly Grebel's conviction as well as his own that Manz expressed in "A Declaration of Faith and Defense," addressed to the civil authorities of Zürich. While this petition may have been written by Manz, as some scholars have contended, in certain paragraphs it sounds exactly like Grebel. The copy in the City Archives of Zürich is not in Grebel's careful hand. It also contains numerous editorial revisions. In all probability it is of composite authorship and expresses the profound conviction of the entire Grebel-led group. In this document the appeal to Scripture is even more explicit. The author asserts that his position on believers' baptism was drawn from the same authority to which Zwingli owed allegiance, the Bible. He denies that the teaching of believers' baptism is seditious. It is even clearer from this document that for the Grebel-led Zürich *Täufer* baptism was not a sacrament in the traditional sense but primarily a symbol of obedient discipleship.

> It is clearly seen what baptism is and to whom baptism should be applied, namely, to one who has been converted by the Word of God, has changed his heart, and henceforth desires to walk in newness of life. . . . From this I have clearly learned and know assuredly, that baptism means nothing else than a dying of the old man, and a putting on of the new, and that Christ commanded to baptize those who had been taught.[3]

"A Declaration of Faith and Defense" denies the validity of infant baptism because of the nature of Christian baptism. In the New Testa-

---

2. "Letters to Thomas Müntzer by Conrad Grebel and Friends," in Williams and Mergal, *Spiritual and Anabaptist Writers,* pp. 80-81.

3. Bender, "The Theology of Conrad Grebel," MQR 12 (January 1938): 47. See also S. C. Wenger, trans., *Conrad Grebel's Programmatic Letters of 1524* (Scottdale, Pa.: Herald Press, 1970).

ment baptism is always for believers; also, there is no commandment of Christ or apostolic example for the baptism of infants. Manz's appeal to the Zürich Council to refrain from the use of force in support of a particular kind of baptism was unavailing.

Grebel began his monograph on baptism from prison at Gröningen. His prison manuscript of 1526 on baptism is not extant. Samuel M. Jackson, however, has successfully reconstructed its outline and essential arguments from Zwingli's attempted refutation, *Catabaptistarum Strophas Elenchus*.[4] In this, his last work, Grebel was concerned with a thorough, scriptural refutation of infant baptism. In combatting Zwingli's arguments, he attempted to prove that no infants could have been included in the household baptisms of the New Testament.[5] The examples of Crispus, the Philippian jailer, and Philip in Samaria are cited as having reference only to adults, or at least to those capable of hearing the Word and believing.

Grebel set forth a suggested order which becomes most pronounced in its tidier development by Hubmaier. According to the Scriptures believing is based upon hearing the Word preached. This, of course, implies a certain degree of maturity and consequently excludes infants. In this last work of Grebel two earlier concepts reappear: the Anabaptists' utter dependence on scriptural authority and the symbolic nature of New Testament baptism. In the light of both concepts, infant baptism was inconceivable.

Before Zwingli began to put his refutation of believers' baptism in print, he assured the recently baptized converts from Zollikon imprisoned in the Augustinian monastery that soon changes would be made in baptism and the mass. At the time both sacraments were still being celebrated in Zürich as they had been for centuries without alteration in vestments or liturgy. Zwingli must have had a very uneasy conscience, for his appeal to the Word of God for the rites and ceremonies of the church was well known and yet he performed the old Latin rites as if nothing had changed, complete with the double signing of

---

4. Bender, *Grebel*, pp. 294-96.

5. The author follows Fritz Blanke and Harold Bender in ascribing the authorship of the anonymous *Taufbüchlein* to Grebel. See Bender's rather complete discussion of the problem in "Theology of Grebel" (pp. 48-52).

the cross, blowing under the eyes, salt placed in the mouth, spittle on the ears and nose, and finally the anointing with oil. He had long since forsaken the traditional theological justification of infant baptism and denied its salvific efficacy. True to his promise, by May, 1525, he had replaced the traditional rites in the Grossmünster with greatly simplified forms of the sacraments. But he still insisted on baptizing infants. He stopped short of Anabaptism, instead launching a sustained attack against the Anabaptists and their "rebaptism."

Zwingli's refutation of Grebel's arguments was extremely weak. But in his attempt to discredit the Anabaptists, he was far more successful. The basic weakness of Zwingli's position was to become even more apparent in the evolving literary debate with Balthasar Hubmaier.

The position of the Swiss Brethren on baptism is clearly enunciated in the Schleitheim Confession. This celebrated Anabaptist confession was drawn up by Michael Sattler and accepted by a representative gathering of German Anabaptists at Schlatten am Randen on February 24, 1527. Yet it faithfully portrays the position of the Swiss Brethren on baptism. Significantly, the article on baptism was the first of the seven to be agreed upon by the Brethren at the conference. It reads, in part:

> Baptism ought to be administered to all who have been taught repentance and a change of life and in truth believe their sins to have been blotted out through Christ . . . and who wish to be buried with him into death that they may be able to rise again with him. To all, then, who ask baptism after this manner . . . for themselves we administer it. By these means are excluded all baptism of infants, the supreme abomination of the Roman Pontif [sic]. For this article we have the testimony and strength of Scripture; we have also the practice of the Apostles.[6]

This sixteenth-century Anabaptist statement on baptism is so clear that an interpretative statement is superfluous. It is impossible to escape the close connection with which the Brethren viewed baptism and discipleship. For the Brethren, believers' baptism was reserved for committed disciples only.

6. McGlothlin, *Baptist Confessions*, pp. 3-4.

Eleven years later, the Swiss Brethren in a public debate with the leaders of the Reformed Church of Bern presented essentially the same view. The debate of 1538 was held ostensibly, to use the words of the Zwinglians, "to find together the truth." However, the debate was held under the auspices of the City Council of Bern, which the Anabaptist participants were forced to acknowledge as the lawful judicature. Hence the objectivity of the state church participants was certainly questionable.

The discussions took place over a six-day period. The agenda included seven articles: "Old and New Testament," "The Ministry," "The Church," "Baptism," "The Oath," "The State," and "The Ban." Clergymen of the Reformed Church were pitted against unlearned Anabaptist laymen, whom they attempted to dazzle and confuse with their learning and sophistry. However, the Anabaptist disputants proved more than a match for the "Doctors." Even though they won none of the ecclesiastics to their banner, they at least were able to maintain their position in spite of intimidation. Their continuous witness through four subsequent centuries shows the depth of conviction which has always marked the Anabaptists of Bern.

In opposition to the usual arguments for infant baptism the Brethren set forth their position, underscoring the basic insights of Anabaptism. First, the nature of baptism rules out the possibility of infant baptism. New Testament baptism requires prior conviction for, and repentance of, sin, and faith in Christ. Baptism is viewed as a symbol of initiation into the church and a sign of the new life which the believer has in Christ. "In other words, baptism is to be administered only after receiving the Holy Spirit; and children, though they are not necessarily condemned, do not have the Holy Spirit."

Second, baptism is a symbol and not a sacrament. It has no meaning where faith in Christ is absent. Third, Christ has set for us an example through his own baptism. Fourth, through the Great Commission, he has explicitly commanded us to teach and baptize. Fifth, baptism is not analogous to circumcision:

> As for the matter of circumcision, it is clear that baptism is not the same as the Old Testament act of initiation, but is its replacement. The analogy should not be pushed too far. Summarizing: Baptism is not the expression of a mechanical covenant theory; it requires a

certain type of personal standing and a personal relation to God, the Father of Jesus Christ.[7]

Once again the debate revealed the priority of the Bible, interpreted christologically, in the formulation of the Anabaptist doctrinal position. Upon the basis of their understanding of the Scriptures, the Swiss Brethren arrived at their view. Believers' baptism, by its very nature, eliminates any possibility of infant baptism.

Balthasar Hubmaier and Baptism

The most able sixteenth-century defender of the Anabaptist position on baptism was Dr. Balthasar Hubmaier of Friedberg. Of the eleven books and pamphlets which he devoted to the ordinances, six relate to baptism. Five of the six were published after Hubmaier went to Nikolsburg. Fortunately for Hubmaier and the Brethren, Simprecht Sorg, surnamed Froschauer, had been forced to leave Zürich because of his Anabaptist convictions. Subsequently he became Hubmaier's publisher. His services made possible a wide distribution of Hubmaier's Nikolsburg writings.

The first work finished at Nikolsburg was "A Speech by Dr. Balthasar Hubmaier von Friedberg Concerning a Book on the Baptism of Infants by Master Ulrich Zwingli at Zürich." Hubmaier indicated how he envisioned his task: "It is easy," he declared, "for me to remove the blocks, stones and boulders from the road. Some were scattered there long ago by the hand of man, and some fell there." After making a slighting reference to Zwingli's latest book on baptism, Hubmaier explained how he planned to remove the stones and boulders that have obscured the biblical revelation. "I wish to put forth in pious writings my reasons, and prove that infant baptism is without any basis in God's Word."[8]

7. Matthijssen, "Bern Disputation," p. 32.
8. The title in German is *Gesprach auf Meister Ulrich Zwinglis Taufbuchlein vom dem Kindertauf* (1526). The quotations are from the English translation of Hubmaier's works by George Diuguid Davidson (1939; microfilmed from typescript), pp. 143-44. I have compared the quotations from Davidson with the translations of Pipkin and Yoder and made changes in Davidson when necessary.

That which appeared an easy task to Hubmaier has been extremely difficult for Christendom to accept. Few are the traditional practices which have been more persistent than infant baptism. These sentences from the hand of Hubmaier might well serve as an introduction to an examination of all his writings on baptism.

Hubmaier's first book devoted exclusively to baptism was completed on July 11, 1525, at Waldshut. *Vom christlichen Tauf (Concerning Christian Baptism)* was by far the most complete exposition of believers' baptism yet to appear. It was polemical in nature, taking issue with the Zwinglian point of view in numerous instances. However, it was not wholly negative. Hubmaier addressed himself to the presentation of a constructive doctrine of believers' baptism.

At the outset, he rejected the scurrilous charge of the Zwinglians:

> But the charge that we boast that we can sin no more after baptism, and such-like things, is a monstrous injustice. For we know that both before and after baptism, we are poor and miserable sinners, and if we say we sin not, we are liars, and the truth is not in us.[9]

But baptism, Hubmaier insisted, is "a public confession and testimony of an inward faith." Baptism is also a pledge of discipleship in which the candidate "promises in the future to live according to the word and command of Christ. But not in human strength, lest that befall him which befell Peter."

Hubmaier was fond of what may be termed "the biblical order." He found the order in relation to John's baptism, but it was also the order followed by the apostles and established by Christ. "The order runs thus," he writes, "first, word; second, obedience; third, amendment of life, or recognition of sins; fourth, baptism; fifth, works."[10] The order is stated differently at various times, depending on the emphasis which Hubmaier had in mind at the moment. A common form in which he sets forth the sequence of acts leading to baptism is: "preach-

9. *Ibid.*, p. 72.

10. *Ibid.*, p. 85. In my own translation of *Vom christlichen Tauf*, I have tried to incorporate the "order" within the text. See also William R. Estep, Jr., ed., *Anabaptist Beginnings (1523-1533)* (Nieuwkoop: B. de Graaf, 1976), pp. 87-90.

ing, hearing, repentance, faith." The complete order includes baptism. After baptism three different terms were used — but always separately, never jointly. They are: good works, church, the Lord's Supper. In the original German edition Hubmaier further emphasizes the biblical order by placing such words as *Wort, Gehör, Glaub, Endrung, Tauff, Erkantnüss,* and *Werk* in the margins of the book. These terms are marked by letters, and the corresponding letters are placed in the text. It is an impressive way of cataloging the scriptural sequence of events leading to baptism, even today.

It would be a mistake to assume that Hubmaier held each of these acts to be part of the saving process. To the contrary, because of the nature of baptism certain events must take place before it and certain others after it. The biblical sequence is accentuated in order to highlight the significance of the baptismal act. Hubmaier believed the divine order is found in the Great Commission and also in Mark 16. "Out of these words it may be readily understood that the mission of the apostles consists of three divisions. Firstly, preaching. Secondly, faith. Thirdly, outward baptism." For Hubmaier there was no question as to which came first. "From this it follows that no one can be so blind or lame that he cannot see and grasp the fact that baptism by water should never be administered without previous profession of faith."[11]

Generally, Hubmaier was very careful to avoid any use of terms that might imply more than a purely symbolic meaning to baptism. Even though he did not always succeed in his desire not to be misunderstood, his use of repetition in attempting clarity becomes monotonous. His style suffered as a result, but no one can successfully accuse Hubmaier of holding a sacramental view of baptism. The following excerpts are typical of the manner in which he continuously stated and restated his position.

Hubmaier, following the typological use of the ark of 1 Peter 3:20, likened the salvation of eight persons by Noah's ark in the Old Testament to baptism in the New. "Similarly we are saved in baptism, which means," he interpreted, taking his cue from Peter, "not the washing of the flesh, but the answer of a good conscience toward God by the resurrection of Jesus Christ, who has ascended into heaven and is seated at the right hand of God." After additional discussion of the necessity

11. *Ibid.,* pp. 94-95, 98.

of faith prior to baptism, Hubmaier summarized his whole argument with these words: "Therefore baptism in water is not what cleanses the soul, but the 'yes,' of a good conscience toward God, given inwardly by faith."[12]

The second chapter of Acts was also interpreted by Hubmaier in a nonsacramental sense:

> Therefore, the baptism in water is called a baptism *in remissionem peccatorum* (Acts second chapter), that is, for the pardon of sins. Not that through it or by it sins are forgiven, but by virtue of the inward "yes" of the heart, which a man outwardly testifies to on submitting to water-baptism, saying that he believes and is sure in his heart that his sins are forgiven through Jesus Christ. The baptism of John was likewise called a baptism of repentance. That is, he who wished to be baptized confessed himself guilty of sin.

Even though Hubmaier refused to attach saving significance to baptism, he did not minimize its importance for the Christian life. Baptism was held obligatory for three reasons: Christ has commanded it; it is a necessary act of personal discipleship; and it is the symbol of corporate discipleship of the visible church.

Hubmaier emphasized that the conversion and baptism of the Ethiopian eunuch show the importance of baptism as an act of obedience by the believer.

> Beyond any doubt, many thousands have been saved who have not been baptized, for the latter was not in their power. But because the treasurer had both water and a baptizer, he was obligated to be baptized according to the command of Christ. Had he not done so, Christ would have considered him a despiser and a transgressor of his word, and would have punished him.[13]

Among the ten reasons in this work given by Hubmaier for the practice of believers' baptism, four emphasize its nature as an act of obedience to the command of Christ. Hubmaier, like the Swiss

12. *Ibid.*, pp. 98-99. See also Estep, *Beginnings*, p. 80.
13. *Ibid.*, p. 108.

Brethren, stressed the relation of baptism to discipleship. He designated the baptismal act by various terms: "Baptism in water in the name of the Father, and of the Son, and of the Holy Ghost — or, in the name of our Lord Jesus Christ, is nothing but a public confession and testimony of an inward faith." It is also called a "vow" by which the new disciple "promises in the future to live according to the word and command of Christ."[14] Baptism is also referred to as a "profession of faith" and a "pledge."

Each of the terms used was intended to convey the meaning of baptism as the deliberate, voluntary act of a committed disciple of Jesus Christ. Therefore, baptism for the believer symbolizes his newness of life and his determination to follow Christ even unto death.

For Hubmaier baptism was not only a symbol of individual discipleship but of corporate discipleship as well. Without it, the visible church could not exist.

> Where baptism in water does not exist, there is no Church, no brother, no sister, no fraternal discipline, exclusion or restoration. I speak here of the visible church as Christ said (Matt. 18). For there must be some outward sign of testimony by which brothers and sisters can know one another, though faith be in the heart alone. By receiving baptism, the candidate testifies publicly that . . . he has submitted himself to his brothers and sisters — that is to the church. If he transgresses, they have power to admonish, punish, exclude and restore.[15]

Hubmaier's view of baptism as the indispensable act of church membership was no passing fancy. It was part of his carefully thought-out doctrine of baptism. The concept of corporate discipleship, of which baptism is the symbol, occurs repeatedly in Hubmaier's subsequent writings. Baptism was not, then, for Hubmaier simply an individual matter by which a person declares his faith. It is also a symbol of his submission to the discipline of the congregation to which he adheres and a prerequisite to the Lord's Supper. Baptism is clearly presented as an act of confession, obedience, individual discipleship,

14. *Ibid.,* pp. 76-77.
15. *Ibid.,* p. 111.

and church membership. All of this is presented in the following quotation:

> Now when a man confesses that he is a sinner, believes in the remission of sins, and has committed himself to a new life, he must then testify outwardly before the church of Christ . . . that he accepts the word of Christ in his heart, and is minded to surrender himself to live in [the] future according to the word, will and law of Christ. . . . Then he must be baptized in water; by which means he publicly professes his faith and purpose. . . . If he should in the future bring reproach or blame upon the name of Christ through public or grievous sins, he promises to submit to punishment by his brethren, according to the command of Christ (Matt. 18). From all this it is easy to see that infant baptism is a deception, invented and introduced by men.[16]

Hubmaier never tired of denouncing infant baptism. He used all the weapons in his arsenal — the Bible, logic, sarcasm, ridicule, the teachings of Christ, and the example of the apostles. Infant baptism was rejected on the basis of the Bible, the nature of baptism, and the nature of the church. In regard to the Bible and infant baptism, he wrote, "I find no text which says go hence into all the world and baptize infants, and teach those who are only a few years old." To those that fear for the infants' salvation if they are not baptized, Hubmaier said, "Not to be baptized does not damn. . . . But not to believe, that damns."[17] Hubmaier was willing to leave the infants "in the hands of a gracious Father." "Into his hands will I commit them," he wrote. "His will be done. And there I leave the matter. Without his will it would do no good for me to be baptized a thousand times. For water does not save."[18]

The baptism of infants, in Hubmaier's understanding, was completely out of step with the New Testament character of baptism. This is his point in the following paragraph.

---

16. *Ibid.*, pp. 132-33.
17. *Ibid.*, pp. 113-14.
18. *Ibid.*, p. 126.

As my Father sent me, so also send I you. As if he would say: He has commanded me to promise to all who believe in me the remission of their sins. . . . With this, the baptism of infants, who have done no sins, does not correspond. It resembles neither the baptism before Christ's resurrection nor the baptism after it, although it be in water. But water is not baptism. Else would the river Rhine be a baptism for him who sails thereon.[19]

Hubmaier pointed out that neither John nor Christ baptized infants. "And no one was baptized by John, or with the baptism of Christ, unless he was previously instructed in the Word of God, and brought to a confession of his sins, and that these sins were forgiven through Christ Jesus." It was his conviction that such a procedure on the part of John, as well as the teaching of Christ in Matthew 28, precludes the possibility of the baptism of infants.

Hubmaier, while recognizing similarities between the baptism of John and baptism as instituted by Christ, treated them as two different kinds of baptism. The discussion offered him an opportunity to deny the common accusation that the Anabaptists were rebaptizers:

Notice . . . [the] difference between the two baptisms. John leads his hearers to a recognition of sin. Then, when they have confessed their sins, he baptizes them and makes them his disciples. In the third place, he points them to Christ. In the fourth place, Christ pardons their sins. In the fifth place, all who believe in this pardon are re-baptized by the apostles of Christ.

That is real Re-baptism, for the baptism of John is, and is called, a baptism, and the baptism of Christ is also a baptism. The sprinkling of infants . . . is no baptism, nor is it worthy of such a name. Therefore it is unjust to say of us that we re-baptize.[20]

It is preposterous, said Hubmaier, to consider infants fit subjects for church membership. The regenerate nature of the church presupposes a certain degree of maturity, personal faith, and volition. Thus infant

19. *Ibid.,* p. 82.
20. *Ibid.,* pp. 92-93.

baptism was summarily dismissed as unscriptural and contrary to the nature of Christian baptism and that of the New Testament church.

From his study of the Scriptures, Hubmaier was so convinced that his position was correct that he did not sufficiently evaluate the arguments of his opponents. This sentiment is revealed in the introduction to his polemical booklet against Ulrich Zwingli's position. He asserted, "It is easy for me to remove the blocks, stones and boulders from the road." Still smarting from the rough treatment which he had received at the hands of his erstwhile friend, he wrote: "And it is necessary for me to attack the deceitful little book that *'Meister Vrich Zwinglen zů Zürch'* has published at Zürich on baptism in water."[21] In this work Hubmaier was at his best. He was always superb as a polemicist. As this and most of his other works reveal, he never freed himself from the scholastic love of theological debate. However, Hubmaier was "scrupulously fair" with his opposition, and his work is remarkably free from the caustic bitterness that characterized his adversary.

In his polemic against Zwingli's *Taufbüchlein vom dem Kindertauf,* Hubmaier set out to prove by the Bible that there is no biblical foundation for the baptism of infants. In this work, as one might expect, infant baptism is treated in much more detail than in his previous work, *Concerning Christian Baptism.* The format of the book is that of a debate. Alternately Hubmaier presented Zwingli's argument and then his own. In the introduction he set forth his appeal to biblical authority.

> As far as my teachings are concerned, the Holy Scriptures shall be my judge. . . . I must speak, for the edification and up-building of the Christian churches, according to the Word of God. For by means of this Zwingli not a few stumbling-blocks have fallen in their way. So I go to the Scriptures, . . . and I will never let the books of men be judges between us.[22]

Like most of Hubmaier's works this one is quite repetitive. It says the same thing at different times in different form in answering the allegations of Zwingli against the Anabaptists and their teachings. Two examples of Hubmaier's style illustrate both the format of the book

21. *Ibid.,* p. 143.
22. *Ibid.,* p. 147.

and the manner in which he avoided the dilemma of accepting the sacramental view of baptism on the one hand and of minimizing the importance of baptism on the other. Zwingli's argument is indicated with a Z and Hubmaier's answer with a B.

> Z. There are some people in our days who have objected to the administration of baptism to all persons, saying that there is nothing in the outward act by which anyone could hope for salvation. We see these people now, for the sake of outward sign, destroying the peace of all Christians, and calling all who contradict them heretics and antichrists.
>
> B. But these rites, like other good works, are not sufficient for salvation, and no one should set his hope upon them. Yet baptism in water is a command of Christ, and no one can deny it. And it is the duty of everyone who believes inwardly to testify to his belief outwardly, before the Christian community. Now when a Christian sees that these things — outward things, to be sure, yet which Christ himself instituted — are set aside, it is his duty to cry out against it ceaselessly, even if that does destroy the worldly peace of the ungodly. For the command of God must be held up and acknowledged, even if the whole world should crash.
>
> Z. Yes, the people that are now being baptized think they are assembling a sinless church.
>
> B. You do us wrong. If we spoke so, we would be mad, we would lead ourselves astray, and the truth would not be in us. (1 John 1) O God! what can such revilings mean: Ascribe not to us sinners a guilt for which I have no less abhorrence than you have.[23]

In this work, Hubmaier allowed Zwingli to bring his most serious charges and faced all of them squarely. One gets the distinct impression that Zwingli could not have presented his own position better if he had been present to do it himself. The following is reminiscent of the first argument cited.

> Z. Pseudo-baptists have sometimes tried to deny that a man can be saved without baptism in water.
>
> B. You are unjust to us. We know very well that salvation depends

23. *Ibid.*, pp. 151, 153.

neither on baptism nor on works of charity. To be unbaptized does not damn one, nor do poor works, but only unbelief. But he who believes will have himself baptized, and will bring forth good fruits.[24]

With obviously devastating effect, Hubmaier used Zwingli's own words and arguments against him. In relation to Zwingli's argument that the baptism of infants is not forbidden in the New Testament, Hubmaier wrote:

> You protest loudly, (and correctly) that Scripture testifies to no purgatory, but only to hell and heaven. Ah! Zwingli! could we not, even here, demand of you a prohibitory law, so that we should not believe in purgatory? By virtue of your own teaching, you must show us a prohibitive word. Else you must reestablish purgatory, accept a new Papacy, and yield to the statements of the Vicar. Else is your present teaching erroneous.[25]

Hubmaier quoted Zwingli's teachings on believers' baptism, indicating time, place, and published source of his alleged opinions. Referring to the position formerly held by Zwingli, Hubmaier said:

> Yes, you have held that opinion, written for it, and preached it in the public pulpit. . . . There are other matters that I will not now mention. But let me ask you one thing: how many years ago were you of that opinion? Perhaps you remember that you had John Faber, Vicar of Constance, on your hands. You had been preaching the gospel purely and clearly for five years. That was in the year 1523. . . . You admitted to me that children ought not to be baptized before they were instructed in the faith. . . . You desired to make an announcement of that fact in your book, as you did in the 18th article on confirmation. Anyone who reads it, will find your judgment clearly expressed.
>
> With us at that time was Sebastian Ruckensperger of St. Gall, at that time Prior at Klingau. You have openly expressed the same opinions in another book: "On Turbulent Spirits," published in the year 1525. . . . Now, my Zwingli, see how your words, your writings

24. *Ibid.*, pp. 164-65.
25. *Ibid.*, p. 159.

and your preaching agree. But may God enlighten you, and us all, and remove your violence from pious people.[26]

In addition to the arguments against infant baptism previously presented in his book *Concerning Christian Baptism,* Hubmaier denied that baptism and circumcision are analogous. In addition, one may dedicate himself to God, he suggests, but he cannot dedicate another. This would be in violation of the Christian religion, which is personal. That which is true of dedication, Hubmaier insisted, is also true of proxy faith. He delivered Zwingli a "low blow" when he suggested that it would be highly precarious to make an infant's salvation depend on the faith of its sponsors. It is ridiculous to assume, Hubmaier asserted, that godfathers can believe for infants. Also, he rejected as unthinkable the idea that infant baptism is simply a pledge of faith to be. It would then be a sign without meaning, like an inn that has a sign in front but no wine inside. Thus the baptism of infants is meaningless and wholly unwarranted by the Scriptures.

Zwingli pointed to the authority of the church as sufficient authorization for infant baptism. But Hubmaier answered: "You must ask the Scriptures, not the church." For Hubmaier the Scriptures take precedence over the church. The church is always under the judgment of the Scriptures. Hubmaier put it this way:

> If I did not believe the gospel, I would never believe the church, since the church is built on the gospel. . . . So says Christ: Thou art Peter, and on this (the faith that thou believest and professest), will I build my church. (Matt. 16) Therefore we must first be instructed in the Word of God that Jesus is the Christ, the Son of the living God. Then on this foundation we may build gold, silver or precious stones — that is, faith and profession. Thirdly, the church is based on this our faith and profession; not our faith in the church. But on the proclaimed Word of God, that God Himself is, and has become man.[27]

In this basic insight, Hubmaier showed himself to be a theologian of no little ability. Explicit Bible teaching on baptism is thus not the

26. *Ibid.,* pp. 166-67.
27. *Ibid.,* pp. 231-32.

only basis for rejecting the baptism of infants. The nature of the gospel and of man's response to it are also reasons. Faith, man's response to the proclaimed Word, is the foundation of the church. Only the faithful are qualified for baptism and church membership.

Hubmaier brought his paper debate to a close with a summary on baptism in general. It is well worth quoting here.

1. No element or outward object in this world can purify the soul; only faith can cleanse the heart of man.

2. So it follows that baptism is no washing away of sins.

3. But, though it cannot wash them away, yet it is of God. So it must be a public profession of an inward faith — a public duty as a sign of new life, to be led henceforth according to the Word of God in so far as God grants us grace.

4. As to whether the children of Christians and children in Old Testament times are the children of God, we leave that to Him who alone knows all things, and we will not usurp his power. Noah's ark is a type of baptism — there is plain Scripture for that. But we have no Scripture comparing it to circumcision. The baptism with which believers are baptized has its doctrine and example in the plain Word of God. So what we can never truthfully be called is Anabaptists. Infant baptism has no grounds for it; therefore it is not of God.[28]

Following this summary, an appendix brings to bear the testimony of Christians who taught believers' baptism in every generation. Thus, Hubmaier clearly demonstrated that believers' baptism was no recent innovation. The practice had solid support in all ages, even from some, such as Oecolampadius and Zwingli, who had come to oppose it.

Four other booklets on baptism were to come from Hubmaier's busy pen before the end of his Nikolsburg stay. Each had its own peculiar purpose to perform in the current pamphlet war over infant baptism. *Eine christliche Lehrtafel* of December 10, 1526, presented certain basic truths of Christian faith, particularly baptism. Hubmaier felt that probably many Roman priests were as ignorant of the Bible and the true nature of the Christian faith as he formerly had been. He

28. *Ibid.*, pp. 201-2.

believed, therefore, that such would benefit immeasurably from his work. He readily confessed his former ignorant status.

> With my own blush of shame I testify and say it openly, that I became a Doctor in the Holy Scriptures without understanding this Christian article which is contained in this booklet, yea, without having read the Gospels or the Pauline epistles to the end. Instead of living waters, I was held to cisterns of muddy water, poisoned by human feet.[29]

In reality, *Eine christliche Lehrtafel* is an Anabaptist catechism presented in the form of a dialogue between Hans and Leonhard. The speakers' names are those of the Lichtenstein barons, Hubmaier's sponsors at the time. The Apostles' Creed is set forth here, as it is elsewhere in Hubmaier's writings, as a minimal statement of the Christian faith. After Hans has given the twelve articles of the creed, Leonhard asks: "What do you want subsequent to faith?" The answer and dialogue comprise a careful definition of Hubmaier's thinking in relation to baptism. Leonhard first asks a question about the kinds of baptism.

> L. How many kinds of baptism are there?
> H. Three.
> L. Which?
> H. The baptism of the Spirit; baptism in water; a baptism in blood.
> L. Which is the baptism of the Spirit?
> H. It is an inward enlightenment of our hearts, given to us of the Holy Spirit, through the living Word of God.
> L. What is water baptism?
> H. It is an outward and public testimony to the inward baptism of the Spirit. A man receives it by receiving the water, when he, in the sight of all, acknowledges his sins. He also testifies hereby that he believes in the pardon of these sins through the death and resurrection of our Lord Jesus Christ. Then he has outwardly designated and enrolled himself, and has been incorporated into the community

---

29. ME, 2:829; the complete title is *Eine christliche Lehrtafel, die ein jeder Mensch, bevor er im Wasser getauft wird, wissen soll* ("A Christian Teacher-Tablet: What Every Man Ought to Know Before He Is Baptized in Water").

of the church by baptism. This is in accordance with the coming of Christ. . . .

And if he should err therein, he will submit to fraternal punishment according to the commandment of Christ. (Matt. 18) That is the entire baptismal vow. Lost for the space of a thousand years, all the time that Satan with his monastic vows and priest's oaths has pressed in and thrust himself into the seat of the Holy.[30]

Thus Hubmaier once again, through the words of Hans, emphasized the close relationship of baptism to discipleship, church membership, and discipline.

Hubmaier's next work contributed nothing new to the baptismal discussion. It only re-emphasized the obligation of the Christian to be obedient to the command of the risen Christ. The full English title is "The Reason and Cause Why Every Man Who Was Christened in Infancy Is Under Obligation to be Baptized According to the Ordinances of Christ, Even Though He Be One Hundred Years Old." It presents thirteen arguments that obligate a person to be baptized as a believer. The thirteen reasons given in this work were intended to be a supplement to Hubmaier's *Taufbüchlein* but were not published until 1527.[31]

The last polemical work which Hubmaier produced on baptism was in refutation of a well-known book against the Anabaptists by Oecolampadius. The book *On Infant Baptism* is quite similar to "A Speech." The format is that of a theological dialogue, and the basis of authority is the same, the Bible. "If you can show me," Hubmaier pleaded, "a single instance of infant baptism in the Bible, I am defeated. Anabaptist doctrine is therefore not new, but derives from Christ."[32]

It is evident from this work that Hubmaier no longer held to "foot washing" as an ordinance. He limited the ordinances of Christ

---

30. Davidson translation, pp. 281-83.

31. ME, 2:829; original title is *Grund und Ursach, dass ein jeglicher Mensch, der in seiner Kindheit getauft ist, schuldig sei, sich recht nach der Ordnung Christi taufen zu lassen ob er schon 100 Jahre alt wäre.*

32. ME, 2:829-30; original title is *Vom dem Kindertauf, Oecolampadius usw., Ein Gespräch der Prädikanten zu Basel, gehalten mit etlichen Kenkennern des Wiedertauf* (1527) was written as a refutation of Oecolampadius's *Ein Gespräch etlicher Praädikanten zu Basel, gehalten mit etlichen Kekennern des Widertaufs* (1525).

to two when he wrote: "I am not speaking of church customs invented by man. Rather do I speak of two ceremonies of Christ, that is, of baptism and of the Supper. We need no more."

Hubmaier never relied more upon a straightforward exegesis of the Scriptures than in this work, a sample of which follows:

> Im. We know that babes are dear to God, and that they have his promise. Why, then, should they not be baptized?
>
> H. Well, because God loves children, you have not proved that they should be baptized. For the Bible on baptism does not apply to them, but to those who believe, and profess their belief with their lips. On this profession Christ has built his church (Matt. 16). This is the sequence: first, Christ — second, the Word — third, faith — fourth, confession — fifth, baptism — sixth, church. . . . What need have infants of another's faith — that of their fathers, mothers, godparents, or of the church? You claim such a thing, but with no basis in the Bible.
>
> Im. It is written (Mark 10); theirs is the Kingdom of heaven.
>
> H. Immelem, I love you from my heart, but I love the truth more. So I must instruct you better in the Scriptures. Show me, where did you ever read in the Bible that Christ said to children: yours is the Kingdom of heaven. You do violence and injustice to Christ and to the Scripture. It is written "of such" and not "of them." . . .
>
> Im. In what then does the error amount? That we do wrong in taking them, by baptism, into Christian community and fellowship?
>
> H. It hinders them from having their own faith. Christ says: he who believes and is baptized. Not "for whom one believes," since if I could believe for another, I could also be baptized for him. For faith is more than baptism. Some people may strut about proudly with a (so-called) "infused faith," but it has no basis in the Bible.[33]

In this work Hubmaier moved a step beyond his previous works in the condemnation of infant baptism. He now declared not only that it has no basis in the Scriptures but that it actually does the infant an injustice. It gives a false sense of security which undoubtedly hinders a child from making the faith of his sponsors his own when he achieves sufficient maturity. This was a well-known argument used by Luther

---

33. Davidson translation, pp. 512, 376-77.

against the indulgence traffic and could not have failed to have effect on those for whom Luther's argument had value.

Hubmaier had yet one more booklet on baptism in his system. It came from the press in 1527 and was entitled "A Formula for Baptizing in Water Those Who Have Been Indoctrinated in the Faith."[34] Perhaps Hubmaier sensed that his time was short. Certainly by anyone's standards the work of the one year he lived relatively unmolested in Nikolsburg was phenomenal, and the world was the richer because of it. Consequently, the Anabaptist movement was not to escape the imprint of Hubmaier's life and teachings for centuries to come. As Johann Loserth has pointed out, Riedemann's *Rechenschaft* closely follows the writings of Hubmaier.[35] The similarity of ideas is particularly apparent in relation to baptism, the Lord's Supper, and the ban. The *Large Chronicle* of the Hutterites also recognizes the indebtedness of the Hutterian Brethren to Balthasar Hubmaier:

> Two hymns are still in our brotherhood which this Balthasar Hübmaier composed. There are also other writings by him from which one learns how he had so forcefully argued the right baptism, and how infant baptism is altogether wrong, all this proved from the Holy Scriptures. Likewise he brought to light the truth of the Lord's Supper, and refuted the idolatrous sacrament and the great error and seduction by it.[36]

Franz Heimann, who has made a detailed study of the influence of Hubmaier upon Peter Riedemann, writes:

> There exists a common Anabaptist understanding both in Riedemann and Hübmaier as far as they deal with the fallen state of man, the inner rebirth in faith, and the testimony of this faith in confession and life, presupposing the freedom of man to obey God's commandments. Beyond that also the teaching concerning the right

---

34. The original title is *Eine Form zu taufen in Wasser die im Glauben Unterrichteten.*

35. Cited by Franz Heimann, "The Hutterite Doctrine of Church and Common Life, A Study of Peter Riedemann's Confession of Faith of 1540, II," MQR 26 (April 1952): 143.

36. *Large Chronicle*, p. 52.

sequence of preaching the Word, hearing, change of life, and baptism, seems to be derived from Hübmaier. Furthermore, Riedemann seemed to have borrowed from him almost in its entirety the polemic against infant baptism (70-77) with all its numerous arguments and reasons. . . . There is also a fairly complete agreement of the *Rechenschaft* with Hübmaier's teachings concerning the "Fellowship of the Lord's Table," whose inner communion must already be present prior to the breaking of the bread. Likewise we find already in Hübmaier the teaching of the Christian brotherhood or church *(Gemeinschaft)*, which exercises inner discipline by brotherly punishment and the ban. It seems fairly apparent that Riedemann knew and used Hübmaier's tracts and books.[37]

Other Anabaptist writers also drank from the Hubmaier fountain; they could hardly do otherwise. Their original contributions, while genuine and helpful in presenting the Anabaptist position on believers' baptism, were relatively insignificant when compared with that of Hubmaier.

37. Heimann, "Hutterite Doctrine," pp. 143-44. It is impossible to agree with Heimann when he writes: "Balthasar Hübmaier, who has a rather isolated position among the early sixteenth century teachers of adult baptism, strongly emphasizes that the sincere belonging to the church is a precondition of salvation, and he places the quasi-sacramental element of forgiveness of sins into the ceremony of baptism proper." This appears to be both a misinterpretation and a misrepresentation of Hubmaier's actual position. It is possible, while ignoring the basic rules of hermeneutics, to so interpret the New Testament. It is true that Hubmaier did place in the baptismal ceremony a pronouncement of the forgiveness of sins after baptism but this was not intended to be a doctrinal exposition of baptism. He had already given that numerous times. What he is doing here is simply emphasizing the recognition of the forgiveness of sins symbolized by the baptismal act in a liturgical form. In baptism the world could see the sign of a true disciple, but without it there was no way either the visible church or the world could have tangible evidence of one's faith. At this point Hubmaier labored to make himself understood, as any careful reading of his works will, I believe, substantiate. I believe Denck reflects Hubmaier's position in the *Widerruf* when he writes in article VII, "Ceremonies are not sinful in themselves, but he who hopes to secure salvation through baptism or the Lord's Supper has a superstitious form of faith." *Denck Schriften,* p. 107.

Baptism in the *Rechenschaft* of 1541

Though his dependence on Hubmaier is clear, Riedemann felt the freedom, as did all Anabaptists, to express Anabaptist beliefs in his own way. The originality of expression is clearly evident in the analogy which Riedemann drew between the faith of Mary and the faith of the new man in Christ Jesus:

> The birth of Christ, however, took place as is said above: through the word that was preached or proclaimed. Mary believed the angel, and through faith received the Holy Spirit, who worked together with her faith so that she conceived Christ, who was thus born of her. Whoever now is to be born in Christian wise, must firstly like Mary hear the word and believe the same, that when his faith is sealed with the Holy Spirit he may be truly accepted into the Church of Christ. In this way also did the apostles.[38]

Riedemann rejected infant baptism for exactly the same reasons that Hubmaier did. He listed six reasons given by pedobaptists for the baptism of infants. Refuting them in typical Anabaptist fashion he took his stance squarely on the Scriptures, which he knew well.

After dispensing with the subject of infant baptism, Riedemann turned his attention to a discussion "Concerning the Baptism of Christ and of His Church." The biblical order, of which Hubmaier made so much, was also insisted upon by Riedemann as necessary to scripturally valid baptism. This baptism Riedemann declared to be "a bath of re-birth." It does not bring or convey the new birth but rather is a sign of that which is already an accomplished fact. Repeating the analogy of the power of faith and the Holy Spirit in Mary's life, Riedemann launched into a discussion of the new birth and the relationship of baptism to the new life. Thus the meaning of the otherwise confusing terminology "bath of rebirth" becomes clear:

> This birth, however, taketh place in this wise. If the word is heard and the same believed, then faith is sealed with the power of God, the Holy Spirit, who immediately reneweth the man and maketh

38. Rideman, *Account,* pp. 68-69.

him live . . . so that the man is formed a new creature. . . . Thus, whosoever is born in this wise, to him belongeth baptism as a bath of re-birth, signifying that he hath entered into the covenant of the grace and knowledge of God.

In a further discussion of baptism and the new birth, Riedemann, by an ingenious stroke, knocked the props from under certain defenders of infant baptism. These had been asserting that infant baptism is analogous to circumcision. He, in effect, said: "You are right, only you have not drawn the analogy clearly in terms of the new covenant." His argument runs thus:

> Therefore we teach that as Abraham was commanded to circumcise in his house, even so was Christ to baptize in his house, as the words that he spoke to John indicate, "Suffer it to be so, for thus it becometh us to fulfill all God's righteousness." Now, just as Abraham could not circumcise in his house before the child was born to him, nor all his seed after him, neither can anyone be baptized in the house of Christ unless he be first born of Christ through the word and faith. But he who is born in this manner, is baptized after he hath confessed his faith.

It is not always clear what Riedemann meant by the term "church of Christ." "Baptism," he wrote, "is acceptance into the Church of Christ."[39] In his baptismal ceremony he used "his kingdom" rather than "his church." The local, visible congregation was certainly meant when he suggested that baptism should take place before the church. Thus it is probable that his teaching at this point is identical to that of Hubmaier. If there are any essential differences between Riedemann's concept of believers' baptism and that of Hubmaier, they are elusive to say the least. There is, therefore, no evident change by Riedemann in the theology of baptism.

---

39. *Ibid.*, p. 78. The preceding quotations are from the same page.

Baptism in the Theology of Pilgram Marpeck

No advance in the theology of baptism can be detected among the Anabaptists until the publication of Marpeck's *Taufbüchlein* of 1542. This was Marpeck's first work after his *Confession of Faith,* written in Strasbourg ten years before.[40] It was the first of several significant publications on controversial tenets of the Brethren as these were held by the Marpeck circle of south German Anabaptists. Marpeck's doctrine of baptism was hammered out in controversy with the Lutherans on one hand and with Casper Schwenckfeld on the other. Undoubtedly Bernhard Rothman and Balthasar Hubmaier were sources upon which Marpeck drew rather heavily. But the presentation of baptism as an integral part of a covenant theology was evidently the product of his own genius.

The key to Marpeck's theology is the term "the new covenant." As circumcision is the sign of the old covenant, baptism is the sign of the new covenant in Marpeck's opinion. Marpeck referred to baptism as "the covenant seal" *(Bundeschliessung).* The covenant seal must be preceded by the circumcision of the heart. For Marpeck, "circumcision in the Old Testament is a *Figur* of circumcision of the conscience of the New Covenant, namely the baptism with the Holy Spirit and with fire."[41] In characteristic fashion Marpeck contrasted the covenant sign of the old covenant with that of the new. The circumcision of Christ is without hands and is the circumcision of the heart as foretold by Jeremiah.

The spiritual circumcision of which Marpeck wrote, unlike that of the old covenant, is not exclusive. It applies to both men and women, to all who are in Christ. The circumcision of the old covenant has the same relationship to the circumcision of the heart as shadow has to substance *(Figur und Wesen).* Water baptism, it follows, is an outward sign of this inner experience referred to as "the circumcision of the hearts." As such, it becomes the seal or sign of one's covenant relationship to God through Jesus Christ.

40. See Wenger, ed., "Pilgram Marpeck's Confession of Faith Composed at Strasbourg," MQR 2 (July 1938): 167-202.
41. *Taufbüchlein,* quoted by Kiwiet, *Marbeck,* pp. 130-31. See also Klassen and Klaassen, *The Writings of Pilgram Marpeck,* pp. 240, 241.

Spiritual circumcision is also synonymous with rebirth *(Wiederge-burt)*, which is the result of faith in Christ. Baptism cannot be applied where faith in Christ is lacking. Marpeck wrote, "Where there is no faith, there is nothing but nothing *[da ist alle ler kain let]* and baptism is no baptism."[42] It was Marpeck's conviction that the baptism act *(Täufhandlung)* is truly baptism only if it is preceded by a conscious personal faith, openly confessed beforehand.

Marpeck also insisted that the confession must be one's own confession, personally believed and formulated, "not a foreign confession *[fremdes Bekenntnis]*, that is to say, not the confession of the sponsors or of the old order of the church."[43] At this point he would disparage the attempts of Hubmaier and Riedemann to use the Apostles' Creed as a suitable prebaptismal confession. Marpeck's view of faith and confession was more dynamic than that reflected in the writings of Hubmaier. At least, he was more careful to spell out in unmistakable terms the necessity of a personal trust in Jesus Christ as the only acceptable faith. Faith here is unmistakably *fiducia*, as contrasted with *assensus* of the scholastics.

Faith finds expression, according to Marpeck, in personal confession. This confession is a confession of regeneration, forgiveness of sins, and of one's own faith in Christ. Thus, a person confesses that he has been born again. The new birth is accomplished through the call of the Holy Spirit which comes to people through the written Word and the preached Word. With the reception of these Words in the heart, a person is born again. The rebirth must in this manner always precede baptism. The resultant confession makes the baptismal act a true baptism which symbolizes the burial of the old man, a putting on of Christ, and an entrance into the church. Thus, for Marpeck, baptism's primary reference is to discipleship. The believer declares that he is forsaking the old life *(abwendung vom alten Leben)* and is turning to the new.

At Strasbourg and again later for the benefit of the Lutherans, Marpeck insisted that the baptism of infants is out of the question. The child knows nothing of the significance of sin, repentance, or the

42. *Ibid.,* p. 128. This is also Leupold Scharnschlager's position as stated in a letter to Michael Leubel in 1532; see Hein, "Two Letters," pp. 165-66.
43. Kiwiet, *Marbeck,* p. 132.

new life. He is incapable of meeting the demands of discipleship. Because baptism has no objective value in itself, and because a child is incapable of faith, infant baptism would be meaningless. Baptism cannot bring faith where there is no faith. Marpeck insisted that children are not damned in their innocent state, for they have not become accountable for their sins.[44]

Baptism for Schwenckfeld was only a superstitious act, but for Marpeck it was the necessary witness of the Spirit to acceptance in the church. Upon being accused by Schwenckfeld of making baptism a sacramental act, Marpeck answered that he had been misinterpreted and misrepresented. He then reiterated that baptism is an act of the church and not a sacramental work. Baptism into the visible church must be preceded by faith, the new birth, and confession. According to Pilgram, baptism derives its importance from the command of Christ given to his church to baptize. Love for Christ then compels obedience. Therefore baptism cannot be a matter of indifference.[45]

While not departing from the characteristic Anabaptist reliance on scriptural exegesis for the support of believers' baptism, Marpeck went beyond mere exegesis. Believers' baptism became for him an indispensable concept within the context of his covenant theology. Therefore, baptism for Marpeck had a threefold relationship: it is the seal or sign of the new covenant, it is a symbol of Christian discipleship, and it is the door into the visible church.[46]

Dutch Anabaptism and Believers' Baptism

Menno Simons's attention was first drawn to the Anabaptists on hearing of the execution at Leeuwarden of Sicke Freerks, a pious tailor. The charge was that he had been baptized a second time. "It sounded strange in my ears," Menno wrote, "that a second baptism was spoken of."[47]

44. *Ibid.,* p. 130, and Wenger, "Marpeck's Confession," p. 194.
45. Kiwiet, *Marbeck,* pp. 137-38. See also Estep, *Anabaptist Beginnings,* p. 167.
46. For a more complete summary of Marpeck's teaching on baptism see Wenger, "Theology of Marpeck," pp. 247-48.
47. *Complete Writings,* p. 7.

Not many years later, Menno himself became a champion of the re-baptizers. However, neither Menno nor Dirk Philips made any original contribution to the theology of baptism. Essentially, both Dirk and Menno presented the same position on the subject. Only the emphases are different. Yet for this reason the teaching of Dutch Anabaptism on baptism is deserving of attention.

In Dutch Anabaptism, the authority for believers' baptism is derived from the command of Christ and the apostolic example.[48] The emphasis upon what is termed the *gottlichen Ordnung* (divine order), of which Hubmaier made so much, reappears in the writings of both Dirk and Menno. Dirk found the order in preaching the Word, hearing the Word, believing, and baptism. Biblical examples include Philip, Peter, Paul, and Silas. This divine order is used to point up two incontrovertible truths in the eyes of the Dutch Mennonites: the absolute necessity of regeneration prior to baptism, and the impossibility of infant baptism. Dirk leaves little room for misunderstanding when he writes:

> The baptism of Christ typifies . . . a putting off of the body of the sins of the flesh, a burial with Christ, and a resurrection by faith to a new spiritual life and being, for in Christ Jesus no outward sign alone avails anything without . . . regeneration and the true Christian life, for by it man becomes united with God, incorporated into the body of Christ and a partaker of the Holy Spirit (John 3:4-10). Hence outward baptism alone avails nothing if the person baptized . . . has not died unto sin, and does not live unto righteousness (Rom. 6:5).[49]

After citing Acts 2:37 and similar passages, Menno offers his interpretation.

> Observe, my elect brethren, how harmonious are both Master and disciples in their teaching, namely, first the birth from above, by which we become children of God (John 1:14); and then the water,

48. Simons, *Christian Baptism,* in *Complete Writings,* p. 237. Cf. Dietrich Philips, "Of the Baptism of Our Lord Jesus Christ," in *Enchiridion,* trans. A. B. Kolb (Elkhart, Ind.: Mennonite Publishing Company, 1910), p. 22.

49. Philips, "Baptism of Christ," pp. 23-24.

by which the obedience of the children of God is signified. Third, the communion of the Holy Ghost, by which we are assured in our hearts of the grace of God, of the remission of sins, and of everlasting life through Christ Jesus our Lord.

In numerous instances Menno repeatedly insisted that baptism has no saving significance. No Anabaptist writer of the sixteenth century made clearer the nonsacramental nature of believers' baptism. The following selection from Menno's voluminous works is typical of many similar statements.

> If we ascribe the remission of sins to baptism and not to the blood of Christ, then we mold a golden calf and place it in the stead of Christ. For if we could be washed or cleansed by baptism, then Christ Jesus and his merits would have to abdicate. . . . For the most holy and precious blood of our beloved Lord Jesus Christ must and shall have the praise, as has been so clearly declared and testified by all the true prophets and apostles, throughout the Scriptures.[50]

Like Riedemann, Dirk referred to baptism as a "bath of regeneration," but he did not interpret this patristic description of baptism sacramentally. To the contrary, he writes:

> Baptism is also a washing of regeneration, because, according to the command and institution of the Lord (John 1:28; 3:5), it belongs to or is for regenerated children of God, that is, true believers. The true believers in Christ, therefore, are the regenerated children of God, but baptism is the washing of regeneration (Tit. 1:5), that is, there the newborn children of God are bathed and washed, but not by the virtue of the elementary or natural water, but by the power of the blood and spirit of Christ Jesus. (1 Pet. 3:20)[51]

Since the Anabaptists could not justify practicing baptism on sacramental grounds, they were forced in controversy with the inspirationists to find its support elsewhere. This they did in the Scriptures and in a biblical theology. The conclusion of Dirk Philips's article "Of

50. *Christian Baptism,* in *Complete Writings,* pp. 243-44.
51. Philips, "Baptism of Christ," pp. 27-28.

the Baptism of Our Lord Jesus Christ" presents the basic apologetic of the Anabaptists for believers' baptism. Dirk called down the wrath of God on those who treat so lightly that which is obviously an ordinance of Christ.

> Therefore we maintain, that our Lord Jesus Christ's ordinance of baptism is ever pleasing to him, and remains as a word and command of God, regardless of the fact that some so fearfully misuse baptism, or that some despise it, whereby they heap upon themselves the wrath of God and will not escape his judgment.[52]

Therefore, believers' baptism was viewed as an act of obedience to the command of Christ on the part of a true disciple. Baptism was also, in the eyes of the Dutch Anabaptists, a symbol of regeneration and a pledge of discipleship. Philips called it "a sign or type of the spiritual baptism, and an evidence of true repentance and a sign of faith in Jesus Christ." He referred to it as "a sacramental sign" and "a covenant sign." He meant that baptism is sacramental in the sense that it testifies to salvation already received. It is a sign of the covenant which is sealed by the Holy Spirit when one commits his life to Christ. It is significant to note the difference between Pilgram Marpeck's heavy emphasis on baptism as a covenant seal and the apparent lack of emphasis by the Dutch Anabaptists. Perhaps the better-trained Philips saw problems here that Marpeck had failed to see. Thus, there follows in Dirk's writings a distinction between the sealing by the Holy Spirit and the sign of that sealing in baptism.[53]

Baptism for Dirk Philips was also important as a necessary element in the constitution of the visible church. Marpeck had found it necessary to work out a clear doctrine of the visible church in his controversy with the Schwenckfelders. Dirk recognized a similar necessity when confronted with David Joris's preaching of a secret discipleship. Dirk argued that the church in the New Testament is not always represented as invisible but is visible as well.

> The apostles, according to the command of the Lord, through the preaching of the gospel, faith and truth, and by proper Christian

---

52. *Ibid.,* p. 66.
53. "The Covenant and Baptism," in *Enchiridion,* p. 452.

baptism, and the power and unity of the Holy Spirit, gathered a church out of all nations (Matt. 28:19, 20; Mark 16:15, 16). This was not an invisible body, for they did not write nor send their epistles in a general or indiscriminate way to all people, but specifically denominating the believers and God-fearing people, and designating many persons by name. How is it possible for all this to be invisible?[54]

Both Menno Simons and Dirk Philips devoted much time to denouncing infant baptism. Menno, like Hubmaier, constantly ridiculed the idea that infant baptism is analogous to circumcision. The Fathers were cited as proof that infant baptism is a postapostolic innovation. In fact, all the familiar arguments of the Swiss Brethren and south German Anabaptists were offered repeatedly by Menno. However, to these Menno added what may be called a moral argument. Referring to the characteristic immorality of his day, he vividly illustrated the superstitious use of infant baptism by godless sponsors and priests. Candidates thus baptized could be expected to repeat the same pattern of conduct after they reached the age of responsibility.

> Yet notwithstanding all this, these same persons carry the children who are thus illegitimately born of such seducers, such immoral rascals and abandoned women, to the baptism, that they may be called Christians and be trained up in the same works and fruits as their unchristian, adulterous parents, in whom and by whom they are conceived and gotten in accursed and damnable adultery.[55]

As Menno emphasized, the age of the candidate is not the primary qualification for baptism but rather his ability to experience regeneration and discipleship. The question is not adult baptism vs. infant baptism but rather believers' baptism vs. unbelievers' baptism. Clearly, Menno's accent was on believers' baptism. The obvious corollary of believers' baptism, however, is that infants cannot possibly be fit subjects for baptism, for they are incapable of discipleship. In the tenderest tones, which transcend the limitations of the printed page, Menno writes,

54. "The Church," in *Enchiridion*, pp. 483-84.
55. *Christian Baptism*, in *Complete Writings*, pp. 251-52.

> Little ones must wait according to God's Word until they can understand the holy Gospel of grace and sincerely confess it; . . . then only is it time, no matter how young or how old, for them to receive Christian baptism. . . . If they die before coming to years of discretion, . . . then they die under . . . the generous promise of grace given through Christ Jesus. Luke 18:16.[56]

Dirk, no less than Menno, held to the conviction that children in their innocency are unfit subjects for baptism and in the case of death are saved by the grace of God.

> Since therefore Christ . . . says that we should become like children, and humble ourselves, it follows without contradiction: First, that children (so long as they are in their simplicity) are innocent and reckoned by God as being without sin. Second, that there is also something good in children (although they have been partakers of the transgression and sinful nature of Adam), namely, the simple and unassuming and humble nature, in which they are pleasing to God (yet purely by grace through Jesus Christ) so long as they remain therein. . . . It is true and indubitable that children as well as adults — the children by their simplicity, the adults by their faith are saved by the grace of our *Lord* Jesus Christ (Acts 15:11).[57]

While there are differing emphases among the Anabaptists, there is a common Anabaptist stance on baptism. And though various arguments from patristics, history, logic, and theology are used, the Scriptures remain the authoritative basis for the Anabaptist doctrine. On the basis of the New Testament, interpreted christologically, baptism is viewed as a witness or testimony of regeneration, a pledge of discipleship, and the door into the visible church. Neither baptism nor the Lord's Supper has sacramental significance. They are signs *(significatum)* which point to Christ, the cross-event, and resurrection. Thus baptism for the Anabaptists is not a "naked symbol." To the contrary, it is rich in symbolic significance relative to the *kerygma,* discipleship, and the church.[58]

---

56. *Ibid.,* p. 241.
57. Philips, "Baptism of Christ," pp. 43-45.
58. The symbolic significance of immersion as a mode of baptism apparently

Believers' baptism, therefore, becomes a necessary element in a highly integrated theology. It is the indispensable act of obedient discipleship without which the church as a visible fellowship cannot exist. The Dutch Mennonite scholar J. A. Oosterbaan expresses well the relation of the doctrine of baptism to Anabaptist theology.

> The connection which the early Anabaptists established between a personally confessed faith and baptism was not merely a peculiarity arising from certain deviate interpretations of Bible texts. The total

----

escaped most sixteenth-century Anabaptists. The pouring of water upon the head of the kneeling believer was the most common method of baptizing. Both means of baptism are mentioned in Marpeck's *Taufbüchlein*. Hubmaier, discussing believers' baptism in the days of the Fathers, mentioned in passing that triune immersion was the common practice at the time of Tertullian. Evidently he believed that immersion was the primitive practice. The mode of baptism was apparently a matter of indifference among sixteenth-century Anabaptists. However, it is likely that immersion was practiced occasionally. As cited in chapter 2, Johannes Kessler, a Reformed minister of St. Gall, reported the baptism of Wolfgang Ulimann by Conrad Grebel in the Rhine River by immersion upon Ulimann's request. Ulimann preceded Grebel to St. Gall and worked with him during a highly successful evangelistic campaign. At the end of two weeks of intensive activity, Grebel led a throng of people to the Sitter River where many were baptized on Palm Sunday, April 9, 1525. Since Ulimann had been immersed by Grebel and both had worked together in St. Gall, it is probable the baptisms on this occasion were by immersion. There was a creek in St. Gall sufficient for pouring but in no way large enough or deep enough for the immersing of candidates. It was Dr. Howard Osgood's opinion that this is why Grebel led the group to the Sitter River, two to three miles distant from the city. See Henry S. Burrage, *The Act of Baptism in the History of the Christian Church* (Philadelphia: American Baptist Publication Society, 1879), p. 141. Vedder held that immersion became the chief mode of baptism among the Swiss Anabaptists. I do not believe, however, that this assertion can be substantiated. He admitted, "Elsewhere [outside of the Ulimann and St. Gall incidents] we find definite proofs of immersion only among the Anabaptists of Augsburg, and in Poland, where the practice was introduced in 1573." *Hübmaier,* p. 144. See Newman, *History of Anti-Pedobaptism,* pp. 336ff., for a discussion of immersion among the antitrinitarian Polish Brethren in 1574 and subsequently. Suffice it to say that among the Anabaptists of Switzerland, south Germany, Moravia, and the Netherlands, the baptismal formula was always trinitarian. Even though the name of Christ may have been used alone in some instances, this was not the prevailing usage and has no theological significance.

Christocentric view of the Bible, the basic ideas of Christology, the reality of the new man in Christ, the church of new-born believers, and baptism upon confession of faith — which is the sign of the change from the old life to the new — all this forms an organic theology which fits together and of which no single part can be missing.[59]

Like spokes of a wheel, the Anabaptist views of the Scriptures, discipleship, and the visible church find their hub in baptism. Baptism was thus the most effective single distinguishing mark of the sixteenth-century Anabaptist movement.

59. Oosterbaan, "Theology of Simons," p. 196.

X

अ   अ

Church and State

ITH THE INTRODUCTION OF BELIEVERS' BAPTISM BY THE SWISS
Brethren, discipleship *(Nachfolge Christi)* became a corporate
experience. At this point the Anabaptist vision of the visible
church, patterned after the apostolic prototype of the New Testament,
became incarnate in history. Henceforth believers' baptism was to serve
as the mark distinguishing the free churches of the Anabaptists from
territorial churches, the so-called *Volkskirchen* or *Landeskirchen* of the
Reformers.

Believers' baptism implied repudiation of the established churches
and also judgment against the inspirationists *(Spiritualisten)*. It not only
set the Anabaptists apart from existing practices but gave the movement
a uniqueness which it had not possessed before. With the formation
of the first Anabaptist congregation was revealed the genius of Anabaptism; it implemented what others only contemplated.

In the distinctive view of the church is seen the most determinative
insight of sixteenth-century Anabaptism. In fact, it is possible, as Littell
has done, to define the Anabaptist movement solely in terms of ecclesiology. "The Anabaptists proper were those in the 'Left Wing' who
gathered and disciplined a 'True Church' *(rechte Kirche)* upon the
apostolic pattern."[1]

However, some other veteran scholars of the Anabaptist move-

---

1. Littell, *Anabaptist View,* p. 47.

ment find its essence elsewhere. Bender holds that the Anabaptist view of the church is "ultimately derivative from its concept of Christianity as discipleship."[2] He contends that the essence of Anabaptism is seen in the concept of *Nachfolge Christi* (discipleship).

On the other hand, Friedmann, the well-known authority on the Hutterites, finds the essence of Anabaptism in a "two world concept." By this phrase he emphasizes that the Anabaptists as Christians felt themselves engaged in an inevitable conflict with the present world order. The kingdom of God was viewed as both the present reign of Christ in the life of the reborn and also a future hope in eschatological dimensions.

> These two views, the kingdom present in every reborn Christian (or present where two or three are assembled in the Master's name), and the kingdom as the new order to be expected at any moment and for which proper preparation is needed, are intermixed in Anabaptist thought just as they are in the original source of that teaching, the Gospels.[3]

The apparent disparity between the three divergent views cited here, which purport to set forth the essence of the movement, indicates two possible insights. First, Anabaptist theology actually is closely interwoven; and second, a case can be made for any one of the three viewpoints. In a sense the Anabaptist concept of the church *(Gemeinde)* can be viewed simply as corporate discipleship. Or it can be viewed as a brotherhood of believers whose citizenship is in heaven but who live upon the earth in an indissoluble tension with this world.

All three of these concepts, of course, are derived from an Anabaptist interpretation of the New Testament. From the earliest documents of the movement, the distinctive Anabaptist concept of the church is discernible.[4] Certainly by the middle of 1524 the concept

2. Bender, "Church," ME, 1:595.
3. "The Doctrine of the Two Worlds," in Hershberger, *Recovery of Anabaptist Vision,* pp. 110-11.
4. See Grebel's letter to Müntzer in Williams and Mergal, *Spiritual and Anabaptist Writers,* pp. 79-82, and Hubmaier's Eighteen Articles in Estep, *Anabaptist Beginnings,* pp. 23-26.

was quite clear, at least in broad outline. By January 21, 1525, the concepts of both discipleship and the church find implementation in the inauguration of believers' baptism. In the historical process apparently both concepts developed simultaneously.

Without a distinctive view of the church, however, it is highly questionable that the Anabaptist version of Christianity would have developed. Neither the concept of discipleship nor that of two worlds would have made Anabaptism distinctive. The Brethren of the Common Life used the concept of *Nachfolge Christi* as the guiding motif for Christian life, as did Thomas à Kempis and other medieval mystics. No new type of institutional Christianity came into existence as a result. The doctrine of two worlds was not absent from the thinking of the inspirationists, but the doctrine of a church patterned after the New Testament example was.

To Franck and Schwenckfeld the implementation of the New Testament pattern of the church was neither possible nor desirable. To Luther and Zwingli, even though desirable, it was clearly impossible. In the final analysis, then, it is the view of the church that distinguishes the Anabaptists from other contemporary reform efforts.[5] This statement does not imply that the essence of Anabaptism can be discovered in the concept of the church per se. The concept of the church must be seen as multidimensional. Not simply abstract theology, it was a living reality within the historical process — in relation to its own fellowship and its orientation to the world.

Visible and Invisible

The thrust of Anabaptist ecclesiology was toward the implementation in history of the visible church. Anabaptism was relatively unconcerned

5. James Leo Garrett in *The Nature of the Church according to the Radical Continental Reformation* (Fort Worth, 1957) delineates four different ecclesiological types within the Radical Reformation. They are: the "gathered church" of the Swiss Brethren; the "church-community" of the Hutterian Brethren; the "church-kingdom-state" of Münsterites and Thomas Müntzer; and "the inward, invisible, universal, spiritual church, ungathered and without external sacraments or worship" of the Franckian-Schwenckfelder tradition. See pp. 11-16.

with the idea of the universal, invisible church. This does not mean that the idea was foreign to Anabaptist thought, for such was not the case. The almost unanimous use of the Apostles' Creed in Anabaptist circles would attest to at least a tacit admission of the concept. There are also many references to the invisible universal church in sixteenth-century Anabaptist literature.

Hubmaier's treatment of the idea is more extensive than that of most other Anabaptists. According to him there are two meanings for the word "church" in the New Testament — the universal and the local. It was Hubmaier's conviction that the universal church is made up of all the regenerate who are "united alone by the Spirit of God." He maintained that the local church, by contrast, is a fellowship under the leadership of a "shepherd or bishop, and assembles for teaching, for baptism, and for the communion." Hubmaier alluded to the human relationship of a mother and daughter to explain the relationship between the universal and the particular church. He suggested that the individual congregation may err but that the universal church cannot.[6]

There are several allusions to the universal church in the writings of other Anabaptists as well. Typical of such references is this from Dirk Philips: "The name church or congregation indicates that it is not only invisible, but also visible, for the term used is 'ecclesia,' that is, a gathering or meeting or congregating together, and the term applied to the person addressing the congregation is 'Ecclesiastes.'"[7] Dirk, unlike other Anabaptists, found the origin of the church in the pre-incarnate Christ and in existence among the angels in heaven and in the Old Testament. Yet his emphasis was on the particular, visible congregation of God. In his book *The Church of God,* Philips was clearly concerned with a delineation of the characteristics of the functioning church as a local gathering of disciples.

The emphasis among the Anabaptists on the local, visible, functioning church *(Gemeinde)* so overshadowed any other concept that Bender feels justified in writing: "The original Anabaptist movement rejected the idea of an invisible church, which was the invention of Luther, holding that the Christian community in any particular place

6. Davidson translation, pp. 287-88.
7. Philips, *Enchiridion,* p. 483.

is as visible as the Christian man, and that its Christian character must be 'in evidence.' "8

Whether or not Anabaptists completely rejected the idea of the invisible church or not, they clearly repudiated the concept taught by Schwenckfeld and Franck. The emphasis of sixteenth-century Anabaptism was on the New Testament concern for the gathered church of the regenerate.

The Fall of the Church

Anabaptists held that the primitive church of the apostles had lost its purity and had ceased to be the church. This catastrophe was referred to as "the fall of the church." Even though this is a common Reformation concept, there is no general agreement as to when the fall occurred. For the Reformers, it took place with the assumption of temporal authority by the papacy. Luther dated the fall with Sabianus and Boniface III, but Zwingli pinpointed it with Hildebrand and the "assertion of hierarchial power." Calvin was inclined to date it with Gregory the Great.9 However, for the Anabaptists, it was the usual procedure to date the fall with the union of church and state under Constantine. An anonymous Anabaptist tract, printed in Augsburg around 1530, asserts, "There was not among the Christians of old at the time of the apostles until the Emperor Constantine any temporal power or sword."10

8. ME, 1:597.

9. Littell, *Anabaptist View,* p. 64.

10. Cited by Hans J. Hillerbrand, "An Early Anabaptist Treatise on the Christian and the State," MQR 32 (January 1958): 31. The entire tract is reproduced photographically in the same issue. I have translated the tract with the help of Miss Ruth Lahotski. The title, like many works at the time, gives a brief digest of the contents: "Disclosure of the Babylonian Harlot and Antichrist's Old and New Mystery and Abomination. Also concerning the Victory, Peace, and Reign of True Christians in their Obedience to the Magistracy, Who carry their Cross with Christ without Rebellion and Resistance in Patience and Love, Brought to the Light of Day for the Glory of God and the Service, Strength, and Improvement of all the Pious and God seekers. (Matt.

The Anabaptist interpretation of the church's fall differed greatly from that of the Reformers. The Reformers apparently accepted uncritically the Roman interpretation of the Constantinian era as a period of the church's triumph. In so doing they fell victim to the Constantinian symbiosis unwittingly embracing a pre-Christian sacral society whose paganism they conveniently overlooked or christened and sought to regulate. For them the Reformation was a revolt against papal authority but not against the Roman concept of the church as an institution. They believed that the old church needed to be cleansed from various abuses and errors, but they did not want to be cut off from its corporate solidarity. Even after their organizational break with Rome was complete, they still felt a sense of continuity with the Roman Church of pre-Reformation days.

In the Reformers' eyes, then, the fall of the church was never complete in the sense that the pre-Reformation Roman Catholic Church had ceased to be the church. This is the reason why the Anabaptists viewed the Reformers as halfway reformers. To them, the Reformers, by introducing the *Landeskirchen,* remained within the fallen church.

To the Anabaptists, the fall of Rome was complete. The union of church and state which was set in motion under Constantine brought all sorts of dire consequences. Infant baptism was one of these. Menno saw the culmination of "the Fall in an Edict of Innocent I, 407 A.D., which made infant baptism compulsory."[11] This is evidently Hubmaier's reference also when he put the following words into the mouth of Hans concerning the baptismal vow in his booklet, "What Every Christian Ought to Know Before Baptism": "That is the entire baptismal vow. Lost for the space of a thousand years, all the time that Satan with his monastic vows and priest's oaths has pressed in and thrust himself into the seat of the Holy."[12]

When infant baptism became the prevailing practice, the character of the church as a fellowship of the regenerate was seriously altered.

---

22) Render to Caesar that which is Caesar's and to God that which is God's. (Prov. 24) Do not Join the Rebellion."

11. Krahn, *Menno Simons* (Karlsruhe: Heinrich Schneider, 1936), p. 136; cited by Littell, *Anabaptist View,* p. 63.

12. Davidson translation, p. 281.

And with the union of church and state and the accompanying use of force to compel conformity to the state church, the fall was complete. To use Verduin's words, "The 'fall' of the Church had so changed the visage of the Bride of Christ as to make her unrecognizable. She who had been sent on a mission of healing and helping had taken on the features of the modern police state."[13]

The Nature of the Church

From the initial stages of the Anabaptist movement there was no hesitancy to cut away the unholy accretions of the ages. The one attempt was to adhere strictly to the apostolic pattern as revealed by the New Testament. Reformation was out of the question. The Anabaptists saw their task as building anew on the original foundation. "Our forebears fell away from the true God and from the one true, common, divine Word, from the divine institutions, from Christian love and life, and lived without God's law and gospel in human, useless, unchristian customs and ceremonies," Grebel wrote. He added that the "evangelical preachers" were also in error. True, they were "antipapal," but their preaching was "not equal to the divine Word nor in harmony with it." He confessed that as long as he read and heard only the views of such preachers, he, too, continued in error. "But after we took Scripture in hand," he explained, then he became aware of the failures of the Reformation. He admonished Müntzer to build his church on "only what may be found in pure and clear Scripture." Grebel's position was characteristic of sixteenth-century Anabaptism.

If the plumb line for the restitution of the church was the New Testament, then what was the foundation upon which the church was to be built? Although stated in different forms, the Anabaptists were agreed that the foundation was Jesus Christ. Hubmaier stated it thus: "As says Paul: no other foundation can any man lay, except what is laid, which is Christ Jesus. (1 Cor. 3) . . . The church is based on this our faith and profession; not our faith in the church. But on the proclaimed

13. Verduin, *Reformers and Their Stepchildren*, p. 45.

Word of God, that God Himself is, and has become man."[14] For Hubmaier the revelation of God in Christ was the foundation of the church, its only foundation. And without the proclamation of the Word of God — the *kerygma* — there could be no church.

Unlike the inspirationists, the Anabaptists desired no new revelation as a basis for rebuilding the church. Like Nehemiah, who returned to rebuild the Temple on the old foundation, they saw themselves as rebuilding the visible church on the original foundation, Jesus Christ. In drawing the analogy between the rebuilding of the Temple in Jerusalem and the rebuilding of the church, Riedemann wrote, "[God] built and established once more a temple for himself, which was separate from all abominations with him, Christ, as the first stone and foundation, upon whom we must all be built."[15]

Dirk Philips also used the same analogy to emphasize the truth that the Anabaptists were not building on a new foundation but on the primeval one. The passage that became an obsession with Menno — finding its place on the flyleaf of everything he ever wrote — was 1 Corinthians 3:11: "For other foundation can no man lay than that is laid, which is Jesus Christ." For Menno the existence of the church rested squarely on the fact of the incarnation.

The Anabaptists believed themselves to be in exactly the same position in relation to the church as were the apostles. The Great Commission was their commission. They were to gather the church through preaching, baptizing, and teaching. This view of the apostolic pattern was enunciated in some form by every Anabaptist writer of consequence from Grebel to Menno Simons. It was most prominent in the writings of Hubmaier but also found a place in the thinking of Dirk Philips: "The apostles, according to the command of the Lord, through the preaching of the gospel, in faith and truth, and by proper Christian baptism, and the power and unity of the Holy Spirit, gathered a church out of all nations (Matt. 28:19, 20; Mark 16:15, 16)."[16]

The Anabaptists were not interested in constructing a church through coercion, either by infant baptism or by the power of the

14. "A Speech," Davidson translation, pp. 231-32.
15. Rideman, *Account*, p. 155.
16. Philips, *Enchiridion*, pp. 483-84.

magistrate *(Obrigkeit)*. They viewed a church so constituted as false and not of Christ. They were concerned with gathering a church of believers who had freely responded to the proclamation of the gospel. They were convinced that only by voluntarily associating themselves together, could believers form a visible church *(Gemeinde)* according to the apostolic pattern of the New Testament.

Hubmaier spelled out the process step by step in his book *Concerning Christian Baptism*. The first mark of the true church, according to Hubmaier, is regeneration. Regeneration must precede church membership. Of course, in Anabaptist thought there can be no scriptural baptism without the prior experience of regeneration, and no church membership without baptism. It, therefore, follows that regeneration must be an accomplished fact before one is enrolled in the visible church. Regeneration is referred to numerous times in sixteenth-century Anabaptist works. Characteristically Anabaptist is the following statement by Dirk Philips.

> Thereafter, the apostle here explains to us what the baptism of Christ signifies, namely, a putting off of the sinful body in the flesh, burial with Christ, and resurrection through faith to a new being of the Spirit. For in Christ Jesus no external sign alone is of any value without true faith, without the new birth, and without a sincere Christlike being, Gal. 5:6; 6:[15]; John 3:3. For it is through this faith primarily that a person is united with God, incorporated into Christ Jesus, and [becomes a] partaker of the Holy Spirit, Rom. 8:10. Therefore, external baptism alone is also not valid in itself if the person being baptized does not believe and is not born anew out of God through Christ Jesus, is not baptized inwardly with the Holy Spirit and with fire, has not died to sin, and does not live in righteousness, John 1:12; Matt. 3:11; Rom. 6:1[-2].[17]

Menno so emphasized the doctrine of regeneration that he might well be termed "the theologian of the new birth." He used terms such as "birth from above," "the new birth," "the spiritual resurrection," "new life," "the second birth," and "the spiritual circumcision of the heart" to show the radical nature of conversion. The regeneration of

17. Cornelius J. Dyck, William E. Keeney, and Alvin J. Beachy, trans. and eds., *The Writings of Dirk Philips* (Scottdale: Herald Press, 1992), p. 76.

which Menno spoke involves repentance, faith, and a new quality of life. It affects vitally the way a person thinks and lives. For Menno its moral and ethical implications were undeniable.

This does not mean that to Menno the new birth is a moral reformation of one's life effected by one's own strenuous efforts. To the contrary, as Oosterbaan has shown, the new birth "had to do with a radical renewal of one's entire person; it is an eschatological event; it is a decided change in one's existence which is possible only by faith in Christ as the New Man."[18] This insight of Oosterbaan seems to be verified by Menno himself in "The New Birth," a tract of 1537: "This regeneration of which we write, from which comes the penitent, pious life that has the promise, can only originate in the Word of the Lord, rightly taught and rightly understood and received in the heart by faith through the Holy Ghost."[19] Is there not also here an echo of Romans 10 and an allusion to the divine order of preaching, hearing, faith, and regeneration?

The second mark of the visible church is baptism. But baptism cannot be administered promiscuously. It can be applied only to those who understand its significance and voluntarily request it. Absence of coercion and dependence on voluntary response *(Freiwilligkeit)* is, as Kiwiet has written, "a main pillar of the free church."[20]

Baptism thus became for the Anabaptists the door into the visible church. This expression seems to have originated with Hubmaier but is found in Riedemann and Marpeck as well. Baptism marks the juncture of individual discipleship and corporate discipleship. By it the believer becomes submissive to the discipline of the church. Without believers' baptism the visible church could not exist. Baptism, while necessary as the initial act of obedient discipleship, is also the indispensable sign of incorporation into the visible fellowship of believers. The significance of baptism as subjecting one to the discipline of the church was clearly set forth in the Schleitheim Confession.

> The ban shall be employed with all those who have given themselves to the Lord, to walk in His commandments, and with all those who

18. Oosterbaan, "Theology of Simons," p. 194.
19. "The New Birth," in *Complete Writings,* p. 92.
20. Kiwiet, *Marbeck,* p. 113.

are baptized into the one body of Christ and who are called brethren or sisters, and yet who slip sometimes and fall into error and sin, being inadvertently overtaken.[21]

Discipline then became a third mark of the true church. By this means the Brethren intended to maintain the integrity of the Anabaptist witness in life and deed. They succeeded so well that they were accused by their enemies of teaching sinless perfection. This accusation Hubmaier categorically rejected: "But the charge that we boast that we can sin no more after baptism, and such like things, is a monstrous injustice. For we know that both before and after baptism, we are poor and miserable sinners."[22]

The Anabaptist insistence on holiness in the Christian life sometimes led to statements that could be interpreted as teaching the possibility of a life completely without sin. Most writers were careful, however, to avoid such a conclusion. A case in point is Dirk Philips. No one was more insistent than he on a high standard of conduct for baptized believers. After quoting a series of passages from both the Old and the New Testaments which enjoin the reader to seek a life of righteousness, he wrote:

> Nevertheless this must be understood with all discretion, for Christians should be holy just as God is holy, and perfect, just as the Father in heaven is perfect. This one may not understand as though Christians could become, or also be, as holy in this time just as God is; but that they should strive after holiness with complete earnestness, just as Paul the apostle did. For he said that he had striven after this with his whole zeal to acknowledge Christ Jesus and the power of his resurrection.[23]

While admitting that sinlessness is impossible in the present life, the Anabaptists insisted that the immorality of the Protestant state churches was obviously sub-Christian. Religious reform by governmental decree did not produce the quality of life exemplified by the apostles or taught in the New Testament. Grebel listed so-called faith without

21. Wenger, "Schleitheim Confession," p. 248.
22. Davidson translation, p. 72.
23. Dyck *et al.*, *The Writings of Dirk Philips*, p. 312.

fruit as one of the issues between the Brethren and the Swiss Reformation in his letter to Müntzer. The failure of the Lutheran Reformation to change the moral standards of its devotees early disillusioned Pilgram Marpeck. It became one of the factors which caused him to leave the Lutherans for the Anabaptists.

The ban was used among the Anabaptists to preserve the quality of life that had become to a high degree distinctive among them. All overt acts of sin were subject to censure. However, force was never to be resorted to in the enforcement of the ban. For the Brethren, love must undergird all actions of the church and nowhere was this more insisted upon than in the use of the ban. Referring to those "who slip sometimes and fall into error, and sin," the Schleitheim Confession recommends:

> The same shall be admonished twice in secret and the third time openly disciplined or banned according to the command of Christ. Mt. 18. But this shall be done according to the regulation of the Spirit (Mt. 5) before the breaking of bread, so that we may break and eat one bread, with one mind and in one love, and may drink of one cup.[24]

The Lord's Supper was inseparably connected with discipline from the very beginning of the Anabaptist movement. This is the significance of Grebel's admonition to Müntzer concerning the Supper: "But if one should be found who is not minded to live the brotherly life, he eats to his condemnation, for he does not discern the difference from another meal. He brings shame on the inward bond, which is love, and on the bread, which is the outward bond." Grebel expresses his concern with the proper observance of the Lord's Supper as a church ordinance. "It is not a mass nor a sacrament. Therefore no one shall receive it alone, neither on a deathbed nor otherwise. Neither shall the bread be locked up, etc., for the use of an individual person, and no one shall take for his own individual use the bread of those in unity — . . . ." Before leaving the subject he returns again to a discussion of the relation of the Lord's Supper to discipline. "It should not be observed except in conformity with Christ's rule in Matthew 18, for then it would not

24. Wenger, "Schleitheim Confession," p. 248.

be the Lord's Supper, for without Matthew 18 everyone runs after the outward, and that which is inward, namely, love, one lets go; . . ."[25]

The same close relationship between discipline and the Lord's Supper was stressed by Hubmaier, Riedemann, and Marpeck. For each of these, the nature of the Lord's Supper precluded participation on the part of one whose conduct had called for censure under the ban. Hubmaier expressed the problem graphically in *A Form for Christ's Supper (Eine Form des Nachtmahls des Christi)*:

> I have fellowship with Christ and all his members, 1 Cor. 10:16, therefore I break bread with all believers in Christ according to the institution of Christ. Without this inner communion in the spirit and in truth, the outward breaking of bread is nothing but an Iscariotic and damnable hypocrisy. It is precisely to this fellowship and commitment of love that the Supper of Christ points, as a living memorial of his suffering and death for us, spiritually signified and announced *[anzaigt]* that by the breaking of bread, the pouring out of the wine, that each one should also sacrifice himself and pour out his blood for the other. Herein will people *[menschen]* recognize that we are truly disciples of Christ, John 13; 14; 15; 16; 17. All the words which Christ spoke about the Last Supper imply this. For just as water baptism is a public testimony of the Christian faith, so is the Supper a public testimony of Christian love.[26]

In the dialogue between Hans and Leonhard, Hubmaier had Hans say: "Let me say at once; the Supper is a sign of brotherly love to which we are obliged."[27] However, the Lord's Supper was more than a symbol of the disciplined fellowship for Hubmaier. It was also a memorial given to the church as a perpetual reminder of the sacrifice of the cross and a promise of Christ's return.[28]

---

25. J. C. Wenger, trans., *Conrad Grebel's Programmatic Letters of 1524* (Scottdale, Pa.: Herald Press, 1970).

26. Pipkin and Yoder, *Hübmaier*, pp. 398-99. While this translation is basically that of Pipkin and Yoder, I have altered it slightly in light of the German text in *Schriften*, pp. 358-59.

27. "What a Man Should Know," Davidson translation, pp. 295-96.

28. *Concerning Christian Baptism*, Davidson translation, p. 135.

In a beautiful passage reminiscent of the Didache, Peter Riedemann in his *Rechenschaft* of 1541 wrote of the Supper. The loaf is formed from the grinding and mingling of many grains of wheat, and the wine comes into existence only with the crushing of individual grapes. Individuality is given up for unity, symbolizing the fellowship of the disciple with his Lord in the church: "Thus, the meal, or the partaking of the bread and wine of the Lord, is a sign of the community of his body, in that each and every member thereby declareth himself to be of the one mind, heart and spirit of Christ."[29]

For Marpeck, the Lord's Supper was a sign of the fellowship, directly related to the discipline of the church. It was a confession of the church's unity in Christ. Marpeck viewed the Lord's Supper as a means of maintaining the purity of the church.[30] This was obviously an allusion to the common Anabaptist prerequisites for participation in the Lord's Supper, which were baptism, right conduct, and fraternal relation with all the brethren of a given congregation.[31]

As early as 1541, Menno Simons wrote *A Kind Admonition on Church Discipline* in which he set forth the doctrine of avoidance or shunning. Up to a point, it is characteristically Anabaptist. Menno emphasized that love must undergird even the act of expulsion from the fellowship and the table of the Lord. The procedure of Matthew 18 must be followed. In cases when the ban is resorted to, the offending brother or sister must be shunned in all unnecessary contacts. To the south German and Swiss Anabaptists, Menno's position seemed unjustifiably harsh. However, Menno felt that in this teaching he was but following the New Testament precedent of the apostles.

> But do not have anything to do, as the holy Paul has taught and commanded, and do not eat, with people who . . . were baptized into the body of Jesus Christ . . . but afterwards, whether through false doctrine or a vain and carnal life, reject and separate themselves from the body and fellowship of Christ, no matter whether it be father or mother, sister or brother, man or wife, son or daughter, no

---

29. Rideman, *Account,* pp. 86-87.
30. Kiwiet, *Marbeck,* pp. 118-19.
31. Rideman, *Account,* pp. 86-87.

matter who he be, for God's Word applies to all alike. . . . We say avoid him if he rejects the admonition of his brethren, done in sighing, tears, and a spirit of compassion and of great love.

A number of sins were listed by Menno which in his opinion would subject the guilty to such treatment. Among these are: the use of the sword; subscribing to the church-kingdom concept of Münster; polygamy; shameful acts such as nakedness; impure living; and, "all fellowship with evil works such as attending the preaching of worldly preachers, infant baptism, worldly Lord's Supper, and similar abominations, as also drunkenness, avarice, fornication, adultery, and unseemly conversation, etc."

To the possible criticism that the Anabaptists were attempting to play God in cutting off certain of the brethren from the church, Menno had this to say: "Wherefore, brethren, understand correctly, no one is excommunicated or expelled by us from the communion of the brethren but those who have already separated and expelled themselves from Christ's communion either by false doctrine or by improper conduct."

Menno felt expulsion and subsequent shunning should be viewed as a temporary remedial measure. The brethren should always be ready for reconciliation with the truly repentant, admonished Menno. "Whoever," he advised, "turns from evil, whether it be false doctrine or vain life, and conforms to the Gospel of Jesus Christ, unto which he was baptized, such a one shall not and may not be expelled or excommunicated by the brethren forever."[32]

It would be unjust to sit in judgment on Menno without realizing something of the historical situation in which he found himself. It was his task to make distinct the true Anabaptists from those whom he termed "false brethren." These false brethren included those adhering to such deviate sects as the Münsterites, Batenbergers, and Davidians. The extreme measures advocated by Menno were certainly accepted as necessary by leaders such as Dirk Philips. These leaders saw on all sides the untold damage wrought by individuals who passed from one group to another, contaminating others by their vacillation. Perhaps, viewed in this light, the practice of shunning is not as harsh and cruel as it

32. *Complete Writings,* pp. 412-13.

might first appear. Nevertheless, it became the source of much bitterness, misunderstanding, and endless divisions among the Mennonites. At last, it was repudiated by the majority.

The ban was introduced in the first place by Anabaptists in order to make radiant another mark of the true church, holiness. And this was interpreted to mean purity of life and doctrine. Thus the Lord's Supper was not only a thanksgiving memorial *(Gedachtnis)* of the death of Christ, a reminder of his sacrificial death on our behalf, and a token of his promised return but also a communion. This unique fellowship is made possible, in spite of the sinful nature of humankind, because of the love of God implanted in the disciple by the indwelling Holy Spirit. "For God works such willing and doing in his believers, Phil. 2:14," wrote Hubmaier, "through the inward anointing of his Holy Spirit, so one stands in complete freedom to will and to do good or evil."[33]

While Hubmaier and the Swiss Brethren were in substantial agreement with Zwingli's memorial view of the *Nachtmal,* there were significant differences. First, the Lord's Supper was closely related to baptism. Hubmaier emphasized the relationship: "For just as water baptism is a public testimony of the Christian faith so is the Supper a public testimony of Christian love."[34] Therefore, the Supper was limited to the baptized believers who recognized the obligations of the faith community. Second, from the depositions taken from the imprisoned Anabaptists during the earliest days of the movement, the Lord's Supper was called a sign of love — and of fellowship in Christ or a communion that binds together the church. Third, the Lord's Supper by 1527 was tied closely to the ban. Both the Schleitheim Articles and the Nikolsburg treatises of Hubmaier indicate that essential to the proper observance of the Supper, the communicate must be in fellowship with his brothers and sisters in Christ. Third, although not in the same category as baptism and the Eucharist, a disciplined discipleship became a mark of believers' churches in contrast with the parish churches of both the Protestants and the Catholics. Franz Heimann has detected this as well.

33. Pipkin and Yoder, *Hübmaier,* p. 400.
34. *Ibid.,* p. 399.

While the spiritual body of Christ always remains immaculate and pure, it is possible that in the empirical church something [impure may enter]. This impure element comes from a member of the church who is no longer a true member of the body of Christ, or probably has never been one, though he yet belongs externally to the congregation. The church has the duty to rid herself of the impure "rotten" members who spoil, if only externally, its purity. And this the church does by the ban.[35]

The congregational principle of church government was born with the Anabaptists of the sixteenth century. The idea finds expression in both the writings of Hubmaier and Grebel by 1524. As early as June, 1524, Hubmaier set forth in the Eighteen Articles ideas that contain the germ of congregationalism. These later found implementation at Waldshut. Article 8 says, "Just as every Christian should believe and be baptized for himself, so it is his privilege to judge from the holy Scriptures if the bread and wine are rightly given him by his pastor." Not only is the right of the individual judgment regarding the faith and practice of the church affirmed; the responsibility of congregational support for the ministers is also insisted on. "It is the duty of church-members, to whom the pure word of God is clearly preached, to provide food and clothing for the ministers."[36]

In a similar vein, Grebel admonished Müntzer in September of the same year. "If your benefices, as with us, are supported by interest and tithes, which are both true usury, and it is not the whole congregation which supports you, we beg that you free yourselves of your benefices. You know well how a shepherd should be sustained." Decisions in the proposed church, he instructed Müntzer, ought to be reached through faith, love, and prayer "without command or compulsion."[37]

The principle of congregational rule was, therefore, set in motion by the Anabaptists of the sixteenth century. The first instance of an established church transferring its allegiance from its former faith to

35. Heimann, "Hutterite Doctrine," p. 46.
36. Vedder, *Hübmaier*, p. 70.
37. Williams and Mergal, *Spiritual and Anabaptist Writers*, pp. 78-79. See also J. C. Wenger, trans., *Conrad Grebel's Programmatic Letters of 1524* (Scottdale, Pa.: Herald Press, 1970), pp. 14-69. Wenger has reproduced not only the German text but also a photostatic copy of the original letters.

Anabaptism was at Waldshut. This event, as Littell indicates, furnishes the historian an illustration of the greatest importance:

> Upon accepting faith baptism as a visible sign of the restored Christian community, Hubmaier resigned as priest and immediately was re-elected as minister by the congregation. This is a most significant point in Anabaptist history, for it marked the beginning of the congregational principle of government.[38]

No type of connectionalism existed among the autonomous congregations of Anabaptists, with the exception of the Hutterites, until Menno reorganized the Mennonites into a more centralized form of church government.

The undergirding motive of life for the Anabaptists was love. It dictated their views of Christian discipleship, the basis of fellowship in the church, and the missionary vision. Christian love was for them the basis of all human relationships. It was love that was initiated by the new relationship of the believer with Christ. This love determined the quality of discipleship which found its validation in the example of Christ. Therefore, it was primarily love that dictated the Anabaptist position on the use of the sword. How could a person in the sixteenth century be a Christian in the Anabaptist understanding of that term and serve as a magistrate? The magistrate often performed the functions of judge, jury, and executioner without the slightest semblance of justice. He played God in realms where he had no jurisdiction. He was more often than not the tool of a corrupt state and a degenerate church. Love could not possibly motivate the actions of such a man.

But the Anabaptists went further. How could one take the sword to kill and still follow Christ, whose teachings on the sword were so clear? From the formative stages of the movement, nonresistance was seen as a mark of the true church. The church must be prepared to suffer. It could never be a party to inflict suffering on any person for any reason.

At this point Hubmaier's Nikolsburg teaching on the sword was clearly out of step with other Anabaptists, however defensible his position may be. Unquestionably sixteenth-century Anabaptism con-

---

38. Littell, *Anabaptist View,* p. 17.

demned almost universally the use of the sword by a Christian. Even when it was condoned by the Hubmaier group, its use was only justified as an act of obedience to the state. The extant sources from sixteenth-century Anabaptism certainly justify Bender's opinion: "The Anabaptist doctrine of nonresistance is not only based on the specific commands of the Sermon on the Mount, but is an outgrowth of this understanding of love as essential in the regenerated nature. This love is not just an inward sentiment, but calls for definite action."[39]

Although often accused of practicing the community of goods, the Swiss, south German, and Dutch Anabaptists denied the charge. Their writings universally attest, however, that love was the basis of fellowship in the church. The practice of love made the sharing of material things a reality. But Christian love does not stop at sharing with those in material need, as Menno so well stated in his *Reply to False Accusations:*

> All those who are born of God, who are gifted with the Spirit of the Lord, who are, according to the Scriptures, called into one body and love in Christ Jesus, are prepared by such love to serve their neighbors, not only with money and goods, but also after the example of their Lord and Head, Jesus Christ, in an evangelical manner, with life and blood.

After alluding to his description of the church and its willingness to share with those in need, Menno wrote, "Behold such a community we teach. And not that any one should take and possess the land and property of the other, as many falsely charge."[40] Of course, the Hut-

---

39. Bender, "Walking in the Resurrection," p. 102. Stayer in his work *Anabaptists and the Sword* questions the traditional treatment of nonresistance among the Anabaptists. He asserts: "At no time in the sixteenth century was there a truly united nonresistant Anabaptist movement. The idea that the several non-resistant sects were part of a larger Martyr Church of the Reformation era was one that began only with the martyrologists of the next century" (p. 334). "Yet," he continues, "by some time around 1565 a single Anabaptist teaching on the Sword had been agreed to by everyone except a very few anachronistic revolu-tionaries, Davidjorites who had effactually opted out of the movement, and the Waterlanders, who were hanging on to the more moderate apoliticism of Menno Simons" (p. 335).

40. *Complete Writings,* p. 558.

terites did teach the community of goods as a mark of the true church. But this was clearly as much a departure from the common practice of most Anabaptists as was Hubmaier's position on the use of the sword.

The concept of love also influenced the Anabaptists greatly in their missionary vision. As nonresistance was love's negative expression, missions became its positive affirmation. In the Anabaptist theology of missions, as in baptism, several convictions converge. As has already been emphasized, the Anabaptists saw faith as a free, uncoerced response to the proclamation of the gospel. Such faith obligates proclamation by those who have experienced the gospel's power and started walking "on the resurrection side of the cross." The love of Christ and the love of one's fellow man compelled a compassionate concern for man's spiritual welfare. This was reinforced by rejection of compulsion and of the role of the state in spiritual matters. Anabaptists saw that the "true Christian is fighting a different battle with different weapons from those of the world."[41] Thus there was formed in the crucible of suffering one of the most aggressive missionary movements in Christian history.

The Anabaptists took the Great Commission seriously. They believed it was binding upon all true disciples of Christ in every age. This was a glaring contrast to the usual views of the Reformers. Menius and Bullinger, for example, were convinced that the Great Commission was binding only on the apostles. As has been shown in previous chapters, the Brethren made much of the Commission as setting forth the "divine order." This is the sequence of events involved in beginning the Christian life. The Commission, of course, sets forth related events in sequence, but it does not explicitly enjoin that sequence as invariable. The "divine order," therefore, is a reasonable inference from the Commission but an inference nonetheless. If the Anabaptists made a major theological point from what the Commission implies, how much more they must have felt compelled to obey its explicit teachings!

And obey they did. Few countries in Europe were without some Anabaptist witness. Into the valleys and cities, the highways and byways, they spread on the Continent and into England with a burning conviction and zeal to preach, teach, baptize, suffer, and die for Christ's sake.

41. Littell, "Anabaptist Theology of Missions," MQR 21 (January 1947): 13.

Of all the Anabaptists, the Hutterites developed the most extensive missionary work. They took advantage of every lull in persecution to enlarge their scope of activity. One of the best known of their missionaries was Claus Felbinger. In his Confession of Faith he gave an admirable statement concerning the missionary motivation of the Hutterites.

> We have been asked by sundry people why we have come into the prince's [of Bavaria] land, and draw people away. My answer is, we do not go only into this land, but into all lands, wherever our language is known, for where God opens a door for us and shows us zealous hearts that truly seek Him, hearts that are discontented with the godless life of the world and would gladly do what is right — there we go, for we have divine cause to do so. For heaven and earth are the Lord's and all men are His; but we have given, surrendered, and sacrificed ourselves wholly to God. Where He sends us and will use us, there we go, in obedience to His divine will, regardless of what we must suffer and endure.[42]

The State and Religious Freedom

If the sixteenth century looked askance at the Anabaptist concept of the church, it was completely unprepared for the Anabaptist view of the state. The radical position of the *Täufer* was undoubtedly beyond the comprehension of most of their contemporaries. Thought patterns of the day were enmeshed in, and determined by, the traditional medieval framework of the Holy Roman Empire. Neither civil nor religious leaders could ordinarily conceive of a stable society that did not have a church-state *(corpus Christianum)* or a state-church, such as Electoral Saxony, Zürich, and Geneva. And yet, the Anabaptists' view of the state was to prove their most far-reaching contribution to the modern world. It is important to see that this view was derived from their view of the church and a corresponding understanding of the Christian faith. Their position was based on Christian involvement — not religious indifference.

For the Anabaptists, the most damaging element in the fall of the

---

42. Friedmann, "Felbinger's Confession," p. 147.

church was its alliance with the state. When church and state were joined, the church ceased to be the church. Anabaptists, in their attempt at a restitution of the apostolic church, did not deny the right of the state to exist. Although ordained of God, the state was not the ultimate authority in all things — it was both temporal and limited. They did deny it any jurisdiction in religious affairs. Therefore, their attitude toward the state was not wholly negative. It was their customary reliance upon biblical authority which saved them from this.

In Romans 13 and similar passages they found a frame of reference within which they attempted to rethink the relationships of Christians, churches, and states. In the Bern Disputation of 1538 the Anabaptist participants made one of the earliest systematic statements on the Anabaptist concept of the state:

> We grant that in the non-Christian world state authorities have a legitimate place, to keep order, to punish the evil, and to protect the good. But we as Christians live according to the Gospel and our only authority and Lord is Jesus Christ. Christians consequently do not use the sword, which is worldly, but they use the Christian ban.[43]

The Schleitheim Confession of some eleven years before is in substantial agreement with this rather negative evaluation of the state's place in human society. In the sixth article the Brethren present expressed their view of the state with a discussion of the sword.

> The sword is ordained of God outside the perfection of Christ. It punishes and puts to death the wicked, and guards and protects the good. In the Law the sword was ordained for the punishment of the wicked and for their death, and the same [sword] is [now] ordained to be used by the worldly magistrates.[44]

The legitimacy of the magistracy was more positively enunciated in the trial of Michael Sattler. He addressed the Catholic authorities at Rottenburg as, "You servants of God." Sattler's conclusion to his defense was both courageous and clever. A part of it reads:

43. Matthijssen, "Bern Disputation," p. 32.
44. Wenger, "Schleitheim Confession," p. 250.

In conclusion, ministers of God, I admonish you to consider the end for which God has appointed you, to punish the evil and to defend and protect the pious. Whereas, then, we have not acted contrary to God and the gospel, you will find that neither I nor my brethren and sisters have offended in word or deed against any authority. Therefore, ministers of God, if you have neither heard nor read the Word of God, send for the most learned men and for the sacred books of the Bible in whatsoever language they may be and let them confer with us in the Word of God.[45]

Sattler did three things in his closing appeal. First, he set forth in a succinct summary the Anabaptist position on the state. He insisted that the state exists to make possible an orderly society among evildoers. It also has the further obligation to protect the righteous which, in this instance, it was not doing. Second, while recognizing the magistrates as "servants of God," he denied by implication that they had jurisdiction in spiritual matters. And third, he challenged his accusers to judge him and themselves on the basis of the only authority the Brethren recognized in spiritual matters, the Bible.

The same note of respect for constituted authority was manifested by Claus Felbinger in his Confession of Faith of 1560. "My lords," he wrote, "first, as you also are servants of God, though outside the perfection of Christ (namely, to take vengeance on evildoers, to punish the evil, and to protect and shelter the devout), God has given the sword into your hand." The Anabaptists had refused to conform to governmental decrees in matters of faith. They were charged, therefore, with being disobedient to constituted authorities, even when they admitted that such were ordained by God. To this charge, Felbinger replied:

> The government should be a shield to the just. For this reason the Lord has placed a sword in its hand, . . . that it may be able to execute its office and protect the just. If it does not do so, God will punish it the harder. Therefore we are gladly and willingly subject to the government for the Lord's sake, and in all just matters we will in no way oppose it. When, however, the government requires of us

45. Williams and Mergal, *Spiritual and Anabaptist Writers,* pp. 141-42.

what is contrary to our faith and conscience — as swearing oaths
and paying hangman's dues or taxes for war — then we do not obey
its command. This we do not do out of obstinacy or pride, but only
out of pure fear of God. For it is our duty to obey God rather than
men. (Acts 5:29)

A systematic thinker, Felbinger discussed nonresistance, the oath,
and freedom of religion in terms of the Anabaptist view. Since the
sword was given to the state for the punishment of evildoers and the
protection of the upright, the Christian could have nothing to do with
it. Because of the plain injunction of Christ, the nature of Christian
discipleship, and the Anabaptist concept of the state, the true Christian
could never take the sword.[46]

46. Friedmann, "Felbinger's Confession," pp. 145ff. The Schleitheim Con-
fession makes unmistakably clear this point in the following paragraphs:
"Thirdly, it will be asked concerning the sword, Shall one be a magistrate
if one should be chosen as such? The answer is as follows: They wished to make
Christ king, but He fled and did not view it as the arrangement of His Father.
Thus shall we do as He did, and follow Him, and so shall we not walk in darkness.
For He Himself says, He who wishes to come after me, let him deny himself and
take up his cross and follow me. Also, He Himself forbids the [employment of]
the force of the sword saying, The worldly princes lord it over them, etc., but not
so shall it be with you. Further, Paul says, Whom God did foreknow He also did
predestinate to be conformed to the image of His Son, etc. Also Peter says, Christ
has suffered (not ruled) and left us an example, that ye should follow His steps.
"Finally it will be observed that it is not appropriate for a Christian to serve
as a magistrate because of these points: The government magistracy is according
to the flesh, but the Christians' is according to the Spirit; their houses and dwelling
remain in this world, but the Christians' are in heaven; their citizenship is in this
world, but the Christians' citizenship is in heaven; the weapons of their conflict
and war are carnal and against the flesh only, but the Christians' weapons are
spiritual, against the fortification of the devil. The worldlings are armed with steel
and iron, but the Christians are armed with the armor of God, with truth,
righteousness, peace, faith, salvation and the Word of God. In brief, as is the mind
of Christ toward us, so shall the mind of the members of the body of Christ be
through Him in all things, that there may be no schism in the body through
which it would be destroyed. For every kingdom divided against itself will be
destroyed. Now since Christ is as it is written of Him, His members must also
be the same, that His body may remain complete and united to its own advancement and upbuilding." Wenger, "Schleitheim Confession," p. 251.

The customary Anabaptist objection to the oath was based on a literal interpretation of Christ's injunction against swearing. However, it also had reference to the qualitative aspects of the Christian witness. For the Christian, the Anabaptists believed the oath was both unnecessary and to a degree impossible of fulfillment. It was unnecessary because the Anabaptist was always under the obligation to tell the truth. It was impossible because no one had power over all circumstances in this life to order them subject to his own will, which an oath in their eyes implied. As the Schleitheim Confession has it: "We cannot fulfill that which we promise when we swear, for we cannot change [even] the very least thing on us."

The separation of church and state was viewed as necessary because of the nature of the church. Only thus could the church be cleansed and freed to be the church under God. The disestablishment of the state churches was for the Anabaptists the minimum requirement in a guarantee of religious freedom. Thus the Anabaptists became the first advocates in the modern era of the institutional separation of church and state. They alone among the sixteenth-century evangelicals made the break with the medieval pattern of church establishment. This even Calvin did not do.

Ultimately, the Anabaptists' movement for religious freedom received its greatest motivation from the conviction that faith cannot be coerced. Shortly before he was beheaded, Claus Felbinger boldly enunciated this Anabaptist precept for the authorities of Landshut. "God wants no compulsory service. On the contrary, He loves a *free, willing heart* that serves Him with a joyful soul and does what is right joyfully."[47]

No one surpassed Hubmaier in proclaiming eloquently or illustrating graphically — through his own tragic experience — that faith cannot be coerced. Before formally becoming an Anabaptist, Hubmaier in 1524 sent forth a plea for religious freedom under the title *Concerning Heretics and Those Who Burn Them.* In this immortal tract he articulated several principles which later became characteristic emphases of the Anabaptists. It was Hubmaier's conviction that both church and state suffer when people are tried and condemned for religious reasons. "The

47. Friedmann, "Felbinger's Confession," p. 149.

law that condemns heretics to the fire builds up both Zion in blood and Jerusalem in wickedness." Faith cannot be forced. "A Turk or a heretic is not convinced by our act, either with the sword or with the fire, but only with patience and prayer."

Hubmaier was in basic agreement with the Schleitheim Confession and the Bernese Anabaptists of 1538 in his support of the common Anabaptist view of the state. The state is ordained of God for the punishment of criminals and the promotion of order in an evil world. For this reason God has given the state the sword. But the state has no authority over a person's religion. Apparently in 1524 Hubmaier had some scruples about a Christian's serving as a magistrate. "But he who is God's cannot injure any one, unless he first deserts the gospel." Hubmaier summed up his entire argument for religious freedom in one sentence. "Now it is apparent to everyone, even the blind, that the law which demands the burning of heretics is an invention of the Devil." The law to which Hubmaier referred was the traditional treatment of heretics in the Holy Roman Empire. A famous lawyer, Philippe de Beaumanoir, expressed it concisely.

> If a lay person believes incorrectly he is to be returned to the true faith by instruction, if he refuses to believe but adheres instead to his wicked error then he shall be condemned as a heretic and burned. But in that event lay justice must come to the aid of the Holy Church; for when anyone is condemned as a heretic by the examinations conducted by the Holy Church then the Holy Church must leave him to lay justice and the lay justice must then burn him, seeing that the spiritual justice ought not to put anyone to death.[48]

In 1526 after a most debilitating imprisonment in Zürich at the hands of his former friend, Ulrich Zwingli, Hubmaier hastened to publish what he termed a "Short Apology." He hoped to erase some

---

48. Vedder, *Hübmaier,* pp. 85-88. See Stayer, *Anabaptists and the Sword,* pp. 141-46. Even though Stayer makes a good case for the *real politic* position of Hubmaier and identifies him very closely with Zwingli, he fails to see the distinctions that are evident in Hubmaier's writings and action. His treatment of Denck shows the same one-sided approach. Stayer has done his research well but his conclusions seem, at times, to be formed upon other grounds.

of the effects of his forced, but nevertheless humiliating, recantation. He referred to Zwingli, who "by capture, imprisonment, suffering and the hangman, tried to teach me the faith." He then reaffirmed his deepening conviction in regard to coercion and faith. "But faith is a work of God and not of the heretics' tower, in which one sees neither sun nor moon, and lives on nothing but water and bread."[49]

Obviously one who had suffered humiliation, imprisonment, and torture as Hubmaier had would be predisposed to champion religious freedom. But it is evident that in Schaffhausen, long before his unexpected experience in Zürich, Hubmaier had given the matter considerable thought. In his abstract of principles, *Concerning Heretics and Those Who Burn Them*, articles 21, 22, and 28 suggest a theological basis for religious freedom more profound than is generally recognized. In article 21, Hubmaier wrote that the Christian's sword is "the Word of God" and not a sword of steel against the criminal. In the next article, it is clear that the judgment and punishment of criminals is the jurisdiction of the secular state or worldly power *(weltlich gwalt)* but in the case of an enemy of God *(gottsfind = Gottesfeind)* who wishes to do nothing other than to forsake the gospel, no one has a right to harm him. Here Hubmaier argues that faith or the lack of it is not within the jurisdiction of secular government. To the contrary, he declared in article 28 that to burn a heretic is in appearance to confess Christ when in reality it is to deny him.[50] Is he not saying that to persecute a person for heresy is to deny the incarnation, for the God revealed in Christ is the God of the invitation, not of coercion?

For the Anabaptists, every person should have the right to believe or not to believe. To be a Turk, Jew, Catholic, or Anabaptist is a privilege to which every person is entitled and for which one is accountable only to God. This position was derived from the Anabaptist conviction that faith cannot be coerced. "Faith is a work of God and not of the heretics' tower." This position explains much in the Anabaptism of the sixteenth century, yet it does not completely explain the steadfastness of the Anabaptists under persecution. Only Anabaptist eschatology can do this.

49. *Ibid.,* p. 141.
50. *Schriften,* p. 99.

Eschatology and the Church

In relating the story of Leonhard Keyser's martyrdom in 1527, Thieleman van Braght wrote: "Having returned to Bavaria, he examined the fruits and doctrine of the Anabaptists, as well as of Zwingli and Luther, and joined himself under the cross to the separated cross-bearing church of the Anabaptists, in the year of 1525."[51]

The terminology used here and elsewhere throughout the *Martyrs' Mirror* is suggestive. It implies that the Anabaptists had come to consider suffering as the mark of Christian discipleship and the true church. They had developed what Ethelbert Stauffer calls a "theology of martyrdom."[52] Their eschatology saved them from utter despair in facing the indescribable suffering which they everywhere experienced from the authorities. Even as Christ suffered, they, too, as his disciples were not to consider themselves immune from a similar fate. As Christ was vindicated in the resurrection, they believed that they, too, would eventually triumph with him.

Their "quiet eschatology," as Littell terms it, manifested itself in both a personal and a universal hope.[53] The Anabaptists could die with the Pauline certitude that "to be absent in the body was to be present with the Lord." Leonhard Schoener's testimony, which he wrote out before his execution in 1528, expresses this concept very well.

> O Lord, there is no sorrow so great that it can separate us from Thee; hence we call upon Thee without ceasing, through Christ thy Son, our Lord, whom Thou out of pure grace, has given us for our consolation, and who has prepared and made known to us the narrow path and the way unto eternal life. Matt. 7:14.

In the second coming of Christ and the final judgment, the Anabaptists believed that the righteous would share the triumph of their risen Lord. The evil world and all its devotees would be condemned. This element is also found in the last writing of Leonhard Schoener: "Eternal glory, triumph, honor and praise be unto Thee now

51. *Mirror*, p. 420.
52. Stauffer, "Anabaptist Theology of Martyrdom," p. 179.
53. Littell, *Anabaptist View*, p. 127.

and in all eternity, and Thy righteousness abide forever. All nations bless Thy holy name, through Christ, the coming righteous Judge of the whole world, Amen. Acts 17:31."[54]

At least three positions can be discerned regarding the return of Christ and the establishment of his millennial kingdom among those called *Wiedertäufer*. The first position is characteristic of the Swiss Brethren and is designated by Littell as "quiet eschatology." These Anabaptists believed in the Lord's return but it never occupied the center of the stage in either their confessions or preaching. Hubmaier, Marpeck, the Hutterites, and the Mennonites seem to have shared this attitude. A second position of fervent but nonviolent chiliasm was that most notably championed by Melchior Hofmann and, to some degree, by Hans Hut. Hofmann's certainty as to when and where the Lord would return to set up his new Jerusalem led to disastrous consequences for him. While Hut appeared ready to wield the sword after the Lord's return, both he and Hofmann held that God must take the initiative in purging the wicked and setting in motion history's last devastating chain of events. The third position is that represented by the followers of Jan Matthys and Jan of Leyden. They could not wait for divine initiative. Therefore they and their followers took matters into their own hands. In this they were the heirs of Thomas Müntzer rather than those of the Swiss Brethren.

What explains the vast gradation between what has been termed normative Anabaptism and the fanatical Münsterites? Of course, the human element (psychological and sociological) cannot be disregarded. Yet the Anabaptism whose history has been the object of this narrative sought and found its guidelines for the church, society, and the individual Christian in the New Testament; whereas Hofmann and his followers, as well as Thomas Müntzer and the Münsterites, turned to the Old Testament as the final source of authority and the interpretative key to history. From the Old Testament they sought to determine the detailed series of events relative to the last days. Once persuaded that they had, indeed, unraveled the mysteries of the Apocalypse with an enthusiasm for the New Jerusalem, born of a mixture of motivations from exasperation to vengeance, they entered into its creation with

54. *Mirror,* p. 425.

complete abandon. Of course this last position was not normative Anabaptism but its aberration.

In common with other evangelicals, apparently all Anabaptists of the sixteenth century believed that the Lord's return was imminent. Judgment which would silence gainsayers and vindicate the righteous was at hand. Hans Schlaeffer, a priest turned Anabaptist, was executed in 1528. In a letter for the admonition of the Brethren, he presented what can be considered typical of most Anabaptists:

> It is a truth not otherwise, than that judgment must first begin at the house of God. I Pet. 4:17. Thus the Holy Scripture is now fulfilled, so that the punishment with which the world is to be visited, is ready and at hand; hence no one ought to be negligent; for the sword is drawn, the bow is bent, the arrow laid upon it, and aim is taken.
>
> By this I do not mean that we are to seek any other refuge, than that whereunto He has sealed us, that we may be assured of the eternal and imperishable kingdom with Him, and forever to possess it with Him in life everlasting; to this may God strengthen us all. Amen.[55]

From the absence of such testimony in many prison epistles, the impression is gained that vindication was not the primary concern of Anabaptists generally. Rather, they felt that regardless of any future judgment within history, they must remain loyal to their insights. Truth to such was its own vindication.

55. *Ibid.*, p. 426.

XI

※   ※

Across the Seas and through the Years

NABAPTIST ANCESTRY HAS BEEN CLAIMED FROM TIME TO TIME
for such widely divergent groups as Unitarians, Baptists,
Quakers, and Communists. Obviously, identification of the
Anabaptists with either the Unitarians or the Communists involves the
loosest possible use of the term "Anabaptist." Antitrinitarian or Uni-
tarian concepts never became characteristic of any major expression of
sixteenth-century Anabaptism, with the possible exception of the Polish
Brethren (Socinians). Virtually the same situation existed in regard to
communism. Communal life has been practiced from 1528 to the
present only by the Hutterites. Other attempts by the Philippites,
Gabrielites, or the more deviate Münsterites began and ended within
a few years. Of course none could be equated with contemporary
communism of Marxist inspiration.

To claim that Baptists and Quakers are direct descendants of the
Anabaptists is to assume that similarity of belief proves causal connections. Such relationship is assumed from something other than historical evidence. However, this is not to deny the pervasive influence of
sixteenth-century Anabaptism upon succeeding generations but to
point up the task of the historian. Therefore, this chapter has a dual
purpose. It attempts to examine the relationship of continental Anabaptism to contemporary religious groups with which it is most closely

267

associated, directly or indirectly; and it seeks to evaluate the impact through these groups of Anabaptist concepts on the modern world.

Lineal Descendants

Dutch Mennonites were reported to have been residents of New Amsterdam as early as 1643. A French Jesuit priest named Jogues, in listing the varieties of religious life in the colony, mentioned the "Anabaptists here called Menists."[1] Although shortly afterward other Mennonites ventured to the New World, the first permanent settlement was not founded until 1683 in Germantown, Pennsylvania.

The Mennonites were few in number and without the services of a regularly ordained minister. They worshiped until 1690 or 1698 with some former German Mennonites who had joined the Quakers.[2] From this Mennonite-Quaker conventicle came the first public protest in the American colonies against slavery. The protest in 1688 was addressed to a meeting of the largest religious group in Pennsylvania, the Quaker Monthly Meeting. Among other things it declared: "Those who hold slaves are no better than Turks."

The petition then proceeded to emphasize the damage which the practice of slavery was likely to do to further immigration. "For this makes an ill report in all those countries of Europe where they hear off, that ye Quackers do here handel men, like they handel there ye cattle and for that reason have no mind or inclination to come hither."[3] Apparently the protest had no immediate effect. Subsequently the Quakers were numbered among the most ardent champions of the antislavery movement.

The first trickle of Mennonite immigrants in the mid-seventeenth century swelled into thousands across three centuries. Today Mennonite colonies may be found from Canada to Paraguay. There are large settlements in north-central Mexico and the midwestern states of the United States. The Mennonites have distinguished themselves in North and South America as excellent farmers. Often exclusive and withdrawn,

---

1. Cited by C. Henry Smith, *The Story of the Mennonites* (revised by Cornelius Krahn; Newton, Kans.: Mennonite Publication Office, 1950), p. 529.

until the present century their influence on the non-Mennonite world has been meager. Their usual choice of farming as a vocation and their exclusiveness have both militated against an effective evangelistic witness.

In spite of these characteristics, however, Mennonites have been the consistent advocates of some basic sixteenth-century Anabaptist principles. Their stand against war is a case in point. The Mennonites' position in this respect was largely negative from the time of the Revolutionary War through World War I. As a result, they have suffered much for their historic nonresistant witness. Usually misunderstood by patriotic neighbors, their motivations have been openly questioned. Frequently they have also been accused of sympathizing with the national enemies — the British during the Revolutionary War and the Germans during World War I.

World War II ushered in a new era in Mennonite church-state relations. While maintaining their nonresistant witness, the Mennonites addressed themselves to the problems presented by the demands and ravages of war. Through the Mennonite Central Committee, they looked for ways to make a positive Christian witness that did not violate their long-standing convictions. The results have been impressive. They have made solid contributions to technological advance in carrying out experiments in many fields at the risk of life. The most gratification came to them in serving in mental hospitals. "As the war progressed," writes C. Henry Smith, "more and more of the units were assigned to mental hospitals. Of the fifty-one such units, the Mennonites administered twenty-five."[4]

One result of service in mental rehabilitation by Mennonites and other conscientious objectors was establishment of the National Mental Health Foundation. The Mennonites have also become interested in establishing mental hospitals as a Christian expression of concern for modern civilization's casualties. However, not all Mennonite young men chose to follow the route of conscientious objector. About half of them chose either regular service or noncombatant military service.

2. See H. Shelton Smith, Robert T. Handy, and Lefferts A. Loetscher, *American Christianity* (New York: Charles Scribner's Sons, 1960), 1:271-73.

3. Smith, *Story of Mennonites,* p. 534.

4. *Ibid.,* p. 814.

What has been said about the Mennonite tendency toward an exclusive, withdrawn, ghetto-like existence is even more true of the Amish and Hutterites. Under the leadership of Jacob Ammann the Amish schism developed in Switzerland during the latter part of the seventeenth century. It represents various degrees of cultural isolation. Few outsiders have sought to understand the deeper principles underlying the old-world folkways of the black-garbed Amish and his sensitive conscience. His fastidious concern with buggies, hooks and eyes, beards, and bonnets has alternately provoked exasperation and mirth in his non-Amish neighbor.

The Amishman is almost always a farmer, and a consistently good one at that. Perhaps his economic success, coupled with his aversion to government regulations, makes him an enjoyable target for tired comics. At any rate, his influence on human existence swirling around him — whether in Pennsylvania, Iowa, or the states in-between — has been slight.

The Hutterites, also lineal descendants of the sixteenth-century Anabaptists, join the Amish in the backwater of what is generally considered cultural progress. Centuries of persecution have forced them more and more into a monastery-like existence. Within Hutterite colonies located in Canada, the Dakotas, and Paraguay, apparently life goes on much as it did four centuries ago. The continued use of German, which was retained during sojourns in Hungary, Transylvania, and Russia, increases isolation from the modern world. This cultural insulation protects the Hutterites from outside influences, but it also prohibits any effective interchange of ideas. Thus, evangelism and appreciable influence on the outside world are also lacking in the Hutterite expression of Anabaptism.

Is, then, the modern world indebted to the Anabaptists to any considerable degree? Have its concepts of freedom, separation of church and state, democracy, and the regenerate church come from this source? If so, the channels of this influence, for the most part, must lie outside those of the lineal descendants. Attention must now be turned to the groups whose ideas bear a striking similarity to the basic insights of sixteenth-century Anabaptism. The first of these is the Baptists.

Baptists and Anabaptists

The relationship of continental Anabaptism to early English Baptists has long been subject to debate. There was a time when many Baptists desired to establish a visible succession back to the apostolic age. Any theory which traced Baptists through Anabaptists found acceptance. However, in recent years it seems to be the vogue to discredit any viewpoint that posits an Anabaptist-Baptist historical relation. The most vocal advocate of this position is Winthrop S. Hudson, formerly professor of church history at Colgate-Rochester Divinity School. Writing for the *Baptist Quarterly*, Hudson said: "It was not until the twentieth century that Baptist historians began to point out . . . that the evidence that the Baptists are not to be confused or identified with the Anabaptists is quite overwhelming."[5]

Hudson not only distinguished English Baptists from the Anabaptists but implied that all Anabaptist influence was repudiated by Helwys. He dismissed as insignificant the contact of early English Baptists with Dutch Anabaptists.

> The insistence upon Believer's Baptism was a logical corollary drawn from the Reformation emphasis upon the necessity for an explicit faith and from the Congregational concept of a gathered church, as well as from the common storehouse of Biblical precept and example, rather than being the result of any supposed Anabaptist influence.[6]

Hudson's position seems to have been taken out of consideration for something other than historical evidence. He admitted this fact in an earlier article:

> By obscuring the theological considerations . . . which determined the attitude of Baptists on political and social issues, the task of dealing . . . with the new problems which have emerged has been made exceedingly difficult. This is true in terms of questions of polity, of providing structural support for a democratic society, of coming

5. Hudson, "Who Were the Baptists?" *The Baptist Quarterly* 16 (July 1956): 304.

6. *Ibid.*, p. 310.

to terms with the major issues of economic life, and it is especially true if unnecessary obstacles are not to be placed in the way of ecumenical discussions.[7]

Does not this admission on Hudson's part seriously jeopardize his position? As St. Amant has insisted, the historian can never allow the message of history to create historical facts. Nor can he ignore or distort those facts in the interest of his own bias.[8] Neither ecumenical interests nor theories of Baptist succession should be allowed to alter the historical record in the least.

Ernest A. Payne, one of England's most prominent twentieth-century Baptist leaders and an able church historian, takes issue with Hudson when he writes:

> No responsible historian "confuses" or "identifies" the seventeenth-century Baptists with the continental Anabaptists of the sixteenth century. By implication Dr. Hudson appears to be denying all similarity or connection. This is, I am convinced, a misreading of history and would deprive the Baptists of one of the main clues to an understanding of their origin and development.

After listing Hudson's four basic propositions, and before proceeding to refute them, Payne offers the following succinct summary of Hudson's position.

> He describes the former [Anabaptists] as stemming from "a few university trained humanists" of an Erasmian type, and the latter [English Baptists] as an offshoot of English Calvinistic Puritanism in its Congregational form. Only by a very selective process, so I believe, can these positions be maintained.[9]

With such prominent Baptist historians in obvious disagreement, others must be exceedingly cautious in seeking a historically valid

---

7. Hudson, "Baptists Were Not Anabaptists," *The Chronicle* 16 (October 1953): 178.

8. Penrose St. Amant, *Christian Faith and History* (Fort Worth, 1954), p. 2.

9. Payne, "Who Were the Baptists?" *The Baptist Quarterly* 16 (October 1956): 339.

solution to the problem. In unraveling the mystery of Dutch and English Anabaptist life and any possible influence on the English Reformation, several questions must be considered. What was the relation of sixteenth-century Anabaptism, first, to the rise of English Separatism; second, to the General Baptists; third, to the Particular Baptists; and fourth, to American Baptists?

Anabaptism and English Separatism

To understand English church life of the sixteenth and seventeenth centuries, it is necessary to distinguish between Puritans and Separatists. The former were devoted to the established Church of England but desired to reform it in the direction of Calvinism. The Separatists, however, regarded the Church of England as apostate. They believed that the only Christian reaction to it was complete withdrawal.

Opinions vary on the extent of influence which the Anabaptists exerted on the rise of English Separatism. It is Latourette's opinion that an Anabaptist contribution to English Separatist movements is undeniable.[10] Scheffer, an erudite Mennonite historian of another generation, was convinced of the indebtedness of English Separatism to Anabaptism. He believed that in Norwich Robert Browne, the father of English Separatism, became addicted to Anabaptist ideas through Dutch Mennonite refugees.

> Among the Dutch Mennonites, who had fled thither from the persecutions in their own country, a new mode of thinking respecting the spirit and organization was brought home to Browne. As his new views were perfectly similar to that of these foreigners, it is evident that he acquired them from these Mennonites.[11]

Two observations militate against an uncritical acceptance of Scheffer's position. Browne, as Scheffer admits, never indicated a de-

10. Kenneth Scott Latourette, *A History of Christianity* (New York: Harper & Brothers, 1953), p. 779.

11. J. De Hoop Scheffer, *History of the Free Churchmen,* ed. William Elliot Griffis (Ithaca, N.Y.: Andrus & Church, n.d.), p. 8.

pendence on the Mennonites. Rather, in 1584 he explicitly denied any relationship with them. Of course, few Englishmen in the sixteenth century would care to admit sympathy with the Anabaptists. Less apparent is the question of the close similarity which Scheffer saw between Browne and the Mennonites. There are some points of similarity, it is true; but these are not so convincing as to necessitate a historical connection. It is Burrage's studied conclusion that the Anabaptist influence on English Separatism before 1612 was slight.[12]

Five decades and many documents after Burrage, a contemporary authority on Anabaptist-Separatist relations, Irvin B. Herst, reverses to some extent his conclusions. When speaking of Anabaptist characteristics revealed in English Separatism, he says: "One may not claim that Anabaptism was the exclusive source of these insights, but the evidence is overwhelming that it was a major influence."[13]

If the above cited statements are carefully weighed, it is clear that very few students of the English Reformation deny an Anabaptist influence on English Separatism. Disagreement is encountered with an evaluation of the nature and extent of this influence.

Very early, England was alerted to the errors of the Anabaptists. By 1531 William Barlow described in detail the Anabaptist movement of the Continent, which he termed "the thyrd faccyon" of the Reformation. Three years later Dutch Anabaptists were known to have taken refuge in England. In fact, they were already actively engaged in propagating their faith by 1534. It is Horst's opinion that "in the 1530's Anabaptism supplanted Lollardy in name as well as in doctrine and became the left wing of the English Reformation."[14] On May 25, 1535,

---

12. Champlin Burrage, *The Early English Dissenters* (Cambridge: The University Press, 1912), 1:68.

13. Irvin B. Horst, "England," ME, 2:220. Horst's work, *The Radical Brethren* (Nieuwkoop: B. de Graaf, 1972), clarifies and enlarges his earlier studies. He writes: "The influence of Anabaptism on Independency and the later Congregational movement can be traced chiefly on the form of church government and the character of church worship and life. Much more radical was its influence on the movement which was to bear the name anabaptist longest; the General Baptists, who were the closest English counterpart to the mainline anabaptists on the Continent (*Täufer*, Mennonites)" (p. 179).

14. Horst, ME, 2:215.

twenty-five Dutch Anabaptists were apprehended at St. Paul's. Fourteen of these were condemned and burned at the stake in London on June 4, 1535. Horst writes that the number of Anabaptists burned by Henry VIII was larger than the number of Lollards burned in the previous century. Perhaps as many as 80 percent of those executed during Mary's reign were Anabaptists. The last large group of Anabaptists to be arrested for their faith in England was apprehended on April 3, Easter Sunday, 1575, at London and Ely.

From time to time Anabaptist preachers were incarcerated in the prisons across the country. Frequently, they were put to death. The first of these seems to have been a Fleming by the name of Bastian, who was arrested for distributing a book around 1534.

In 1538, the English authorities learned that the Anabaptists had published and distributed a book on the incarnation. For this effrontery, they were asked to leave the country. Some were seized and burned. Among them was one of their leaders, Jan Matthijsz, who was burned at Smithfield on November 29, 1538.[15] Joan Boucher, whom Cranmer failed to win for the Church of England, was also burned at the stake on May 2, 1550. It seems, therefore, that continental Anabaptists were present and not without influence in England from about 1534.

Anabaptist ideas became commonplace in England from several sources. The Anabaptists themselves were not inactive. Many pamphlets and books were written against them. Government proclamations also carried descriptive accounts of their beliefs. Cranmer indicated a wide acquaintance with Anabaptist ideas and vocabulary. He used both in his *Catechismus* of 1548, obviously seeking to gain the Anabaptist ear.[16] The most important creedal formulation of the Church of England, the Forty-two Articles of 1553, included no less than seventeen articles

---

15. *Ibid.*, pp. 215-18. See Horst, *Radical Brethren*, pp. 183-84, for a copy of the order which authorized the arrest of "Bastiane, a flemmying, whiche is sayd to be the byshop & reder to the Anabaptistes." The order also lists the names of John Raulinges, Paule Baughton, Andrew Pierson, "a scottische man, an organ-maker," John Clarke, John Gough, George Jonson Botchard, Nicholas Whilar, and Harry Bonar.

16. C. Burrage, *Early English Dissenters,* pp. 47-48.

directed against Anabaptism. If Anabaptists were not strong contenders for the minds and hearts of Englishmen, it would hardly have been necessary to give so much attention to their teachings.[17]

Several ministers of the Church of England held to one or more Anabaptist teachings. One of these, John Bale, wrote in the defense of an Anabaptist, Peter Franke, who was burned at the stake in Colchester. Bale also spoke favorably of Balthasar Hubmaier in a tract written against Edmund Bonner and published in Zürich in 1543. "Of Balthasar Hiebmeir Pacimontanus ys the thyrde cathechysme, whom in dede I knowe not but by name, as I have redde yt in other mennys writinges. But I conceyve here the better opynyon of hym, for that my lorde hath condemned him amonge these menne, whose doctryne I knowe to be pure and perfyght."[18] Perhaps what is even more significant, Bale in a later work, *A brief and faithful declaration of the true faith of Christ* (1547), while denying that he had become an Anabaptist, presented arguments for believers' baptism based on the Great Commission.[19]

Henry Hart, a leader of a congregation of dissenters in Kent, succeeded in getting three of his tracts printed. Hart and his fellow nonconformists were well known. In contemporary accounts they were referred to as Anabaptists. They were also accused of Pelagian heresy and libertinism. From Hart's own tract, printed in 1548 and reprinted in 1549, it is clear that he, like Menno Simons and Hubmaier, writes for the sheep — not for Shepherds or wolves. His emphasis is a practical one that points up the necessity of the new birth, which comes with faith-commitment to Christ, and a subsequent life of obedient discipleship. He is a champion of the doctrine of free will and the individual's responsibility to decide for Christ and to remain faithful to him. Horst

17. Horst, *Radical Brethren*, p. 170. Horst also writes: "Anabaptism in England was closely related to the Melchiorite Wing of the movement, and this spiritualistic climate doubtless furthered a nonseparating type of anabaptism, even though intense persecution did not occur except in Mary's reign" (p. 174).

18. Cited by Horst, *ibid.*, p. 94.

19. Irvin B. Horst, *Anabaptism and the English Reformation to 1558* (Nieuwkoop: B. de Graaf, 1968), pp. 106-7. Robert Barnes and John Lambert are two other Church of England clergymen Horst names. The convictions of these two come across more clearly than Bale's and without as much equivocation.

writes: "The themes of following Christ, obedience to the commands of Scripture, nonconformity to the world, and the willing acceptance of suffering, are dominant throughout."[20] Even though Hart may not have practiced believers' baptism or established churches according to the Anabaptist model, it seems fairly obvious that his teachings regarding free will, the new birth, and discipleship were true to Anabaptist insights. Thus, he and his brethren appear to have been correctly labeled by Hart's adversaries.

In refuting the Anabaptists, John Knox gave wide publicity to their concepts in his book *An Answer to a great number of blasphemous cavillations written by an Anabaptist and adversarie to God's eternal Predestination,* published in 1560. Champlin Burrage professes to be at a loss as to the author of the book Knox attempts to refute. But Horst is certain Robert Cooche is the target.[21]

It seems beyond reasonable question that Anabaptists and Anabaptist ideas were current in England for the greater part of the sixteenth century. The question which now must be dealt with is whether there is any evidence to support a theory of Anabaptist influence on early English Separatism.

The nature of the first English Separatist conventicles is still in doubt. Two were known to have existed at Bocking in Essex and at Faversham in Kent by mid-century. Together they numbered some sixty persons. When arrested in 1551, these Separatists admitted that they had refused to take communion in the Church of England for two years.[22]

From the available records not a great deal is known about the doctrinal position of those arrested. However, they were antipredestinarian. They were accused of Pelagianism, which was probably assumed because of their emphasis upon free will and human responsibility. If Henry Hart's works are indicative of the theological complexion of the "Kent sectaries," they were Anabaptist in their soteriology and concept of the ethical requirements of the Christian life, if not in the practice of believers' baptism and the implementation of an Anabaptist church

20. Horst, *Radical Brethren,* p. 129.
21. Horst, *Anabaptism and English Reformation,* p. 62.
22. C. Burrage, *Early English Dissenters,* p. 53.

order. The church under the cross — suffering in order to serve —
however, was taught and practiced. Hart spent much time in prison.[23]
Another of their leaders, Humphrey Middleton, was burned at the stake
during the reign of Queen Mary.[24]

Much more is known about two nonconformist churches of London. The Separatist Congregation of Richard Fitz was termed the Privy
Church of London. At the time Fitz's church was discovered, there was
another conventicle of strictly Puritan sentiment. Some members of
this Plumber's Hall congregation later became Separatists and united
with the Privy Church.

The two churches should not be confused, even though members
of both groups were arrested and jailed for their clandestine operations.
The Plumber's Hall congregation intended no separation from the
Church of England. A promise to that effect was given by the pastor,
William Bonam, and twenty-four of his fellow-believers before their
discharge from Brydewell prison in 1569. They promised not to observe
communion "in anie howse, or other place, Contrarie to the state of
religion nowe by publique authoritie established, or contrarie to the
Lawes of this Realme of *England*."[25] In addition, they pledged not to
meet separately or to preach against the practices of the established
church. On the other hand, the Fitz congregation was Separatist from
the beginning.

Three extant documents of this church reveal its guiding concepts.[26] The first of these is the principle that the "blessed and glorious
worde" shall alone determine the faith and practice of the church. This
meant the "abolishinge and abhorringe all tradicions and inuentions of
man." Thus the principle of restitution of the church in the light of
the New Testament is clearly set forth.

23. Horst, "England," ME, 2:217.
24. C. Burrage, *Early English Dissenters*, p. 53.
25. *Ibid.*, 2:11-12.
26. *Ibid.*, pp. 13-18; in chronological order: "The order of the priuye
churche in London, whiche by the malice of Satan is falselie slaundred, and euell
spoken of"; "The Separatist Covenant of Richard Fitz's Congregation"; "O Englande, yf thou returne, returne vnto me, saythe the Lorde, Ieremy"; the last
document appears to have been a petition addressed to Queen Elizabeth on behalf
of the Separatists in 1571.

The idea of the suffering church under the cross as a mark of true discipleship is a recurring theme in the three documents. In the document termed by Burrage, "The Separatist Covenant of Richard Fitz's Congregation," the following words emphasize this concept. "They doo persecute our sauiour Iesus Christ in his members. Actes. 9. verses .4. and .5 2 Corinth. 1. verse .5. Also they reiecte and despyse our Lorde and sauiour Iesus Christ. Luke. 10. verse .16." The "Covenant" closes with a moving prayer which embodies the two concepts mentioned above.

> God geue vs strength styl to stryue in suffryng vndre the crosse, that the blessed worde of our God may onely rule, and haue the highest place, to cast downe strong holdes, to destroy or ouerthrow policies or imaginations, and euery high thyng that is eralted [exalted] against the knowledge of God, and to bryng in to captiuitie or subiection, euery thought to the obedience of Christ. &c. 2. Corinth. 10 verses .4. and .5. &c, that the name and worde of the eternall our Lorde God, may be exalted or magnified aboue all thynges. Psalm. 138. verse .2.[27]

Positively, Richard Fitz in "The order of the priuye church in London" gave a three-point outline which he believed the foregoing principles dictate.

> Fyrste and formoste, the Glorious worde and Euangell preached, not in bondage and subiection, but freely, and purelye. Secondly to haue the Sacraments mynistred purely, onely and all together according to the institution and good worde of the Lorde Iesus, without any tradicion or inuention of man. And laste of all to haue not the fylthye Cannon lawe, but dissiplyne onelye, and all together agreable to the same heauenlye and allmighty worde of oure good Lorde, Iesus Chryste.[28]

Negatively, the followers of Fitz, after his death in prison, enumerated the practices which they considered the works of Antichrist. Among these are listed "forked cappes, & tipetes, surplices, copes, starche cakes, [godfathers and godmothers], and popishe holy days."

27. *Ibid.,* p. 15.
28. *Ibid.,* p. 13.

The reference to godfathers and godmothers might imply some question about the propriety of infant baptism. Yet the appeal of the petitioners was made to the constituted authority to destroy and consume "the manners, fashions, or customes of the papistes." This is clearly Calvinistic in tone and not Anabaptist. The covenant enjoins the Lord's people "to go forewarde to perfection," which might indicate an Anabaptist interpretation of the Christian life. The polity was congregational as was that of many Anabaptist churches on the Continent. It called, however, for a threefold ministry of pastor, deacon, and elder, again indicating possible Calvinistic influence.

The members of the congregation, addressing the Queen, referred to themselves as "a poore congregation whom god hath separated from the churches of englande." They made clear their judgment of the established church, speaking of "the mingled and faulse worshipping therin vsed, out of the which assemblies the lord our onely saviour hath called vs."[29] It is quite evident that the Fitz church was made up of Englishmen who were formerly members of the Church of England. For the sake of their deep religious convictions, they had separated themselves from the church of their childhood. They possessed many concepts that were common to the Anabaptists, but there are others that are obviously not Anabaptist. It is possible that an Anabaptist influence was exerted from some source as yet unknown in the formation of the Fitz congregation. However, it would be a mistake to refer to this church as either an Anabaptist or a Congregational church. It was neither, as far as available documents indicate.

The fate of the little church is unknown. Perhaps its members suffered in the same way as those whose imprisonments and death they mourned, such as Richard Fitz, their pastor, and Thomas Bowlande, their deacon. Six prisons are named as places known to the petitioners where a great multitude of the "lordes servantes" had suffered. Undoubtedly, these confined Anabaptists as well as Puritans and Separatists. It would be strange, indeed, if those who shared common cells and suffered from the same intolerant hands did not exchange ideas. New insights into biblical truth, at least, continued to crop out in the ever-rising stream of English Separatism.

29. *Ibid.*, pp. 16-17.

Ten years were to pass between the disappearance from history of the Privy Church and the appearance of Browne's Separatist Church at Norwich. Very little is known about English Separatism during the interim other than the arrest of twenty Anabaptists of London and Ely and subsequent execution of some of their number. Before going to Norwich, Robert Browne was a radical Puritan moving toward Separatism.[30] Having heard that there were those inclined to his point of view in Norwich, he went there in the summer of 1580. His friend of like sympathies, Robert Harrison, accompanied him. By the beginning of the following year, Browne began to gather "his companie" together. In "early spring of 1581" they separated themselves completely from the Church of England.

Norwich at this time was the center of radical Puritanism. St. Andrews was practically a Congregational church within the Anglican establishment. The radical nature of the Puritan movement here may have been due to the influence of the Mennonites in the area. Norwich had long been the refugee center for continental Anabaptist groups. As has been indicated, Scheffer believed Browne to have been influenced directly by the Mennonites. "In 1571," he writes, "no fewer than 2925 Dutch and Walloon or Belgian Protestant people were established at Norwich."[31] He assumed that Browne's position was so similar to that of the Mennonites that dependence was obvious. This opinion has long been shared by many others.

Horst comes close to the same position. However, he admits that "conclusive evidence has never been presented" but that "it is on theological and spiritual grounds that the evidence is more convincing."[32] Certainly Browne's view of the church, with the possible exception of baptism, was very close to the Anabaptist concept. His view of the magistrate also sounds quite familiar to those who are acquainted with the teachings of continental Anabaptists. Is it an Anabaptist or a Puritan who speaks through the following words concerning the responsibilities and limitations of the magistracy?

---

30. *Ibid.*, 1:95.
31. Scheffer, *History of Free Churchmen*, p. 8.
32. Horst, ME, 2:219.

Yet may they doo nothing concerning the Church, but onelie ciuile, and as ciuile Magistrates, that is, they haue not that authoritie ouer the Church, as to be Prophetes or Priestes, or spiritual Kings, as in all outwarde Iustice, to maintain the right welfare and honor thereof, with outward power, bodily punishment, & ciuil forcing of men. And therefore also because the church is in a common wealth, it is of their charge: that is concerning the outward prouision and outward iustice, they are to look to it, but to compell religion, to plant churches by power, and to force a submission to Ecclesiastical gouernement by lawes & penalties belongeth not to them.[33]

Browne, instead of taking his persecuted flock to Scotland or to the vicinity of his former Puritan comrades, as some of the devout suggested, led them to Holland. Perhaps this indicates sympathy with the Mennonite view. Some years later, after suffering numerous imprisonments in Scotland and England, the battle-worn preacher at last returned to the Church of England. The similarity between the ideas of this erratic, yet courageous, soul and those of the Mennonites seems to have been more than coincidental.

There are two other facts that make the theory of Mennonite influence upon Browne even more plausible. The first is a phenomenon that accompanied the rise of the Brownists. With the emergence of Separatism, Anabaptists in England almost completely vanished.[34] The second is the prevalence of Anabaptist ideas among the Brownists and Barrowists. For example, the Barrowists (followers of Henry Barrowe) were charged by the authorities with denying the validity of the "Sacraments of Babtisme & the Lords supper, as they are administred now in the Church of England."[35] The Barrowists went so far as to withhold their children from baptism and refused to use the Lord's Prayer. Their practice of discipline, the taking of an offering for the suffering brethren of their number, and the use of a lay ministry are all practices reminiscent of the continental Anabaptists.

Horst holds that Henry Barrowe, a prominent Separatist leader

---

33. Quoted by C. Burrage, *Early English Dissenters*, 1:105.
34. Horst, ME, 2:220.
35. C. Burrage, *Early English Dissenters*, 2:20.

in London during the last decade of the sixteenth century, was Ana-baptist in every point with the exception of baptism.[36] However, the question of baptism among the Barrowists is not a closed one. R. Alison in his *A Plaine Confvtation of A Treatise of Brownisme*, printed in London in 1590, says that Browne did not in plain words "require a baptising againe, yet their successors [the Barrowists] in their established Church attempted it."[37] Alison claimed that his information came from the Barrowists themselves.

From the available evidence, it seems more than mere chance that the Separatist movement in England bore such a close resemblance to sixteenth-century Anabaptism. Apparently some segments within English Separatism only lacked a more favorable climate in order to emerge into fully developed Anabaptist churches.

The Rise of English Baptists

With the conversion to Separatism of Francis Johnson, an able Puritan divine, a new era in the development of the English Separatist movement began. It was the discovery and confiscation by Johnson of Barrowe and Greenwood's work, *Plaine Refvtation*, that led to his new alignment. As Governor Bradford puts it,

> At length he met with something that began to work upon his spirit. . . . In the end he was so taken . . . [that] he crossed the seas and came to London to confer with the authors, who were then in prison, and shortly after executed. After which conference he was so satisfied and confirmed in the truth, as he never returned to his place any more at Middleburg, but adjoined himself to their society at London, and was afterwards committed to prison, and then banished; and in conclusion coming to live at Amsterdam, he caused the same books, which he had been an instrument to burn, to be new printed and set out at his own charge.[38]

36. Horst, ME, 2:219.
37. Quoted by C. Burrage, *Early English Dissenters*, 1:127.
38. *Ibid.*, pp. 140-41.

In Francis Johnson, the Barrowists had gained a champion. It is hardly possible to deny the impact of the *Plaine Refutation* upon the subsequent course of his life.

After the deaths of Barrowe, Greenwood, and Penry many of the Barrowists sought refuge in Holland, as the Brownists and Puritans had done before them. The first group of new English immigrants left England for Holland in 1593, while Johnson was still in prison. This new Separatist migration apparently settled first at Campen, where a significant schism took place. By 1594 a part of the original congregation which had settled at Campen became Anabaptist in practice as well as belief.

The pronounced affinity of English Separatists for Anabaptist ideas now clearly manifested itself.[39] If believers' baptism had not actually been practiced in England by the Barrowists, at least there appears to have been the desire for such action as early as 1590.[40] Once in Holland, some of the Barrowists evidently were influenced by the Mennonites to adopt believers' baptism. Henoch Clapham, a contemporary witness, wrote of these early developments among the Barrowists:

> About thirteen yeares synce, this Church through persecution in England, was driven to come into these countreyes. A while after they were come hither divers of them fell into the heresies of the Anabaptists (which are too common in these countreys) and so persisting were excommunicated by the rest. Then a while after that againe, many others (of whom I think he speaketh here), some elder, some younger, even too many, though not the half (as I vnderstand)

39. Scheffer, *History of Free Churchmen*, p. 30: "In fact, the Brownists had much more sympathy with the Mennonites, than with the Reformed. They found they were one in sentiment. The views of both on the origin and organization of the Christian Church; its absolute autonomy; its order and government; the general suffrage of its members, but above all, its discipline were in substance identical. They had the same almost idolatrous exaltation of scriptures, the same aversion to symbolical books, the same institution of unpaid teachers and pastors, the same tendency to distinguish themselves from other children of the world by simplicity of dress and purity of morals. No one need wonder at this. It was at Norwich that Browne was indoctrinated with these principles."

40. C. Burrage, *Early English Dissenters*, 1:126-27.

fell into a schisme from the rest, and so many of them as continewed therein were cast out.[41]

Evidently the first division took place as early as 1594 and the other secessions followed at Naarden before Johnson's arrival in Holland around 1597.

This is the first English Anabaptist congregation of which there is any reliable information. Rebaptism was first practiced by one who then baptized the rest. Burrage quotes from Henoch Clapham's work published in 1600 entitled *Antidoton: or A Soveraigne Remedie Against Schisme and Heresie:*

> Touching the Anabaptists, they stand not partaking in the matter (as doth the Brownist) but they exufflate or blow off our Baptisme, so well as Ordination. . . . And so, one baptizeth [From margin: "I knew one such, and sundry can witness it."] himselfe (as Abraham first circumcised himselfe: mary, Abraham had a commandement; they haue none, nor like cause) and then he baptizeth other.[42]

The influence of this exiled English Anabaptist church was widespread. Not only were the Barrowists back home informed of the schisms and the issues which involved the "ancient [Johnson] church," but the Anabaptists themselves energetically propagated their views among their friends and relatives. Thomas Mitchell returned to Norwich, evidently for the purpose of advancing the cause on English soil. His visit was not without results. Among others, a certain John Neale seems to have embraced Anabaptism in the wake of Mitchell's visit. There is also a real possibility that John Smyth was first influenced toward believers' baptism by the English Separatists-turned-Anabaptist. It is thought that Thomas Odal, later a member of Smyth's Anabaptist congregation of Amsterdam, was one of the English Anabaptists in Campen. There is a possibility that Leonard Busher, who became quite prominent in later English Baptist life, was also one of the Campen group.[43]

41. Quoted in *ibid.,* p. 156.
42. *Ibid.,* p. 223.
43. *Ibid.,* pp. 222-25.

Even though much of the history of the first English Anabaptist congregation in Holland remains obscure, there is an abundance of information about John Smyth and his church. It is this church that is of such great importance to the history of English Baptists and the free church movement.

In 1594, the year the first English Anabaptist church was formed in Holland, John Smyth was ordained by Bishop Wickham. Smyth had received his B.A. and his M.A. degrees at Christ's College, Cambridge. In Michaelmas term of 1594, he was selected as fellow of Christ's College, a position he held until 1598. During these four years at Cambridge he proved to be an able teacher and was publicly identified with the Puritan majority at the University.[44]

Smyth next was city preacher in Lincoln, an enviable position and far more remunerative than the vicarship of a local parish. At Lincoln his services must have been very satisfactory, at least for some of his supporters. After a period of two years he was declared city lecturer for life. Only five weeks later, however, this unprecedented action was revoked; Smyth was relieved of his duties on October 13, 1602. He had raised the ire of certain city fathers with some remarks in the course of his sermons which they took as a personal affront.[45] Actually Smyth was the victim of a political struggle in which he became identified with the losing faction.

It is significant that Smyth at this time was in no sense a Separatist. To the contrary, as a good Puritan he set himself against toleration in any form. He had become convinced that toleration of many religions gave the devil an opportunity to push the kingdom of God "out of doores." Therefore, to the magistrates, Smyth ascribed the responsibility to punish heretics and advance the cause of true religion. "The Magistrates should cause all men to worship the true God, or else punish them with imprisonment, confiscation of goods, or death as the qualitie of the cause requireth."[46]

It is difficult to follow Smyth's movements from his dismissal at

44. W. T. Whitley, *The Works of John Smyth* (Cambridge: The University Press, 1915), 1:34-37.
45. *Ibid.,* p. xlv.
46. *Ibid.,* p. 166.

Lincoln to his move to Gainsborough, also in Lincolnshire. During the early months of his residence at Gainsborough, he supported himself and his family by the practice of medicine. The condition of the local Anglican parish weighed heavily on his conscience. The vicarage was held by Jerome Phillips. Although he received the income, he did not discharge the duties required, either in person or by proxy.

Therefore, Smyth stepped into the breach. In the light of the situation it is easy to see why he acted. However, he had not secured a license from the Anglican bishop. Instead of being commended for his devotion and zeal, he was severely reprimanded. Thus the course of Separatism was almost forced on a previously staunch Puritan. His experiences had brought him into increasing conflict with the establishment.

Smyth and his followers spent nine months in deliberation, consultation with many friends, and a fresh searching of the Scriptures. By the end of 1606 they drew up a church covenant after the example of the Old Testament saints.

> They shooke of this yoake of antichristian bondage, and as ye Lords free people, joyned them selves (by a covenant of the Lord) into a church estate, in ye fellowship of ye gospell, to walke in all his wayes, made known, or to be made known unto them, according to their best endeavours, whatsoever it should cost them, the Lord assisting them.[47]

Apparently the Gainsborough church met in two congregations. One was at Gainsborough under the leadership of Smyth. The other, at Scrooby, was under the leadership of a former Puritan minister of Norwich, John Robinson, and a layman, Richard Clyfton. The persecuting measures of James I and Bishop Bancroft drove the new Separatist church to consider seeking a refuge in Holland. Opinions began to crystallize in this direction by the summer of 1607, when some of their number were arrested and confined for a time in York Castle. However, the actual move apparently did not begin until 1608. The Gainsborough group then arrived in Amsterdam, where Francis John-

---

47. *Ibid.*, p. lxii.

son's church had been worshiping since 1597. Soon after the arrival of the Gainsborough and Scrooby Separatists and their companions, new developments began to occur in Smyth's congregation.

Before going to Holland, in 1607 Smyth published a book entitled *Principles and inferences concerning The visible Church,* in which he defined a church as follows: "A visible communion of Saincts is of two, three, or moe Saincts joyned together by covenant with God & themselves, freely to vse al the holy things of God, according to the word, for their mutual edification, & Gods glory."[48] This concept of the church as held by Smyth was soon to undergo a drastic change. As early as 1608 he published a work under the title *The Differences of the Churches of the separation.* He set forth six points of difference between his church and the "Ancient Church" of Johnson. The most serious difference apparent at this time was in regard to the ministry. Of this difference Smyth writes: "Wee hould that the Presbytery of the church is vniforme: & that the triformed Presbytetie [Presbyterie] consisting of three kinds of Elders viz. Pastors Teachers Rulers is none of Gods Ordinance but mans devise."[49] Before the end of the year or at the very beginning of the next year, Smyth was to introduce the most revolutionary change of all, believers' baptism.

Early in 1609 or late in 1608 Smyth and his congregation unchurched themselves and reconstituted the church upon the basis of believers' baptism instead of a church covenant. John Robinson wrote in 1617 of this action:

> Mr. Smith, Mr. Helw[ys] the rest haveing vtterly dissolved, & disclaymed their former Ch: state, & ministery, came together to erect a new Ch: by baptism: vnto which they also ascribed so great virtue, as that they would not so much as pray together, before they had it. And after some streyning of courtesy, who should begin. . . . Mr. Smith baptized first himself, & next Mr. Helwis, & so the rest, making their particular confessions.[50]

What influenced Smyth and his small congregation to take such

48. C. Burrage, *Early English Dissenters,* 1:233.
49. *Ibid.,* p. 235.
50. Quoted in *ibid.,* p. 237.

a drastic step? It could bring nothing but sorrow upon sorrow and forever separate them from their fellow Separatists. Was this the logical outworking of Separatism? If so, why did all Separatists not adopt such a procedure and reconstitute their churches after the pattern of the continental Anabaptists?

Doubtless on learning firsthand of the defections to Anabaptism from Johnson's church, Smyth was forced for his own satisfaction to search the Scriptures anew. Once convinced of the rightness of the new position, he wasted no time instructing his congregation. The church was then reconstituted on personal confessions of faith and baptisms. Smyth based his action squarely on the New Testament and the example of Christ and the apostles. Before, he had found the precedent in the Old Testament for constituting a church on a covenant. His former practice gave way to his new understanding.

To his former co-laborer, Richard Clyfton, he wrote that infants are not to be baptized because "there is neither precept nor example in the New Testament that they were baptized by John or Christ's disciples. Only they that did confess their sins and confess their faith were baptized."[51] The practice of infant baptism was further denied on the basis of the order of the Great Commission. Also baptism was seen as the seal of the new covenant, which applies only to believers. Because infants are incapable of belief, the new covenant cannot possibly apply to them. Infant baptism is therefore a "profanation."

The second major portion of Smyth's argument in his letter of 1610 to Clyfton is concerned with the proper constitution of a church. He argued that since the "defection of Antichrist," churches must be constituted after the example of the apostles. True baptism is one, but the baptism of "Antichrist is not true baptism." Therefore, he argued, false ministry and false worship, which included infant baptism, must be renounced.

The first major division of Smyth's argument against infant baptism is quite familiar to the student of Anabaptist history. Smyth's arguments for believers' baptism are identical to those offered by the Anabaptists since 1524. If there were no circumstances to indicate a

51. Walter H. Burgess, *John Smith, the Se-Baptist, Thomas Helwys, and the First Baptist Church in England* (London: James Clarke & Co., 1911), pp. 149-50.

possible relationship between Smyth and the Mennonites, it would be necessary to attribute the similarity of their positions to other factors. Conceivably, Smyth could have arrived at his position from his own private study of the Scriptures, apart from any outside stimulus. In the light of the historical context, this is highly unlikely.

In the first place, Smyth had been in Holland about a year before arriving at his new position. Scheffer has written that Smyth and his small congregation "were surrounded by at least three Mennonite churches: that of the Flemish, of the Frisons, of the United High German and Waterlanders. Particularly with the least [sic] one, Smyth had already come in contact. From it he borrowed his views on the ministry, nay, even on baptism itself."[52]

Possibly the English Anabaptists, formerly of Johnson's church, provided a stimulus to examine New Testament teaching on baptism. Smyth's act of self-baptism had been anticipated by them. Some Mennonite influence seems undeniable at this point. The source of his doctrine of the church had changed. In Gainsborough he had led the Separatists to follow the Old Testament in constituting the church on the basis of a covenant. This was a Separatist's pattern. In Amsterdam, on the basis of the New Testament, he rejected the covenant and constituted a church on believers' baptism. Here he followed an Anabaptist pattern. He apparently did not seek baptism from one of the neighboring Mennonite churches because he had not yet felt any necessity for such action. Nor was he prepared at this time to accept the Hofmannite Christology of his Mennonite friends.[53]

Smyth did not seek approval for his actions on the grounds of Mennonite practice but on the authority of the New Testament itself. It is not altogether accurate, therefore, to say that he "borrowed" these ideas from the Mennonites. Doubtless they caused him to rethink his doctrine of the church in the light of the New Testament. Yet it was the New Testament which convinced him of the error of his former action and the necessity of the new step which he and his followers took in 1609.

Ensuing controversy with Richard Clyfton forced Smyth to re-

52. Scheffer, *History of Free Churchmen*, p. 112.
53. Burgess, *John Smith*, p. 178.

think his self-baptism. The result was renunciation of his former action and a petition to the Waterlander Mennonites for admission into their fellowship. Before this step had been taken, Smyth had led his church from Calvinism into the acceptance of the general atonement and other views associated with James Arminius. While at first rejecting the Hofmannite Christology, he finally capitulated on this point also. He was now prepared to accept with only slight alteration the whole of Mennonite theology. Since Smyth had come to recognize the Waterlander church as a true church, only one step remained. He declared his own baptism invalid and for the sake of order sought baptism at the hands of the Mennonites. The majority of his church followed his lead, but the Mennonites declined to accept the group at this time. The break between Smyth and Helwys, which had begun with Smyth's adoption of Hofmannite Christology, was now complete.[54]

A minority of the Smyth church, led by Thomas Helwys and John Murton, excommunicated Smyth and the majority in 1610. The Helwys group numbered no more than ten. This small congregation, with such an unpromising beginning, established on English soil a church from which the General Baptists of England trace their beginning.

Helwys rejected Smyth's request for Mennonite baptism. This does not mean that he threw overboard every conviction that Smyth and his congregation had reached in Holland. To the contrary, the General Baptists were to reflect in both their basic tenets and practices their indebtedness to John Smyth and the Mennonites. Some even continued to hold to a Hofmannite Christology, and others rejected Helwys's position on the sword. However, Helwys's conviction that a magistrate, whose authority was limited to secular affairs, could be a member of the "Christ's church" became at the same time the most divisive issue between the English Baptists and the Mennonites and his most creative theological contribution to a distinctive Baptist witness.[55] A compara-

54. *Ibid.*, pp. 175-84.
55. See James R. Coggins, *John Smyth's Congregation* (Scottdale, Pa.: Herald Press, 1949), and Paul Toews, ed., *Mennonites and Baptists* (Winnipeg: M B Canada, 1993), for more information on Smyth, Helwys, and the Mennonite connection.

tive study of Helwys's confession of 1611 and that of the Smyth congregation of 1612 reveals both striking similarities and significant differences.[56] Helwys listed four points at which he took issue with Smyth.

I. that Christ took his flesh of Marie, having a true earthlie, naturall bodie.

II. that a Sabbath or day of rest is to be kept holy everie first day of the weeke.

III. that ther is no succession or privilege to persons in the holie things.

IV. that magistracie, being an holy ordinance of God, debarreth not any from being of the Church of Christ.[57]

Helwys did not know it, but on each of the disputed points except the second there were continental Anabaptists who agreed with him. The only point uniquely his was the idea of the Puritan Sabbath. In connection with his view of the Sabbath, he also advocated the weekly observance of the Lord's Supper, which was contrary to Mennonite usage. In his first confession of faith, he was one with Smyth in denying original sin. Article three reads: *"Quod Deus necessitatem peccandi nemini imponit:"* and article four, *"Quod nullum sit peccatum per generationem a parentibus nostris."*[58] In a later edition of the confession, Helwys changed article four to read, "men are by nature the children of wrath, born in iniquitie and in sin conceived, wise to all evil, but to good they have no knowledge."[59] But other aspects of a quasi-Arminian soteriology were retained.

For the time being, Helwys was content to remain in Amsterdam. He was thinking through the differences between his congregation and that of John Smyth, on the one hand, and those of the other English Separatists, on the other. He was still in Amsterdam on July 8, 1611. Chr. Lawne's *Prophane schism* states that at that time there were three congre-

---

56. See William L. Lumpkin, ed., *Baptist Confessions of Faith* (Philadelphia: Judson Press, 1959), pp. 114-42.

57. Scheffer, *History of Free Churchmen,* p. 170.

58. *Synopsis fidei verae Christianae Ecclesiae Anglicanae Amsterodamiae* (Amsterdam, 1611), p. 1, as reproduced in full by Scheffer in *ibid.,* p. 215.

59. Cited by Scheffer in *ibid.,* p. 170.

gations of "English Mennonites" in Amsterdam: "Mr. Smyth, an Anabaptist of one sort, and Mr. Helwise of another, and Mr. Busher of another."[60]

Apparently sometime in 1612, Helwys and his followers returned to England. Possibly it was the death of Smyth that finally convinced him that the mission of his church was to bear witness to the new-found faith in his native land. Further, he had become convinced that a disciple of the Lord should not seek to escape persecution. Perhaps he had never intended to remain in the Netherlands in the first place. News from England was not encouraging. Two dissenters had been executed there in the spring of 1611. In spite of a foreboding future, Helwys and his small group had settled in or just outside the walls of London at Spitalfield by the end of 1612. The following year he was imprisoned in Newgate Prison.

Shortly after his return to England Helwys published a little book entitled *The Mistery of Iniquity*, which set forth for the first time in England the concept of complete religious freedom. With rare courage the former country squire of Broxtowe Hall sent a copy of his new book with an inscription to King James I. In words as eloquent as they are bold, Helwys admonished the king to heed a principle that must have been strange to one of James's background.

> Heare, o king, and dispise not ye counsell of ye poore, and let their complaints come before thee. The king is a mortall man, and not God therefore hath no power over ye immortall soules of his subiects, to make lawes and ordinances for them, and to set spirituall Lords over them.
>
> If the king have authority to make spirituall Lords and lawes, then he is an immortall God, and not a mortall man.
>
> O king, be not seduced by deceivers to sin so against God whome thou oughtest to obey, nor against thy poore subiects who ought and will obey thee in all things with body life and goods, or els let their lives be taken from ye earth.
>
> God save ye king.
>
> *Spittlefield*   THO: HELWYS[61]
> *neare London.*

60. *Ibid.*, p. 171.
61. *A Short Declaration of the Mistery of Iniquity* (London: Grayes Inne,

In the year of Smyth's death, his basic teachings on religious liberty, the nature of the church, relation of the church to the state, primacy of the New Testament, believers' baptism, salvation, and discipleship found vigorous expression among those who had excommunicated him. The major differences between the two groups centered around the validity of Smyth's self-baptism and the possibility of church membership for a Christian magistrate. Helwys accepted the basic Anabaptist position on separation of church and state and religious freedom. He did not, however, reject the use of the oath; nor did he hold that a magistrate was automatically disqualified for church membership. This positive orientation of the doctrine of separation of church and state made possible a transmission of Anabaptist concepts into the English-speaking world of the seventeenth century. In this form, they were to shape to a considerable degree the culture of the Western world.

In 1612 an Englishman could read a vigorous plea for complete religious liberty and the separation of church and state. Helwys was the author of this historic statement, the first to be published in English. It is found in the informal table of contents entitled "The principal matter handled in the *Booke of the Mistery of Iniquity.*" The Church of Rome is identified with the first beast of Revelation 13, and the Church of England with the second. Helwys then discussed the authority of the king and its limitations.

> What Great Power and authority: what honor, names & titles God hath given to the King.
>
> That God hath given to the K. an earthly kingdome with all earthly power against the which, none may resist but must in all thinges obey, willingly, either, to do, or suffer.
>
> That Christ alone is K. of Israell, & sitts vpon Davids Throne, & that the K. ought to be a subject of his Kingdome.
>
> That none ought to be punished either with death or bonds for transgressing against the spirituall ordinances of the new Testament,

---

1612), reproduced from the copy presented by Helwys to King James, now in the Bodleian Library (London: Kingsgate Press, 1935), unnumbered page.

and that such Offences ought to be punished onely with spiritual sword and censures.[62]

To whom was Helwys indebted for this basic Baptist principle? John Smyth is the most obvious answer. Smyth had been his pastor since Gainsborough days. It was he who had led him from Puritanism to Separatism. From Separatism he had led him to adopt believers' baptism and the Anabaptist concepts of the church and state. In Helwys is it not the voice of Smyth that is heard? Compare Smyth's position as revealed in article 84 of "Propositions and Conclusions concerning True Christian Religion, containing a Confession of Faith of certain English people, living at Amsterdam."

That the magistrate is not by virtue of his office to meddle with religion, or matters of conscience, to force or compel men to this or that form of religion, or doctrine: but to leave Christian religion free, to every man's conscience, and to handle only civil transgressions (Roman. XIII), injuries and wrongs of man against man, in murder, adultery, theft, etc., for Christ only is the king and lawgiver of the church and conscience. (James iv.12).[63]

There is one important difference between Helwys's position regarding the magistrate and that of Smyth. While Smyth's position became identical with that of the Waterlander Mennonites, Helwys's understanding was closer to that of Balthasar Hubmaier. The typical Mennonite conviction was that a Christian could not be a magistrate. Helwys disagreed. Since the magistracy was ordained of God for an orderly society, a magistrate could not be justifiably barred from the church. After setting forth his position on the lawfulness of the magistracy in *A Declaration of Faith of English People Remaining at Amsterdam in Holland* of 1611, Helwys declared: "And therefore they may bee members off the Church off CHRIST, reteining their Magistracie, for no Hoile Ordinance off GOD debarreth anie from being a member off CHRISTS Church."[64]

62. *Ibid.*
63. William L. Lumpkin, ed., *Baptist Confessions of Faith* (Philadelphia: The Judson Press, 1959), p. 140.
64. *Ibid.*, pp. 122, 123.

In this same confession Helwys states that the magistrates "beare the sword off God, — which sword in all Lawful administracions is to bee defended and supported by the servants off God that are vnder their Goverment." He further departed from the practice of Dutch Mennonites by making the oath a permissible act in the Christian life.

Without question, Helwys was largely dependent on Smyth for his theology. Both Smyth and Helwys were dependent on the Mennonites for the determinative features of what was to become known as Baptist faith and practice. However, on the separation of church and state there is a significant difference between Helwys and the Mennonites. A more positive orientation of the Christian toward the state became, under the creative touch of Helwys, characteristic of Baptists.[65] Subsequently, the Baptists of England and America were to become vocal, consistent, and effective champions of religious freedom and church-state separation.

Helwys died in prison by 1616. But before his death others had caught his vision and had begun to proclaim essentially the same message in the inhospitable English climate. Noteworthy among the new prophets was Mark Leonard Busher, a leader among the English Anabaptists in Amsterdam as early as 1611.[66]

Leonard Busher brought his manuscript on religious freedom from the press in 1614. *Religions Peace: A Plea for Liberty of Conscience* has sometimes been erroneously referred to as the "earliest known publication" advocating religious freedom. Even though *Religions Peace* was by no means the earliest treatise advocating religious freedom, it was certainly the most balanced and closely argued treatise on the subject published to that date. Busher argued from the conviction that religious freedom is "no civil favor to be granted or withheld by the whim of the king; it is a God-given right of man and is essential because

65. See Harry Leon McBeth, "English Baptist Literature on Religious Liberty to 1689" (unpublished Th.D. thesis; Fort Worth, 1961) for an incisive study of the Baptist concept of religious liberty as revealed in English Baptist literature to 1689.

66. C. Burrage, *Early English Dissenters*, 1:243, 244 n. 2, cites the fact that Christopher Lawne in *The Prophane Schisme of the Brownists or Separatists* (1612), quotes from a letter by Cvth. Hvtten written on July 8, 1611, which reads: "Master Smith an Anabaptist of one sort, and master Helwise of another, and master Busher of another . . . to speake nothing of Pedder, Henrie Martin, with the rest of those Anabaptists" (p. 56).

of the very nature of Christianity."[67] Apparently Busher's book was published in London, but he was probably in the Netherlands at the time. He was an Englishman who spent the remainder of his life in Holland for conscience' sake.[68]

It was, therefore, John Murton and not Leonard Busher who became leader of the English Baptists on the death of Helwys. Murton had been the faithful co-laborer of Helwys from Amsterdam days. He shared Helwys's convictions. In devotion to the cause, courage, and suffering, he was Helwys's true heir. It appears that he spent the better part of thirteen years in prison, from 1513 to 1625, where he evidently died. After his death, Murton's widow returned to Amsterdam and united with the Mennonites on September 26, 1530, "without further baptism." Fortunately for the cause of religious freedom, few General Baptists followed her example.

The deaths of Helwys and Murton did not mean the end of the struggle for religious freedom. English Baptists were yet to find ardent and eloquent spokesmen for their cause. Among these Roger Williams emerged on the American scene. He became the most prominent of many able religious and political architects of the seventeenth century. The inspiration for much of his thought and work apparently came from the General Baptists and through them from the continental Anabaptists. At least Williams's writings often bear a striking resemblance in both content and vocabulary to earlier Anabaptist works on religious freedom.

67. McBeth, "English Baptist Literature," p. 47. See also *Religions Peace,* as reprinted with a new preface in *Tracts on Liberty of Conscience and Persecution, 1614-1661,* ed. Edward Bean Underhill (London: The Hanserd Knollys Society, 1846), pp. 1-181.

68. See C. Burrage, *Early English Dissenters,* 1:276-80. The nationality of Busher has been a matter of debate among historians for some time. In 1964 I examined a letter Busher wrote in Dutch from Delft to the Waterlander Mennonite congregation when he was 78 years of age. This letter proves conclusively that Busher was an Englishman. His advanced age and the contents of the letter suggest that he remained in Holland from the early part of the century to the end of his life. The letter was at that time in the Mennonite Archives in Amsterdam. See also Keith L. Sprunger, *Trumpets from the Tower* (Leiden: E. J. Brill, 1994), p. 19. Sprunger has discovered that Busher was still referred to as living in the Waterland Mennonite Archives as late as 1651. The 1614 edition of *Religions Peace,* according to Sprunger, was printed in Amsterdam.

The resemblance between Williams and Hubmaier may be seen by comparing excerpts from *Bloudy Tenent* of 1644 and *Concerning Heretics* of 1524. Roger Williams:

> All civil states, with their officers of justice, in their respective constitutions and administrations, are proved essentially civil, and therefore not judges, governors, or defenders of the spiritual, or Christian, state and worship.
>
> . . . It is the will and command of God that, since the coming of his Son the Lord Jesus, a permission of the most Paganish, Jewish, Turkish, or anti-christian consciences and worships be granted to all men in all nations and countries: and they are only to be fought against with that sword which is only, in soul matters, able to conquer: to wit, the sword of God's Spirit, the word of God.[69]

Balthasar Hubmaier:

> Verily, it is still no excuse (as they chatter) that they turn the godless over to the worldly power, for those who do this sin even more grievously. John 19.
>
> For every Christian has a sword against the godless, that is, the Word of God, Eph. 6, but no sword against the criminal.
>
> Therefore, it is well and good that the secular authority puts to death the criminals who do physical harm to the defenseless, Romans 13. But no one may injure the unbeliever *[gotssfind]* who wishes nothing for himself other than to forsake the gospel.[70]

The basis of Williams's political theory was religious concern — concern for the souls of people, including the Jew and the Turk. The same concern motivated the continental Anabaptists and the General Baptists. In the introductory statement to the *Bloudy Tenent,* articles 9 through 12, Williams evaluated the union of church and state. The

---

69. Roger Williams, *The Bloudy Tenent of Persecution for Cause of Conscience Discussed,* ed. Edward Bean Underhill (London: The Hanserd Knollys Society, 1848), pp. 1-2.

70. Balthasar Hubmaier, *Concerning Heretics and Those Who Burn Them,* Articles 20-21 in *Hübmaier Schriften,* p. 98. Vedder's translation, *Hübmaier,* pp. 85-87, is accurate and complete enough for most purposes.

inevitable denial of religious freedom is "the occasion of civil war, ravishing of conscience, persecution of Christ Jesus in his servants, and the hypocrisy and destruction of millions of souls." This state of affairs, he contended, disclaims "our desires and hopes of the Jews' conversion to Christ" and denies "that Jesus Christ is come in the flesh."[71]

Paralleling Williams's views is the thrust of Hubmaier's argument against persecution in *Concerning Heretics and Those Who Burn Them,* "The law that condemns heretics to the fire builds up both Zion in blood and Jerusalem in wickedness." Hubmaier expresses concern for the salvation of the hated Turk in these words: "We should pray and hope for repentance, as long as man lives in this misery. . . . A Turk or a heretic is not convinced by our act, either with the sword or with fire, but only with patience and prayer." Persecution for religious reasons, Hubmaier taught, "is in appearance to profess Christ (Tit. 1., 10,11), but in reality to deny him."[72]

That Williams and Hubmaier emphasized essentially the same points in these cited references is fairly obvious. However, the question of Williams's relationship with continental Anabaptism is still an open one. It is possible that similarities do not show direct dependence. Indeed, Williams, dealing with the same problems as those of the sixteenth-century Anabaptists, might have reached similar convictions on his own.

However, Williams was undoubtedly familiar with English Baptist works on religious freedom. He also had spent many hours as a boy observer in the courts of England. Ample opportunity was thus afforded him for wide acquaintance with the variety of religious opinions held by heretics condemned by the law. He also possessed a knowledge of several languages, including Dutch, opening avenues of knowledge closed to the ordinary Englishman. It is entirely possible, through the English Baptists and other channels, that Williams learned about continental Anabaptist concepts of religious liberty. Knowledge of the General Baptists could account for the concepts listed above. That Williams was well acquainted with the General Baptist contributions in the struggle for freedom is fairly certain.

71. Williams, *Bloudy Tenent,* p. 2.
72. *Schriften,* p. 98. See also Estep, *Anabaptist Beginnings,* pp. 49-53, for the author's translation of *Concerning Heretics* (1524).

Williams even incorporated an anonymous Baptist petition for religious freedom, presented to the crown in 1620, in his *Bloudy Tenent.* He may not have known the name of the author. He had been informed that "The Humble Supplication" had been written in milk on paper, which served as stoppers to the bottles, by a close prisoner of Newgate. "In such paper," Williams wrote, "written with milk, nothing will appear; but the way of reading it by fire being known to this friend who received the papers, he transcribed and kept together the papers, although the author himself could not correct, nor view what himself had written."[73]

To "The Humble Supplication" Williams gave the title "Scriptures and Reasons Against Persecution in Cause of Conscience." In all probability its anonymous author was John Murton.[74] In this prison manuscript of 1620 the argument for religious freedom is based on the command of Christ and the teachings of the New Testament. Further appeal is made to the possibility of salvation of the vilest from the historical precepts of kings, bishops, and Reformers; and the examples of the Old Testament saints. Its imagery is typically Anabaptist. From the parable of the tares and the wheat the writer argued for liberty of conscience as Hubmaier had done years before. Notice the writer's opening statement: "Because Christ commandeth, that the tares and wheat, which some understand are those that walk in the truth, and those that walk in lies, should be let alone in the world. Matt. xiii.30,38, &c."[75] Compare this with two statements from Hubmaier:

> So it follows now that the inquisitors are the greatest heretics of all, since, against the teaching and example of Christ they condemn heretics to the fire, and before the time of harvest root up the wheat with the tares.[76]

The extent of Williams's indebtedness to the General Baptists and to the continental Anabaptists may never be fully known. It is obvious, however, that he became the most effective instrument for transplanting

73. Williams, *Bloudy Tenent,* p. 36.
74. McBeth, "English Baptist Literature," p. 54.
75. Williams, *Bloudy Tenent,* p. 10.
76. *Schriften,* p. 98.

their characteristic doctrines of church and state to the New World. Even more significant was his choice when opportunity developed to establish a new colony. He rejected the Puritan theocracy and the Old World *corpus Christianum* as equally invalid. For the first time in history a government was formed embodying the principles which the English Baptists had come to champion.

While Williams was busy seeing *The Bloudy Tenent of Persecution* through the press in England, the Particular Baptists brought out their first confession of faith, known as the London Confession. Printed by Matthew Simmons in 1644, the title reads: The Confession of Faith of Those Churches which are commonly (though falsely) called Anabaptist; . . ."[77] The Particular Baptists reflect a further development within English Separatism. Growing out of the Independent Church of Henry Jacob, the radical party, which began to emerge as early as 1630, by 1638 had arrived at the conviction that only believers were fit subjects for baptism. Baptism by immersion was inaugurated by 1641. Thus an exceedingly remarkable development had taken place. For the first time Calvinism and Anabaptism merged to produce a new and different religious configuration in seventeenth-century England. The London Confession of 1644, according to Glen H. Stassen, offers some clues as to the nature and source of the changes that brought about this new Baptist movement.[78]

For the greater part of the Reformation era, English religious life was dominated by Calvinistic influences. The earlier "free will" ideology, stemming from Anabaptist, Lollard, and Erasmian influences, had fallen back in the face of the vigorous Calvinism characteristic of Puritans, Independents, and Separatists alike. It appears that only the General Baptists and a few other extremely small groups still held to an "Arminian" soteriology. Somehow the Separatists, coming out of the Jacob-Lathrop-Jessey church, came under the influence of Anabaptist ideas most commonly associated with the rapidly growing General Baptist movement. The result was a modification of their Calvinism and an adoption of concepts and practices heretofore held only by the

---

77. Lumpkin, *Baptist Confessions,* p. 153.
78. Glen H. Stassen, "Anabaptist Influence in the Origin of the Particular Baptists," MQR 36, no. 4 (October 1962): 322ff.

continental Anabaptists and General Baptists. It is Stassen's opinion that the changes came about as a result of the influence of either Menno Simons's *Foundation Book* or of the writing of an individual who reflected a similar position.

A comparison of Helwys's Confession of 1611 with the London Confession will reveal the striking similarity between the two confessions and also some marked differences. The two confessions are very close in concept and even in wording on biblical authority, ecclesiology, baptism, and the magistracy. On soteriology, the Calvinism of the True Confession of 1596 overshadows the alterations. Yet, as Stassen observes, "Thus the Baptists sharpened Calvinism when it gave glory to the act of God in Christ, and they softened it where it detracted from their conception of God as the One who acted in Christ."[79] On baptism the framers of the London Confession spell out the mode of baptism in detail. This is a departure from both the true Confession and the General Baptist confessions. Articles XXXIX and XL read, without the supporting Scripture references:

> Article XXXIX
> That Baptisme is an Ordinance of the new Testament, given by Christ, to be dispensed (a) onely upon persons professing faith, or that are Disciples, or taught who upon a profession of faith, ought to be baptized.

> Article XL
> The way and manner of the dispensing of this Ordinance (c) the Scripture holds out to be dipping or plunging the whole body under water: it being a signe, must answer the thing signified, which are these: first, the washing the whole soule in the bloud of Christ: Secondly, that interest the Saints have in the death, buriall, and resurrection; thirdly, together with a confirmation of our faith, that as certainly as the body is buried under water, and riseth againe, so certainly shall the bodies of the Saints be raised by the power of Christ, in the day of the resurrection, to reigne with Christ.

A marginal note is added,

79. *Ibid.*, p. 333.

The word *Baptizo,* signifying to dip under water, yet so as with convenient garments both upon the administrator and subject, with all modestie.[80]

The article on the magistracy is not as clear on the limitations of that office and the guarantee of religious liberty as either Smyth's confession of 1612 or Helwys's *Mistery of Iniquity.* Subsequent confessions of the Particular Baptists were to reflect more clearly the General Baptist position on both ecclesiology and religious liberty. Such progression within Particular Baptist life tends to indicate dependence upon the General Baptists for those features that called forth this new expression of English Baptist life.[81]

The English Quakers

Colonial America felt the impact of another religious development which has often been associated with the Anabaptists, the Quakers. Their founder, George Fox, acknowledged no indebtedness to human sources for his new movement. However, circumstances associated with the rise of the Society of Friends are suggestive. Many ideas which Fox began to emphasize were current in contemporaneous movements. Fox, consciously or unconsciously, partook of a varied religious menu served up by Seekers, Familists, and General Baptists. Apparently, a group of "shattered Baptists" at Nottinghamshire became the channel through which he and his followers were infected with the Anabaptist heresy.[82]

---

80. Lumpkin, *Baptist Confessions,* p. 167.

81. Among the English Separatists only the Baptists developed an explicit theology relative to believers' baptism, the church, and religious liberty. Of course, all of these concepts find validation in the New Testament, but most Separatists could not see this because they read their Bibles with Calvinistic glasses. See also W. R. Estep, Jr., "Anabaptists and the Rise of English Baptists," *The Quarterly Review* 28, no. 4 (October 1968), and 29, no. 1 (1969), for a more complete discussion of Baptist origins. In addition, see William Estep, "Sixteenth-Century Anabaptism and the Puritan Connections: Reflections upon Baptist Origins," in Paul Toews, ed., *Mennonites and Baptists* (Winnipeg: Kindred Press, 1993), pp. 1-38.

82. See William C. Braithwaite, *The Beginnings of Quakerism* (Cambridge: The University Press, 1955), pp. 43ff.

However, the Quaker movement was not simply a pale reflection of some previous religious development but something new under the sun. The genius of George Fox and the influence of diverse groups account in part for the characteristic emphases of the Quakers.

The Quaker contribution to life in America is perhaps better known than that of any other group discussed in this chapter. There is no necessity, therefore, to repeat an already familiar story. Quakers and Mennonites found an undeniable affinity for one another in Pennsylvania. Subsequently many Mennonites were caught up in the enthusiasm of the early Friends and became Quakers themselves. To some degree this represented a repudiation of certain aspects of their Anabaptist heritage. Ideologically, at least, the Quakers are closer to quietistic inspirationists, such as Sebastian Franck and Casper Schwenckfeld, than they are to the Swiss Brethren.[83]

The Church of the Brethren

The Church of the Brethren, commonly known as Dunkards, is more closely related to sixteenth-century Anabaptism than are the English Quakers. Late in the seventeenth century, circumstances in Germany resembled those in England during the reign of the Stuarts. These gave rise to a new German Baptist movement.

Actually, the Dunkards represent a number of converging influences. All the original members were Pietists, advocates of the revival that swept Germany through the work of Spener and Francke. Formerly members of the Reformed and Lutheran churches, a radical group of Pietists denounced their former baptism. Out of a sense of obedience to Christ they adopted believers' baptism. Since the Mennonites in the area did not immerse, the Pietist group re-established baptism on their own by trine immersion. Hochmann, their most effective leader, was

83. Many fine works detail various facets of the Quaker development. However, John Nickalls, ed., *The Journal of George Fox* (Cambridge: The University Press, 1952); William Tallack, *George Fox, the Friends, and the Early Baptists* (London: S. W. Partridge, 1868); and William C. Braithwaite, *The Beginnings of Quakerism,* ed. Henry J. Cadbury, 2nd ed. (Cambridge: The University Press, 1955), are basic.

in prison at the time; therefore Alexander Mack probably baptized the group.

The Dunkards were designated "New Baptists" in order to distinguish them from the Mennonites or "Old Baptists." From their meager beginnings in 1708, they suffered the severest reprisals for their courageous witness. Increasingly they found Germany an inhospitable land. Their Mennonite brethren, who had left Crefeld some years before for Pennsylvania, wrote back glowingly of the freedom which they had found in the New World. The Brethren soon joined them. Between 1719 and 1729 almost the entire movement was transplanted from Europe to North America.[84]

Naturally the vanguard of the movement settled near their former Mennonite neighbors of Crefeld in Germantown, Pennsylvania. Although slow to organize churches in their new environment, once they regained their spiritual momentum the Brethren began to make their presence felt. Through the Sauers, an early Brethren family, the first German Bible printed in America and the first German newspaper using German type were published. Even before the Revolutionary War the Dunkards had begun to move south, carrying with them their earnest piety and their nonresistant witness. Like the Mennonites, the Brethren lost heavily to other denominations. Many were absorbed by their Baptist neighbors. But a sizeable and influential denomination has persisted and shows promise for the future.

The Anabaptist Heritage

Today the Anabaptist heritage is not the sole possession of some inconspicuous sect in the backwater of civilization. Rather, it is the prized possession of every free society of the twentieth-century world. While the twin concepts of religious freedom and the institutional separation of church and state have found expression in a number of constitutions and declarations of human rights in various governments and in the United Nations Organization, the implementation of these principles

---

84. Donald F. Durnbaugh, *European Origins of the Brethren* (Elgin, Ill.: Brethren Press, 1958), p. 281.

is by no means universal. To the contrary, in this last decade of the twentieth century these ideals seem further from realization than at the beginning of the century. Even with the decline of communism and the breakup of the Soviet Union, religious freedom has failed to flourish in many countries. Instead, formerly established churches have rapidly attempted to regain their hegemony at the expense of freedom for any alternate expression of religious faith. Fanatics among Muslims, Hindus, Sikhs, and Zionists apparently would rather kill than grant co-existence to those of other religious persuasions. Even in the United States some Christians of the believers' church heritage seem to have become disillusioned with freedom in the face of the moral collapse of Western civilization, as if the institutional separation of church and state were the root of the problem. In face of the realities of the age, does the Anabaptist heritage make sense any more, even if it once did? The answer to this question from the Anabaptists of the sixteenth century cannot help but be a resounding *"Jawohl!"*

In the face of increasing acts of terror against believers and evangelical churches in almost every country and on every continent, it appears that the message of the Anabaptists who insisted that Christ alone is "the Lord of the church and conscience" has yet to be heard — and if heard, to be accepted — in many nations of our fragmented world. A few moments' reflection should convince even the most skeptical that where one is not free to hear and respond to the gospel, there can be no true freedom — or responsible citizenship. If the Anabaptists teach us anything, it is that those who fear freedom and court the governments of this world in the interest of a more moral or "Christian" state are placing their faith in a broken reed. For the Anabaptists, there is only one way, the way of the cross, for the church to become "salt, light, and leaven" in any society, and in every age.

🏃   🏃

Bibliography

Source Materials

Atkinson, James, ed. and trans. *Luther: Early Theological Works.* Philadelphia: The Westminster Press, 1962.

Burrage, Champlin. *The Early English Dissenters.* Vol. 2. Cambridge: The University Press, 1912.

Cramer, S., and Pijper, F., eds. *Bibliotheca Reformatoria Neerlandica.* 10 vols. 's-Gravenhage: Martinus Nijhoff, 1909.

Davidson, G. D. *The Writings of Balthasar Hübmaier.* 3 vols. Liberty, Mo.: reproduced by microfilm, 1939.

Denck, Hans. *Schriften, Quellen und Forschungen zur Reformationsgeschichte Herausgegeben vom Verein für Reformationsgeschichte.* Band XXIV, 1. Teil Bibliographie von Pfarrer Georg Baring (Gütersloh: C. Bertelsmann Verlag, 1955); 2. Teil Religiöse Schriften Herausgegeben von Walter Fellmann (Gütersloh: C. Bertelsmann Verlag, 1956); 3. Teil Exegetische Schriften Gedichte und Briefe Herausgegeben von Walter Fellmann (Gütersloh: Verlagshaus Gerd Mohn, 1960).

Dyck, Cornelius J., Keeny, William E., and Beachy, Alvin S., ed. and trans., *The Writings of Dirk Philips.* Scottdale, Pa.: Herald Press, 1992.

Egli, Emil, and Schoch, Rudolf, eds. *Johannes Kessler's Sabbata mit kleineren Schriften und Briefen.* St. Gallen: Huber, 1902.

307

Estep, William R., Jr., ed. *Anabaptist Beginnings (1523-1533): A Source Book.* Vol. 16. Nieuwkoop: B. de Graaf, 1976.

————, ed. *The Reformation: Luther and the Anabaptists.* Broadman Press, 1979.

Fast, Heinold, ed. *Der linke Flügel der Reformation.* Bremen: Carl Schünemann Verlag, 1962.

Fellmann, W., ed. *Hans Denck Schriften.* Gütersloh: C. Bertelsmann Verlag, 1956.

Franz, Günther. *Thomas Müntzer Schriften und Briefe.* Gütersloh: Verlagshaus Gerd Mohn, 1968.

Friedmann, Robert, trans. "Claus Felbinger's Confession of Faith Addressed to the Council of Landshut, 1560." *The Mennonite Quarterly Review* 29 (April 1955): 141-61.

————. "The Oldest Church Discipline of the Anabaptists." *The Mennonite Quarterly Review* 29 (April 1955): 164.

Harder, Leland, ed. *The Sources of Swiss Anabaptism.* Scottdale, Pa.: Herald Press, 1985.

Helwys, Thomas. *A Short Declaration of the Mistery of Iniquity.* London: Grayes Inne, 1612. Reproduced by Kingsgate Press (London), 1935.

Hillerbrand, Hans J. "An Early Anabaptist Treatise on the Christian and the State." *The Mennonite Quarterly Review* 32 (January 1958): 31.

Hutterian Brethren, ed. and trans. *The Chronicle of the Hutterian Brethren.* Vol 1. Riften, N.Y.: Plough Publishing House, 1987.

Jenny, Beatrice. "Das Schleitheimer Täuferbekenntnis 1527." In *Schaffhauser Beiträge zur väterlandischen Geschichte,* ed. *Historischen Verein des Kantons Schaffhausen.* Thayngen: Verlag Karl Augustin, 1951.

Kepler, Thomas S., ed. *Theologia Germanica.* Cleveland: World Publishing Company, 1952.

Klassen, William, and Klassen, Walter, ed. and trans. *The Writings of Pilgram Marpeck.* Scottdale, Pa.: Herald Press, 1978.

Liechty, Daniel. *Early Anabaptist Spirituality.* New York: Paulist Press, 1994.

Lumpkin, William L. *Baptist Confessions of Faith.* Philadelphia: The Judson Press, 1959.

McGlothlin, W. J. *Baptist Confessions of Faith*. Philadelphia: American Baptist Publication Society, 1911.

Muralt, Leonhard von, and Schmid, Walter, eds. *Quellen zur Geschichte der Täufer in der Schweiz*. Vol. 1. Zürich: S. Hirzel Verlag, 1952.

Philips, Dietrich. *Enchiridion*. Trans. A. B. Kolb. Elkhart, Ind.: The Mennonite Publishing Company, 1910.

————. *Enchiridion oder Handbuchlein von der Christlichen Lehre und Religion*. Neu-Berlin: Christian Moser, 1851.

Pijper, F., ed. "De geschriften van Dirk Philipsz." In *Bibliotheca Neerlandica Reformatoria*. Vol. 10. 's-Gravenhage: Martinus Nijhoff, 1914.

Pipkin, H. Wayne, and Yoder, John H., ed. and trans. *Balthasar Hübmaier: Theologian of Anabaptism*. Scottdale, Pa.: Herald Press, 1989.

Rideman, Peter. *Account of our Religion, Doctrine, and Faith*. Trans. Kathleen E. Hasenberg. London: Hodder & Stoughton, Ltd., 1950.

————. *Rechenschaft unserer Religion, Lehre und Glaubens*. Alberta: Verlag der Hutterischen Brüder Gemeine., 1962.

Smith, H. Shelton, Handy, Robert T., and Loetscher, Lefferts A. *American Christianity*. Vol. 1. New York: Charles Scribner's Sons, 1960.

Underhill, Edward Bean. *Tracts on Liberty of Conscience and Persecution, 1614-1661*. London: The Hanserd Knollys Society, 1846.

Wenger, John Christian, ed. *The Complete Writings of Menno Simons*. Trans. Leonard Verduin. Scottdale, Pa.: Mennonite Publishing House, 1956.

————, trans. *Conrad Grebel's Programmatic Letters of 1524*. Scottdale, Pa.: Herald Press, 1970.

————. "Pilgram Marpeck's Confession of Faith Composed at Strasbourg." *The Mennonite Quarterly Review* 12 (July 1938): 167-202.

————. "The Schleitheim Confession of Faith." *The Mennonite Quarterly Review* 19 (October 1945): 248.

Westin, Gunnar, and Bergsten, Torsten, eds. *Balthasar Hübmaier Schriften*. Gütersloh: Verlagshaus Gerd Mohn, 1962.

Whitley, W. T. *The Works of John Smyth*. Vol. 1. Cambridge: The University Press, 1915.

Williams, George Huntston, and Mergal, Angel M., eds. *Spiritual and Anabaptist Writers*. Philadelphia: The Westminster Press, 1957.

Williams, Roger. *The Bloudy Tenent of Persecution for Cause of Conscience*

Discussed, ed. Edward Bean Underhill. London: The Hanserd Knollys Society, 1848.

Yoder, John H. *The Legacy of Michael Sattler.* Scottdale, Pa.: Herald Press, 1973.

Zieglschmid, A. F. J., ed. *Das Klein-Geschichtsbüch der Hutterischen Brüder.* Philadelphia: Carl Schurz Memorial Foundation, 1947.

————. *Die älteste Chronik der Hutterischen Brüder.* New York: Carl Schurz Memorial Foundation, 1943.

Zwingli, Huldreich. *Huldreich Zwingli's Werke.* Ed. Melchior Schuler and Joh. Schulthess. Vols. 1, 5, 7. Zürich: Friedrich Schulthess, 1828.

Special Works on the Anabaptists

Armour, Rollin Stely. *Anabaptist Baptism: A Representative Study.* Scottdale, Pa.: Herald Press, 1966.

Bauman, Clarence. *Gewaltlosigkeit im Täufertum.* Leiden: E. J. Brill, 1968.

————. *The Spiritual Legacy of Hans Denck.* Leiden: E. J. Brill, 1991.

Bax, E. Belfort. *Rise and Fall of the Anabaptists.* New York: Macmillan, 1903.

Blanke, Fritz. *Brüder in Christo: Die Geschichte der ältesten Täufergemeinde.* Zürich: Zwingli-Verlag, 1955.

————. *Brothers in Christ.* Trans. Joseph Norden Haug. Scottdale, Pa.: Herald Press, 1961.

Braght, Thieleman J. van. *The Bloody Theatre or Martyr's Mirror of the Defenceless Christians.* Trans. I. Daniel Rupp. Lancaster, Pa.: American Publishing Society, 1879.

Clasen, Claus Peter. *Anabaptism, A Social History, 1525-1618.* Ithaca: Cornell University Press, 1972.

Davis, Kenneth Ronald. *Anabaptism and Asceticism: A Study in Intellectual Origins.* Scottdale, Pa.: Herald Press, 1974.

Dosker, Henry Elias. *The Dutch Anabaptists.* Philadelphia: The Judson Press, 1921.

Egli, Emil. *Die Züricher Wiedertäufer zur Reformationszeit.* Zürich: Friedrich Schulthess, 1878.

Friesen, Abraham. *Thomas Muentzer, A Destroyer of the Godless.* Berkeley: University of California Press, 1990.

Grätz, Delbert L. *Bernese Anabaptists.* Scottdale, Pa.: Herald Press, 1953.

Gross, Leonard. *The Golden Years of the Hutterites.* Scottdale, Pa.: Herald Press, 1980.

Hershberger, Guy F., ed. *The Recovery of the Anabaptist Vision.* Scottdale, Pa.: Herald Press, 1957.

Hillerbrand, Hans Joachim. *A Bibliography of Anabaptism, 1520-1630.* Elkhart, Ind.: Institute of Mennonite Studies, 1962.

————. *A Bibliography of Anabaptism, 1520-1630, A Sequel — 1962-1974.* St. Louis: Center for Reformation Research, 1975.

Horsch, John. *The Hutterian Brethren.* Goshen, Ind.: The Mennonite Historical Society, 1931.

Horst, Irvin Buckwalter. *The Dutch Dissenters: A Critical Companion to Their History and Ideas.* Leiden: E. J. Brill, 1986.

————. *The Radical Brethren: Anabaptism and the English Reformation to 1558.* Nieuwkoop: B. de Graaf, 1972.

Klaassen, Walter. *Living at the End of the Ages.* New York: Institute for Anabaptist and Mennonite Studies. Conrad Grebel College, Waterloo, Ont., n.d.

————, ed. *Anabaptism Revisited.* Scottdale, Pa.: Herald Press, 1992.

Krahn, Cornelius. *Dutch Anabaptism: Origin, Spread, Life and Thought (1450-1600).* The Hague: Martinus Nijhoff, 1968.

Littell, Franklin Hamlin. *The Anabaptist View of the Church.* Boston: Starr King Press, 1958.

————. *The Free Church.* Boston: Starr King Press, 1957.

————. *A Tribute to Menno Simons.* Scottdale, Pa.: Herald Press, 1961.

Packull, Werner O. *Studies in Anabaptist and Mennonite History: Mysticism and the Early South German–Austrian Anabaptist Movement (1525-1531).* Vol. 19. Scottdale, Pa.: Herald Press, 1977.

Rempel, John D. *The Lord's Supper in Anabaptism.* Scottdale, Pa.: Herald Press, 1993.

Smith, C. Henry. *The Story of the Mennonites.* Rev. Cornelius Krahn. Newton, Kans.: Mennonite Publication Office, 1950.

Smithson, R. J. *The Anabaptists.* London: James Clarke, 1935.

Stayer, James M. *Anabaptists and the Sword.* Lawrence, Kans.: Coronado Press, 1972.

————. *The German Peasants' War and Anabaptist Community of Goods.* London: McGill-Queen's University Press, 1991.

Verduin, Leonard. *The Reformers and Their Stepchildren.* Grand Rapids: Wm. B. Eerdmans Publishing Company, 1966.

Wenger, John Christian. *Glimpses of Mennonite History and Doctrine.* Scottdale, Pa.: Herald Press, 1947.

Williams, George Huntston. *The Radical Reformation.* 3rd ed. Kirksville, Mo.: Sixteenth Century Journal Publishers, Inc., 1992.

Windhorst, Christof. *Täuferisches Taufverständnis.* Leiden: E. J. Brill, 1976.

Yoder, John Howard. *Täufertum und Reformation in der Schweiz.* Karlsruhe: Verlag H. Schneider, 1962.

——. *Täufertum und Reformation im Gespräch.* Zürich: EVZ-Verlag, 1968.

Zeman, Jerold Knox. *The Anabaptists and the Czech Brethren in Moravia 1526-1628.* The Hague: Mouton, 1969.

Zijpp, N. van der. *Geschiedenis der Doopsgezinden in Nederland.* Arnhem: Van Loghum Slaterus, 1952.

Biographies

Bauman, Clarence. *The Spiritual Legacy of Hans Denck: Interpretation and Translation of Key Texts.* Leiden: E. J. Brill, 1991.

Bender, Harold. *Conrad Grebel.* Goshen, Ind.: The Mennonite Historical Society, 1950.

——. *Menno Simons.* Scottdale, Pa.: Herald Press, 1956.

Bergsten, Torsten. *Balthasar Hübmaier, Seine Stellung zu Reformation und Täufertum 1521-1528.* Kassel: J. G. Oncken Verlag, 1961.

——. *Balthasar Hübmaier.* Valley Forge, Pa.: Judson Press, 1978.

Friesen, Abraham, and Goertz, Hans-Jürgen, eds. *Thomas Müntzer.* Germany: Wissenschaftliche Buchgesellschaft, 1978.

Goertz, Hans-Jürgen, ed. *Profiles of Radical Reformers.* Kitchener, Ont.: Herald Press, 1982.

Gritsch, Eric W. *Thomas Müntzer: A Tragedy of Errors.* Minneapolis: Fortress Press, 1989.

Horsch, John. *Menno Simons.* Scottdale, Pa.: Mennonite Publishing House, 1916.

Kiwiet, Jan J. *Pilgram Marbeck.* Kassel: J. G. Oncken Verlag, 1957.

Koolman, J. ten Doornkaat. *Dirk Philips, 1504-1568*. Haarlem: H. D. Tjeenk Willink & Zoon N.V., 1964.

Krahn, Cornelius. *Menno Simons*. Karlsruhe: Heinrich Schneider, 1936.

Krajewski, Ekkehard. *Leben und Sterben des Zürcher Täuferführers, Felix Mantz*. Kassel: J. G. Oncken Verlag, 1958.

Littell, Franklin Hamlin. *Landgraf Philipp und die Toleranz*. Bad Nauheim: Im Christian-Verlag, 1957.

Moore, John Allen. *Anabaptist Portraits*. Scottdale, Pa.: Herald Press, 1984.

————. *Der Starke Jörg*. Kassel: J. G. Oncken Verlag, 1955.

Pater, Calvin Augustine. *Karlstadt as the Father of the Baptist Movements: The Emergence of Lay Protestantism*. Canada: University of Toronto Press, 1984.

Potter, G. R. *Zwingli*. Cambridge: Cambridge University Press, 1978.

Rilliet, Jean. *Zwingli, Third Man of the Reformation*. Trans. Harold Knight. Philadelphia: The Westminster Press, 1959.

Snyder, C. Arnold. *The Life and Thought of Michael Sattler*. Scottdale, Pa.: Herald Press, 1984.

Vedder, Henry C. *Balthasar Hübmaier*. New York: G. P. Putnam's Sons, 1905.

General Works

Bainton, Roland H. *Here I Stand*. New York: Abingdon Press, 1950.

————. *The Travail of Religious Liberty*. New York: Harper & Brothers, 1958.

Barth, Karl. *Die Kirchliche Lehre von der Taufe*. Zürich: Evangelischer Verlag AG, 1953.

————. *Die Taufe als Begründung des Christlichen Lebens*. Zürich: EVZ-Verlag, 1967.

Braithwaite, William C. *The Beginnings of Quakerism*. Cambridge: The University Press, 1955.

Burgess, Walter H. *John Smith, the Se-Baptist, Thomas Helwys, and the First Baptist Church in England*. London: James Clarke, 1911.

Burrage, Champlin. *The Early English Dissenters*. Vol. 1. Cambridge: The University Press, 1912.

Coggins, James R. *John Smyth's Congregation*. Waterloo, Ont.: Herald Press, 1991.

Cullmann, Oscar, *Die Tauflehre des Neuen Testament*. Zürich: Zwingli-Verlag, 1948.

Durnbaugh, Donald F. *European Origins of the Brethren*. Elgin, Ill.: Brethren Press, 1958.

Dyck, Cornelius J., and Martin, Dennis D., eds. *The Mennonite Encyclopedia*. Scottdale, Pa.: Herald Press, 1990.

Estep, William R. *Renaissance and Reformation*. Grand Rapids: Wm. B. Eerdmans Publishing Company, 1986.

Garrett, James Leo. *The Nature of the Church according to the Radical Continental Reformation*. Fort Worth, 1957.

———, ed. *The Concept of the Believers' Church*. Scottdale, Pa.: Herald Press, 1969.

———. *A Fellowship of Discontent*. New York: Harper & Row, 1967.

Hoop Scheffer, J. G. de. *History of the Free Churchmen*. Ed. William Elliot Griffis. Ithaca, N.Y.: Andrus & Church, n.d.

Jackson, Samuel Macauley. *Huldreich Zwingli*. New York: G. P. Putnam's Sons, 1900.

Latourette, Kenneth Scott. *A History of Christianity*. New York: Harper & Brothers, 1953.

Lindsay, Thomas M. *A History of the Reformation*. 2 vols. Edinburgh: T. & T. Clark, 1907.

Manschreck, Clyde Leonard. *Melanchthon: The Quiet Reformer*. Nashville: Abingdon Press, 1958.

Mueller, William A. *Church and State in Luther and Calvin*. Nashville: Broadman Press, 1954.

Payne, Ernest A. *The Teaching of the Church Regarding Baptism*. London: SCM Press, 1954.

Reid, J. K. S. *Baptism in the New Testament*. Chicago: Henry Regnery, 1940.

St. Amant, Penrose. *Christian Faith and History*. Fort Worth, 1954.

Smith, Preserved. *The Age of the Reformation*. New York: Henry Holt, 1920.

Strand, Kenneth A. *German Bibles Before Luther*. Grand Rapids: Wm. B. Eerdmans Publishing Company, 1966.

Sprunger, Keith L. *Trumpets from the Tower: English Puritan Printing in the Netherlands, 1600-1640.* Leiden: E. J. Brill, 1994.

Toews, Paul, ed. *Mennonites and Baptists.* Winnipeg, Man., and Hillsboro, Kans.: Kindred Press, 1993.

Vedder, Henry C. *A Short History of the Baptists.* Philadelphia: The American Baptist Publication Society, 1907.

Wallbank, T. Walter, and Taylor, Alastair M. *Civilization Past and Present.* New York: Scott, Foresman, 1942.

Wappler, Paul, *Thomas Müntzer in Zwickau und die Zwickauer Propheten.* Gütersloh: Gerd Mohn, 1966.

Watts, Michael R. *The Dissenters.* Oxford: Oxford University Press, 1978.

Westin, Gunnar. *The Free Church through the Ages.* Trans. Virgil Olson. Nashville: Broadman Press, 1958.

Whitley, W. T. *A History of British Baptists.* London: Charles Griffin, 1923.

Wilbur, Earl Morse. *A History of Unitarianism: Socinianism and Its Antecedents.* Cambridge, Mass.: Harvard University Press, 1945.

Williams, George Huntston. *The Radical Reformation.* Philadelphia: The Westminster Press, 1962. Third Rev. Ed. Kirksville, Mo.: Sixteenth Century Publishers, Inc., 1992.

————. *La Reforma Radical.* Mexico City: Fondo de Cultura Economica, Mexico, 1983.

Zuck, Lowell H., ed. *Christianity and Revolution.* Philadelphia: Temple University Press, 1975.

Articles

Bender, Harold S. "The Anabaptist Vision." In *The Recovery of the Anabaptist Vision,* ed. G. F. Hershberger, p. 33. Scottdale, Pa.: Mennonite Publishing House, 1957.

————. "Church." In *Mennonite Encyclopedia,* 1:594-97.

————. "The First Anabaptist Congregation: Zollikon, 1525." *The Mennonite Quarterly Review* 27 (January 1953): 28.

————. "Historiography of the Anabaptists." *The Mennonite Quarterly Review* 31 (April 1957): 88-104.

————. "Pilgram Marpeck." *Mennonite Encyclopedia,* 3:494-95.

————. "The Theology of Conrad Grebel." *The Mennonite Quarterly Review* 12 (January 1938): 47.

————. "Walking in the Resurrection." *The Mennonite Quarterly Review* 35 (April 1961): 102.

Bossert, Gustav, Jr. "Michael Sattler." In *Mennonite Encyclopedia,* 4:433-34.

————. "Michael Sattler's Trial and Martyrdom in 1527." *The Mennonite Quarterly Review* 25 (July 1951): 205.

————. "Wilhelm Reublin." In *Mennonite Encyclopedia,* 4:304-7.

Bratcher, Robert G. "The Church of Scotland's Report on Baptism." *The Review and Expositor* 54 (April 1957): 205-22.

De Wind, Henry A. "A Sixteenth Century Description of Religious Sects in Austerlitz, Moravia." *The Mennonite Quarterly Review* 29 (January 1955): 44-53.

Estep, W. R. "The Anabaptist View of Salvation." *Southwestern Journal of Theology* 20 (Spring 1978): 32-49.

Estep, W. R., Jr. "Von, Ketzern und ihren Verbrennern: A Sixteenth Century Tract on Religious Liberty." *The Mennonite Quarterly Review* 43 (October 1969): 271-82.

Friedmann, Robert. "Christian Sectarians in Thessalonica and Their Relationship to the Anabaptists." *The Mennonite Quarterly Review* 29 (January 1955): 54.

————. "Claus Felbinger's Confession of 1560." *The Mennonite Quarterly Review* 39 (April 1955): 141-61.

————. "Conception of the Anabaptists." *Church History* 9 (October 1940): 351-52.

————. "The Encounter of Anabaptists and Mennonites with Anti-Trinitarianism." *The Mennonite Quarterly Review* 22 (July 1948): 145.

————. "The Philippite Brethren." *The Mennonite Quarterly Review* 32 (October 1958): 272.

————. "Riedemann." In *Mennonite Encyclopedia,* 4:326-27.

Heimann, Franz. "The Hutterite Doctrine of Church and Common Life, A Study of Peter Riedemann's Confession of Faith of 1540." *The Mennonite Quarterly Review* 26 (January/April 1952): 35, 143.

Hein, Gerhard, ed. "Two Letters by Leupold Scharnschlager." *The Mennonite Quarterly Review* 17 (July 1943): 168.

Horst, Irvin B. "England." In *Mennonite Encyclopedia*, 2:220.

Hudson, Winthrop S. "Baptists Were Not Anabaptists." *The Chronicle* 16 (October 1953): 178.

————. "Who Were the Baptists?" *The Baptist Quarterly* 16 (July 1956): 304.

Keeney, William. "Dirk Philips' Life." *The Mennonite Quarterly Review* 32 (July 1958): 172.

Kiwiet, Jan J. "The Life of Hans Denck (*ca* 1500-1527)." *The Mennonite Quarterly Review* 31 (October 1957): 240.

————. "The Theology of Hans Denck." *The Mennonite Quarterly Review* 32 (January 1958): 278.

Klassen, William. "Pilgram Marpeck in Recent Research." *The Mennonite Quarterly Review* 32 (July 1958): 211-14.

Krahn, Cornelius. "The Conversion of Menno Simons, a Quadricentennial Tribute." *The Mennonite Quarterly Review* 10 (January 1936): 46.

————. "Historiography." In *Mennonite Encyclopedia*, 2:751-69.

Littell, Franklin Hamlin. "Anabaptist Theology of Missions." *The Mennonite Quarterly Review* 21 (January 1947): 13.

————. "Protestantism and the Great Commission." *Southwestern Journal of Theology* 2 (October 1959): 26-42.

Loserth, Johann. "Balthasar Hübmaier." In *Mennonite Encyclopedia*, 2:826.

————. "Hans Hut." In *Mennonite Encyclopedia*, 2:846.

————. "Jakob Hutter." In *Mennonite Encyclopedia*, 2:851.

Matthijssen, Jan P. "The Bern Disputation of 1538." *The Mennonite Quarterly Review* 22 (January 1948): 30.

MaCoskey, Robert A. "The Contemporary Relevance of Balthasar Hübmaier's Concept of the Church." *Foundations* 6 (April 1965): 99-103.

Neff, Christian L. "Felix Manz." In *Mennonite Encyclopedia*, 3:472.

————. "George Blaurock." In *Mennonite Encyclopedia*, 1:354.

————. "Melchior Hofmann." In *Mennonite Encyclopedia*, 2:779-81.

Neff, W. F. "Hans Denck." In *Mennonite Encyclopedia*, 2:35.

Oosterbaan, J. A. "The Theology of Menno Simons." *The Mennonite Quarterly Review* 35 (July 1961): 191-92.

Oyer, John S. "Anabaptism in Central Germany." *The Mennonite Quarterly Review* 35 (January 1961): 37.

Payne, Ernest A. "Who Were the Baptists?" *The Baptist Quarterly* 16 (October 1956): 339.

Quiring, Horst. "The Anthropology of Pilgram Marpeck." *The Mennonite Quarterly Review* 9 (October 1935): 162-63.

Ramaker, A. J. "Hymns and Hymn Writers among the Anabaptists of the Sixteenth Century." *The Mennonite Quarterly Review* 3 (April 1929): 114.

Sommer, John L. "Hutterite Medicine and Physicians in Moravia in the Sixteenth Century and After." *The Mennonite Quarterly Review* 27 (April 1953): 119-23.

Stauffer, Ethelbert. "The Anabaptist Theology of Martyrdom." *The Mennonite Quarterly Review* 19 (July 1945): 179.

Vos, Karel. "Leenaert Bouwens." In *Mennonite Encyclopedia*, 3:305.

Wenger, John C., ed. "A Letter from Wilhelm Reublin to Pilgram Marpeck, 1531." *The Mennonite Quarterly Review* 23 (April 1949): 70-73.

———. "The Life and Work of Pilgram Marpeck." *The Mennonite Quarterly Review* 2 (July 1938): 147.

———. "The Theology of Pilgram Marpeck." *The Mennonite Quarterly Review* 12 (July 1938): 207ff.

Williams, George Huntston. "Studies in the Radical Reformation (1517-1618): A Bibliographical Survey of Research since 1939." *Church History* 27 (April 1958): 124-60.

Yoder, John Howard. "The Turning Point in the Zwinglian Reformation." *The Mennonite Quarterly Review* 32 (April 1958): 128-40.

———. "Dirk Philips." In *Mennonite Encylopedia*, 2:65.

———. "Hans de Ries." In *Mennonite Encyclopedia*, 4:330.

———. "Obbe Philips." In *Mennonite Encyclopedia*, 4:10.

Zijpp, N. van der. "Apostles' Creed." In *Mennonite Encyclopedia*, 1:137.

Unpublished Works

Brandsma, Nan Auke. "The Transition of Menno Simons from Roman Catholicism to Anabaptism as Reflected in His Writings." Unpublished B.D. thesis, Baptist Theological Seminary, Rüschlikon-Zurich, Switzerland, 1955.

Kirkman, Ralph Everett. "The Anabaptists: Their Historical Roots and Relation to the English Baptist Movement." Unpublished M.A. thesis, Baylor University, Waco, Texas, June 1951.

McBeth, Harry Leon. "English Baptist Literature on Religious Liberty to 1689." Unpublished doctoral thesis, Southwestern Baptist Theological Seminary, Fort Worth, Texas, 1961. (Published under the same title by Arno Press, 1980)

Index